JOB READY PYTHON®

JOB READY PYTHON®

HAYTHEM BALTI
CO-AUTHORED BY KIMBERLY A. WEISS

WILEY

About the Authors

Haythem Balti is the dean of education solutions at the mthree Global Academy and director of curriculum at Software Guild. Haythem created courses used by thousands of mthree and Software Guild graduates. He earned his doctorate in computer engineering and computer science from The University of Louisville.

Kimberly A. Weiss is a senior instructional designer at the mthree Global Academy and a veteran course developer, specializing in computer science courses since 2002. She was an assistant professor in computer science for over ten years before deciding to focus exclusively on course design. She has worked with multiple universities and in corporate training settings to develop interactive instructional content appropriate for the target learners and course goals.

About the Technical Writer

Bradley Jones is the owner of Lots of Software, LLC. He has programmed in a variety of languages and tools ranging from C to Unity on platforms ranging from Windows to mobile and includes the web as well as a little bit of virtual reality for fun. In addition to programming, he has authored books on C, C++, C#, Windows, the web, and many more technical topics and a few nontechnical topics. Bradley has been recognized in the industry as a community influencer and has been recognized as a Microsoft MVP, a CODiE Judge, an international technology speaker, a bestselling technical author, and more.

About the Technical Editor

Doug Holland is a software engineer at Microsoft with over twenty years of experience designing and developing software. He really enjoys applying the art and science of software engineering to real-world problems and holds a master's degree from Oxford University in software engineering.

Acknowledgments

Although Kim and Haythem are the main authors of this book, this book would not have been possible without the hard work of the content development and instruction teams at the Software Guild and mthree.

Contents

About the Authors   v

About the Technical
Writer   v

About the Technical
Editor   v

Acknowledgments   vi

Introduction   xvii

PART I: Getting Started with Python   1

Lesson 1: Setting Up a Python Programming Environment   3

Python Overview   4

Using Replit Online   4

    Creating a Replit Account   5

    Creating a Python Program in Replit   7

    Running a Python Program in Replit   9

    Other Replit Tasks   11

      Renaming Your Code File   11

      Saving Your Coding File Locally   12

      Creating a New File for Your
       Python Project   12

      Adding Files to Your Python
       Project   13

      Returning to Replit   13

      Getting More Help for Replit   14

Getting Started with Jupyter
Notebook   14

    Installing Anaconda Jupyter
    Notebook   15

    Creating a New Jupyter Notebook
    File   16

    Renaming a Jupyter Notebook
    Project File   18

    Saving a Python File Locally   19

    Opening an Existing Jupyter
    Notebook File   20

A Quick Look at Visual Studio Code   21

    Obtaining Visual Studio Code   21

    Adding the Python Extension
      to Visual Studio Code   22

Using Python from the Command Line   24

Summary   26

Exercises   26

    Exercise 1: Say Hello   27

    Exercise 2: What's It Do?   27

    Exercise 3: Counting   27

    Exercise 4: Fruity Code   28

Lesson 2: Understanding Programming Basics   29

The Future of Computer Programming   30

    What Is Programming?   30

    What Is a Program?   30

    Computational Thinking   31

Programming Languages   32

    Common Components   33

      Statements   33

      Syntax   33

      Reserved Words   34

      Operators   35

    Hello, World!   36

Data Types and Variables   37

    Data Types   37

Text	38
Numbers	38
True/False	39
Date/Time	39
Data Collections	39
Variables	40
Reserving Memory	42
Variables and Data Types	43
Constants	44
Example 1: Area of a Circle	44
Example 2: Tax Rate	45
Example 3: Output Messages	45
Summary	46
Exercises	46
Exercise 1: Daily Tasks	47
Exercise 2: Python Programming	47

Lesson 3: Exploring Basic Python Syntax — 49

Using with Single-Line Commands	51
Using Semicolons	52
Continuing with Backslash	54
Working with Case Structure	55
Adding Comments	56
Using the Input Function	57
Storing Input	59
Understanding Variable Types	61
Displaying Variable Values	62
Naming Variables	64
Summary	65
Exercises	65
Exercise 1: Displaying Text	66
Exercise 2: Follow the Comments	66
Exercise 3: Fixing the Code	66
Exercise 4: Broken Variables	67
Exercise 5: Broken Names	67
Exercise 6: Where Are You?	67

Lesson 4: Working with Basic Python Data Types — 69

Review of Data Types	70
Number Data Types	70
Identifying Data Types	72
Mathematical Operations	74
PEMDAS	77
Common Math Functions	81
Math Library Functions	83
Using Numbers with User Input	86
Boolean Types and Boolean Operations	89
Convert to Boolean	90
Logic Operations	92
Comparative Operators	95
Summary	96
Exercises	97
Exercise 1: Prompting the User	97
Exercise 2: Manipulated Math	97
Exercise 3: Integers Only	98
Exercise 4: Current Value	98
Exercise 5: Simple Interest	98
Exercise 6: True or False	99
Exercise 7: Playing with Numbers	99
Exercise 8: Do the Math	99
Exercise 9: Street Addresses	100

Lesson 5: Using Python Control Statements — 101

Control Structures Review	101
Understanding Sequence Control Structure	102
Understanding Selection Statements	103
Understanding Conditional Statements	106
If-Else Statements	108
Working with Nested Conditions	109

Embedding Conditions	112
Summary	114
Exercises	114
Exercise 1: Are You Rich?	115
Exercise 2: Cats or Dogs	115
Exercise 3: True or False Quiz	115
Exercise 4: For Every Season...	115
Exercise 5: Company Picnic	116

Lesson 6: Pulling It All Together: Income Tax Calculator   117

Getting Started	118
Step 1: Gather Requirements	118
Values in Use	119
User Interface	119
Other Standards	120
Step 2: Design the Program	120
Step 3: Create the Inputs	120
Step 4: Calculate the Taxable Income	122
Step 5: Calculate the Tax Rate	124
Add a Conditional Statement	125
Create Nested Conditionals	127
Step 6: Update the Application	133
What About Negative Taxable Incomes?	134
Does Code Compare to Standards?	136
Step 7: Address the UI	136
On Your Own	139
Summary	139

PART II: Loops and Data Structures   141

Lesson 7: Controlling Program Flow with Loops   143

Iterations Overview	144
The Anatomy of a Loop	144
The for Loop	145

The while Loop	146
Unexecutable while Loop	148
for vs. while Loops	149
Strings and String Operations	151
Determining the Length of a String	152
Splitting a String	153
Storing Characters	154
Comparison Operators in Strings	155
Concatenating Strings	158
Slicing Strings	159
Searching Strings	163
Iterating through Strings	164
Summary	167
Exercises	167
Exercise 1: Separating Your Fruits	168
Exercise 2: Keeping It Short	168
Exercise 3: Fruit Finder	168
Exercise 4: It's Divisible	169
Exercise 5: Identify the Numbers	169
Exercise 6: And the Total Is...	169
Exercise 7: Multiplication Tables	169
Exercise 8: Sum of Prime Numbers	169
Exercise 9: One Letter at a Time	170
Exercise 10: Length without len()	170
Exercise 11: Count the Numbers	170
Exercise 12: Fizz Buzz	170

Lesson 8: Understanding Basic Data Structures: Lists   173

Data Structure Overview—Part 1	174
Creating Lists	175
Determining List Length	179
Working with List Indexes	179
Negative Indexing in Lists	182
Slicing Lists	184
Using the Slice Object	187
Adding Items to a List	189
Inserting List Items	190
Removing List Items	192

Deleting versus Removing Items	194
Popping Instead of Removing	195
Concatenating Lists	196
List Comprehension	197
Sorting Lists	199
Copying Lists	200
Summary	202
Exercises	202
Exercise 1: All About You	203
Exercise 2: Shopping List	203
Exercise 3: List Deletion	203
Exercise 4: List Modification	203
Exercise 5: A Complete List Program	203

Lesson 9: Understanding Basic Data Structures: Tuples 205

Tuples and Tuple Operations	206
Syntax of Tuples vs. Syntax of Lists	206
Tuple Length	208
Tuple Index Values	209
Negative Indexing in Tuples	210
Slicing Tuples	212
Immutability	213
Concatenating Tuples	216
Searching Tuples	217
Summary	218
Exercises	219
Exercise 1: Creating Tuples	219
Exercise 2: Modifying Tuples	219
Exercise 3: Where's Waldo?	220
Exercise 4: A Complete Tuple Program	220

Lesson 10: Diving Deeper into Data Structures: Dictionaries 223

Data Structure Overview—Part 2	224
Getting Started with Dictionaries	224
Generating a Dictionary	227
Retrieving Items from a Dictionary	230
Using the keys() Method	233
Using the items() Method	234
Reviewing the keys(), values(), and items() Methods	236
Using the get() Method	239
Using the pop() Method	241
Working with the in Operator	245
Updating a Dictionary	246
Duplicating a Dictionary	249
Clearing a Dictionary	254
Summary	255
Exercises	255
Exercise 1: Working with Text	256
Exercise 2: Separating the High from the Low	256
Exercise 3: High and Low All in One	257
Exercise 4: Self-Assessment	257

Lesson 11: Diving Deeper into Data Structures: Sets 259

Sets	260
Retrieving Items from a Set	261
Adding Items to a Set	262
Creating an Empty Set	262
Understanding Set Uniqueness	263
Searching Items in a Set	265
Calculating the Length of a Set	267
Deleting Items from a Set	268
Clearing a Set	270
Popping Items in a Set	272
Deleting a Set	273
Determining the Difference Between Sets	274
Intersecting Sets	277
Combining Sets	278
Summary	279

Exercises 279
   Exercise 1: Line by Line 280
   Exercise 2: Adding New Names 280
   Exercise 3: Popping Accounts 280
   Exercise 4: Everywhere That
      Mary Went... 280
   Exercise 5: Self-Assessment 281

Lesson 12: Pulling It All Together: Prompting for an Address   283

Step 1: Getting Started 284
Step 2: Accept User Input 285
Step 3: Display the Input Value 286
Step 4: Modify the Output 287
Step 5: Split a Text Value 288
Step 6: Display Only the House
   Number 290
Step 7: Display the Street Name 291
Step 8: Add the Period 292
Summary 293

Lesson 13: Organizing with Functions   295

Functions Overview 295
Defining Functions in Python 296
Function Syntax 300
Default Input Values 301
Parameter Syntax 303
Arbitrary Arguments 304
Keyword Arguments 306
Arbitrary Keyword Arguments 306
Summary 308
Exercises 309
   Exercise 1: Lower Numbers 309
   Exercise 2: This Will Be 309
   Exercise 3: Finding the Largest 310
   Exercise 4: Simple Calculator 310
   Exercise 5: Which Is Greater? 310

PART III: Object-Oriented Programming in Python   311

Lesson 14: Incorporating Object-Oriented Programming   313

Object-Oriented Programming
   Overview 314
Defining Classes 314
   Attributes 315
   Methods 316
Creating Objects 316
Working with Methods 319
Class Attributes 324
   Working with Static Methods 326
   Working with Class Methods 328
Summary 330
Exercises 330
   Exercise 1: Create Your Own Class 331
   Exercise 2: Classy Vehicles 331
   Exercise 3: Streamlined Banking 331
   Exercise 4: Using a Calculator in
      Class 331

Lesson 15: Including Inheritance   333

Understanding Inheritance 334
Creating a Parent Class 335
Creating a Child Class 335
Inheriting at Multiple Levels 338
Overriding Methods 340
Summary 343
Exercises 344
   Exercise 1: Basic Inheritance 344
   Exercise 2: Adding Attributes 344
   Exercise 3: Creating More Children 345

Exercise 4: Dogs and Cats   345
Exercise 5: Hourly Employees   345
Exercise 6: File System   347

Lesson 16: Pulling It All Together: Building a Burger Shop   349

Requirements for Our Application   350
Plan the Code   350
Create the Classes   351
Create the Food Item Class   352
   Create a Burger Class   353
   Create a Drink Class   354
   Create a Side Class   354
   Create a Combo   355
   Create the Order Class   356
Create the Main File   357
   Create order_once   358
   Order a Burger   359
   Add a Drink   360
   Add Sides   362
   Order a Combo   363
Display the Output   364
Tie the Code Files Together   364
Summary   368

PART IV: Data Processing with Python   369

Lesson 17: Working with Dates and Times   371

Getting Started with Dates and Times   372
   Creating a Variable for a Date   372
   Creating a Variable for Time   375
   Creating a Variable for Both Date and Time   375
Getting the Current Date and Time   376
Splitting a Date String   377
Using datetime Attributes   379
Creating Custom datetime Objects   380

Compare datetime Values   381
Working with UTC Format   383
Applying Timestamps   384
Arithmetic and Dates   387
Calculating the Difference in Days   388
Using Date without Time   390
Using Time without Date   392
Summary   394
Exercises   394
   Exercise 1: Displaying Dates   394
   Exercise 2: Leap Years   395
   Exercise 3: The Past   395
   Exercise 4: Unix Dates   395
   Exercise 5: Yesterday, Today, and Tomorrow   395
   Exercise 6: Setting Future Days   395
   Exercise 7: Five Seconds in the Future   395
   Exercise 8: Date Calculators   396
     Calculator 1: Time Duration   396
     Calculator 2: Add or Subtract Time from a Date   397
     Calculator 3: Age Calculator   397

Lesson 18: Processing Text Files   399

File Processing Overview   401
Introduction to File Input/Output   402
   The input() Function   402
   The open() Function   402
   The read() Method   403
   The write() Method   403
   The close() Method   403
   The print() Function   403
Processing Text Files   404
Opening a File   404
Reading Text from a File   406
   Use the read() Method to Limit the Content   406

Reading Lines   408
    Iterating through a File   410
Add Content to a File   412
Overwriting the Contents of a File   415
Creating a New File   417
Using the os Module   418
Deleting a File   419
Summary   421
Exercises   421
    Exercise 1: Reading Lines   422
    Exercise 2: Combination of the Two   422
    Exercise 3: Combination
      of Them All   422
    Exercise 4: Listing Lines   422
    Exercise 5: Longest Word   422
    Exercise 6: Listing Text   423
    Exercise 7: Text in Reverse   423

Lesson 19: Processing CSV Files   425

Reading CSV Files   426
Using the DictReader Class   430
Creating a Dataset List   432
Using writerow()   434
Appending Data   436
Writing Rows as Lists   439
Writing Rows from Dictionaries   440
Summary   444
Exercises   444
    Exercise 1: Reading Lines   444
    Exercise 2: Company Stocks   444
    Exercise 3: Rearranging Files   445
    Exercise 4: Pop Music Evolution   445
    Exercise 5: All About Cars   446

Lesson 20: Processing JSON Files   447

Processing JSON Files   448
Creating a JSON File with dump()   448
Converting to JSON with dumps()   449

Formatting JSON Data   450
Using json.loads()   452
Iterating through JSON Data   454
Reading and Writing JSON Data   457
Summary   460
Exercises   461
    Exercise 1: Company Bank Account   461
    Exercise 2: Formatted Account
      Information   461
    Exercise 3: Nobel Prizes   461
    Exercise 4: New York Restaurants   462
    Exercise 5: Movies   463

PART V: Data Analysis and Exception Handling   465

Lesson 21: Using Lambdas   467

Creating a Lambda Function   468
Working with Multiple Inputs   469
Placing Lambda Functions inside
    a Function   471
Using the map() Function   472
Combining Map and Lambda
    Functions   475
Using the filter() Function   477
Combining a Filter and a Lambda   479
Using the reduce() Function   480
    Specify an Initial Value   482
    Using reduce() with Comparison
      Operations   484
Summary   486
Exercises   486
    Exercise 1: Computing the
      Square Root   487
    Exercise 2: Converting a Text File
      to Uppercase   487
    Exercise 3: Determining Prime   487
    Exercise 4: Identifying Absolute
      Value   487

Exercise 5: Highest Number 487
Exercise 6: Lowest Number 487
Exercise 7: Last Key 487
Exercise 8: Highest Value 488
Exercise 9: Sum of Even 488
Exercise 10: Sum of Positive
    Numbers 488
Exercise 11: Highest Stock Market
    Volume 488
Exercise 12: Bad Stock Market Day 488
Exercise 13: Highest Opening Price 488
Exercise 14: Highest Price at
    Closing 489
Exercise 15: Self-Assessment 489

Lesson 22: Handling Exceptions   491

Built-In Exceptions 492
Working with try and except 493
Working with Multiple Excepts 495
Combining Exception Types 498
Using Multiple Operations in a try 500
Using the raise Keyword 501
Exploring the General Exception
    Classes 502
Adding finally 505
Summary 506
Exercises 506
Exercise 1: Typing Numbers 507
Exercise 2: Current Value 507
Exercise 3: Reading Lines 508
Exercise 4: Concatenating Files 508
Exercise 5: Creating a List from
    a File 508
Exercise 6: Self-Assessment 508

Lesson 23: Pulling It All Together: Word Analysis in Python   511

Examine the Data 512
Read the Data 514
Tokenize the Dataset 517
Tokenize an Input String 518
Tokenize an Input Review 521
Tokenize the Entire Dataset 522
Using the Tokenize Functions 523
Count the Words in Each Review 524
Word Count for an Input List of
    Words 524
Word Count an Input Review 525
Word Count for the Dataset 526
Summary 528

Lesson 24: Extracting, Transforming, and Loading with ETL Scripting   531

ETL Scripting in Python 532
Design and Implement Custom
    ETL Scripts 532
The extract Class 534
Adding the extract.fromCSV
    Method 534
Creating the extract.fromJSON
    Method 536
Creating the extract.fromMySQL
    Method 538
Creating the extract.fromMongoDB
    Method 542
Verify the extract.py Module 544
Using Our Script as an External
    Module 545
The transform Class 546
Defining the transform Class 546

Creating the head and tail
  Methods   547
Renaming a Column   551
Removing a Column from the
  Data Source   552
Renaming Multiple Columns   556
Removing Multiple Columns   558
Transforming the Data   563
The load Class   569
Creating the load.toCSV Method   570
Creating the load.toJSON Method   572
Creating the load.toMYSQL
  Method   574
Creating the Load.toMONGODB
  Method   578
Summary   582
Exercises   582
Exercise 1: Transforming CSV to
  CSV   583
Exercise 2: Transforming CSV to
  JSON   583
Exercise 3: Transforming JSON to
  CSV   583
Exercise 4: Transforming JSON to
  JSON   583
Exercise 5: Removing an Attribute   583
Exercise 6: Renaming an Attribute   583
Exercise 7: Confirming an Attribute   584

**Lesson 25: Improving ETL
Scripting**   **585**
Converting to Static Methods for the
  extract Class   586
Converting to Static Methods for
  the transform Class   588
Converting to Static Methods for
  the load Class   592

Adding Exception Handling in the
  extract Class   594
Creating a Custom Extractor for
  the extract Class   601
Summary   607
Exercises   608
Exercise 1: Revisiting Lessons
  Learned   608
Exercise 2: Day of Week   608
Exercise 3: Date Validity   609
Exercise 4: Listing Duplicates   609
Exercise 5: Removing Duplicates   609
Exercise 6: Transforming Names   609

PART VI: Appendices   **611**

Appendix A: Flowcharts   **613**
Flowchart Basics   613
Sequences   613
Branches   614
Loops   615
Common Flowcharting Shapes   615
Flowcharting Example   616
Additional Flowchart
  Elements   618

**Appendix B: Creating
Pseudocode**   **621**
What Is Pseudocode?   621

**Appendix C: Installing
MySQL**   **623**
MySQL Installation   623
Download and Install MySQL   623
Configure MySQL   624
Configure MySQL Router
  Options   626

Configure Samples and
Examples 627
Verify the Installation 628
The MySQL Notifier 630

Appendix D: Installing Vinyl DB 631

Database Structure 631
Create the Database 632

Appendix E: Installing MongoDB 637

Installing MongoDB Community
Server 637
Running MongoDB 642

Appendix F: Importing to MongoDB 643

Index 645

Introduction

With the proliferation of data in the past decade, Python emerged as a viable language for data processing and analysis. Its simple syntax and powerful toolbox and libraries make Python the standard language for data.

There are many reasons why learning Python is great choice:

- As a general-purpose language, Python runs on all platforms and operating systems, which makes Python programs and applications very portable.

- Python is widely used around the globe and benefits from a huge online community that is highly active. Python is number 3 at the time of this writing in the Tiobe index.

- Python is the standard language for data analysis, data engineering, and data science. If you want to become a data developer, learning Python is a must as it provides many built-in and external libraries that allow you to develop machine learning models or ETL processes, or analyze some data.

> **NOTE** You can find the Tiobe index for Python at `https://www.tiobe.com/tiobe-index/`.

A Python Course within a Book

This book contains a full-fledged Python course that is used by the mthree Global Academy and the Software Guild to train our alumni in Python and other topics, such as data analysis and data science.

Features to Make You Job Ready

Job Ready Python provides an overview of the Python language and teaches how to leverage the basics of Python to create Python programs that can process and analyze data.

If you read through this book, enter the code listings, and try the code, then you will get an experience like many other books. If you also take a hands-on approach to doing the exercises, you will be better able to take what you learned to the next level.

Most importantly, this book (as well the *Job Ready* series) goes beyond what many books provide by including lessons that help you pull together everything you are learning in a way that is more like what you would find in the professional world. This includes building a more comprehensive example than what you get in the standard short listings provided in most books. If you work through the "Pulling It All Together" lessons, then you will be better prepared for many of those Python jobs that are available.

WHAT DOES THIS BOOK COVER?

As mentioned, this book is a complete Python course. It is broken into several parts, each containing a number of lessons. By working through the lessons in this book, you will not only learn Python programming, but you will be preparing yourself for a job in Python programming.

Part I: Getting Started with Python   The first part of this book focuses on getting you set up to use Python. This will include help for installing Python and setting up the tools you will need to work through this book. You will also be shown how to enter and run Python programs. This section also provides an overview of the basics of Python including syntax, basic data types, and control statements.

Part II: Loops and Data Structures   The second part of this book focuses on loops and data structures. This will include a deep dive into the different types of loops that exist in Python, such as `for` loops and the `while` loop. Moreover, this section will cover the basic data structures in Python, including lists, tuples, dictionaries, and sets. These four data structures provide the foundation of all programs that store and process data. Finally, we will learn how to create and leverage functions to create reusable code.

Part III: Object-Oriented Programming in Python   The third part of this book focuses on object-oriented programming (OOP), an important and powerful concept in Python and many other programming languages. You will leverage Python and OOP concepts such as inheritance to create classes and build elegant and reusable solutions to complex programs.

Part IV: Data Processing with Python   The fourth part of this book digs into processing data and working with files using Python. You will start with learning about lambdas, which provide some functional programming capabilities to Python. This coverage includes the use of maps, the reduce function, and filters. This will be followed by teaching you how to access and use data from various file types including text files, CSV files, and JSON.

Part V: Data Analysis and Exception Handling   The fifth part of this book teaches you a key concept for ensuring users of your programs have a good experience: exception handling. You will learn about exceptions and how to use them to handle errors within your Python programs. Finally, everything you have learned will be leveraged to design and develop an extract-transform-load (ETL) Python library that can be used to read and write data to and from various sources, as well as perform standard transformation and processing on the data.

Part VI: Appendices   The final part presented in this book is additional material for your reference. This includes a number of appendices that provide supplemental information on flowcharts and creating pseudocode. There are also appendices to help guide you through installing various database programs used within the book, including MySQL, the Vinyl DB, and MongoDB.

READER SUPPORT FOR THIS BOOK

There are several ways to get the help you need for this book.

Companion Download Files

As you work through the examples in this book, you should type in all the code manually. This will help you learn and better understand what the code does.

However, in some lessons, download files are referenced. You can download the files from `www.wiley.com/go/jobreadypython`.

How to Contact the Publisher

If you believe you have found a mistake in this book, please bring it to our attention. At John Wiley & Sons, we understand how important it is to provide our customers with accurate content, but even with our best efforts an error may occur.

In order to submit your possible errata, please email it to our Customer Service Team at `wileysupport@wiley.com` with the subject line "Possible Book Errata Submission."

PART I

Getting Started with Python

Lesson 1: Setting Up a Python Programming Environment

Lesson 2: Understanding Programming Basics

Lesson 3: Exploring Basic Python Syntax

Lesson 4: Working with Basic Python Data Types

Lesson 5: Using Python Control Statements

Lesson 6: Pulling It All Together: Income Tax Calculator

Lesson 1

Setting Up a Python Programming Environment

As mentioned in the introduction, this book is designed to give you a thorough understanding of the Python programming language and its rich set of libraries, and to expose you to application development using Python. In order to do this, you'll need a tool to enter and run your Python programs. In this first lesson, we point to tools and show you how to get started using them.

LEARNING OBJECTIVES

By the end of this lesson, you will:

- Know of a few Python tools that are available.
- Learn where you can access an online Python tool to enter and run Python scripts.
- Create and run your first Python script.

> **NOTE** Don't worry if you don't understand some of the jargon and code presented in this lesson. Rather, focus on setting up your programming environment as described in this lesson. The rest of this book will focus on teaching you the jargon and code!

PYTHON OVERVIEW

Python is a general-purpose programming language that is interpreted. Python balances ease and comprehension with power and speed. With its focus on speed for developing applications, it has become a significant tool for software development. When working with Python, you write programs that are then executed using Python. The programs are generally saved as text files with a .py extension and interpreted using the Python program.

Because Python is open source, there are several development environments and distributions that can be used to write Python programs. To program Python you need either a text editor or an integrated development environment (IDE) as well as a Python interpreter. In many cases, if you install an IDE, it will install Python for you as well. You can also install the Python interpreter on your system and use any text editor you want.

In this lesson, we will cover installing Python and some publicly available tools. Before showing how to install Python locally, we'll introduce Replit, which is an integrated development environment you can use online without installing anything locally. It is relatively easy to use and includes everything you need to get started learning Python. We'll also show you how to install two other development environments, Anaconda Jupyter Notebook and Microsoft Visual Studio Code, which are also free. Finally, we'll show you how to install Python on its own to use via the command line of your operating system.

> **NOTE** We show several tools in this lesson; however, you don't need to use all of them. The objective is to show you several tools and let you decide which one to use. If you are unsure which to use, we recommend starting with Replit.

USING REPLIT ONLINE

Replit is a popular online IDE used to learn many programming languages including Python. By using Replit, you can enter your Python code and run it without installing anything locally on your machine. This means you can start programming Python immediately and will be able to access your programs and the tools from any computer with internet access.

> **NOTE** Replit was originally called Repl.it, but changed its name around 2021. It also changed its URL from Repl.it to Replit.com at the same time.

Creating a Replit Account

You can find Replit at www.Replit.com. When you land on this page, you should be greeted with a page similar to Figure 1.1.

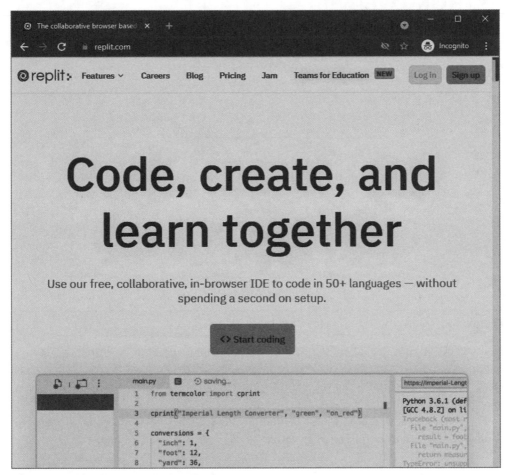

Figure 1.1: The Replit.com home page

You will notice a button in the middle of the page labeled < > *Start coding*. Clicking this button will take you to a dialog asking you to log in. This is similar to clicking the *Log in* button on the top-right corner of the page. Before you can start coding with Replit, you need to sign up for an account. Thankfully, Replit offers a free account that should provide you with everything you need to complete this book. Clicking either button will present a dialog similar to Figure 1.2.

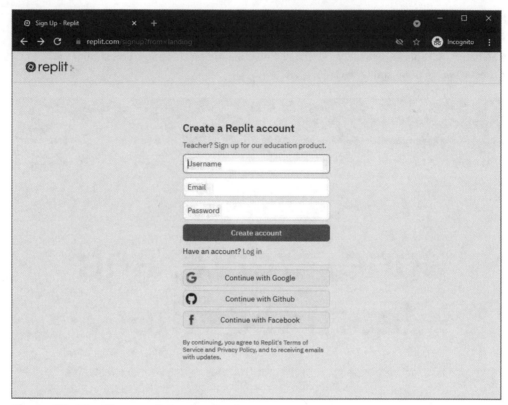

Figure 1.2: The Sign-up dialog for Replit

If you plan to use Replit, you should create an account by entering a username that is between 2 and 15 characters, a valid email address to use to verify the account, and a password. Enter the information and click the *Create account* button. Alternatively, you can log in using a Google, GitHub, or Facebook ID.

If you've entered acceptable information for your account, then the sign-up process should take you to the Replit desktop with a welcome dialog similar to Figure 1.3.

> **NOTE** You might see a slightly different flow for initially setting up Replit. You might be prompted with a survey that contains questions related to what you plan to do with Replit. Replit will to customize the IDE based on your answers to these questions.

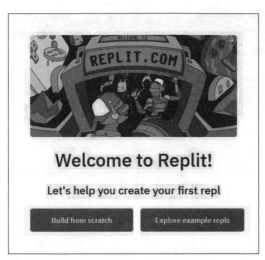

Figure 1.3: The Replit welcome dialog

Creating a Python Program in Replit

In the welcome dialog, you are offered the options to build from scratch or to explore example repls. Select *Build from scratch* to continue. This should greet you with a dialog to build your first repl as shown in Figure 1.4, which is simply a program area within the Replit IDE.

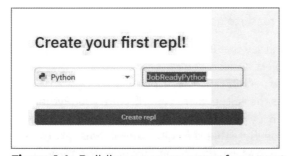

Figure 1.4: Building a new program from scratch

You should select Python from the drop-down menu and enter a name for your repl in the second box. In Figure 1.4, we entered **JobReadyPython**. You can do the same. With the language selected and name provided, click *Create repl* to continue.

Your first repl work area will be created and you'll be dropped into the Replit desktop. More importantly, because you selected Python, the desktop will be preconfigured to allow you to write Python code. The desktop is shown in Figure 1.5.

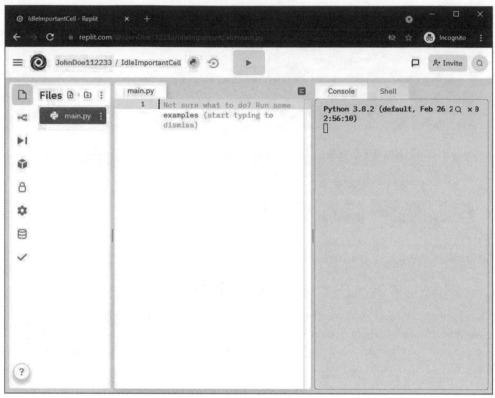

Figure 1.5: Replit desktop with Python ready to go

If you look at the Replit desktop, you will see that it is presented in three sections. The far left is the Files dialog and icons for project options. You can see in Figure 1.5 that your Python project was started with one file by default called main.py.

The middle section has a tab that shows the editor where you will write your Python code. Currently the tab shown has the main.py file displayed. If you click to the right of the number 1, you will be able to enter code. Note that the editor shows some text there; however, it is not part of your file and as soon as you type something, it will go away. You can click that text if you want to see some examples.

The right side of the desktop shows the Console window. The Console window is where the output from running your program will be displayed. Using the IDE, you will write programs in the middle section, then click the run button (▶) at the top of the screen. The results (or errors) will then be displayed in the right dialog area.

To see this in action, enter Listing 1.1 into the main.py file in the middle dialog on the IDE. This is basic Python code used to print statements. You will need to make sure you use the same capitalization and spacing.

LISTING 1.1

Using the Replit editor

```python
print("This is my first Python program!")
print("It is beautiful!")
```

When you enter this, you will notice that the Replit editor will provide you helpful information as shown in Figure 1.6. This is one of the benefits of using an IDE.

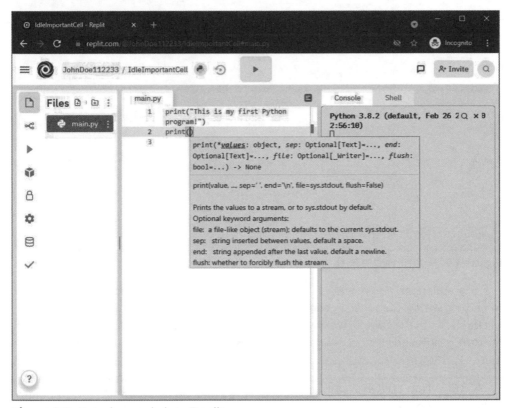

Figure 1.6: Entering code into Replit

Running a Python Program in Replit

Once you've entered the code from Listing 1.1, click the run button (▶) at the top. The print function you are using displays text to the console, so you will see the text that was within the quotes displayed on the right side of the IDE as shown in Figure 1.7.

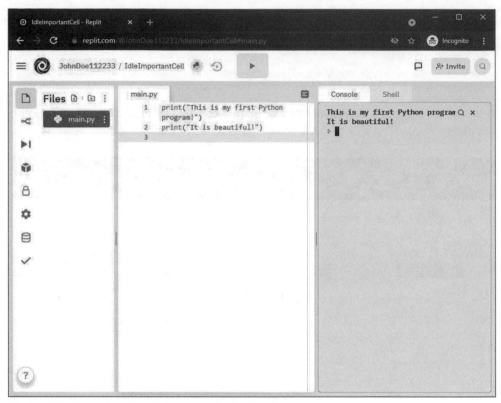

Figure 1.7: Running the Python script in Replit

Congratulations! You've entered and executed your first Python program. If you type something wrong, then you might get an error when you run the program. If so, that error will be shown in the Console window instead of the expected results. You can read what the error states and possibly determine what was done wrong.

> **NOTE** When an IDE shows an error, it might include a line number. The line number shown might not be the line that had the issue, but often will be close. If you leave off the closing parenthesis on the second line of code, the error you receive will likely indicate line 3 because the interpreter didn't know the parenthesis was missing until it got to line 3.

Other Replit Tasks

It is beyond the scope of this book to teach you everything about Replit; however, the following sections present a few core tasks you will find useful as you work through the code within this book using the Replit IDE. These include:

- Renaming your code file
- Saving your code file
- Adding additional files to a Python project
- Getting more help for Replit

Renaming Your Code File

The default name for the Python file was main.py. You can change this name to any name you'd like, but you should leave the extension as .py to indicate it is a Python program.

To rename the source code file, click the three dots to the right of the file name in the Files dialog on the left side of the IDE. This will display a menu as shown in Figure 1.8.

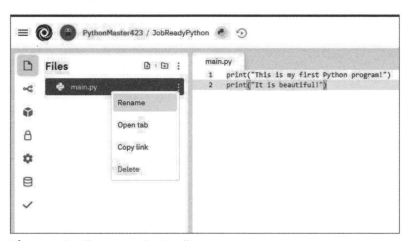

Figure 1.8: Files menu in Replit

You can click *Rename*, which will then allow you to rename the file directly in the Files dialog. You'll notice that this menu also gives you the ability to delete the file as well.

If you rename your main.py file, you'll find that Replit will no longer run the program. By default, Replit runs the file called main.py, so if you rename it, Replit will give an error in the console when you use the Run button.

You can get around this issue by running the program in the Shell tab in the right pane of the IDE. Using the Shell is like running a program from an operating system command line.

To run a Python script from the command line, you type **python** followed by the filename with its extension. To run the script in MyFirstProgram.py, you would enter the following in the Shell:

python MyFirstProgram.py

Because MyFirstProgram.py is the renamed main.py we created earlier, it will display the same output. Figure 1.9 shows the Replit Shell with the command entered and the resulting output.

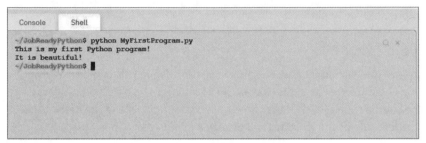

Figure 1.9: Running Python in the Replit Shell

NOTE The Shell is case sensitive, so you need to type python in all lowercase and the filename case must match what you used to save the file.

Saving Your Coding File Locally

If you'd like to save a copy of your source code to your local machine, you can either copy and paste from the online IDE, or you can download everything in your project in a compressed zip file.

To download the project, click the three dots to the right of the word *Files* at the top of the Files dialog. This will provide a menu similar to Figure 1.10 that will allow you to download your code. Once downloaded, you can uncompress the zip file to get to your individual files.

Creating a New File for Your Python Project

As you work through the lessons in this book, your projects will become more complex. Many lessons will have you enter and run one listing at a time, but as you build more advanced programs, you will need to create additional files to hold your scripts. Replit will let you create multiple files.

You can create an additional file by clicking the *Add file* icon (⊕) in the Files dialog. This will prompt you for the name of the new file as shown in Figure 1.11. You can enter the new filename into the open box and press *Enter* to create it.

Figure 1.10: Downloading a project from Replit

Figure 1.11: Creating a new file

Adding Files to Your Python Project

In addition to creating new files, you can also upload files to your project. These files might be database files, images, text files, or additional source files. You can do this by clicking the three dots to the right of the word *Files* at the top of the Files dialog to bring up the menu you saw in Figure 1.10. From the displayed menu, you can upload a file or a folder into your project. Clicking the menu option will bring up the file dialog for your operating system and let you select the file you want to include.

Returning to Replit

The scripts you create in Replit will remain online at `Replit.com`. If you leave `Replit.com` or if you load `Replit.com` from a different site or browser, you might not return to the workspace you've seen earlier, but rather you might land on a page similar to Figure 1.12. If so, you can click the *My repls* option on the left menu to find your project. Once your project is displayed, you can select it to return to the IDE you saw earlier in this lesson.

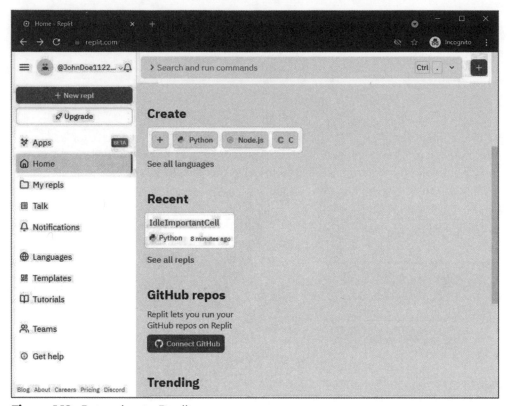

Figure 1.12: Returning to Replit

Getting More Help for Replit

As mentioned earlier, it is beyond the scope of this book to teach you everything that Replit can do. That could be an entire book of its own. At this point, you know enough to enter the code from the lessons in this book and run them. If you want to learn more about Replit, you can click the menu and select either the *Tutorials* option or *Get Help*. Both will provide links to additional sources of information.

GETTING STARTED WITH JUPYTER NOTEBOOK

Jupyter Notebook is another development environment that can be used to write Python programs. The following section covers installing the Anaconda Distribution, which is an open-source IDE that includes Python 3 and several libraries. The key difference between Anaconda and Replit is that you can install Anaconda on your local machine instead of using it online.

To install the Anaconda Distribution, start at the Anaconda downloads page for the Individual Edition at `https://www.anaconda.com/products/individual`. On this page, you can click the *Download* button to download the latest version of the installation package for your computer. There are downloadable versions for Windows, macOS, and Linux.

Installing Anaconda Jupyter Notebook

When the download is complete, open the file and follow the instructions to install Anaconda using the default settings. Once the software is installed, you will need to choose a development environment that allows Python programs to be written. One of the most popular development environments is Jupyter Notebook, which is installed as part of the Anaconda Distribution.

After you have installed the Anaconda Distribution, you will be able to open Jupyter Notebook from the Windows Start menu, as shown in Figure 1.13.

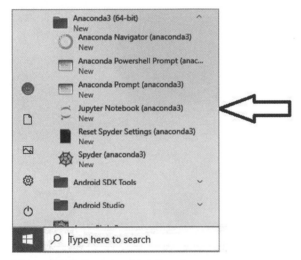

Figure 1.13: Jupyter Notebook

> **NOTE** If you are using a Mac, open the Anaconda Navigator app and launch Jupyter Notebook from there.

When you open Jupyter Notebook, a script will run in a command window and the user interface will open in a browser window. You should leave the command window open while you work, but you can minimize it if it is in your way. If you close the command window, you will have to restart Jupyter Notebook to continue working.

The user interface opens in your default browser, and you will see a list of folders stored on your computer similar to Figure 1.14.

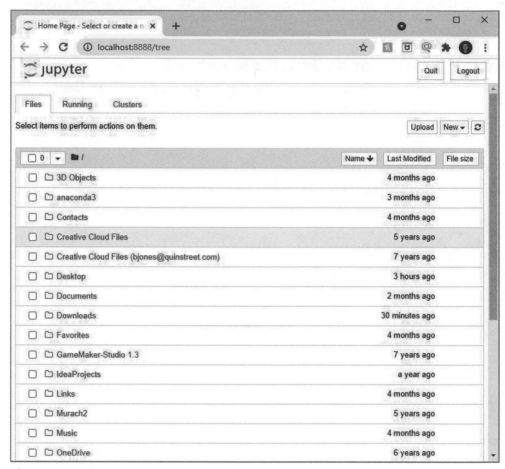

Figure 1.14: The Jupyter Notebook interface

Creating a New Jupyter Notebook File

To create a Python file in Jupyter Notebook, you will need to navigate to the location where you want to create it first. Once there, you can create and run a Python script.

Start by opening the folder where you want to save the new file in the Jupyter Notebook. You can click and navigate to the folders displayed in the browser interface you saw in Figure 1.14. For example, we clicked the *Documents* folder to navigate into it. You can also create new folders by clicking the *New* drop-down option on the upper-right area of the interface as shown in Figure 1.15.

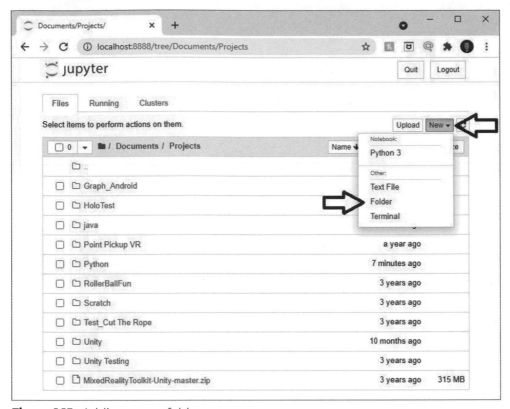

Figure 1.15: Adding a new folder

Once you have navigated to the folder where you want your file, you can add the file by clicking the *New* button in the upper-right corner again and then clicking Python 3. You can see this option at the top of the menu shown in Figure 1.15.

The new file will open in a new tab in your browser as shown in Figure 1.16. The new file will include one cell ready for you to use.

Let's display a "Hello, World!" message using the Python `print` command:

```
print ("Hello, World!")
```

After typing the code in the first cell, click the *Run* button in the toolbar at the top of the page or use the keyboard shortcut Shift+Enter to view the result. The output will appear in a new block immediately under the code cell. In this case, "Hello, World" will appear under the active cell as shown in Figure 1.17.

You will see that a new cell is created after running the code. You can either enter new code into the new cell, or you can click your existing cell and make changes. If you want to run the same cell again, click it, then click the *Run* button again.

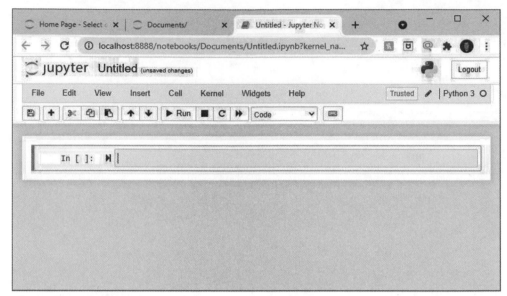

Figure 1.16: The new Python file in Jupyter Notebook

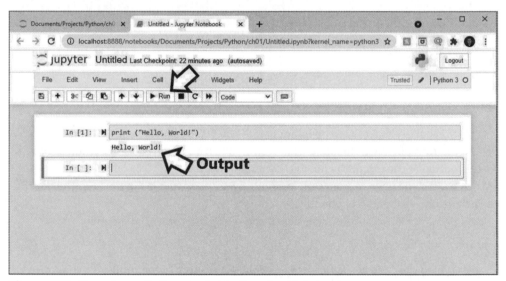

Figure 1.17: Running a Python script in Jupyter Notebook

Renaming a Jupyter Notebook Project File

You can rename the file by clicking the title at the top of the page. A popup window will open, as shown in Figure 1.18, allowing you to enter a new name for the file. Enter the name you want to use and click *Rename*.

> **NOTE** You can also select *File* and then *Rename...* from the menus to rename the file.

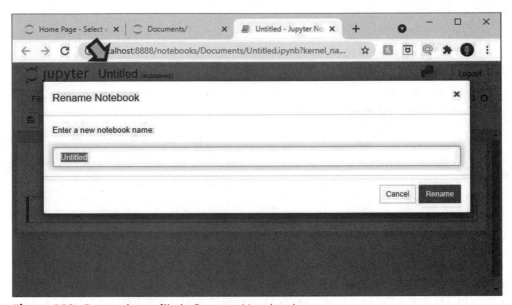

Figure 1.18: Renaming a file in Jupyter Notebook

The new name will appear at the top of the window when the page is opened. The new file will also appear in the list of files in the current folder.

You can save your work as a Jupyter Notebook file by pressing Ctrl+S or selecting *File* and then *Save and Checkpoint* from the menu. You can also click the disk icon. After closing the saved file, you should notice it listed in the folder. In the case of Figure 1.19, we renamed the file "Hello World." You can see it is now saved as a Jupyter Notebook file.

Saving a Python File Locally

You can save your code as a Python file (.py extension) when you have the file loaded in a window. You simply need to select *File* then select *Download as* followed by selecting *Python (.py)* from the menus as show in figure 1.20. This will save a copy of the code in the current file in text format with a .py extension.

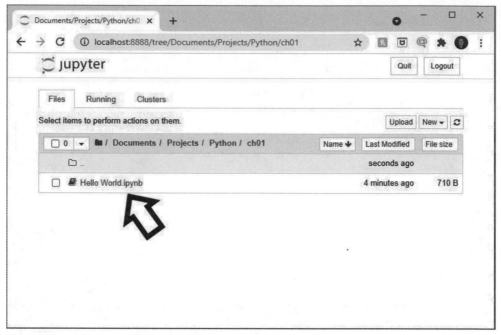

Figure 1.19: The new file in the folder

Opening an Existing Jupyter Notebook File

As you could see in Figure 1.19, Jupyter Notebook files use the filename extension `.ipynb`, which your computer will not recognize if you try to open a file directly from the file manager. To open an existing file, you will need to start Jupyter Notebook using the previous steps. When you see the list of folders in your browser window, you can again navigate to find the file you want to open. For example, if you want to open a file named `HelloWorld.ipynb` that is in `Documents/Projects/Python/ch01`, you would navigate by clicking each folder in the path: *Documents*, then *Projects*, then *Python*, then *ch01*. Once there, you should see the file.

To open the file, simply click it. The file will open in a new editor tab, leaving the folder tab open so you can easily switch back to it if you wish.

> **ADDITIONAL RESOURCES**
> **NOTE** For more information about Jupyter Notebook, see the Jupyter Notebook Documentation at `http://jupyter-notebook-beginner-guide.readthedocs.io/en/latest/what_is_jupyter.html`.

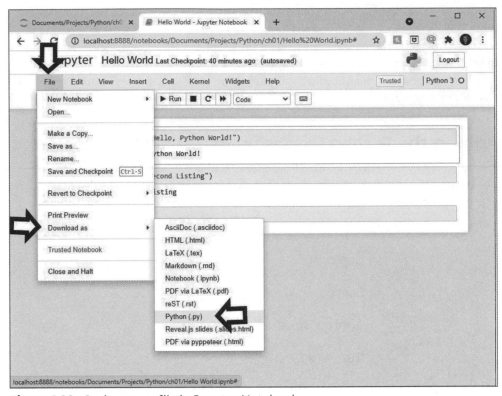

Figure 1.20: Saving a `.py` file in Jupyter Notebook

A QUICK LOOK AT VISUAL STUDIO CODE

You've now seen Replit, which can be used online without installing anything locally, and you've seen Anaconda Jupyter Notebook, which you can use locally. There are other IDEs that are available as well. Microsoft Visual Studio Code allows you to get started coding Python at no cost.

Visual Studio Code is a powerful IDE that lets you run Python scripts on Windows, macOS, and Linux. As an added bonus, it can be used for many other programming languages. Note that this is just one of many IDEs that are available for you to use. It is beyond the scope of this book to discuss how to use Visual Studio Code; however, we will walk through downloading a copy and adding the Python extension.

Obtaining Visual Studio Code

You can obtain a copy of Visual Studio Code at `https://code.visualstudio.com/`. When you arrive at this page, you will find an option to download a copy. You should select, download, and install the stable version for your operating system.

After downloading the Visual Studio Code program, you can run it to install the IDE. When you run the installation, you will first be asked to accept the licensing agreement, and then to set the location where you want the program files installed on your computer, to select a system folder, and to select additional tasks such as creating a desktop icon.

When you first run Visual Studio Code, you will be greeted with a welcome screen and possibly release notes.

Adding the Python Extension to Visual Studio Code

In order to be able to fully use Visual Studio Code for Python, you need to add an extension to the IDE. You can do this by clicking the *Extensions* icon on the left side of the page or pressing Ctrl+Shift+X. Figure 1.21 shows the icon that you should click.

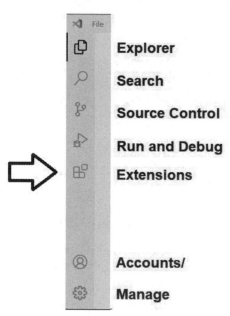

Figure 1.21: The Extensions icon

When you click the *Extensions* icon, you will be prompted with the Extensions dialog in the left pane of the IDE as shown in Figure 1.22. This dialog shows the language support that has been installed and provides a prompt for you to search for additional extensions within the Marketplace. You can enter **Python** into the search box and press Enter to start the search.

When you search for Python, you will likely receive a number of search results. These are different Python tools and extensions written by a variety of people and organizations. We recommend you select "Python" with Microsoft as the developer. You can click the *Install* button to the right, as indicated in Figure 1.23, to start the installation of the extension.

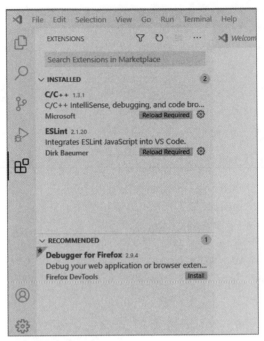

Figure 1.22: The Extensions dialog

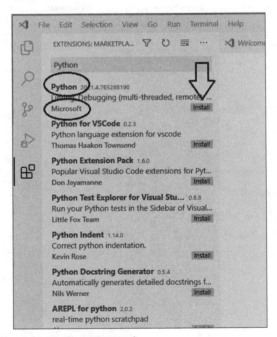

Figure 1.23: Installing the Python Extension

The extension will be installed and a welcome page with details on the extension will be displayed. The welcome page should also present you with a Python getting started page.

> **NOTE** Again, it is beyond the scope of this book to detail using Visual Studio Code. You can find help and tutorials through links on the Help menu of the IDE. This includes a number of introductory videos.

USING PYTHON FROM THE COMMAND LINE

If you installed Jupyter Notebook or Visual Studio Code to your local machine, then you should already have Python installed as well. If you did not install a Python IDE locally, you can download and install Python on its own.

You can find the Python files at `https://www.python.org/downloads/`. When you land on this page, it will have a button to download the current version of Python, similar to what is shown in Figure 1.24. There are also links to get to the download files for other operating systems.

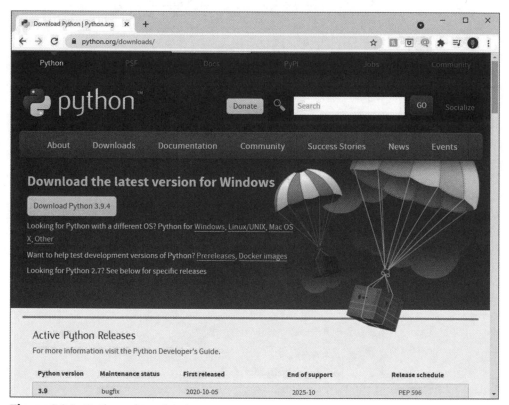

Figure 1.24: Python download page

To install Python, download and run the file for your operating system. If you run this on Windows, you will be greeted with the Setup wizard as shown in Figure 1.25.

Figure 1.25: The Python Setup wizard

It is recommended that you click the two checkboxes on this dialog box to install the launcher for all users and to add Python to PATH so that it can be accessed from any folder on your system using the command line. If you want to change the location where it will be installed, you can click the *Customize installation* link. The customization link will also let you add or remove some of the features being installed. It is recommended that other than checking the two boxes on the main dialog in Figure 1.25, you should use the default values for everything else.

Click *Install Now* to start the installation. This will start the installation and display a status bar as shown in Figure 1.26.

Once the installation is complete, a dialog box will be displayed indicating success. You can click the *Close* button. At this point, you've installed Python to your system and can close the dialog box.

With Python installed, you can now run Python scripts from the command line. To do that, navigate to the directory where a Python file is saved. At the command line, type **python** followed by the full name of the file. If the file is called hello.py, type:

```
python hello.py
```

Python will then run the script and display the output.

> **NOTE** If you are using Windows 10 or later, you can also look for Python in the Microsoft Store and download it from there.

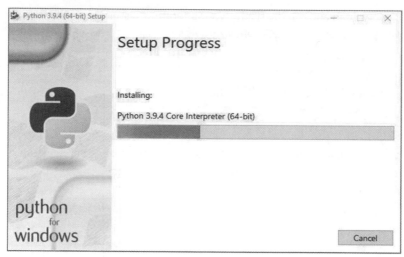

Figure 1.26: Installing in progress

SUMMARY

In this lesson, you learned about a number of integrated development environments (IDEs) that can be used to code and run Python scripts. Three different tools were presented as well as information provided on installing Python to run from the command line. If you are unsure which tool to use, we recommend starting with Replit as it is readily available online and doesn't require any installation.

Now that you have completed Lesson 1, you should

- Know of a few Python tools that are available.
- Learn where you can access an online Python tool to enter and run Python scripts.
- Create and run your first Python script.

EXERCISES

Most lessons will conclude with one or more exercises that you can do to help confirm your understanding of the lesson. You should complete each exercise before moving on to the next lesson. The exercises in this lesson are:

Exercise 1: Say Hello

Exercise 2: What's It Do?

Exercise 3: Counting

Exercise 4: Fruity Code

> **NOTE** Software development skills build on each other, so many of the exercises in future lessons might also require an understanding of the skills and tools presented in earlier lessons.

Exercise 1: Say Hello

Sign up for a Replit account and enter Listing 1.1 presented in this lesson. Run the listing and confirm you get the results shown in the lesson. Change the text that is within the quotes to display your name.

If you installed a different IDE, then enter Listing 1.1 into it and execute the code. Again, confirm you get the result shown in the lesson.

Exercise 2: What's It Do?

Enter the code in Listing 1.2 into an IDE and run it. What is the output?

LISTING 1.2

What's It Do?

```
x = 2
while(x < 100000):
  print(x)
  x = x**2
```

You will want to make sure that you enter the code exactly as shown. You should include all spaces and punctuation. You should also make sure that you use the same case for the characters. Print is not the same as print.

> **NOTE** Hint: If you entered everything correctly, five numbers should be displayed when the script is run.

Exercise 3: Counting

Enter the code in Listing 1.3 into an IDE and run it. What is the output? Don't worry about what the code is actually doing. Rather, focus on entering the code into your IDE and having it run.

LISTING 1.3

Counting

```
print("Getting ready to count...")
for x in range(10):
  print("I'm counting and at ", x) # make sure to indent this line!
print("Done counting!")
```

Again, make sure you enter the code exactly as presented. When you run the script, you should see output similar to the following:

```
Getting ready to count...
I'm counting and at  0
I'm counting and at  1
I'm counting and at  2
I'm counting and at  3
I'm counting and at  4
I'm counting and at  5
I'm counting and at  6
I'm counting and at  7
I'm counting and at  8
I'm counting and at  9
Done counting!
```

Exercise 4: Fruity Code

Enter Listing 1.4 and run it. Again, focus on entering the code into your IDE and running it. You'll learn more about what this code is doing in later lessons.

LISTING 1.4

Fruity code

```
fruit = input("Enter your favorite fruit and press Enter: ")
print("Your favorite fruit is ", fruit)
```

When you run this, the output should look like the following, except with the fruit you enter:

```
Enter your favorite fruit and press Enter: pear
Your favorite fruit is  pear
```

Understanding Programming Basics

This lesson provides an overview of general concepts related to the world of computer programming. The information presented will help you understand basic concepts that are common to all types of programming, regardless of the language you use to write computer code, as well as give you some basic tools that you can use to design your own programs.

LEARNING OBJECTIVES

By the end of this lesson, you will be able to:

- Explain basic concepts in computer programming, including computational thinking and creating algorithms.
- Identify concepts that are relevant to most computer languages, including reserved words, operators, statements, and syntax.
- Describe what a variable is and how languages use data types.

THE FUTURE OF COMPUTER PROGRAMMING

One of the most important parts of working in the field of computer programming is understanding that things change. The change may be slow, or it may happen overnight, but it is often said that the only certainty in the field of computer science is that things will change. Even considering the marvels that today's society already takes for granted, new technology is always on the horizon.

Virtual reality allows people to work as if they are in an office, exercise as if they are in a gym, and check out new places as if they traveled there, all from the comfort of their living room.

Anyone who chooses to work in technology must be willing to continue learning. Not only is new hardware invented every day, but software and software programming languages are also in a constant state of revision and evolution. Although the basic concepts of software development will not change in the foreseeable future, the way people implement those concepts will change drastically. It is quite likely that some of the elements taught in this text will be obsolete in a year or two.

Good software developers keep up with what is happening in the field, and there are lots of resources available to do so. Here are some examples:

- Magazines and newsletters allow professionals to read about upcoming technology. Many electronic newsletters are free, and you can always unsubscribe in the future if you decide one isn't useful to you.

- Many developers produce podcasts that cover specific topics in software development. You can subscribe and listen while commuting or doing housework.

- You might also want to find or form groups that meet regularly to discuss current industry topics. These groups are not only a source of information for changes in the field but can also help members network for job opportunities. This includes both local in-person groups and online groups through social media or meeting software such as Meetup.

What Is Programming?

Programming in general is nothing more than telling something (noun) to do something (verb), normally with the goal of solving a problem. In the context of this book, we will be programming a computer.

What Is a Program?

Computers can compute anything that is computable. We can use computations to analyze data, create websites, and automate machine responses. Programming allows us to provide an efficient and tunable set of instructions for the computer to perform tasks that solve problems. In fact, from a developer's perspective, a program is often referred to as a **solution**.

In reality, humans can do everything that a computer can do, given the right set of instructions and a way to implement those instructions. However, since a computer can perform these instructions billions of times per second, it takes us much longer. Humans are also notoriously bad at following instructions, even with extensive programming, which is why we make significantly more mistakes than computers do.

At the same time, computers can literally do only those things we tell them to do, so they follow any instruction without fail. Even so-called "smart" computers that appear to learn new behavior on their own depend on input to adapt those behaviors. That means that if a computer makes a mistake, it is the fault of the person (or more likely, person**s**) who wrote the instructions or created the dataset.

These devices also seem limitless in what they can do, but in fact, there are limitations. They can do things quickly, but some parts, such as the processor and RAM, are faster than other parts, like hard drives and network connections. They also can't perform any task with incomplete instructions or inadequate resources, even if they have the instructions required to complete the task. A program designed to predict the next Oscar winner will fail if it does not have enough data, and a self-driving car will crash if it does not have adequate sensors to know what else is on the road. These failures are due to the program design, not because a machine is performing the task rather than a human.

Computational Thinking

The term **computational thinking** refers to a design approach that focuses on the steps required to solve a problem. It is essentially a way of thinking that allows us to break a larger problem down into smaller, more approachable problems, and we then use those smaller problems as stepping-stones to solving the larger problem at hand.

One aspect of computational thinking is *planning things in advance*, to be sure that resources are available when you need them. For example, when you leave for work or school in the morning, you take your briefcase or backpack, not because you need them on the commute but because you know you *will* need the contents when you arrive at your destination. Similarly, you likely take your car keys out of your pocket or check that you have your bus pass, to make sure that you have the resources you need to get there in the first place.

Another skill is using **algorithms**. While TV shows and movies about computers can make it sound like an algorithm is a complicated computer process, an algorithm is simply a set of instructions with a predefined goal. When you put together a model, build a piece of boxed furniture, or even follow a recipe to make a meal, you are using an algorithm that someone else wrote. As a software developer, you will have to define algorithms for your solutions, and you can start doing that now, even without a computer or any knowledge of programming languages.

Writing instructions for other humans is relatively easy because we can assume that most humans share some basic knowledge that they can build on. When a recipe tells you to add a cup of flour, it assumes that you know what a cup is, where the cup is stored in your kitchen, where the flour is stored in your kitchen, how to tell when the cup is full of flour, and that you should put the flour in the bowl *without* the cup itself.

Writing an algorithm for a computer, however, is more complicated because *a computer has no background knowledge*. If we were to write a program to make a pizza, for example, it would have to include detailed instructions on where to find the cup, where to find the flour, how to tell when the cup is full, and how to transfer the flour from the cup to the bowl.

> **NOTE** To see a humorous approach to writing an algorithm to make a peanut butter sandwich, watch the video at https://youtu.be/Ct-100UqmyY.

PROGRAMMING LANGUAGES

Programming languages are the way we humans communicate, instruct, and interact with computers. Just as computers have evolved over the decades, the languages we use to communicate with them have evolved. There are many different languages that software developers can choose from today; however, all of them have similar components and structures.

Computers themselves use only series of binary digits (which we often represent as 1s and 0s). Every "decision" that a computer makes, every instruction that it follows, and every action that it performs is broken down into a series of "yes" or "no" questions, with the answers being derived as 1 or 0. For this reason, the original programmers used binary values (like punch cards and magnetic tapes) to feed instructions into computers.

Over time, developers have created programming languages that are easier for humans to read and write, and software developers have many different languages to choose from today. The following is a short list of common programming languages, but there are many more:

- C
- C++
- C# (pronounced *C sharp*)
- Java

- JavaScript
- Python
- Swift
- Go

Modern programming languages are heavily based on natural human language, especially English, and as a result, they share some characteristics. However, because we need the instructions to be clear and unambiguous when we give them to a computer, programming languages are more structured than human languages are.

Computers, however, still speak only binary. This means that regardless of the language we choose to use to write a program, that program must be converted to binary before the computer can read and execute its instructions. Modern languages include a **compiler** that translates the computer code the developer has written into binary code that the computer can read.

Common Components

All modern programming languages include four basic components: statements, syntax, reserved words, and operators.

Statements

Each instruction in a program is called a **statement**, and each statement has a specific purpose within the program. A statement can perform a calculation, define a variable or a constant, start a loop, create a class or method, or make a decision.

Syntax

The **syntax** component works together with the statements. A language's syntax includes the rules that we must follow to write statements in that language, including the order in which the words appear in a statement, the use of upper- and lowercase letters, punctuation, spaces, and even indents.

Human languages also rely on syntax to create meaning. Consider how the commas are used (or not used) in the following sentences:

- I love baking, my family, and my friends.
- I love baking my family and my friends.

Without the commas, the second sentence takes on a disturbingly different meaning.

Similarly, in English, changing the word order completely changes the meaning in the following sentences:

- The cat caught the fly.
- The fly caught the cat.

And if we put the words in a random order, the sentence has no meaning at all:

- Cat the caught fly the.

Another important aspect of syntax is the use of spaces. In English, we generally use spaces to separate words, but our concept of a *word* is more flexible than what a programming language considers a word. For example, it is common in English to use names that include two or more separate words, like "Rockefeller Center" or "Michael Jones."

Because programming languages are more rigid, we cannot include spaces in things that we name, like variables or classes. When we want to name something in a program, and the name should include two or more human words, we can use one of the following strategies:

- Use an underscore where we would normally use a space, like `total_price`.

- String the words together but use capitalization to identify individual words. There are two options for this scenario:

  - **camelCase:** Use a lowercase letter at the start of the name, then capitalize each word following the first word.

  - **PascalCase:** Capitalize each word in the name.

- Use only lowercase or uppercase for all letters, like `roomarea` or `TOTALPRICE`

The last option is generally discouraged because it is harder for humans to read words that don't have appropriate spacing between them.

Most programming languages are also case-sensitive (meaning that `totalPrice` is not the same as `TotalPrice`), so it's a good idea to establish a naming convention early in the development process and follow that convention everywhere going forward. Specific languages normally have recommended naming conventions, and everyone on the development team should agree on and follow the same naming convention.

Each language has its own syntax variations. For example, in Java, any statement must end in a semicolon, while in Python, semicolons are generally optional, and you can simply hit Enter at the end of a statement instead. Part of learning a language (or learning a second language) is to identify the syntax requirements for that language.

> **NOTE** This lesson is providing you with an overview of concepts. As you progress through this book, you'll learn more about some of the terms being used here. Don't be concerned at this time if you don't know what things like variables or classes are.

Reserved Words

All computer languages have **reserved words**, words that are specific to the compiler for that language and that have a predefined meaning to the compiler. These are also sometimes referred to as **keywords**. Because these words have specific meanings within the language, we cannot use them for other purposes when we write our own programs.

While each language has its own set of reserved words, some common examples include the following:

- **IF** is used to indicate that the algorithm must make a decision based on the status of a given value. This is similar to how we use the word in English: "*If* it is raining, I will stay home today."

- **WHILE** is used to indicate that an instruction (or set of instructions) should repeat as long as a given condition is met. This is similar to English: "*While* it is raining, I will stay home."

- **PRINT** generates output to the user. In the early days of computing, output was always printed on paper, but today, many languages use a variant of *print* to create output on a monitor or similar screen.

You can normally find the reserved words for any language in the documentation for that language, which is nearly always available online.

Operators

All computer languages rely heavily on **operators**. An operator is a symbol that will allow some sort of comparison or manipulation to occur between values. We call a statement that includes an operator an **operation**.

Math operators are the most common:

- + (addition)
- - (subtraction)
- * (multiplication)
- / (division)
- % (modulus; the remainder of a division operator)

All languages also use an order of precedence for statements that include more than two operators. You should remember the acronym "Please Excuse My Dear Aunt Sally," which reminds us that math operations are executed in the order of parentheses first, then exponents, multiplication and division, and finally addition and subtraction.

Programming languages also rely heavily on **comparison operators**, which we use to compare one value to another to determine if a statement is True or False. The most common include:

- = (equal to)
- != (not equal to)

- > (greater than)
- < (less than)
- >= (greater than or equal to)
- <= (less than or equal to)

Another common category is truth operators, which are also used to determine whether a given statement is true or false:

- && (AND)
- || (OR)
- ! (reverses the truth of the value, so !FALSE is TRUE)

Hello, World!

A common first step when learning a new programming language is to produce the phrase "Hello, world!" on a screen or printer. This exercise introduces the learner to the basic syntax of the new language, as well as some reserved words.

The code snippets in Listings 2.1 through 2.3 show how this instruction is written in different languages. In each example, most of the words *except* "Hello, world!" are reserved words for that language.

LISTING 2.1

Python

```
print "Hello, world!"
```

LISTING 2.2

Java

```
public class Hello {
    public static void main(String[] args) {
        System.out.println("Hello, World!");
    }
}
```

LISTING 2.3

C#

```
using System;

namespace HelloWorldSample
{
    class Program
    {
        static void Main(string[] args)
        {
            Console.WriteLine("Hello World!");
        }
    }
}
```

Read through each of these examples and see if you can identify any similarities. Can you tell what each reserved word does in the snippet? How do the languages differ in their use of punctuation, such as commas, semicolons, brackets, and parentheses?

DATA TYPES AND VARIABLES

Modern programming languages depend on the use of variables and constants to know what values the program should use when performing an operation. When learning a programming language, it is important to understand how data is stored as well as understand the common data types used.

Data Types

Many instructions in a computer program rely on **values**. For example, a standard addition operation requires three values: the two numbers that will be added together and the resulting sum.

```
1 + 2 = 3
```

A basic print statement will generally include only one value, however: the value that the instruction will display to the user.

```
print("Hello, world!")
```

An `if` statement may include only two values that are compared to each other to determine if the statement is True or False.

```
if a > b
```

The values themselves have a variety of **data types** that determine if the computer can execute the statement or not. While programming languages vary somewhat in what data types they support and how the data types are identified, the most common include:

- Text
- Numbers
- True/False
- Date/Time
- Data collections

Different programming languages use different terms for these concepts, but the concepts themselves show up in any programming language.

Text

Text is exactly what it sounds like: values that are made up of letters, punctuation, symbols, and even numbers. In computer programming, we often use the term **string** to refer to a text value because the value itself is composed of a string of individual characters.

An example is shown in the following statement:

```
print("Hello, world!")
```

In this case, the value that will print is the string inside quotation marks:

```
Hello, World!
```

Strings can include numbers when we don't plan to perform mathematical operations on the value. For example, a zip code (10045) or a phone number (905-555-4785) is normally treated as a string because we aren't likely to add them together or find their square root.

Numbers

Values that we plan to do math with must be treated as numbers in any programming language. Most languages also distinguish between **integers** and **decimal** values:

- An integer is a whole number with no digits to the right of the decimal place, like 4 or 8467. We are most likely to use integers to count things (like items in an inventory) and when we only want to consider whole objects rather than partial objects.

- Decimal values, also called **doubles** or **floats** in some languages, allow values to the right of the decimal place, even if a given real value does not have any. We use decimal values for anything related to money, such as prices or wages, to be sure that we can store the entire number, including all decimal places. We also normally use decimal values when we are measuring things, including length and weight, so that we are not limited to whole units.

Although we can treat numbers like text (especially numbers that are used for identification rather than as mathematical values), no language allows the use of text as numbers.

True/False

Conditional operations (including if-statements) depend on whether a value is True or False. For example, the value of c in the following statement would be either True or False, depending on the values assigned to a and b:

```
a > b = c
```

We often refer to these as **Boolean values**. They typically translate as True or False, but they can also be represented as Yes/No, On/Off, or even 1/0. Because there are only two options, we also refer to these as *binary values*.

Date/Time

As humans, we tend to think of dates as something on a calendar, with months, days, and years, while time includes hours, minutes, and seconds. However, computers need a more digital approach to this concept. In most systems, Date/Time is a single data type that functions more as a combined number than as distinct pieces. In a common approach, calendar values are represented as digits to the left of the decimal place, where each unit is a day; and hours, minutes, and seconds are values to the right of the decimal place, representing a part of the day.

The key part of using Date/Time data is conversion between the way humans represent the value (for example: "02/07/2020 12:57") and how computers represent the value to perform calculations using that value. As programmers, we have to define the date format humans are using so that the program knows how to interpret and display the value.

Data Collections

We often use data collections in programming, and most languages support the use of data collections as a data type. A **data collection** is just what it sounds like: a collection of individual values treated as a single unit. Common examples include *lists*, *sets*, and *arrays*.

Some languages, like Python, allow a data collection to include items of different data types. In the following Python example, the list named `list_of_items` includes string values, an integer, and a float:

```
list_of_items = ["Kate", "124 W Main Street Boston", 24, 4.0]
```

Other languages, including Java and C#, require that all items in a collection have the same data type, and you must declare that data type when you create the collection. These languages are referred to as "strongly typed" and they generally help to ensure that data is treated as the type expected, such as treating a number as a number and not as a character. The following example creates an array of integers named `teamScores` in Java:

```
int[] teamScores = {
    2, 45, 4, 8, 99,
    23, 67, 1, 88, 42
};
```

Data collections allow us to use a defined group of values as a single unit, such as a class roster or an inventory list, while also allowing us to manage and retrieve individual values within that collection.

Variables

Imagine that you were asked to design a program that would calculate the amount of carpeting needed for a customer's order and then use that amount to calculate the total cost of the order. Given that Bob Smith's floor is 10 feet by 20 feet and that the selected carpet is $2 per square foot, you could represent this as:

```
10 * 20 = 200
200 * 2 = 400
```

The result is that Bob owes $400 for his carpeting.

Now assume that Mary Jones also wants new carpet, but her room is 15 feet by 25 feet, and the carpet she wants is $1.75 per square foot. If we use only the values, we have to write the program over again from scratch:

```
15 * 25 = 375
375 * 1.75 = 656.25
```

While this looks like a very simple program and it doesn't take that long to write it all over again, most programs are considerably more complicated. For that reason, developers prefer to use more abstract values that can be recycled, rather than real values that must be updated each time we run the program.

We can describe the steps used to calculate the total cost using the following statements:

1. Multiply the *length* of the room by the *width* of the room to produce a total *square footage*.

2. Multiply the *square footage* by the *carpet price* to produce the *total cost*.

Writing it out like this shows us that our program uses five different values:

- Length
- Width
- Total square footage
- Carpet price
- Total cost

In this case, we are using **variables** to represent the values we need for our program. They are called variables because the exact value can vary each time we run the program and their values can change between the start of a program and the end of a program.

When we use variables, we create code that is more reusable than if we hard-code the values in the program like we did in the first two examples. Using pseudocode, our program could look something like:

```
length * width = total_footage
total_footage * price = total_cost
```

We would then add steps to input values for length, width, and price, as well as output the final cost at the end:

```
length = [user_input_length]
width = [user_input_width]
price = [user_input_price]

length * width = total_footage
total_footage * price = total_cost

print total_cost
```

While this may look more complicated than the two lines of code we started with, this program will now work for any room and any carpet, as long as we have those values on hand before we run the program. More importantly, as the software developer writing the program, we don't need to know what those values will be. As an added advantage, anyone (even someone who knows nothing about the code or the program) can easily tell what the program is supposed to do, because the variable names are more meaningful than the values themselves.

Reserving Memory

Another role of variables is in the preparation stage of running a program, and in this respect, you can think of a variable as a place setting at a table. If you are holding a dinner party, you likely know in advance how many people plan to attend. Even before you start cooking the meal, you may set out dinner places at the table, to be sure you have enough room for every person. While you may end up seating different people in different places, you reserve the spaces in advance to be sure that you know where to find them when you need them.

We use variables in a similar way when writing a computer program. When we **declare a variable** (as in the previous statement `length = [user_input_length]`), we reserve a spot in the computer's memory, and we give that spot a name. When we reference the variable later (`length * width`), the program uses the variable's name to find that spot in memory and retrieve the value that is currently stored there.

To extend the dinner place setting example somewhat, consider that the contents of that place setting may change as the meal progresses. For example, the starting course might be soup, and then the main dish would replace the soup dish in a later course.

Variables work the same way in that the value assigned to a variable may change as the program progresses. For example, when you purchase items in a grocery store, you can normally see the total sale value change each time the cashier scans another product. The pseudocode for this program might look something like what is presented in Listing 2.4.

LISTING 2.4

Pseudocode for a grocery store program

```
purchase_total = 0
product_price = 0

//while loop calculates subtotal until last product is scanned
while products to buy
    product_price = [upc_scan]
    purchase_total = purchase_total + product_price
    print purchase_total
```

```
print purchase_total

end program
```

In the following line, the current value of `purchase_total` is replaced by a new value that includes the price of the most recent product scanned:

```
purchase_total = purchase_total + product_price
```

This effectively updates the current total each time a new product is scanned into the order so that the final `purchase_total` reflects the total price of all products included in the order. When the program retrieves that final value, it pulls it from the same memory spot that started with a value of 0.

Note that this also means we only need two variables (`purchase_total` and `product_price`), regardless of the number of items the customer purchases. If we couldn't reuse variables like this, we would need separate placeholders for the price of each item and separate placeholders for each subtotal.

Variables and Data Types

Programming languages differ in how variables work with data types. These will generally use either dynamic or static typing.

Dynamic Typing

Some languages, like JavaScript and Python, automatically assign data types to a variable based on the value assigned to the variable. They also change the data type of the variable if a value with a different data type is assigned to the variable later in the program. This is called **dynamic typing**.

For example, the following series of statements is valid in Python:

```
x = 75 // data type integer (int)
x = 6.458 // data type float
x = "Hello, world!" // data type string (str)
```

Because we use the same variable (x) in each of these statements, the final value of x would be "Hello, World!" if we were to run this code in Python.

Static Typing

In other languages, including Java and C#, you must assign a data type to a variable when you declare it, and values stored in the variable must be appropriate for that data type. Because the data type cannot change once the variable has been declared, we refer to this as **static typing**.

The following examples declare a series of variables in Java:

```
// create an integer variable named quantity with the value 75
int quantity = 75;

// create a float variable named price with the value 6.458
float price = 6.458;

// create a string variable named greeting with the value "Hello, world!"
String greeting = "Hello, world!";
```

Note that in this snippet, each variable has a different name. If we were to use the same name for each variable (as in the previous Python example), we would have problems in Java. A float value stored in an integer variable would have the values to the right of the decimal place truncated (or deleted), and it simply isn't possible to store text in a variable defined as a number.

> **NOTE** Static typing is also known as strongly typed.

Constants

While most values used in a program should be incorporated as variables (even when you know the value up front and that value is not likely to change), there are times when we should use constants instead.

When we use constants, we are essentially **hard coding** the value into the program in a way that will make it difficult to change in the future. This means that we need to think through the use of constants carefully before we use them.

The following are three examples of using hard-coded constants.

Example 1: Area of a Circle

When calculating the area of a circle, you use the formula:

$$A = \pi\ r^2$$

In this formula, you would use a variable for area (A) and for the circle's radius (r), because both values will change from one circle to the next, but π has a fixed value that will never change. In this case, we would use a constant to represent the value of π, rather than a variable.

Example 2: Tax Rate

A given state currently has a state sales tax rate of 4%, and it's had the same sales tax rate for several decades. In fact, there is no evidence that the tax rate is likely to change in the future.

While this might seem like a constant value that could be hard coded into a program (on the grounds that it is not likely to be different in the future), it is much better to err on the side of caution and use a variable that is assigned the value of 4%. That will allow for future changes to the tax rate, as well as make the program easier to adapt to a variety of states with different sales tax rates.

In addition, using a variable makes the code more readable. Other developers looking through the code would see a variable named something like `state_sales_tax` and understand immediately what the value represents, while the purpose of a constant value like `0.04` would be less transparent.

Example 3: Output Messages

Messages that are displayed to the user are not necessarily variables: most of them are defined once in a program and will not change, even if they are used in multiple places. However, you can have a variety of messages in the same program, and you are likely to use different messages in different programs.

As an example, you might have a prompt that requests that the user enter their name when the program starts:

```
print("Hi! Please enter your name: ")
```

This is fine as long as this is the only message you want the user to see. However, you may decide to make things more interesting by using phrases like "Good morning!" or "Good afternoon!" instead of just "Hi!" This would require the use of a variable, and the logic would look something like this:

```
if time between 5am and noon
    greeting = "Good morning!"
else if time from noon to 5pm
    greeting = "Good afternoon!"
else if time between 5pm and 9pm
    greeting = "Good evening!"
else
    greeting = "Good night!"

print(greeting + "Please enter your name: ")
```

In this example, we use a variable with an if-statement to determine which greeting is appropriate based on the time of day. We then combine the variable's value with a constant ("Please enter your name:") to produce the output the user will see when they start the program.

SUMMARY

Many software developers will say that programming is part art and part science. Much like the renowned painter Pablo Picasso made use of tools like canvases and brushes to convey his images to the world, programmers use tools like computers and their peripherals to execute their instructions. The code and its design represent the art. The execution of the code with the application and the peripherals represent the science.

Modern programming languages are written to be more human friendly than the binary code that computers use to process instructions, and each language has its own reserved words and syntax. Learning to write computer programs means becoming familiar with how to write instructions in the selected language. This includes learning the language's reserved words, how statements are written, and what syntax is required.

As you work through this book and learn to write Python programs, you'll find that the things covered in this lesson will be revisited in detail. You'll learn how each is applied with Python to create your own masterful programs in the same way Picasso created his masterful art pieces.

Now that you have completed Lesson 2, you should be able to

- Explain basic concepts in computer programming, including computational thinking and creating algorithms.

- Identify concepts that are relevant to most computer languages, including reserved words, operators, statements, and syntax.

- Describe what a variable is and how languages use data types.

EXERCISES

The exercises here provide you with additional practice to deepen your application of the concepts learned in this lesson and to achieve the objectives for this lesson.

It is recommended that you complete each exercise as described. The exercises are:

Exercise 1: Daily Tasks

Exercise 2: Python Programming

Exercise 1: Daily Tasks

As you go through routine tasks over the next few days, think through and define algorithms for those tasks. Consider writing the steps out for the following tasks:

- Tie shoes
- Load a dishwasher
- Make a bed
- Create a peanut butter and jelly sandwich

How would you write the steps for these tasks for a computer? Write the steps and see if another person can follow them exactly as they are written.

Exercise 2: Python Programming

In the previous lesson, you learned how to enter and run a Python application. Enter the following code in Listing 2.5 and run it. Note that the listing uses comments, variables, reserved words, operators, and other programming elements. You'll learn more about these through the rest of this book.

LISTING 2.5

A Python program

```python
# A short python program
user_input_length = input("Enter a length (whole number): ")
user_input_width = input("Enter a width (whole number): ")
user_input_price = input("Enter a price (numbers and decimal only): ")

length = int(user_input_length)
width = int(user_input_width)
price = float(user_input_price)

# Do calculations
total_footage = length * width
total_cost = total_footage * price

# display results
print("-----------------")
print("Length: ", length)
print("Width: ", width)
print("Total Footage: ", total_footage)
print("Total Cost: ", total_cost)
```

When you run this program, you will be prompted to enter three numbers.

Lesson 3
Exploring Basic Python Syntax

In this lesson, we will start programming Python. We will begin with an introductory look at Python syntax, comments, variables, user input, and data types.

LEARNING OBJECTIVES

By the end of this lesson, you will be able to:

- Create one-line and multiline expressions to perform basic tasks in Python.
- Include comments in a Python program.
- Declare and use variables in a Python program.
- Write a Python program that accepts user input.

> **NOTE** As you go through this and future lessons, you will need an integrated development environment, as mentioned in Lesson 2. We recommend that you enter each listing from the book into your development environment and run the code. The best way to learn is by doing, so you should enter and play with the code by making changes and seeing the results.

There are a number of key terms you will see in this lesson. These include the following:

- **Syntax** refers to the order in which letters, words, and characters appear in the code, including when to use punctuation symbols that serve as operators (like semicolons, brackets, parentheses, and slashes). While all programming languages have syntax rules, they are different from one language to another. Putting words in the wrong order or including characters in the wrong place leads to syntax errors that prevent the code from running.

- **Comments** are code within Python that does not execute. Comments can be used to explain Python code, or make it more readable, or you can use comments during testing.

- **Variables** are names given to areas within memory used to store information.

- **User input (*input* function)** allows the developer to ask the program user for input. You can use the input function to tell the program to stop and wait for the user to input data.

- **Data types** determine the "type" or format (such as a number versus a letter) of information stored within the memory space versus variables that are names given to areas within memory used to store information.

- **Commands** are statements that direct an application to take some specific action when executed.

- **Operators** are symbols used to execute arithmetic or logical computations.

- **Snippet** is a term used in programming that describes a smaller portion of programming code. Snippets will not typically run on their own and must be included in a larger code block to work.

USING WITH SINGLE-LINE COMMANDS

When writing Python scripts, we normally write one statement per line, where a statement is a complete command. Python executes each statement in the order they appear in the code. The syntax would be:

Command	line 1 parameter
Command	line 2 parameter

As a Python developer, you may be tasked with developing or maintaining a variety of functions within code. Let's say you are tasked with building a banking application for a financial institution to communicate information with customers and facilitate transactions. The Python code in Listing 3.1 prints two messages using the `print()` command.

LISTING 3.1

Printing in Python

```
print("Hello, welcome to the banking portal.")
print("In this portal, you can handle all your banking needs.")
```

When you run this code, the following is displayed:

```
Hello, welcome to the banking portal.
In this portal, you can handle all your banking needs.
```

You should copy the code from the listing into your IDE and run it. For example, you can copy it into Repl.it, which was covered in Lesson 1, and click Run to see the output in Figure 3.1.

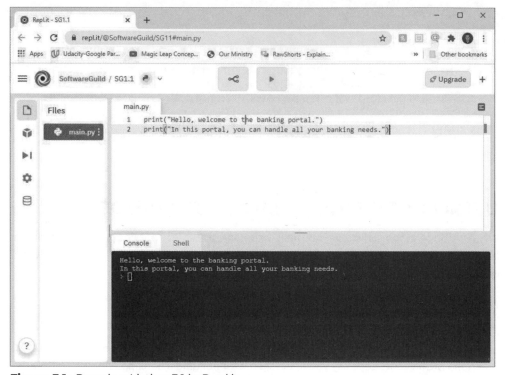

Figure 3.1: Running Listing 3.1 in Repl.it

You should experiment with the `print()` command by changing one or both statements and adding at least one more `print` statement.

USING SEMICOLONS

We can choose to terminate statements with a semicolon. Semicolons are optional as long as we have only one statement per line. A semicolon in Python denotes separation, rather than termination. It allows you to write multiple statements on the same line:

```
command('Statement1'); command('Statement 2'); command('Statement3')
```

As an example, you can enter multiple `print` statements on the same line separated by a semicolon:

```
print("Hello, world!"); print("How are you doing?")
```

If you enter this snippet of code into your IDE and run it, you'll see the expected output:

```
Hello, world!
How are you doing?
```

In a banking application, you may need to communicate information to customers using multiple lines of code. Let's look at how you can create a menu of options. As we continue building on our banking application, we want to add a menu system. Consider what syntax is needed to create a code snippet that allows the following messages to be displayed:

```
Hello, welcome to the banking portal.
In this portal, you can handle all your banking needs.
Please enter a selection from the following menu
Type Login to log in
Type Quit to quit
```

To create this menu of text, you can use several print statements as you've seen before. Adding a semicolon at the end of each line will help denote that each line is separate. Listing 3.2 provides a solution. Enter this listing and run it to see that it matches the expected output.

LISTING 3.2

Banking application menu

```
print("Hello, welcome to the banking portal.");
print("In this portal, you can handle all your banking needs.");
print("Please enter a selection from the following menu");
print("Type Login to log in");
print("Type Quit to quit");
```

As mentioned, a semicolon is not actually required at the end of a command (also known as an instruction) unless there are several instructions written on the same line. This means you could remove the semicolons in Listing 3.2 and the code would execute in the same manner. In fact, the following snippet:

```
print("Hello, welcome to the banking portal");print("In this portal, you can handle all your banking needs")
```

is the same as

```
print("Hello, welcome to the banking portal")
print("In this portal, you can handle all your banking needs")
```

In a banking application, you may need to communicate information to customers with multiple lines of code. Let's make the code from Listing 3.2 more concise by using semicolons this way. Since we can write more than one instruction on the same line, we must use a semicolon at the end of each instruction as shown in Listing 3.3.

LISTING 3.3

A more concise banking application menu

```
print("Hello, welcome to the banking portal.");print("In this portal, you can
handle all your banking needs.");print("Please enter a selection from the
following menu");print("Type Login to log in");print("Type Quit to quit");
```

> **NOTE** While Listing 3.3 is more concise, so is the ability to easily maintain code. Making it easier to read code makes it easier to maintain code, so it is good to balance conciseness with maintainability.

CONTINUING WITH BACKSLASH

If an instruction uses more than one line, we can use the backslash operator (\) as the last character of the line. Python interprets the line following a backslash as a continuation of the instruction.

Listing 3.4 shows an example of an instruction that is written on several lines.

LISTING 3.4

A multiline instruction

```
print("This is a loooooooooooonggggggggggggg \
stringgggggggggggggggggggggggggggggggggg")
```

When we run this listing, the following output is displayed:

```
'This is a loooooooooooonggggggggggggg stringgggggggggggggggggggggggggggggggggg'
```

As we continue to build our banking app, experimenting with output and how users will view our information is important. Also, we can experiment with how our code will be formatted for those on our team to review as it relates to editing and maintaining our code.

Enter Listing 3.5 into your IDE.

LISTING 3.5

A broken multiline instruction

```
print(
"Hello, welcome to the banking portal.
```

```
In this portal, you can handle all of your banking needs.
Please enter a selection from the following menu. Type Login to log in. Type Quit
to quit"
)
```

When you run this listing, you will get an error similar to the following:

```
File "main.py", line 2
    "Hello, welcome to the banking portal.
                                          ^
SyntaxError: EOL while scanning string literal
```

How would you fix the code in a way that keeps the instruction on four separate lines? The answer is to use the backslash as shown in Listing 3.6.

LISTING 3.6

The multiline banking instructions

```
print(
"Hello, welcome to the banking portal. \
In this portal, you can handle all of your banking needs. \
Please enter a selection from the following menu. Type Login to log in. Type Quit
to quit" \
)
```

WORKING WITH CASE STRUCTURE

Everything in Python is case-sensitive. "Print" is not the same as "print." The code will report an error for the Print command since Python will only recognize lowercase print as a valid command. Enter and run Listing 3.7 to see the result of this in action.

LISTING 3.7

Showing case sensitivity of Python

```
print("This will be displayed.")
Print("This will throw an error.")
```

When this code is executed, we see that Print is not the same as print. The second line of code throws an error for the Print command because it is not a valid Python command. The following is the output from running Listing 3.7:

```
This will be displayed.
--------------------------------------------------------------------------------
NameError                               Traceback (most recent call last)

<ipython-input-7-2793b3127a9b> in <module>

     1 print("This will be displayed.")

----> 2 Print("This will throw an error.")

NameError: name 'Print' is not defined
```

> **NOTE** Quite often, you will be taking over and maintaining a section of
> code that you did not write. You may need to trace errors in the code. As
> you have seen in this lesson, formatting, syntax, and case can all make a
> difference in whether or not your code works properly.

ADDING COMMENTS

We use comments to document our code. It is a common industry practice to add comments to code. This ensures a higher level of continuity and ease of working with code. If we know who did what, why, and when, it makes the code easier to work with. We have other sources for documentation that are more detailed and laid out, but short segments of comments in our code can be invaluable for explaining what is going on.

You may not be the only person working in the code as you develop. Comments allow us to communicate with others by leaving "invisible notes" among the code.

In Python, comments begin with a hash symbol (#) and allow us to add notes that the code interpreter will ignore and not attempt to run. Comments are for those who are working with us to explain updates, actions, reasoning, and other issues that can help us as we work together with other developers to maintain an application.

Python will ignore all text to the right of the hash symbol, but it *will* read the next line if there is no hashtag on that line. In Listing 3.8, the first two lines are comments.

LISTING 3.8

Using comments

```
# this is a comment
# this is another comment
print("This is an instruction.")
```

When you execute this code, you'll see that the first two lines are ignored:

```
This is an instruction.
```

Going back to our banking scenario, we can add comments above the code we've created to document who wrote the code, when the code was written, and when the code was last edited. This is done as shown in Listing 3.9.

LISTING 3.9

Updated banking menu with comments

```
# add comment with the date where you added this code
# example: Written by Robert Smith on 05/07/2020
# example: Last edited on 05/08/2020
print("Hello, welcome to the banking portal.")
print("In this portal, you can handle all your banking needs.")
print("Please enter a selection from the following menu.")
print("Type Login to log in.")
print("Type Quit to quit.")
```

> **NOTE** The hash symbol (#) is also known as the number sign, hash sign, or pound sign.

USING THE INPUT FUNCTION

Most useful programs accept inputs from some source, process these inputs, and then output results to some destination. We can use the input() function in Python to ask for user input. The syntax of the input() function is:

```
input(prompt)
```

where the *prompt* is a string that represents optional text or a message that will be displayed before the input is obtained.

When the input() function executes, the optional text or message (if specified in quotation marks) will display on the output screen to ask a user to enter an input value. Program flow will be stopped until the user has given an input. Any data entered as input will be converted into a string. For example, if an integer value is entered, the input() function will still convert it into a string.

In the following example, we want to get input from the user:

```
input("How are you? ")
```

When this line of code executes, the text in quotes is displayed and the computer waits for the user to enter something. Figure 3.2 shows what would be seen if the user responded with **"I am great!"**

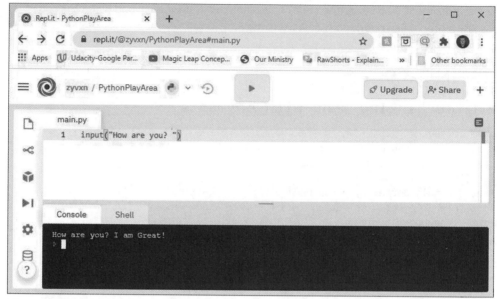

Figure 3.2: Using the input() function

Input is extremely important and one of the fundamental areas where we create inter-activity in our applications. Think of a form on a website, an online shopping experience, or the search function in an application; these are all areas where input is a key component of giving users the ability to create content, produce output, and perform actions.

Listing 3.10 is a better example. Going back to our banking example, let's use the input() function to ask the user to login or quit. Remember, this input isn't being stored yet, so nothing will happen when you enter anything, and you will not be able to store it for later use.

LISTING 3.10

Adding input() to our menu

```python
print("Hello, welcome to the banking portal.")
print("In this portal, you can handle all your banking needs.")
print("Please enter a selection from the following menu.")
print("Type Login to login")
print("Type Quit to quit")
input("Enter Login or Quit: ")
```

Now when this listing is executed, the user will be prompted to enter **Login** or **Quit**.

> **TIP** Because the user input happens immediately after the text displayed placed in the input( ) function, it is good to include a space at the end of the quote so that the entered text isn't flush against the prompt.

STORING INPUT

Storing input is an important process within the execution of an application. In Listing 3.10, while we prompt the user to enter a value, and while the user is able to enter that value, nothing is done with it. The input( ) function returns to us the value the user entered, but in the case of Listing 3.10, nothing was done with it.

When we want to store a series of input values, we can associate each input with a variable. We have a number of actions that we can do with the data that is captured. This can include analyzing, changing, or otherwise manipulating it during our program's execution. Using the created variable, we can reference the value received from the user.

In Listing 3.11, we once again use the input( ) function, but this time we create two variables, firstname and lastname, and associate an input statement with each variable.

LISTING 3.11

Storing input in a variable

```
firstname = input("Please enter your first name: ")
lastname = input("Please enter your last name: ")
print("Your name is:")
print(firstname + " " + lastname)
```

When Listing 3.11 is executed, the user is prompted to enter their first and last name, which are stored in variables called firstname and lastname. The values that were entered are then printed to the screen by passing the variables to the print( ) function. If the first name **Mary** is entered, and the last name **Smith** is entered, then the output should look like the following:

```
Please enter your first name: Mary
Please enter your last name: Smith
Your name is:
Mary Smith
```

In looking at the banking menu that was presented in Listing 3.10, the user is asked to
either Login or Quit; however, the input is never captured. To capture the user's response,
we can again use a variable. Listing 3.12 shows the updated banking menu that captures
the user's input in a variable called selection.

LISTING 3.12

Capturing the menu selection

```
print("Hello, welcome to the banking portal.")
print("In this portal, you can handle all your banking needs.")
print("Please enter a selection from the following menu.")
print("Type Login to log in")
print("Type Quit to quit")
selection = input("Enter your selection now: ")
print(selection)
```

When this listing is executed, the user is prompted to enter a selection, which will then
be printed as shown:

```
Hello, welcome to the banking portal.
In this portal, you can handle all your banking needs.
Please enter a selection from the following menu.
Type Login to log in
Type Quit to quit
Enter your selection now: Login
Login
```

UNDERSTANDING VARIABLE TYPES

As you have now seen, we use variables to store data in programs. Unlike other programming languages, Python has no command for declaring a variable. Rather, a variable is created the moment you first assign a value to it. For example:

```
variable = "John"
x = "John"
nbr = 42
age = 29
```

Because Python uses *dynamically typed* variables, we do not have to assign data types to them. Python automatically determines the appropriate data type based on the value associated with a variable.

Variables are used to store values during the course of the execution of our application. As we have already seen, variables can store user input, but they are also a way to store other things as well such as the result of calculations for future use and recall.

We usually define variables at the beginning of a program so that we have them available to use in statements and calculations in later parts of the program. Two of the most common store types are strings (the programming term for text) and numbers.

In Listing 3.13 we will examine storing several values with a few variables to illustrate the capabilities of Python to store and handle the various data types.

LISTING 3.13

Declaring variables

```
t=0       #a variable that stores an integer
message="Hello World"  #a variable that stores a string
tax_rate=0.06 #a variable that stores fractional numbers
isFromNH = False  #a variable that stores Boolean values True or False
pets = ["Maya","Marley"] #a variable that stores a list of strings
winning_numbers= [45,7,25,7,2,6,4,11]  #a variable that stores a list of integers
```

> **NOTE** Remember that the # symbol indicates the start of a comment. Everything starting with the # and going to the end of the line is ignored.

Running this code block will not produce any output because the code simply defines variables that could be used by other processes later in the program. This listing does, however, demonstrate the process of creating variables of several different data types including an integer, a string, a float value, a Boolean, a list of strings, and a list of integers. You'll learn more about many of these types in the next lesson.

DISPLAYING VARIABLE VALUES

After we have defined a variable, we can use the `print()` command to display the contents of the variable. You've seen `print()` used already, so the format should be familiar:

```
print( output_variable )
```

For example, the following defines a variable and prints its value:

```
x = "fun"
print( "Python is" + x )
```

This results in the following being printed:

```
Python is fun
```

Using variables to change and customize the output is important. Data can have a drastic effect on the functionality of our application, as it can affect what the user will see on-screen.

Generally, the more that we can customize our output, the more likely users will be to adopt and support that application. Tailoring an application to a user's needs is important and will definitely make attitudes toward our application more favorable.

In Listing 3.14 we use a series of `print()` commands to display the value of each variable that we had created in Listing 3.13 to the user's screen when the user runs the code. As we will see, setting variables to the proper value and outputting the proper formatting for a variable is important. Giving users the right message and the right formatting can prevent information from being missed.

LISTING 3.14

Printing different variable types

```
t = 0     #a variable that stores an integer
print(t)
message="Hello World"  #a variable that stores a string
print(message)
tax_rate=0.06 #a variable that stores fractional numbers
print(tax_rate)
isFromNH = False  #a variable that stores Boolean values True or False
print(isFromNH)
pets = ["Maya","Marley"] #a variable that stores a list of strings
print(pets)
winning_numbers= [45,7,25,7,2,6,4,11]  #a variable that stores a list of integers
print(winning_numbers)
```

The output from the print() function is impacted by the type of data stored in the variable. When you run Listing 3.14, the following is expected:

```
0
Hello World
0.06
False
['Maya', 'Marley']
[45, 7, 25, 7, 2, 6, 4, 11]
```

If we revisit the banking menu, we can add a few additional variables as well as work with the print formatting. In Listing 3.15, three variables are added to the code that will store the following:

- Version of the banking portal. We will start at version 1.1.

- Bank Name. Use a bank name of your choice.

- A variable named isLogged that is equal to False.

LISTING 3.15

The banking menu with variables and more formatting

```
pversion = 1.1
bname="Digital Bank"
isLogged = False
print("Hello, welcome to "+bname)
print("You are using the banking portal version ");print(pversion)
print("In this portal, you can handle all your banking needs.")
print("Please enter a selection from the following menu.")
print("Type Login to log in")
print("Type Quit to quit")
selection=input("")
print("You have selected")
print(selection)
```

The expected output, assuming "**Login**" is entered, is:

```
Hello, welcome to Digital Bank
You are using the banking portal version
1.1
In this portal, you can handle all your banking needs.
Please enter a selection from the following menu.
Type Login to log in
Type Quit to quit
Login
You have selected
Login
```

NAMING VARIABLES

Python has strict naming rules for variables, including the following:

- Variable names may use uppercase or lowercase letters, numeric digits, or the underscore character. No other characters are allowed.
- Variable names must start with a letter or underscore.
- Variable names are case sensitive.

In addition to these rules for the names of variables, Python allows variable names to have unlimited length. While longer names can be useful to make variable names meaningful, it is best practice to keep variable names relatively short whenever possible. Very long names can be hard to reuse because they take more time to key out and because the length makes it more likely that errors will occur when rekeying the name.

In Listing 3.16, three valid variables and two invalid variables are created. Python will throw an error for the last two variables because they do not meet the criteria described earlier.

LISTING 3.16

Declaring variables

```
age = 33 #correct
_age = 33 #correct
__age = 33 #correct
5_age = 33  #incorrect
-age = 33 #incorrect
```

When you run this listing, you will get the following error:

```
File "<ipython-input-4-813e410b451b>", line 4
5_age = 33  #incorrect
 ^
SyntaxError: invalid token
```

Note that if you are using an IDE to run Listing 3.16, the IDE informs you of the syntax error even without having run the listing. For example, in Figure 3.3 you can see that the Repl.it IDE shows that there is a problem because the variable in the fourth line has a squiggly line underneath it.

> **NOTE** In Figure 3.3, only the first error was highlighted with a squiggly line. You might find that when you fix one error, others are identified!

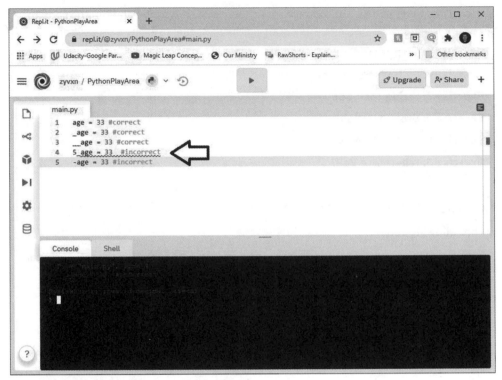

Figure 3.3: Syntax error in an IDE

SUMMARY

In this lesson, we looked at the basics of writing a program in Python, including syntax, accepting user input, and storing values in variables.

Now that you have completed Lesson 3, you should now be able to:

- Create one-line and multiline expressions to perform basic tasks in Python.

- Include comments in a Python program.

- Declare and use variables in a Python program.

- Write a Python program that accepts user input.

EXERCISES

The following exercises provide additional practice to deepen your application of the concepts learned in this lesson and to achieve the objectives of this lesson.

It is recommended that you complete each exercise as described and run the code to make sure it works as expected before starting the next exercise. The exercises are:

Exercise 1: Displaying Text

Exercise 2: Follow the Comments

Exercise 3: Fixing the Code

Exercise 4: Broken Variables

Exercise 5: Broken Names

Exercise 6: Where Are You?

Exercise 1: Displaying Text

Fix the following code:

```
Print("Hello, welcome to the banking portal.")print("In this portal, you can
handle all of your banking needs.")
print("Please enter a selection from the following menu.")
Print("Type Login to log in")
print("Type Quit to quit")
```

Exercise 2: Follow the Comments

Starting with the code blocks provided here, add to the code as needed to follow the instructions in the comments. You may add necessary code, but you should not delete any of the existing code. Run each block to make sure it works as expected before going to the next block.

```
# Add a new line of code that displays the text in quotation marks
# to an output block without repeating the text in quotation marks.
output = "I love Python!"

# your code below this line
# Display only the text Python is fun! to an output block
# without deleting any of the existing code
print("Python is fun!")
print("Python is also easy!")
```

Exercise 3: Fixing the Code

Each of the following code blocks includes at least one error that will prevent it from running. Fix the errors and test to make sure the code runs as expected. Comments at the top of each block will tell you what the code should do.

```
# display the text in quotation marks to an output block
Print("Python is fun!")
# Display the text in quotation marks to an output block
# without moving any of the existing code to a different line
print("Python is fun!") print("Python is also easy.")
# Display the text in quotation marks to an output block
# without moving any of the existing code to a different line
print
("Python is fun!")
# Change each variable name to an appropriate name for Python.
# Do not use the same variable name more than one time.
1-name = "Rebecca" # first name
&_name = "Roberts" # last name

# After changing the variable names, update the code below
# to print out each name.
print(1-name)
print(&_name)
```

Exercise 4: Broken Variables

Fix the following code to create three valid variable names. Add print() statements to display the values associated with each variable and run the code to verify that there are no errors.

```
-name="Alex"
__age = 35
2_list_of_states = ["Kentucky", "New Jersey"]
```

Exercise 5: Broken Names

Fix the following code to create valid variable names:

```
thisisavalidvariablenamealthoughitisverylong=5
thisIsASecondVariableNmeThatIsVeryLong = "help"
print(thisisavalidvariablenamealthoughitislong)
print(thisIsASecondVariableNameThatIsVeryLong)
```

Exercise 6: Where Are You?

Create a script that prompts the user for the name of the state where they were born and the name of the state where they live now. Save each value in its own variable and display the input values to the user.

Lesson 4
Working with Basic Python Data Types

Python supports a variety of basic data types that determine how content in a program will work and interact. This lesson covers variables typed as numbers and Booleans. The lesson also introduces operators and how to use them to change the value of a variable to produce an updated output.

LEARNING OBJECTIVES

By the end of this lesson, you will be able to:

- Use a variety of data types in Python, including numbers and Booleans.
- Use Python to perform operations using numbers.
- Use Python to perform logic operations using Booleans.

REVIEW OF DATA TYPES

Every modern programming language uses data types to determine what actions are possible for specific values in a program. For example, numbers can be used in mathematical calculations while Boolean values can be used to create conditional activities within a program.

In programming languages like Java and C#, programmers must explicitly define the variable's type when they declare a variable. Python, however, automatically types variables, which means that it logically assigns a data type to the value of a variable based on the value itself. In other words, if we define a variable using just a number, Python treats it as a number. If we put the value in quotation marks, Python treats it as a string.

Within this lesson, we will review the concept of variables, and then explore how Python processes numbers that are stored in numerically typed variables. There are a few key terms within this lesson to be aware of:

- **Variables** are areas within memory used to store information.
- **Data types** determine the "type" of data stored within the memory space.
- **String data types** are sequences of character data.
- **Binary arithmetic operations** are commands that perform mathematical operations, such as addition (+), subtraction (–), multiplication (*), and division (/).

NUMBER DATA TYPES

Python supports several numeric data types, including integers and floats. *Integers* are the numbers that include 0, positive whole numbers, and negative whole numbers. Integer literals in Python are written without commas, and a leading negative sign indicates a negative value. *Floats* are any real number in math consisting of a whole number, a decimal point, and a fractional part.

Variables are areas within memory used to store information. Variables can store various types of data. Variables, and their declarations, tell the application what data type is going to be used and how that data can be referenced and manipulated. In programming, we say we are going to "declare a variable." However, there is no variable declaration in Python! Python allows us to assign a value to a variable, and it comes into existence.

Because Python assigns type automatically based on the value entered, if we use an integer as the value for a variable, Python will treat the value as an integer. If the value includes digits to the right of the decimal place, Python will treat the number as a float.

Listing 4.1 shows how to declare number variables using a variety of number types.

LISTING 4.1

Declaring number variables

```
age = 33               # integer
tax_rate = 0.06        # float type
coordinates = 1+3.4j  # complex type z : a+b*j
print(age)
print(tax_rate)
print(coordinates)
```

In this listing, three variables are created and used called age, tax_rate, and coordinates. Each of these is assigned a value. age is assigned an integer, tax_rate is assigned a float, and coordinates is assigned a complex type. When you run this listing, you see the following results:

```
33
0.06
(1+3.4j)
```

Data types are important to define in any application, but they are especially important for financial applications since the calculations and programming can depend on the data type. The difference between integers and decimals can be problematic if not handled properly. Transactions and financial statements use decimals, and an integer wouldn't store decimals when a float would.

Consider the scenario in Listing 4.2, which creates variables to be used in a banking application.

LISTING 4.2

Variables for a banking application

```
acctBal=13445;
savInterest=.025;
months=12;
alphanum=1+52.4j;
print(acctBal);
print(savInterest);
print(months);
print(alphanum);
```

Listing 4.2 creates a variable to store an account balance, an interest rate (which is a decimal percentage), and a month. It also stores an alphanumeric variable. The listing then prints the value of each as shown in the following output:

```
13445
0.025
12
(1+52.4j)
```

IDENTIFYING DATA TYPES

Because Python handles typing in the background, we sometimes need to know what type Python has assigned to a given value. We can use the type function to get the type of a variable. For example, if we had a variable called val, we could get its type as follows:

```
type(val)
```

We could print the type that is returned using the print() function:

```
print(type(val))
```

During the development of our banking application, there are times our developers might want to ensure the type is being defined as they expect, to ensure that subsequent calculations achieve their desired results. Listing 4.3 includes a series of values with number data types as well as a variable defined as a string. We use the type function to identify the type for each variable.

While most of the examples here are numbers, a string value is also included to show Python's flexibility in assigning a type to variables. String variables are discussed in detail later in this lesson.

LISTING 4.3

Checking a variable's type

```
a = 5  #int type
b = 6.7 #float type
c = 1+2j #complex type
d = "2020" #string type inside quotation marks
print(a)
print(type(a))
print(b)
```

```
print(type(b))
print(c)
print(type(c))
print(d)
print(type(d))
```

When you execute this listing, you'll see that the value of the variable is displayed followed by its type:

```
5
<class 'int'>
6.7
<class 'float'>
(1+2j)
<class 'complex'>
2020
<class 'str'>
```

If we apply what was shown in Listing 4.3 to our banking example, we can begin to set up variables to hold account information. We can then use the type function to confirm that we are storing what we expect as shown in Listing 4.4.

LISTING 4.4

Creating variables for banking

```
acctBal = 13445;
savInterest = .025;
months = 12;
alphanum = 1+52.4j;
numString = "12345"
print(type(acctBal));
print(type(savInterest));
print(type(months));
print(type(alphanum));
print(type(numString));
```

The output from executing this listing shows the data types created for each variable:

```
<class 'int'>
<class 'float'>
<class 'int'>
<class 'complex'>
<class 'str'>
```

As you can see, our account balance (`acctBal`) and months are stored as integers, and the interest on a savings account (`savInterest`) is stored as a float.

MATHEMATICAL OPERATIONS

Now that we have reviewed variables and discussed numeric typed variables, let's take a look at how Python supports binary arithmetic operations on numerically typed data. Expressions provide an easy way to perform operations on data values to produce other data values. The operands of an expression are evaluated, and its operator is applied to such values to compute the value of the expression.

Python supports the following types of operators:

- Arithmetic operators
- Comparison (relational) operators
- Assignment operators
- Logical operators
- Bitwise operators
- Membership operators
- Identity operators

Let's take a look at several mathematical operators and how you might use them in code. Arithmetic expressions consist of operands and operators that are familiar from your study of algebra:

- Addition (+)
- Subtraction (−)
- Multiplication (∗)
- Division (/)
- Modulus (%)
- Floor division (//)
- Exponents (∗∗)

> **NOTE** Modulus returns the remainder from a division equation. For example, the remainder of dividing 5 by 2 would be 1. The floor division operator returns the integral part of a division equation. For example, the floor division value of dividing 5 by 2 would be 2.

In Listing 4.5, examples of several different arithmetic operations are presented. Note that we declare the initial variables in the first two lines and then perform a series of operations using those variables, assigning each result to a new variable.

LISTING 4.5

Arithmetic operations

```
a = 50
b = 6
c = a + b # sum of a and b
d = a - b # difference between a and b
e = a * b # product of a and b
f = a / b # quotient of a and b
g = a // b # floored quotient of a and b
h = a % b  # remainder of a / b
i = a ** b # a to the power of b

print(c)
print(d)
print(e)
print(f)
print(g)
print(h)
print(i)
```

In this listing, you can see that several variables are created. The first two (a and b) are simply assigned values. After that, the variables that are created are assigned the result of an equation. When Listing 4.5 is executed, you see the results of the operations as shown here:

```
56
44
300
8.333333333333334
8
2
15625000000
```

Now that we know the mathematical operations that Python uses, let's add a few variables to our banking example's code and perform some mathematical calculations that might be encountered when doing banking. In Listing 4.6, the print() statements are removed that were added in the previous banking code. The `alphanum` variable has also been removed.

LISTING 4.6

Updated banking program with numeric variables

```
acctBal = 13445;
locBal = 16000;
savBal = 4000;
savInterest = .025;
locInterest = .098;

months = 12;
years = 8.5;
numString = "12345"

result1 = acctBal+savBal-locBal;
print(result1);
result2 = acctBal-locBal*locInterest;
print(result2);
result3 = savBal*months*savInterest;
print(result3);
result4 = acctBal/savBal/locBal;
print(result4);
result5 = savBal*1+savInterest/months**years;
print(result5)
```

In this listing, in addition to the account balance (`acctBal`) that we had before, we have added numeric variables for a line of credit balance called `locBal` as well as a numeric variable for a savings balance called `savBal`. These are each assigned values. Decimal variables for interest rates have also been added that can be applied to the local balance as well as the savings balance. The other value added was a number of years (`years`) that can be used within the calculations.

After creating these variables, the code performs several calculations and prints the result:

- Account balance (`acctBal`) plus savings balance (`savBal`) minus line of credit balance (`locBal`).

- Account balance (`acctBal`) minus the line of credit balance (`locBal`) multiplied by the line of credit interest percentage (`locInterest`).

- Savings balance (savBal) multiplied by variable for months (months) and multiplied again by the savings interest rate (savInterest).

- Account balance (acctBal) divided by the savings balance (savBal) divided by the line of credit balance (locBal).

- Savings account balance (savBal) multiplied by 1 plus the savings interest rate (savInterest) divided by the months variable (months) set to the power of the year variable (years).

When Listing 4.6 is executed, the results of the calculations are presented:

```
1445
11877.0
1200.0
0.000210078125
4000.000000000017
```

> **NOTE** You might notice that the results of the calculations don't seem correct. Continue to the next section to learn more about what is happening.

PEMDAS

In Listing 4.6, we didn't get the results we expected or wanted for some of the mathematical expressions. Python, like other mathematical systems, follows the precedence rules of PEMDAS when evaluating statements that include more than one operation. PEMDAS refers to the order in which each operation is evaluated:

- Any operations inside **P**arentheses are evaluated first; if there are nested parentheses, Python starts with the innermost set of parentheses and works its way out.

- **E**xponents (which use the operator ∗∗) are calculated after any operations in parentheses and before any other operations.

- **M**ultiplication and **D**ivision come next.

- **A**ddition and **S**ubtraction are evaluated last.

Let's look at a couple of examples of PEMDAS in action. First, let's look at **a** plus **b** times **c**:

```
a + b * c
```

If we do not include parentheses, Python evaluates this expression in the following order:

1. b times c

2. a plus the result of b times c

If we want Python to perform the addition first, that operation must be inside parentheses:

```
(a + b) * c
```

Another example is the remainder of a divided by b to the power of c:

```
a % b ** c
```

If we do not include parentheses at all, Python evaluates this expression in the following order:

1. b to the power of c

2. Divide a by the result of b to the power of c

3. Save the remainder of the previous step

If we want Python to find the remainder first and calculate the remainder to the power of c, we have to put the modulus operation in parentheses:

```
(a % b) ** c
```

Consider the code in Listing 4.7 and predict the values that are calculated for d, e, f, and g before looking at the output.

LISTING 4.7

Predict the output of the calculations

```
a = 10
b = 20
c = 30

d = a - b * c
print("a - b * c:")
print(d)
```

```
e = (a - b) * c
print("a - (b * c)")
print(e)

f = a % b ** c
print("a % b ** c:")
print(f)

g = (a % b) ** c
print("(a % b) ** c:")
print(g)
```

This listing illustrates the points made earlier by including both an equation without parentheses and then the addition of the parentheses. As you can see, when this listing is executed the output is different as a result of the parentheses:

```
a - b * c:
-590
a - (b * c)
-300
a % b ** c:
10
(a % b) ** c:
1000000000000000000000000000000000
```

The proper order of operations is paramount to the foundational math elements in most programs, and this includes our banking application. Imagine if the incorrect order was performed, and the result was providing a customer thousands or millions of dollars instead of the several dollars that would result from the compound interest calculation.

As mentioned previously, the code in our banking application in Listing 4.6 might not have evaluated properly, or at least the way we wanted it to operate. Specifically, if you look at the last formula that performs a calculation with the savings account and interest, there is an incorrect result due to the default order in which the math is performed. In our banking application, we need to adhere to the proper calculations to have a valid result. We want the banking application to apply the correct amount of interest, not accidentally give the customer millions of dollars due to a coding error!

To correct the code, we will need to add parentheses to control the order of operation. In Listing 4.8, we'll update the bank application to correct the `print` statement's equation to match the following equation:

- Compound Interest Calculation: (S = Savings, m = months, i = savings interest, y = years)
  - `S(1 + (i / m))^my`

We will also perform the following calculations and print the results of each:

- Savings plus account balance, minus line of credit
- Account balance minus line of credit balance, times line of credit interest
- Savings interest rate divided by months, add 1, then to the power of months times years

LISTING 4.8

Fixing the bank application calculations

```
acctBal = 13445;
locBal = 16000;
savBal = 4000;
savInterest = .025;
locInterest = .098;
months = 12;
years = 8.5;
numString = "12345"

compInt = savBal*((1 + (savInterest/months))**(months*years))
print(compInt)
result1 = (savBal+acctBal)-locBal
print(result1)
result2 = (acctBal-locBal)*locInterest
print(result2);
result3 = ((savInterest/months)+1)**(months*years)
print(result3);
```

We can see in the listing that the calculations described have been added and that parentheses have been used to ensure the order of operations is what we want. When this listing is executed now, we get the following results:

```
4945.971040318913
1445
-250.39000000000001
1.2364927600797282
```

While these results are definitely more accurate, they could be presented in a cleaner manner. For example, it would be good to round the numbers to fewer decimal points.

COMMON MATH FUNCTIONS

In Python, there are many useful functions and other resources organized in libraries of code that we call modules. A *function* is simply a piece of code called to perform a task. The math module includes several functions that perform basic mathematical operations.

Following is a list of several built-in math functions included in Python:

- `pow(a, b)`: Calculates **a** to the power of **b**; alternative of **a******b**
- `round(a)`: Rounds **a** to the nearest integer
- `round(a, b)`: Rounds **a** to **b** decimal points
- `bin(a)`: Converts a decimal value **a** to its binary value

You can use these functions in the same way that you have used the `type` and `print` functions. You simply call them and pass the corresponding values. In Listing 4.9, a number of values are set into variables and then used with these methods.

LISTING 4.9

Using Python math functions

```
a = 10
b = 20
c = 15.578
d = 15.494
e = 15.50000
f = pow(a, b)
g = round(c)
h = round(d)
i = round(e)
j = round(d, 1)
k = bin(a)

print(f)
print(g)
print(h)
print(i)
print(j)
print(k)
```

You should step through this listing to see how each call to each of the math functions works. For example, the `pow` function is called with `a` and `b`, which are 10 and 20, respectively. As a result, the power of a to b (thus 10 to the power of 20) is calculated. The result of 100000000000000000000 is then printed.

Next, the listing focuses on the round function. The round function is called with three different values to show you that it is rounding and not simply truncating. These values are set to g, h, and i and then printed. The fourth time the round function is also called, a second parameter of 1 is included that indicates that the rounding should go to one decimal position. The result is that 15.494 is rounded to 15.5.

Finally, the listing does a call to the bin function. The binary function converts a decimal number to a binary (base 2) value.

When this listing is executed, the final results are:

```
100000000000000000000
16
15
16
15.5
0b1010
```

In our banking application, for better display of the results, we should round the resulting values. The users are not going to need to see values such as 4945.971040318913 in their account balances. Let's take the code from Listing 4.7 and update it as specified here:

- Compound interest result rounded up to two decimal places.
- Account balance minus line of credit balance, times line of credit interest with the result rounded down.
- Line of credit interest multiplied by months and years, plus 1, times the line of credit balance with the result rounded up to one decimal place.

Listing 4.10 presents the updated application with these rounding rules added.

LISTING 4.10

The banking application with rounding added

```
acctBal = 13445;
locBal = 16000;
savBal = 4000;
savInterest = .025;
locInterest = .098;
months = 12;
```

```
years = 8.5;
numString = "12345"

compInt = savBal * ((1 + (savInterest/months))**(months*years))
print(round(compInt,2))
result1 = (savBal+acctBal)-locBal
print(result1)
result2 = (acctBal-locBal)*locInterest
print(round(result2,2));
result3 = ((savInterest/months)+1)**(months*years)
print(result3);
result4 = ((locInterest*months*years)+1)*locBal
print(round(result4,1))
```

Now when we execute our listing, the results look much better:

```
4945.97
1445
-250.39
1.2364927600797282
175936.0
```

MATH LIBRARY FUNCTIONS

The arithmetic operations and functions described earlier are inherent to Python, but sometimes we need to perform more advanced operations. Python includes a separate math library, which includes a variety of additional functions that must be imported before a script can use it. Some of these functions and constants in the math library are presented in Table 4.1.

Table 4.1 Some of the Math Library Functions and Constants

Function	Description
ceil(x)	Returns the smallest integer greater than or equal to x
cos(x)	Returns the cosine of x where x is in radians
e	Returns Euler's number (2.718....)
fabs(x)	Returns the absolute value of x
floor(x)	Rounds a float value of x down to the closest integer and returns that value
gcd(x, y)	Returns the greatest common divisor of two integers (x and y)
isqrt(x)	Returns a square root of x after it has been rounded downward to the nearest integer

Function	Description
pi	Returns the mathematical constant for pi, which is the ratio of the circumference of a circle to its diameter (3.141592653589793)
pow(x, y)	Returns x raised to the power of y
sin(x)	Returns the sin of x where x is in radians
sqrt(x)	Returns the square root of x
tan(x)	Returns the tangent of x where x is in radians
trunc(x)	Removes all values to the right of the decimal point in x to create an integer, which is returned

> **NOTE** For a complete list of the math module methods and constants, you can go to the online documentation at `https://docs.python.org/3/library/numeric.html`.

To complete these more advanced operations, we must import Python's math module using the syntax `import math`. Details about the `import` function are outside the scope of this lesson; however, we will see how these functions can be used in our own code. Listing 4.11 imports the math module and uses several of these functions.

LISTING 4.11

Using math module functions

```
import math  #we need to import the math module before using it

a =  6.1
print(a)
b = math.trunc(a) #the integral part of the float
print(b)
c = math.floor(a) #round down
print(c)
d = math.ceil(a) #round up
print(d)
print(math.pi) #print the value of pi
```

In the first line of this listing, we import the math module using the `import` keyword so that we will have access to the functions it contains. We then set a value of a to 6.1 so that we can use it to illustrate several functions. We set b equal to the truncated value of a by calling `trunc()`. We round a down using the `floor()` function and place the result in c.

Finally, we round a upward using the `ceil()` function and place that value into d. All these values are printed along with the math functions' value for pi:

```
6.1
6
6
7
3.141592653589793
```

> **NOTE** The `import` keyword will be covered in more detail later in this book.

Looking back at our banking scenario, typical functions involve transferring transaction amounts, calculating interest and rates, calculating current balances after transactions, and then rounding amounts to the appropriate result as needed. Now that we have the math library added to the mix, we can perform additional calculations that we might encounter while working within a banking scenario. In Listing 4.12, we will start with a blank slate to create a Python script that does a few financial calculations using a few of the new functions we now have access to.

LISTING 4.12

A new banking Python script

```python
import math;

loan1=12383.89
loan2=48339.99
roundLoanA = math.ceil(loan1*.078)
roundloanB = math.floor(loan2*.19)
print(roundLoanA+roundloanB)
```

This listing starts by importing the math module so that we have access to the math functions. It then sets up two variables, `loan1` and `loan2`, representing the balances of two loans. With our loan amounts in place, we multiply our loans by what could be considered interest rates. In this case, we multiply `loan1` by .078. we also round `loan1` up and store the result in a variable named `roundLoanA`. With `loan2` we multiply by .19 and round down. The result is then stored in a new variable named `roundLoanB`. With our calculations completed, we print the sum of `roundLoanA` and `roundLoanB`.

The output from executing this listing is:

```
10150
```

USING NUMBERS WITH USER INPUT

Python automatically assigns the *string data type* to user input, even when the input includes only numeric characters. In Listing 4.13, we prompt the user to enter a number—the year they were born—and Python returns that value.

LISTING 4.13

When were you born (with error)?

```
year_born = input("Enter the year you were born: ")
current_year = input("Enter the current year: ")
print(type(year_born))
print(type(current_year))

age = current_year - year_born

print("Your age is:")
print(age)
```

When you execute this listing, you will find that you can enter the year you were born and the current year without any issue. When Python is asked to subtract the `year_born` from the `current_year`, in order to calculate the user's age, Python reports an error. You can see this in the output:

```
Enter the year you were born: 1985
Enter the current year: 2021
<class 'str'>
<class 'str'>
Traceback (most recent call last):
  File "main.py", line 6, in <module>
    age = current_year - year_born
TypeError: unsupported operand type(s) for -: 'str' and 'str'
```

We see this error because both input values are string values, and Python cannot perform mathematical operations on string values. This means that we must convert user input from a string to a numeric data type before we can use the values in a mathematical operation. We can do this using the built-in `int()` or `float()` function, depending on the values we are using.

Listing 4.14 is the same as the previous example, except that we convert the input values and store them as `born_int` and `current_int`. We then use the converted values in the math operations.

LISTING 4.14

When were you born (without error)?

```python
year_born = input("Enter the year you were born: ")
current_year = input("Enter the current year: ")

# convert the strings into integers
born_int = int(year_born)
current_int = int(current_year)

age = current_int - born_int

print("Your age is:")
print(age)
```

Now when we run the listing, the math is completed without error and the result is displayed:

```
Enter the year you were born: 1985
Enter the current year: 2021
Your age is:
36
```

> **NOTE** Although the math is completed without error in Listing 4.13, did you find the problem with the program? The program doesn't take into account the month.

Returning back to the banking application, there are often many calculations that are being performed such as checking a customer's debt-to-income ratio for loan or credit card applications or how much interest is being accrued. Listing 4.15 prompts the user to enter a monthly debt payment and a monthly gross income amount.

LISTING 4.15

Calculating a debt ratio

```python
monthlyDebt = input("Enter the monthly debt payments: ");
grossIncome = input("Enter the gross monthly income: ");
```

```
#Convert the strings to integers
debtInt = int(monthlyDebt);
incomeInt = int(grossIncome);

diRatio = debtInt / incomeInt;
print(diRatio);
```

The numbers that are entered by the user are used to calculate a debt-to-income ratio for a loan by dividing the monthly debt payments by the gross monthly income. Before doing the calculation, we apply what we just learned by converting the entered numbers to integer values using the `int()` function.

Listing 4.15 converted the values to integers. In Listing 4.16, we return to calculating the simple interest of an account. In this case, we ask the user to enter the balance of the account, the rate of interest, and a period of time in years. This information will be used in the calculations.

LISTING 4.16

Calculating the simple interest

```
acctBal = input("Please enter an account balance: ");
intRate = input("Please enter an interest rate: ");
time = input("Please enter a period of time in years: ");
acctInt = int(acctBal);
rateInt = float(intRate);
timeInt = int(time);
result = acctInt * rateInt * timeInt;
acctBal = result + acctInt;
print(acctBal);
```

Note that this listing is simplistic in that it does not compound the interest. Rather, it simply multiplies the balance, rate of interest, and period of time and adds it to the original balance. After doing the calculation, the result is displayed:

```
Please enter an account balance: 1000
Please enter an interest rate: .05
Please enter a period of time in years: 10
1500.0
```

NOTE In this listing, we used the float() function to convert the interest rate. It is worth considering whether float() or int() should have been used. In this case, you need to consider what value the reader is going to enter and what format they will be using. For example, if the interest rate is 5%, will they enter 5, .05, or some other value?

BOOLEAN TYPES AND BOOLEAN OPERATIONS

Now that we have discussed numeric number types, we will continue our discussion of data types in Python with *Boolean* data types. Boolean types have values that are either True or False. These two basic values are very powerful because they allow us to create complex conditional operations that allow a program to produce specific outcomes based on the state of other variables when we run the code.

> **NOTE** Boolean data types are generally used when the values of expressions produce "Yes" or "No" answers. Python supports True or False Boolean values.

We can declare Boolean variables by assigning a value to a name, just like we do for other variables. As shown in Listing 4.17, if the value is True or False, Python treats the value as a Boolean type (bool).

LISTING 4.17

Creating Boolean variables

```
bool1 = True
bool2 = False
print(bool1)
print(type(bool1))
print(bool2)
print(type(bool2))
```

You can see in this listing that two variables are created called bool1 and bool2. They are assigned the values of True and False, respectively. To show that these are created as Booleans, the value in each variable is printed followed by its type:

```
True
<class 'bool'>
False
<class 'bool'>
```

Convert to Boolean

We can use the built-in bool() function to convert values into a Boolean value of True or False. In general, bool() will return True unless the value passed to it is the value of 0, False, None, or an empty object. For example, the following call to bool() returns True:

```
bool("Hello")
```

Listing 4.18 shows a few additional examples of bool() in action.

> **NOTE** We will cover None and empty objects in more detail later in this book. An example of an empty object is a string with nothing in it: "".

LISTING 4.18

Using bool()

```
a = 0
b =  1
print(a)
print(bool(a))
print(b)
print(bool(b))
print(bool("Hello")
```

In the first part of this example, we see that the value 0 corresponds to False, while any value that is not 0 corresponds to True. The output confirms this:

```
0
False
1
True
True
```

> **NOTE** bool() is a primitive type, meaning that the value (True/False in this case) is stored directly in the variable. A *Boolean function* returns the Boolean value True or False.

Listing 4.19 goes further with the bool() function. In this listing, several additional values are passed to bool() and the results are printed.

LISTING 4.19

Using bool() some more

```
test = 0
print(test,':',bool(test))
test = [1]
print(test,':',bool(test))
test = []
print(test,':',bool(test))
test = 1.1
print(test,':',bool(test))
test = "1"
print(test,':',bool(test))
test = False
print(test,':',bool(test))
test = True
print(test,':',bool(test))
test = 'Easy string'
print(test,':',bool(test))
test = ""
print(test,':',bool(test))
test = ''
print(test,':',bool(test))
```

In this expanded listing, we start by assigning a value to the variable test. The first time we assign test the value of 0. We then pass test to bool() and print the value. The print function is printing three things when it is called. First it is printing the value stored in test, then it is printing a colon (:), then it is printing the value returned from the call to bool(test).

After printing the information, a new value is assigned to test. A new print is used to display the results again. This is done with a number of different values with the last two being empty strings. The output lets you see which evaluated to True and which evaluated to False:

```
0 : False
[1] : True
[] : False
1.1 : True
1 : True
False : False
True : True
Easy string : True
 : False
 : False
```

> **TIP** Experiment with Listing 4.19. Change the values assigned to test and see what the results are from the call to bool( ).

LOGIC OPERATIONS

You have now been introduced to various operations that Python can process, and we have discussed mathematical operations. Now let's discuss logic operators. Python inherently supports logical operations on Boolean types, including and, or, and not.

Standard logic operations include the following:

- and: A binary statement where both values must be True for the operation to evaluate as true. Otherwise, the operation evaluates as False.

- or: A binary statement where either or both values must be True for the operation to evaluate as True. The operation evaluates as False only if both values are False.

- not: A unary statement that returns the opposite of the original value.

The code in Listing 4.20 helps to illustrate these logical operations.

LISTING 4.20

Using the logical operators

```
a = True
print(a)

b = False
print(b)

c = not a
print(c)

d = a or b
print(d)

e = a and b
print(e)
```

When this listing is executed, you can see the values that are printed when each of the lines is executed:

```
True
False
```

```
False
True
False
```

By reviewing the output from the code in Listing 4.20, you should be able to answer the questions shown in Listing 4.21. When this listing is running, you should answer whether the outcome of each statement will be True or False and then compare your predictions to the results that are then shown.

LISTING 4.21

Is it True or False?

```
a = input("What is the output of the following operation (True and True)? ")
aTest = True and True
print("True and True = ", aTest)

b = input("What is the output of the following operation (False or False)? ")
bTest = False or False
print("False or False = ", bTest)

c = input("What is the output of the following operation (False and False)? ")
cTest = False and False
print("False and False =", cTest)

d = input("What is the output of the following operation (not False)? ")
dTest = not False
print("not False = ", dTest)

e = input("What is the output of the following operation ( (not False) or \
False )? ")
eTest = ( (not False) or False )
print("(not False) or False = ", eTest)

f = input("What is the output of the following operation ( (not True) and (not \
False) )? ")
fTest = ( (not True) and (not False) )
print("(not True) and (not False) = ", fTest)
```

The following shows the results of executing the code. Note that the answer you enter will not impact the actual results that show the correct answers:

```
What is the output of the following operation (True and True)? True
True and True =  True
```

```
What is the output of the following operation (False or False)? False
False or False =  False
What is the output of the following operation (False and False)? True
False and False = False
What is the output of the following operation (not False)? x
not False =  True
What is the output of the following operation ( (not False) or False )? x
(not False) or False =  True
What is the output of the following operation ( (not True) and (not False) )? x
(not True) and (not False) =  False
```

Before moving on, consider functionality that could be added to our banking application. When working with a user of the application, it is likely that a number of questions would need to be asked such as the following:

- Do you have a savings account?

- Do you have a checking account?

- Would you like to create a savings account?

- Would you like to create a checking account?

In the case of these questions, you would likely want to create Boolean variables to store the user's answers to be used throughout the rest of the application. Listing 4.22 presents these questions to the user and saves the values into variables for later use.

Listing 4.22

Querying a banking customer

```
savings = input("Do you have a savings account?: ");
checking = input("Do you have a checking account?: ");
opensave = input("Would you like to open a savings account?: ")
opencheck = input("Would you like to open a checking account?: ")
print(savings);
print(type(savings));
print(checking);
print(type(checking));
print(opensave);
print(type(opensave));
print(opencheck);
print(type(opencheck));
```

The output from this listing shows the values that the user entered and the resulting data type:

```
Do you have a savings account?: Yes
Do you have a checking account?: No
Would you like to open a savings account?: No
Would you like to open a checking account?: Yes
Yes
<class 'str'>
No
<class 'str'>
No
<class 'str'>
Yes
<class 'str'>
```

These answers can be used later in our banking application when doing comparisons such as transaction validity or to check conditions such an account or applicant meeting certain conditions.

COMPARATIVE OPERATORS

Let's continue to expand our knowledge of operators with this exploration of comparative operators. Python uses *comparative operators* to compare the values of two objects and return True or False. The operators are:

`<`	Less than
`<=`	Greater than or equal to
`>`	Greater than
`>=`	Greater than or equal to
`==`	Equal to
`!=`	Not equal to
`Is`	Equal to (equality)
`is not`	Not equal to (inequality)

In Listing 4.23 a value is assigned to each of the variables a and b and then a variety of comparisons is performed between the two values with each result equating to True or False.

> **NOTE** Python supports both == and is for equality statements and != and is not for inequality statements.

LISTING 4.23

Using the comparison operators

```
a = 6
b = 5
print("Is a greater than b?", a > b)           #greater than
print("Is a less than b?", a < b)              #less than
print("Is a greater or equal to b?", a >= b)   #greater or equal
print("Is a less or equal to b?", a <= b)      #less or equal
print("Is a equal to b (option 1)?", a == b)       #test for equality
print("Is a equal to b (option 2)?", a is b)       #test for equality
print("Is a not equal to b (option 1)?", a != b)     #test for inequality
print("Is a not equal to b (option 2)?", a is not b) #test for inequality
```

When you execute this listing, you can see the results of each comparison:

```
Is a greater than b? True
Is a less than b? False
Is a greater or equal to b? True
Is a less or equal to b? False
Is a equal to b (option 1)? False
Is a equal to b (option 2)? False
Is a not equal to b (option 1)? True
Is a not equal to b (option 2)? True
```

> **TIP** Change the values of a and b in Listing 4.23 so that they match and see what the results are when you run the script again.

Imagine in our banking application that a user initiates a transaction to transfer money, but there is not enough money in the account for the transfer. A comparative operator could be used to check the validity of the transfer or whether other numbers don't match.

SUMMARY

Python supports a variety of basic data types that determine how content in a program will work and interact. This lesson covered variables typed as numbers and Booleans. It introduced operators and taught us how we can use operators to change the value of a variable to produce an updated output.

Now that you have completed Lesson 4, you should now be able to:

- Use a variety of data types in Python, including numbers and Booleans.
- Use Python to perform operations using numbers.
- Use Python to perform logic operations using Booleans.

EXERCISES

The exercises here will give you the opportunity to practice the skills and tools presented in this lesson, with the objectives of this lesson.

Note that software development skills build on each other, so many of the activities here will also require skills and tools presented in earlier lessons. The exercises here include:

Exercise 1: Prompting the User

Exercise 2: Manipulated Math

Exercise 3: Integers Only

Exercise 4: Current Value

Exercise 5: Simple Interest

Exercise 6: True or False

Exercise 7: Playing with Numbers

Exercise 8: Do the Math

Exercise 9: Street Addresses

Exercise 1: Prompting the User

Create a program that prompts the user to enter a number and then displays the type of the number entered (e.g., complex, integer, or float).

For example, if the user enters 6, the output should be `int` (for integer).

Exercise 2: Manipulated Math

Update the following code so that the result is equal to 576. Do not change any of the existing values or operators or the order in which they appear.

```
# do not change the order in which the numbers and
# operators appear in the next line
```

```
result = 5 + 3 ** 2 * 9

print(result) # the output should be 576
```

Exercise 3: Integers Only

Create a program that prompts the user for a float number and returns the integer portion of the floating number.

Exercise 4: Current Value

Write a program that calculates and displays the current value of a deposit for a given initial deposit, interest rate, how many times interest is calculated per year, and the number of years since the initial deposit.

The program should prompt the user for each of the values and use the following formula to calculate the current value of the deposit:

```
V = P(1 + r/n)^nt
```

where

V = value
P = initial deposit
r = interest rate as a fraction (e.g., 0.05)
n = the number of times per year interest is calculated
t = the number of years since the initial deposit

The program should display each of the values entered in a meaningful way to the user (so that the user can easily see what each value represents, along with the results of the calculation).

Exercise 5: Simple Interest

Write a program that prompts the user for a principal amount, the rate of interest, and the number of days for a loan, and then calculates and returns the simple interest for the life of the loan. Use the formula:

```
interest = principal * rate * days / 365
```

Exercise 6: True or False

Create a program that displays three statements that evaluate to `True` and three statements that evaluate to `False`.

Example:

```
a = 0
b = 1

Output: a < b = True
```

Exercise 7: Playing with Numbers

Create a program that prompts the user for a number and calculates the following:

- The Boolean of the number entered
- The binary equivalent of the number entered
- The square root of the number entered

The program should display the following to the user:

- The number the user entered, in a phrase like, "You selected `value`."
- The Boolean of the number, in a phrase like, "The Boolean of your number is `value`."
- The binary equivalent of the number, in a phrase like, "The binary equivalent of your number is `value`."
- The square root of the number, in a phrase like, "The square root of your number is `value`," with the value rounded to three decimal places.

Exercise 8: Do the Math

Create a program that completes the following tasks:

- It prompts the user for a series of five integers.
  - The user must be prompted for five numbers.
- After the fifth entry, the program stops prompting for values and performs the following calculations:
  - The product of the integers
  - The average of the integers
  - The sum of the integers

- After performing the calculations, the program should display the following to the user:

  - The values the user entered

  - Each of the calculations, using a phrase that identifies the value

Exercise 9: Street Addresses

Write a program that performs the following steps:

- Start with a street address that includes a building/house number, the name of the street, and the type of street (e.g., Street, Avenue, Boulevard, etc.).

  - You can use any address you wish, and abbreviations are acceptable.

  - An example is 25 Main Street.

- Display the full address to the user.

- Display the house number only in a phrase like, "The building or house number is 25."

- Display the street name in a phrase like, "The street name is Main Street."

Lesson 5
Using Python Control Statements

Python supports a variety of control structures that determine how content in a program will work and interact. This module explores those control structures that make creating algorithms possible.

LEARNING OBJECTIVES

By the end of this lesson, you will be able to:

- Use an `if` statement to determine the outcome of a program.
- Use an `if–else` statement to define two potential outcomes.
- Use nested `if` statements to define more than two potential outcomes.

CONTROL STRUCTURES REVIEW

Computers understand only machine language, which uses only binary code (represented as 0s and 1s for humans), but it is hard for humans to write code in binary. As a result, programmers create algorithms within a specified programming language (such as Python) that instruct the computer on the specific actions to take to reach the desired outcome. As programmers code and subsequently compile the code, the compiled code translates from the high-level language (in this case, Python) to the machine-level language that can be understood by the computer. This translation from high-level to low-level language allows the computer to execute the directions given.

In order for a problem to be "computable," an algorithm must be constructed. If programmers are unable to build an algorithm, we say that the problem cannot be computed. However, if the problem is solvable, the instructions can be presented using three important **control structures**:

- Sequence
- Selection
- Iteration

Python supports these structures in various forms. Essentially, a control structure controls the flow of data through the program.

As you work through this lesson, there are a number of key terms you will see. These include the following:

- **Sequence control structures** are sequential line-by-line executions of program code within a program.

- **Selection control structures** allow programmers to ask questions, and then, based on the result, perform different actions.

- **Conditional operators** are used within an if statement block for numeric comparisons.

UNDERSTANDING SEQUENCE CONTROL STRUCTURE

A sequence control structure is the simplest of the three control structures that we will discuss in this lesson. Essentially, a **sequence control structure** is a sequential line-by-line execution of program code within a program. The syntax of a sequence control structure would simply be:

```
statement 1
statement 2
statement 3
```

A sequence might carry out a series of print statements or a set of mathematical calculations. Figure 5.1 shows how the data flows sequentially through the structure.

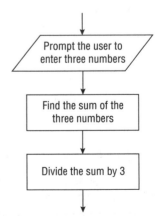

Figure 5.1: Sequence control structure

The code in Listing 5.1 provides an example of the sequential flow of data through a Python application.

LISTING 5.1

Sequential flow of data

```
print((2 + 3) * 4)
print(2 ** 10)
print(6 / 3)
print(7 / 3)
print(7 // 3)
print(7 % 3)
print(3 / 6)
print(3 // 6)
print(3 % 6)
print(2 ** 100)
```

Python will execute these statements in the order shown, from top to bottom. As a result, the output will be printed in the same order that the print statements appeared:

```
20
1024
2.0
2.3333333333333335
2
1
0.5
0
3
1267650600228229401496703205376
```

> **NOTE** Sequence statements are the code statements used to execute code within the sequence structure. Because of the simplicity of sequence statements, our banking application utilizes sequences to control the flow of data through the application. We can use a sequence of statements to display application instructions to users as they log in.

UNDERSTANDING SELECTION STATEMENTS

In every programming language, it is essential to be able to execute an appropriate block of code depending on some condition. **Selection statements**, which are the code statements used to execute code within the selection structure, allow programmers to ask questions and then, based on the result, perform different actions. Most programming languages provide dual versions of this construct: the `if` and the `if-else`. An example of a binary selection uses the `if-else` statement.

The `if` statement creates a basic conditional statement that executes a block of code if a condition is `True`, using the syntax:

```
if condition:
    statement
```

where the `condition` is a statement that can evaluate to either `True` or `False`. If the condition evaluates as `True`, Python will execute the statement that follows. If the condition evaluates as `False`, Python will skip that statement and go on to the next set of instructions.

In some cases, we may want to test whether the condition is `False` rather than only testing for `True`. For this reason, we often explicitly state the outcome of the condition. For example, if we explicitly want to test for True, we can use the statement:

```
if condition == True:
```

Otherwise, when we want to test for `False`, we can use:

```
if condition == False:
```

We frequently use flowcharts to create a visual representation of the steps a program will follow when there is an `if` statement, using a diamond to represent the condition, as shown in Figure 5.2. The diamond typically has one input, a question that evaluates to yes (`True`) or no (`False`), with one output for each possibility.

> **NOTE** You do not have to use flowcharts if you don't want to, but they can be beneficial to help you step through a program, both before you start to write the code and to troubleshoot statements that produce unexpected results.

The code in Listing 5.2 presents an example of an `if` statement in Python. Note that we use a simple condition called `condition` to test for `True`, and we provide another conditional statement that will produce a different output if the condition is `False`.

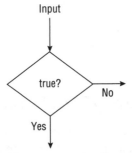

Figure 5.2: The flow of an `if` statement

LISTING 5.2

Using an if statement in Python

```python
password = "admIn"
condition = (password == "admin")

# if condition is equal to True, which means the password is correct
if condition:
    print("password correct")
#if condition is equal to False, which means the password is not correct.
if condition == False:
    print("password incorrect")
```

In this listing, you can see that a password is set to "admIn" in the first line. Note that while this makes a great example, you'd never actually want to code a password into a listing like this. Having said that, this listing then checks to see if the assigned password is equal to the string "admin." If the value in password does equal admin, then the value set to the variable condition will be True. If they are not equal, then the value set to condition will be False.

In this case, the result is False because Python is case-sensitive, so *admIn* is not the same as *admin*. This means the first if statement evaluates to False, so its print statement is skipped, and program control flows to the next if statement. That if statement is true because condition does equal False. As such, that print statement is executed, producing the following output:

```
password incorrect
```

If you change the check in the second line to see if the password is equal to "admIn," then the condition will evaluate to True. Figure 5.3 shows the logic of the code from Listing 5.2 using a flowchart.

These types of structures are critical for authentication in our banking application. In the real world, our banking application would likely use a database to store user credentials that would be stored as a "hash" value for security. A hash is a value that has been converted to a number in a secure way in that the process cannot be reversed to reveal the password.

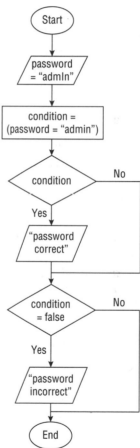

Figure 5.3: Flowchart for Listing 5.2

In our scenario we don't have any mechanism to store credentials, so we are specifying variables to act as user credentials to provide a similar experience. Our banking application needs to ensure that unauthorized users are not permitted access, and this ultimately requires that the selection statements evaluate to True for the username and password combination.

UNDERSTANDING CONDITIONAL STATEMENTS

The simplest form of selection is the if statement. We sometimes refer to this as a binary selection since there are two possible paths of execution.

A standard if-else block uses only one condition. If that condition is True, the first set of instructions are followed. If that condition is False, the instructions in the else block are followed. The header line within the statement begins with the keyword if accompanied by a Boolean expression and ends with a colon (:). We refer to the indented statements that follow as a block. The first statement that is not indented marks the end of the block.

Statements inside the first block of statements are executed in order if the Boolean expression evaluates to True. The first block of statements is skipped if the Boolean expression evaluates to False, and instead, the statements under the else clause are executed.

> **NOTE** An unlimited number of statements may appear under the two clauses of an if statement, but there must be at least one statement in each block.

We often use conditional operators within conditional statements. The most common *conditional operators* that we can use within an if statement block for numeric comparisons are listed in Table 5.1.

Table 5.1 Python Conditional Operators

Operator	Definition
>	Greater than
>=	Greater than or equal to
<	Less than
<=	Less than or equal to
==	Equal to
!=	Not equal to

Let's consider an example of a conditional operator in action. Listing 5.3 presents a single condition: age >= 16. If the person's age is greater than or equal to 16, the person can drive. If the person is younger than 16, they cannot drive.

LISTING 5.3

Can a person drive?

```
age = 21

condition = (age >= 16)
#condition will evaluate to True or False

if condition == True:
    #True if the value of the age is greater or equal to 16
    print("This person is allowed to drive.")

else:
    #False if the value of the age is less than 16
    print("This person is NOT allowed to drive.")
```

Looking at the code, you can see that we set a variable for age to the value of 21. We could have asked the user to enter their age as well. We then compare the age to see if it is greater than or equal to 16 and set the True or False result into the variable called condition. Using an if statement, we see if the condition is True. If it is, a message is printed. If the condition is not True, then the else code block is executed, and a different message is printed. The output from running the listing with an age of 21 is:

```
This person is allowed to drive.
```

If you change the age to a value less than 16 in the first line, then the if statement will evaluate to False and the else code block will be executed.

NOTE You might have noticed that in Listing 5.2, the if statement simply said if condition. In Listing 5.3 the if statement was presented as if (condition == True). These are equivalent statements. Because the if statement is checking for a True value, adding the "== True" is somewhat redundant. Adding the "== True" does, however, make it clearer what the code is doing.

Conditional statements can have many uses within our banking application; they can be employed to provide analysis or error handling. For example, the banking application could be programmed to spot irregularities using conditional operators such as whether the amount in a transfer equals more than the account balance or whether the user specifies the wrong account number.

IF-ELSE STATEMENTS

When we use a simple `if` statement, we evaluate a single condition and produce an outcome based on the state of that condition. While we can include a series of `if` statements (and even build complex conditions by comparing individual `if` conditions), this approach has the disadvantage that Python will evaluate each statement as it goes through the code, even if only one of the statements can logically be true.

Another approach is to use an `if-else` statement instead of two (or more) individual `if` statements. The advantage of `if-else` is that the `else` part of the statement will be evaluated only when the `if` condition is not met. If the initial condition is met, Python can skip the remaining code in the block, which can help speed up the runtime of the code. However, a standard `if-else` block supports only two outcomes: one for situations where the condition is `True` and the other for situations where the condition is `False`.

In the example in Listing 5.4, we compare a stored username with a guessed username. In this scenario, there are only two possible outcomes: either the usernames are the same or they are not.

LISTING 5.4

Checking a username

```
correct_username="admin"
guessed_username = "Admin"

if correct_username == guessed_username:
    #This will only display if the guessed username is equal
    # to the correct username
    print("Access Granted")
else:
    #This will only display if the guessed username is not equal
    # to the correct username
    print("Access Denied")
```

While we could use two separate `if` statements to compare the values, the `if-else` structure allows us to state the comparison exactly one time. If the values are the same, Python will display the "if-true" response and skip over the `else` portion of the statement. If the initial `if` statement is false, Python skips the instructions in that block and goes straight to the `else` block to execute the instructions there.

When you look at the code in Listing 5.4, you can see that the `correct_username` and `guessed_username` are not the same. As such, the condition goes to the else block and the output displayed is:

```
Access Denied
```

WORKING WITH NESTED CONDITIONS

Python uses the `elif` keyword as a contraction of "else if," which allows us to string together many different conditions, each of which must be True or False on their own. The syntax for using an `elif` is:

```
if expression1:
    statement(s)    # Expression1's code block

elif expression2:
    statement(s)    # Expression2's code block

elif expression3:
    statement(s)    # Expression3's code block

else:
    statement(s)
```

While `if` and `if-else` provide acceptable ways to produce a specific outcome based on current conditions, they are most useful for situations where the outcome is clear (`True` or `False`), and it is harder to include gray areas in the conditions. In reality, though, we often need a program to choose between a variety of outcomes rather than just one or two.

A program requirement could be to provide a specific statement based on a person's income, yet there is also a need to include options for income ranges—to apply income-dependent discounts for childcare—or something that Python can display as an error message if the user enters a value that cannot represent an age (like a name or a date). The `elif` operator allows us to nest a series of conditions in a conditional block and produce one of several different options.

While the construction must include at least one `elif` statement, it can contain as many as necessary to address all the positional conditions.

When evaluating this structure, Python does the following:

1. If the condition in `expression1` evaluates to `True`, Python executes the statement(s) in `expression1`'s code block and skips the rest of the code in the structure.

2. If `conditional1` is `False`, Python evaluates each `elif` statement in sequence until it finds a condition that is `True`. It then executes the instructions for that `elif` statement and skips the rest of the code in the structure.

3. If none of the conditions are `True`, Python executes the instructions in the `else` block.

In Listing 5.5, we use `elif` in a short code snippet. The listing starts with a word and then compares that word to a sequence of other words.

LISTING 5.5

Using elif

```
color="morning"

if color=="red":
    print("The color is red.")
elif color=="blue":
    print("The color is blue.")
elif color=="yellow":
    print("The color is yellow.")
else:
    print("Please enter a valid color.")
```

If the word stored in `color` matches one of the expected words, Python will tell us what color the word represents. If the stored word does not match any of the expected words, the user will see a prompt to enter a more appropriate value. In this case, when the listing is executed, you will see:

```
Please enter a valid color.
```

In Listing 5.6, we update Listing 5.5 to be more practical. In this listing, the user is prompted to enter a color and then an appropriate message is displayed depending on the color.

LISTING 5.6

Selecting a color

```
color=input("Please enter a color [red, green, yellow, blue, pink]: ")
if color == "red":
    print("The color is red.")
elif color == "green":
    print("The color is green.")
elif color == "yellow":
    print("The color is yellow.")
elif color == "blue":
    print("The color is blue.")
elif color == "pink":
    print("This color is pink.")
else:
    print("Please enter a valid color that is on the list.")
```

It is worth noting that Listing 5.6 could have been created by using just if-else statement and not elif. Listing 5.7 presents the code without elif. As you can see by comparing Listing 5.6 to 5.7, the elif statements make our code much cleaner and easier to read.

LISTING 5.7

Selecting a color with if-else

```
color=input("Please enter a color [red, green, yellow, blue, pink]: ")
if color == "red":
    print("The color is red.")
else:
  if color == "green":
    print("The color is green.")
  else:
    if color == "yellow":
      print("The color is yellow.")
    else:
      if color == "blue":
        print("The color is blue.")
      else:
        if color == "pink":
          print("This color is pink.")
        else:
          print("Please enter a valid color that is on the list.")
```

The usage of elif is valuable in reducing the overhead requirements of the code and reducing the complexity of the if-else statements. Let's again consider the banking application we've been creating. Imagine our banking application has a loan processing module that looks at the applicant and rates them based on their creditworthiness. The elif statement could provide for the "gray areas" and allow for different results depending on the applicant's situation, such as a higher interest rate if their credit is low, or shorter-term limits if they don't have any credit.

We'll create a piece of our banking application where we perform the following steps:

1. Create a variable and ask the user for a credit score.

2. If the score is less than or equal to 450, we will print: "This credit score is very low."

3. If the score is greater than 450 but less than or equal to 650, we will print: "This credit score is low."

4. If the score is greater than 650 but less than or equal to 800, we will print: "This credit score is good."

5. If the score is above 800 to a maximum of 850, we will print: "This credit score is excellent."

6. Finally, if the value doesn't match any of those ranges, the program should tell the user to input a valid credit score.

Listing 5.8 presents our code for checking the user's credit score.

LISTING 5.8

Checking a credit score

```
creditscore = int(input("Please enter a credit score: "))

if creditscore <= 450:
    print("This credit score is very low.")
elif creditscore <= 650 and creditscore > 450:
    print("This credit score is low.")
elif creditscore <= 800 and creditscore > 650:
    print("This credit score is good.")
elif creditscore > 800 and creditscore <= 850:
    print("This credit score is excellent.")
else:
    print("Please enter a valid credit score between 0 and 850")
```

This listing starts by prompting the user to enter their credit score. The first line of code might look complicated, but it is similar to code you've seen. The input() function is prompting the user to enter a value. The value that is retuned by the input() function is passed to the int() function, which changes it from a string to an integer. This integer is then placed in the variable creditscore. That is all accomplished in the first line of code.

The entered value is then processed through the checks within the if and elif conditions. You can see that the conditional operators are used to evaluate the creditscore against the various values. If none of the conditions evaluates to True, then the else code block is executed, which asks the user to enter a valid score between 0 and 850.

> **TIP** Remember that Python always treats user input as a string, but you can't compare strings to numbers.

EMBEDDING CONDITIONS

In the following code, a variable is created that has the value True or False, and we used the variable in the conditional statement:

```
condition = (age >= 16)
    #condition will evaluate to True or False
if condition == True:
```

We can streamline this code by embedding the condition directly in the if statement like this:

```
if age >= 16:
```

Listing 5.9 repeats the driving age example given in Listing 5.3, except that the conditional statement is embedded in the if statement rather than existing as a separate variable.

LISTING 5.9

Embedding conditions

```
age = 21

if age >= 16:
    #True if the value of the age is greater or equal to 16
    print("This person is allowed to drive.")

else:
    #False if the value of the age is less than 16
    print("This person is NOT allowed to drive.")
```

As before, when this listing is executed the same output is displayed:

```
This person is allowed to drive.
```

In Listing 5.10, a second listing is presented to illustrate an embedded condition. In this listing, a new Python method is used called string.isupper(). This built-in method evaluates the case of a characters in a string. It returns True if the characters are all uppercase and False if they are not.

Our program prompts the user to enter a single letter. If the character is uppercase, display the message "The user entered an uppercase letter." If the character is lowercase, display the message "The user entered a lowercase letter."

LISTING 5.10

Checking the case of the character

```
letter=input("Please enter a single letter: ")
if letter.isupper():
    print("The user entered an uppercase letter.")
else:
    print("The user entered a lowercase letter.")
```

When this listing is run, you should get the expected output as shown in the following two examples:

```
Please enter a single letter: r
The user entered a lowercase letter.

Please enter a single letter: R
The user entered an uppercase letter.
```

> **TIP** Python supports the methods `string.isupper()` and `string.islower()` to evaluate the case of characters in a string. You will learn more about methods in a separate lesson.

SUMMARY

In order for a problem to be "computable," an algorithm must be constructed. If programmers are unable to build an algorithm, we say that the problem cannot be computed. However, if the problem is solvable, the instructions can be presented using three important control structures: sequence, iteration, and selection. Python supports these structures in various forms. Essentially, a control structure controls the flow of data through the program.

In this lesson, we explored those control structures that make creating algorithms possible.

Now that you have completed Lesson 5, you should be able to:

- Use an `if` statement to determine the outcome of a program.
- Use an `if-else` statement to define two potential outcomes.
- Use nested `if` statements to define more than two potential outcomes.

EXERCISES

The following exercises are provided to allow you to demonstrate the objectives for this lesson.

You should complete each exercise and make sure that the code runs without errors. The exercises here include:

Exercise 1: Are You Rich?

Exercise 2: Cats or Dogs

Exercise 3: True or False Quiz

Exercise 4: For Every Season...

Exercise 5: Company Picnic

Exercise 1: Are You Rich?

Write a program that asks the user how much money they have in their wallet. The program should output "You're rich!" if the user inputs $20 or more and "You're broke!" if the input is less than $20.

Exercise 2: Cats or Dogs

Write a program that performs the following steps:

1. Ask the user if they own any cats. (Yes/No answer)

2. Ask the user if they own any dogs. (Yes/No answer)

3. If the user's responses indicate that they have both cats and dogs, output "You must really love pets!"

4. Otherwise, the output should be "Maybe you need more pets."

The last step will apply if the user has cats but not dogs, dogs but not cats, or neither cats nor dogs.

Write two different versions of this program: one that uses only if statements and another that uses if-else statements.

Exercise 3: True or False Quiz

Create a program that asks the user a few questions to which the user will respond either True or False. Display all the questions with the correct answer and the user's answers at the end of the program, along with the user's correct response rate (number of questions answered correctly/number of questions).

Exercise 4: For Every Season...

Write a program that uses elif to produce five different possible outcomes based on a single user input:

1. Ask the user what season it is (fall, winter, spring, or summer).

2. If the user enters fall, output "I bet the leaves are pretty there!"

3. If the user enters winter, output "I hope you're ready for snow!"

4. If the user enters spring, output "I can smell the flowers!"

5. If the user enters summer, output "Make sure your AC is working!"

6. If the user enters a value that does not correspond to a season, output "I don't recognize that season."

The user should be able to enter the name of the season in any case and the program will still work.

Challenge: After you have the program working as describe here, modify the program so that the user can enter either "fall" or "autumn" and get the same result.

Exercise 5: Company Picnic

Your company has organized a morale event. They're hosting a picnic and field day in the park, and of course, they want to play team-building games.

To do that they want to assign the attendees to certain teams based on their last name. They've already chosen the team names, but they want you to write a program that will sort each person into the correct team.

Here are the specs:

- If a person's name starts with A, B, C, or D, then they are on the team "Red Dragons."

- If the name starts with E, F, G, or H, they are on the team "Dark Wizards."

- If the name starts with I, J, K, or L, they are on the team "Moving Castles."

- If the name starts with M, N, O, or P, they are on the team "Golden Snitches."

- If the name starts with Q, R, S, or T, they are on the team "Night Guards."

- If the name stars with U, V, W, X, Y, or Z, they are on the team "Black Holes."

Here's an example of the output:

```
What's your last name? Weasley
Aha! You're on the team "Black Holes"!
Good luck in the games!
```

The example uses the person's last name, but you can choose to use first names if you prefer. You may also use a different output message as long as it clearly states what team the person is on.

> **TIP** Make sure to test the program using at least two names from each group to make sure it works as expected.

Pulling It All Together: Income Tax Calculator

In this lesson, we pull together many of the concepts from the previous lessons. Instead of presenting new information on Python, we will walk through a real-world application that uses what you've already learned. In this code-along, we will walk through the steps to create a calculator that determines a person's income tax based on their income.

> **NOTE** Important!
> The information in this code-along is based on U.S. Tax Law for the year 2020. If you choose to update this calculator for a different year, you should find current values for the year you want to use. However, this specific calculator will work only for individuals with relatively simple income based only on wages and tips. A more advanced calculator would be needed for more complicated returns, including other forms of income and tax credits or deductions. Consult a tax expert or business analyst for more advanced tax return requirements.

LEARNING OBJECTIVES

By the end of this lesson, you will be able to:

- Demonstrate understanding of basic Python tools, including using syntax basics, defining variables, and accepting user input.

- Explain basic Python data types and describe the differences between each data type.

- Use numbers and number operations in a Python application.

- Use Boolean values in a Python application, especially in the use of conditional statements.

- Use conditional statements to determine the outcome of a program.

GETTING STARTED

To complete this code-along, you will need an IDE that supports Python 3, such as one of the following:

- Jupyter Notebook (part of the Anaconda Distribution)
- IDLE
- Visual Studio Code

While you can use an online tool like Replit to test small blocks of code, we recommend that you get in the habit of using an installed IDE for larger programs.

As you work through this code-along, make sure that you understand each step before going on to the next step. For steps that involve writing code, all code should work before you go to the next step. Run the code frequently to check for problems and fix problems as soon as you find them.

STEP 1: GATHER REQUIREMENTS

Before you begin to write code for any program, you should take the time to identify the requirements and expected use of that application. When you are working with a client, you should agree on the requirements early in the process, both to be sure that you understand what the client expects and to ensure that your final program meets those expectations.

In this case, the client wants a simple income tax calculator that will calculate the tax obligation for an individual, single filer, based only on income from wages and tips, as reported on a U.S. W-2 form. Remember that for many people, calculating income tax can be complicated by other forms of income, such as dividends and interest payments, so if you were going to create a calculator for more complicated returns, you should consult a tax expert to understand how other forms of income can affect a tax return.

Values in Use

For this example, we are using values from U.S. Tax Law for the year 2020. If you want to calculate income taxes for another year, you may need to update the values used in the calculations.

Specifically, we are assuming the following values to calculate taxable income based on gross income:

- All taxpayers are allowed a $12,200 standard deduction.

- For each dependent, a taxpayer is allowed an additional $2,000 deduction.

U.S. tax rates vary based on the amount of money earned. In 2020, the values in Table 6.1 are used to calculate a person's income tax based on their taxable income.

Table 6.1 2020 Tax Rates

Rate	Income for Single Individuals
10%	Up to $9,875
12%	$9,876 to $40,125
22%	$40,126 to $85,525
24%	$85,526 to $163,300
32%	$163,301 to $207,350
35%	$207,351 to $518,400
37%	$518,401 or more

User Interface

We want the program to accept the following input values from the user:

- Gross income

- Number of dependents

At this point, we will also assume that the user will access the program through a terminal window, rather than through a form.

Other Standards

The number standards are as follows:

- Gross income must be entered to the nearest cent.
- The taxable income is expressed as a decimal number.
- The tax due is expressed as an integer.

All text that appears to the user should use correct grammar and spelling.

STEP 2: DESIGN THE PROGRAM

After finalizing what the program will do, you should take time to design the program. Designing a program can include pseudocode or flowcharts. Let's start with pseudocode that describes the actions the program will perform:

```
User Input: gross income
User Input: number of dependents

taxable income = gross income - 12,200 - (2000 * number of dependents)
tax due = amount calculated from tax table

print tax due
```

You may find it useful to create a flowchart for yourself that identifies these steps. Remember that you only need a pencil and paper to create a flowchart, but it can help you visualize what the program will do and identify the required steps in the program.

> **NOTE** Appendix A provides more information on flowcharts, and Appendix B provides additional information on creating pseudocode.

STEP 3: CREATE THE INPUTS

When writing a program, it is good practice to break it up into smaller pieces. You can then build the pieces individually, testing that they work as expected as you go. If you try to write an entire program in one go (even a relatively short program like the one we are working on here), you may end up with errors that are hard to trace. If you get each piece working without error before going on to the next piece, it is easier to troubleshoot problems when they happen.

For the code-along, we are using 35987.65 for the gross income value, with two dependents, except where stated otherwise. When you test the code with input values, you can use different values to see what happens.

We'll start by creating the user inputs. We know that we want the user to enter their gross income and we need to save the input in a variable:

```
# define user input
gross_inc = input("Enter your gross income from your W-2 for 2020: ")
```

Let's also add a `print` statement so that we can verify that the correct value was stored. Your code should now look like Listing 6.1.

LISTING 6.1

Prompting for the income

```
# define user input
gross_inc = input("Enter your gross income from your W-2 for 2020: ")
print(gross_inc)
```

Add this code to your IDE and run the program. It should prompt you for a value and display that value immediately after you have entered it.

```
Enter your gross income from your W-2 for 2020: 35987.65
35987.65
```

Once this code works, we can create the prompt for the number of dependents and add it to our code as shown in Listing 6.2.

LISTING 6.2

Adding additional prompt

```
# define user input
gross_inc = input("Enter your gross income from your W-2 for 2020: ")
print(gross_inc)

num_dep = input("How many dependents are you claiming? ")
print(num_dep)
```

The output should now look like:

```
Enter your gross income from your W-2 for 2020: 35987.65
35987.65
How many dependents are you claiming? 2
2
```

Once the input statements work to collect the values correctly, we can remove the `print` statements. We'll just comment them out as shown in Listing 6.3 in case we need to restore them later.

LISTING 6.3

Commenting out the print statements

```
# define user input
gross_inc = input("Enter your gross income from your W-2 for 2020: ")
# print(gross_inc)

num_dep = input("How many dependents are you claiming? ")
# print(num_dep)
```

The program will still accept the user input values, but it will not display those values.

STEP 4: CALCULATE THE TAXABLE INCOME

We know from the planning step that the formula for taxable income is:

```
taxable income = gross income - 12,200 - (2000 * number of dependents)
```

The values 12,200 and 2000 come from U.S. tax calculations for the year 2020.

Remember that using variables not only saves values to a named memory location, but if we name them correctly, they can help us better map a formula to an operation. In this case, you can see in Listing 6.4 that we have the variables `gross_inc` and `num_dep` that we have plugged into the statement, and we then assign the result of the calculation to a new variable. We can also print out the result to help us make sure that the value is appropriate.

LISTING 6.4

Adding the taxable income formula

```
# define user input
gross_inc = input("Enter your gross income from your W-2 for 2020: ")
# print(gross_inc)
```

```
num_dep = input("How many dependents are you claiming? ")
# print(num_dep)

#calculate taxable income
tax_income = gross_inc - 12200 - (2000 * num_dep)
print (tax_income)
```

If you run this program Python will return an error:

```
--------------------------------------------------------------------------
TypeError                                 Traceback (most recent call last)
<ipython-input-7-cf539198992d> in <module>
----> 1 tax_income = gross_inc - 12200 - (2000 * num_dep)
      2 print (tax_income)

TypeError: unsupported operand type(s) for -: 'str' and 'int'
```

Remember that Python treats any user input as text (or *string*) values and as with most other programming languages, it cannot perform mathematical operations (like subtraction and multiplication) using string values. We need to update our code to convert the input values to numbers.

We know from step 1 that the income should allow decimal places. This means that the number value should be a float. We can convert that value easily in Python:

```
gross_inc_float = float(gross_inc)
```

The number of dependents, however, should be a whole number—a person is either a dependent or not. We can use the int function to convert the input:

```
num_dep_int = int(num_dep)
```

Let's update the code to include these conversions and to use the new variables. Listing 6.5 shows our updated listing.

LISTING 6.5

Adding conversions

```
# define user input
gross_inc = input("Enter your gross income from your W-2 for 2020: ")
# print(gross_inc)

num_dep = input("How many dependents are you claiming? ")
# print(num_dep)
```

```
# convert the input values to numbers
gross_inc_float = float(gross_inc)
num_dep_int = int(num_dep)

# calculate taxable income
tax_income = gross_inc_float - 12200 - (2000 * num_dep_int)
print (tax_income)
```

You should get the following value, if you use the same inputs that we used earlier in the code-along:

```
19787.65
```

STEP 5: CALCULATE THE TAX RATE

The next step is to calculate the tax due for the person whose values we are using. We know that the income tax rate is dependent on the taxable value itself, using the values from Table 6.1 presented in step 1.

Here's where things get complicated, though. In U.S. tax law, the taxable income is sliced into values that match the tax table presented in Table 6.1, and each slice uses the appropriate tax rate for that slice. For example, if a person's taxable income is $80,000, the tax due is calculated as follows:

- The first $9,875 is taxed at 10%:

  ```
  9875 * .1 = 987.6
  ```

- The amount from $9,876 through $40,125 is taxed at 12%:

  ```
  40145 - 9875 = 30270
  30270 * .12 = 3632.4
  ```

- The remainder is taxed at 22%:

  ```
  80000 - 40125 = 39875
  39875 * .22 = 8772.5
  ```

- We then add up the three values to get the total tax due:

  ```
  tax_due = 987.6 + 3632.4 + 8772.5
  tax_due = 13392.5
  ```

Let's look at how to code this, breaking it up into slices (or *tiers*). The first tier is for taxable incomes of less than $9,875. Because this is the first tier, we simply multiply the taxable income by 10% to calculate the tax due. We'll add that to our program as shown in Listing 6.6.

LISTING 6.6

Adding the first tier of the tax calculation

```
# define user input
gross_inc = input("Enter your gross income from your W-2 for 2020: ")
# print(gross_inc)

num_dep = input("How many dependents are you claiming? ")
# print(num_dep)

# convert the input values to numbers
gross_inc_float = float(gross_inc)
num_dep_int = int(num_dep)

# calculate taxable income
tax_income = gross_inc_float - 12200 - (2000 * num_dep_int)
print (tax_income)

# calculate tax due
tax_due = tax_income * 0.1

# print the result
print(tax_due)
```

If you test this with a gross income of $20,000 and two dependents, you should get the following output:

```
Enter your gross income from your W-2 for 2020: 20000
How many dependents are you claiming? 2
3800.0
380.0
```

Add a Conditional Statement

Now that we understand the math, we can make the program more flexible. Specifically, we want it to look at the taxable income, determine the correct tax rate for that value, and use that tax rate to calculate the tax due. That requires us to use conditional statements. Because this step is a bit complicated, we're only going to look at the taxable income for now. Once we understand what's going on, we can incorporate the code into the earlier version of the program.

Create a new program that includes only the basics of calculating the tax due based on the taxable income but ignore the deductions at this point. We'll start with $4,000 as shown in Listing 6.7, which is in the 10% tier.

LISTING 6.7

Taxing 4000

```
tax_income = 4000
tax_due = tax_income * 0.1

# print the result
print(tax_due)
```

This should give us a result of `400.0`, which is a 4000 income value multiplied by the 0.1 tax rate.

Now let's update the code to calculate a taxable income that is in the 22% tier. In this case, we first need an *if* clause for the 10% tier:

```
tax_income = 4000

if tax_due <= 9875
    tax_due = tax_income * 0.1
tax_due =       # calculation for 22% tier

# print the result
print(tax_due)
```

The calculation is a bit complicated. We first calculate 10% of the first $9,875:

```
9875 * .1
```

We then subtract 9875 from the taxable income and calculate 12% of that value:

```
(tax_income - 9875) * .12
```

We then add those values together to calculate the tax due:

```
tax_due = (9875 * .1) + ((tax_income - 9875) * .12)
```

Update your code in Listing 6.7 to include this calculation and use a taxable income value that falls into the 22% tier. Listing 6.8 shows the updated code.

LISTING 6.8

Adding the second tier logic

```
tax_income = 35000

if tax_income <= 9875:
    tax_due = tax_income * 0.1
tax_due = (9875 * .1) + ((tax_income - 9875) * .12)
```

```
# print the result
print(tax_due)
```

If you start with a taxable income value of 35000, the result should be:

```
4002.5
```

Now that we understand the math from one tier to the next, we can add the next tier.

Create Nested Conditionals

To handle more than two options in a conditional construction, we use nested conditionals. Because the tax table is a series of "up to" values, we can simply use less than or equal to (<=) conditional statements that correspond to the highest value on the current tier.

In Python, we use `elif` to create nested conditions between the initial condition and the `else` value. Let's start by making the 12% tier an *elif* statement, which we've done in Listing 6.9.

LISTING 6.9

The second tier using an elif statement

```
tax_income = 35000

if tax_income <= 9875:
    tax_due = tax_income * 0.1
elif tax_income <= 40125:
    tax_due = (9875 * .1) + ((tax_income - 9875) * .12)

# print the result
print(tax_due)
```

Run the code to make sure you get the same result we saw before:

```
4002.5
```

Now add the 22% tier as shown in Listing 6.10.

LISTING 6.10

Adding the 22% tier

```
tax_income = 80000

if tax_income <= 9875:
    tax_due = tax_income * 0.1
```

```
elif tax_income <= 40125:
    tax_due = (9875 * .1) + ((tax_income - 9875) * .12)
elif tax_income <= 85525:
    tax_due = (9875 * .1) + ((40125 - 9875) * .12) + (tax_income - 40125) * .22)

# print the result
print(tax_due)
```

Now it's getting even more complicated, so look at the code to make sure you understand it. To calculate the tax for values between 40125 and 85525, we perform the following steps:

1. Calculate 10% of the first tier's maximum value:

   ```
   9875 * .1
   ```

2. Calculate 12% of the second tier's maximum value:

   ```
   (40125 - 9875) * .12
   ```

3. Calculate 22% of what's left:

   ```
   ((tax_income - 40125) * .22)
   ```

4. Add the three values together.

Let's do the same thing for the 24% tier as shown in Listing 6.11.

LISTING 6.11

Adding the 24% tier

```
tax_income = 150000

if tax_income <= 9875:
    tax_due = tax_income * 0.1
elif tax_income <= 40125:
    tax_due = (9875 * .1) + ((tax_income - 9875) * .12)
elif tax_income <= 85525:
    tax_due = (9875 * .1) + ((40125 - 9875) * .12) + ((tax_income - 40125) * .22)
elif tax_income <= 163300:
    tax_due = (9875 * .1) + ((40125 - 9875) * .12) + ((85525 - 40125) * .22) +
((tax_income - 85525) * .24)


# print the result
print(tax_due)
```

Note that we're seeing a lot of repetition here. We know that 10% of 9875 is always 987.5, and we keep reusing values like 40124 and 9875. In fact, you likely copied and pasted code from one `elif` to the next and then updated as necessary.

Whenever we see repetition like that, we should also see the opportunity to introduce variables. Using variables will not only simplify our code by removing repetition, but the variables themselves will also make the code easier to read. Variables can also make the code more flexible.

In 2020, we have fixed ranges for each tier, but it's possible that those ranges will be different in other years. If we use variables instead of constants, we only have to update those values in one place rather than replacing every instance of each value with a new value.

We'll start by creating variables that reference the highest value in each tier. Create these above the `if` block as shown in Listing 6.12 so that we can use them in the calculations.

LISTING 6.12

Declaring high range value variables

```
tax_income = 150000

max10 = 9875
max12 = 40125
max22 = 85525
max24 = 163300
max32 = 207350
max35 = 518400

if tax_income <= max10:
    tax_due = tax_income * 0.1
#[…]
```

We can also calculate the maximum tax due for each tier and assign those values to variables as shown in Listing 6.13.

LISTING 6.13

Using variables calculating maximum tier taxes

```
tax_income = 150000

max10 = 9875
max12 = 40125
max22 = 85525
```

```
max24 = 163300
max32 = 207350
max35 = 518400

tier10_tax = max10 * .1
tier12_tax = tier10_tax + ((max12 - max10) * .12)
tier22_tax = tier12_tax + ((max22 - max12) * .22)
tier24_tax = tier22_tax + ((max24 - max22) * .24)
tier32_tax = tier24_tax + ((max32 - max24) * .32)
tier35_tax = tier32_tax + ((max35 - max32) * .35)

if tax_income <= max10:
    tax_due = tax_income * 0.1
#[…]
```

Here, we calculate the maximum tax due for each tier by adding the maximum for the previous tier and calculating the remaining tax rate based on the current tier.

Now we can replace the hard-coded values in the calculations with the appropriate variable as shown in Listing 6.14.

LISTING 6.14

Updating tax calculations with variables

```
tax_income = 150000

max10 = 9875
max12 = 40125
max22 = 85525
max24 = 163300
max32 = 207350
max35 = 518400

tier10_tax = max10 * .1
tier12_tax = tier10_tax + ((max12 - max10) * .12)
tier22_tax = tier12_tax + ((max22 - max12) * .22)
tier24_tax = tier22_tax + ((max24 - max22) * .24)
tier32_tax = tier24_tax + ((max32 - max24) * .32)
tier35_tax = tier32_tax + ((max35 - max32) * .35)


if tax_income <= max10:
    tax_due = tax_income * 0.1
elif tax_income <= max12:
    tax_due = tier10_tax + ((tax_income - max10) * .12)
```

```
elif tax_income <= max22:
    tax_due = tier12_tax + ((tax_income - max12) * .22)
elif tax_income <= max24:
    tax_due = tier22_tax + ((tax_income - max22) * .24)
elif tax_income <= max32:
    tax_due = tier24_tax + ((tax_income - max24) * .32)

# print the result
print(tax_due)
```

It should be easy to see that the code is much simpler, but it's also worth taking the time to examine the code to see what it's doing. First, each of the `if`/`elif` clauses references the maximum value for that tier. The appropriate maximum value is also used to calculate the amount of taxable income for the current tier:

```
elif tax_income <= max24:
    tax_due = tier22_tax + ((tax_income - max22) * .24)
```

Second, most of the math required for each of the `elif` results is already done for us when we define the tier tax values, because those expressions calculate the highest possible tax due for each tier. We can then simply include that value in the next tier when we calculate the tax due:

```
elif tax_income <= max24:
    tax_due = tier22_tax + ((tax_income - max22) * .24)
```

Finally, should the maximum value for a given range be changed in the future, we only have to change the values assigned to the max variables, which is much more efficient than having to replace every instance where that value is used in the code.

Now let's finish out the code with the remaining tiers. Try to do it on your own, and then check your code against the code shown in Listing 6.15.

LISTING 6.15

Tax calculation with remaining tiers added

```
tax_income = 150000

max10 = 9875
max12 = 40125
max22 = 85525
max24 = 163300
max32 = 207350
max35 = 518400
```

```
tier10_tax = max10 * .1
tier12_tax = tier10_tax + ((max12 - max10) * .12)
tier22_tax = tier12_tax + ((max22 - max12) * .22)
tier24_tax = tier22_tax + ((max24 - max22) * .24)
tier32_tax = tier24_tax + ((max32 - max24) * .32)
tier35_tax = tier32_tax + ((max35 - max32) * .35)

if tax_income <= max10:
    tax_due = tax_income * 0.1
elif tax_income <= max12:
    tax_due = tier10_tax + ((tax_income - max10) * .12)
elif tax_income <= max22:
    tax_due = tier12_tax + ((tax_income - max12) * .22)
elif tax_income <= max24:
    tax_due = tier22_tax + ((tax_income - max22) * .24)
elif tax_income <= max32:
    tax_due = tier24_tax + ((tax_income - max24) * .32)
elif tax_income <= max35:
    tax_due = tier32_tax + ((tax_income - max32) * .35)
elif tax_income > max35:
    tax_due = tier35_tax + ((tax_income - max35) * .37)

# print the result
print(tax_due)
```

Note that the last `elif` block uses only a greater-than symbol rather than less than or equal to. This is because any income above $518,400 is taxed at the 37% rate. There is no maximum value set on this range, so we can't compare it to a highest possible value (which is also why we didn't initialize a `max37` variable).

Test your code with a variety of taxable incomes in each range. For testing purposes, your results should match those shown in Table 6.2.

Table 6.2 Taxes Due Based on Tier

Taxable Income	Tax Due
$9,000	$900.00
$35,000	$4,002.50
$50,000	$6,790.00
$100,000	$18,079.50
$200,000	$45,015.50
$400,000	$114,795.0
$700,000	$223,427.00

STEP 6: UPDATE THE APPLICATION

Now that we have the tax due calculations finalized, we can incorporate them into our original program. Because we used the same `tax_income` variable in the calculations, we simply need to add the new code to the existing program, replacing the original tax due calculation as shown in Listing 6.16.

LISTING 6.16

Tax program with updated tax calculation

```python
# declare the variables
max10 = 9875
max12 = 40125
max22 = 85525
max24 = 163300
max32 = 207350
max35 = 518400

tier10_tax = max10 * .1
tier12_tax = tier10_tax + ((max12 - max10) * .12)
tier22_tax = tier12_tax + ((max22 - max12) * .22)
tier24_tax = tier22_tax + ((max24 - max22) * .24)
tier32_tax = tier24_tax + ((max32 - max24) * .32)
tier35_tax = tier32_tax + ((max35 - max32) * .35)

# define user input
gross_inc = input("Enter your gross income from your W-2 for 2020: ")
# print(gross_inc)

num_dep = input("How many dependents are you claiming? ")
# print(num_dep)

# convert the input values to numbers
gross_inc_float = float(gross_inc)
num_dep_int = int(num_dep)

# calculate taxable income
tax_income = gross_inc_float - 12200 - (2000 * num_dep_int)
print (tax_income)

#calculate tax due
if tax_income <= max10:
    tax_due = tax_income * 0.1
```

```
elif tax_income <= max12:
    tax_due = tier10_tax + ((tax_income - max10) * .12)
elif tax_income <= max22:
    tax_due = tier12_tax + ((tax_income - max12) * .22)
elif tax_income <= max24:
    tax_due = tier22_tax + ((tax_income - max22) * .24)
elif tax_income <= max32:
    tax_due = tier24_tax + ((tax_income - max24) * .32)
elif tax_income <= max35:
    tax_due = tier32_tax + ((tax_income - max32) * .35)
elif tax_income > max35:
    tax_due = tier35_tax + ((tax_income - max35) * .37)

# print the result
print(tax_due)
```

Note that we added the variables at the beginning of the application. It is common practice to define variables early in an application to ensure that they are available when they are needed in the application itself. Grouping them together like this can also help with debugging in case we need to look at how a variable was originally declared and initialized.

After updating the code, test it a couple more times to make sure it produces the expected results. Remember that the complete code starts with gross income and calculates deductions to determine the taxable income.

What About Negative Taxable Incomes?

Another problem that the tax calculator doesn't solve is situations where the taxable income is less than zero. For example, if a person earns $10,000 gross income and has two dependents, their taxable income is −$6,200. Note that this is a logic error, not a syntax error. Entering the values 10000 and 2 for the initial income values in our program will not cause Python to throw an error. In fact, it will clearly tell you that the person owes −$620, an amount that doesn't really make sense.

In U.S. tax law, a person whose taxable income is less than 0 owes no taxes at all. We can update our program to take this into account as shown in Listing 6.17.

LISTING 6.17

Adjusting for low incomes

```
# initialize the variables
max10 = 9875
max12 = 40125
```

```
max22 = 85525
max24 = 163300
max32 = 207350
max35 = 518400

tier10_tax = max10 * .1
tier12_tax = tier10_tax + ((max12 - max10) * .12)
tier22_tax = tier12_tax + ((max22 - max12) * .22)
tier24_tax = tier22_tax + ((max24 - max22) * .24)
tier32_tax = tier24_tax + ((max32 - max24) * .32)
tier35_tax = tier32_tax + ((max35 - max32) * .35)

# define user input
gross_inc = input("Enter your gross income from your W-2 for 2020: ")
# print(gross_inc)

num_dep = input("How many dependents are you claiming? ")
# print(num_dep)

# convert the input values to numbers
gross_inc_float = float(gross_inc)
num_dep_int = int(num_dep)

# calculate taxable income
tax_income = gross_inc_float - 12200 - (2000 * num_dep_int)
print (tax_income)

if tax_income <=0:
    tax_due = 0
elif tax_income <= max10:
    tax_due = tax_income * 0.1
elif tax_income <= max12:
    tax_due = tier10_tax + ((tax_income - max10) * .12)
elif tax_income <= max22:
    tax_due = tier12_tax + ((tax_income - max12) * .22)
elif tax_income <= max24:
    tax_due = tier22_tax + ((tax_income - max22) * .24)
elif tax_income <= max32:
    tax_due = tier24_tax + ((tax_income - max24) * .32)
elif tax_income <= max35:
    tax_due = tier32_tax + ((tax_income - max32) * .35)
elif tax_income > max35:
    tax_due = tier35_tax + ((tax_income - max35) * .37)

# print the result
print(tax_due)
```

Run the program with a few lower numbers to make sure it produces the correct results without errors.

Does Code Compare to Standards?

As a final check on the code, compare what we have to the expected standards. Specifically, the number standards are as follows:

- Gross income must be entered to the nearest cent.
- The taxable income is expressed as a decimal number.
- The tax due is expressed as an integer.

We do allow the user to enter a float value for the gross income, and we do have the program express the taxable income as a decimal number. However, you should have noticed at least one example where the tax due included a value after the decimal point.

We can fix this by converting the calculated value to an integer. In Python, this conversion will cause the number to use standard rounding procedures (rounding up for values where the decimal value is .5 or higher and rounding down otherwise). Update the print statement for the tax due:

```
# print the result
print(int(tax_due))
```

Run the code a few times with different inputs to ensure that the tax due is expressed as an integer.

STEP 7: ADDRESS THE UI

Once you have the program working as you expect, you should take time to improve the user interface (UI). We've done this a little by clearly stating what data the user should enter, but we also want to clean up the output a little.

In this case, we want the program to clearly state what values were input as well as the calculated values, using phrases that identify the values. At this point, we can uncomment the earlier print statements we used for testing and embellish them to make them more meaningful:

```
# define user input
gross_inc = input("Enter your gross income from your W-2 for 2020: ")
print("Your gross income is $" + gross_inc + ".")

num_dep = input("How many dependents are you claiming? ")
print("You have " + num_dep + " dependents.")
```

Here we include the $ symbol as part of the first `print` statement, so that the symbol appears in front of the number and the result looks like money. We also include a period at the end of each statement. The output statements should look like the following:

```
Your gross income is $35987.65.
You have 2 dependents.
```

We also want to clearly state the taxable income:

```
# calculate taxable income
tax_income = gross_inc_float - 12200 - (2000 * num_dep_int)
print ("Your taxable income is $" + tax_income + ".")
```

Note that the first two `print` statements work fine. The program should prompt you for the value and display that value in the print sentence.

The taxable income statement will not work as written, though. Just as we cannot perform math with string values (which is why we had to convert the input values to numbers), we cannot concatenate a string with a number. This means that we must convert the number to a string, using the `str` function:

```
print ("Your taxable income is $" + str(tax_income) + ".")
```

This should generate a statement like the following:

```
Your taxable income is $19787.65.
```

Now let's do something similar with tax due:

```
# print the result
print ("Your tax due is $" + str(int(tax_due)) + ".")
```

Note here that Python allows us to convert the float value to an integer and then convert the integer to a string in a single step. This gives us the following:

```
Your tax due is $2177.
```

Now let's finalize the program with all the `print` statements in a logical order at the end of the program as shown in Listing 6.18. This isn't absolutely necessary, but it helps keep the code more organized. It's also easier to update a program if similar pieces of code are grouped together.

LISTING 6.18

Our completed tax program

```
# initialize the variables
max10 = 9875
max12 = 40125
```

```python
max22 = 85525
max24 = 163300
max32 = 207350
max35 = 518400

tier10_tax = max10 * .1
tier12_tax = tier10_tax + ((max12 - max10) * .12)
tier22_tax = tier12_tax + ((max22 - max12) * .22)
tier24_tax = tier22_tax + ((max24 - max22) * .24)
tier32_tax = tier24_tax + ((max32 - max24) * .32)
tier35_tax = tier32_tax + ((max35 - max32) * .35)

# define user input
gross_inc = input("Enter your gross income from your W-2 for 2020: ")

num_dep = input("How many dependents are you claiming? ")

# convert the input values to numbers
gross_inc_float = float(gross_inc)
num_dep_int = int(num_dep)

# calculate taxable income
tax_income = gross_inc_float - 12200 - (2000 * num_dep_int)

if tax_income <=0:
    tax_due = 0
elif tax_income <= max10:
    tax_due = tax_income * 0.1
elif tax_income <= max12:
    tax_due = tier10_tax + ((tax_income - max10) * .12)
elif tax_income <= max22:
    tax_due = tier12_tax + ((tax_income - max12) * .22)
elif tax_income <= max24:
    tax_due = tier22_tax + ((tax_income - max22) * .24)
elif tax_income <= max32:
    tax_due = tier24_tax + ((tax_income - max24) * .32)
elif tax_income <= max35:
    tax_due = tier32_tax + ((tax_income - max32) * .35)
elif tax_income > max35:
    tax_due = tier35_tax + ((tax_income - max35) * .37)

# report the results to the user
print("Your gross income is $" + gross_inc + ".")
print("You have " + num_dep + " dependents.")
print ("Your taxable income is $" + str(tax_income) + ".")
print ("Your tax due is $" + str(int(tax_due)) + ".")
```

Using the previous input values, the output should look like the following:

```
Enter your gross income from your W-2 for 2020: 35987.65
How many dependents are you claiming? 2
Your gross income is $35987.65.
You have 2 dependents.
Your taxable income is $19787.65.
Your tax due is $2374.
```

ON YOUR OWN

Once you have the program working from this lesson, check results using different input values—both lower and higher. Feel free to use a calculator to spot-check results to make sure the results are correct.

Also consider that tax rates and the tax table can change from one year to the next. We looked at using variables to store the maximum value for each tier as well as the maximum tax due for each tier, but there are still some hard-coded values that could potentially change, and which are repeated throughout the program. For example:

- Can you refactor the program to use variables for the percentages for each tier?
- Can you refactor the program to use a variable for the personal deduction and the dependent deduction values?
- How could you handle changes to the range or percentage tax value for each tier?

Also keep in mind that code style can vary drastically from one developer to the next. The program here shows one solution, but there are many other ways to approach a problem like this one and at least as many ways to solve it. The important take-aways here include:

- Understand what you want the code to do to solve the problem at hand.
- Understand how the code solves that problem.
- Write code so that it is easy to read, especially by other developers.
- Write code that is reasonably free of repetition or reused values and calculations.

SUMMARY

In this lesson we pulled together many of the concepts you had seen in the previous lessons into a working application. We walked through the steps to create a calculator that determines a person's income tax based on their income. You added variables to make it easier for you to update the program in the future for different tax rates.

Now that you have completed Lesson 6, you should be able to

- Demonstrate understanding of basic Python tools, including using syntax basics, defining variables, and accepting user input.

- Explain basic Python data types and describe the differences between each data type.

- Use numbers and number operations in a Python application.

- Use Boolean values in a Python application, especially in the use of conditional statements.

- Use conditional statements to determine the outcome of a program.

PART II

Loops and Data Structures

Lesson 7:   Controlling Program Flow with Loops

Lesson 8:   Understanding Basic Data Structures: Lists

Lesson 9:   Understanding Basic Data Structures: Tuples

Lesson 10: Diving Deeper into Data Structures: Dictionaries

Lesson 11: Diving Deeper into Data Structures: Sets

Lesson 12: Pulling It All Together: Prompting for an Address

Lesson 13: Organizing with Functions

Lesson 7
Controlling Program Flow with Loops

Python supports a variety of control structures that determine how content in a program will work and interact. This lesson continues the exploration including additional control structures that make creating algorithms possible. The lesson concludes with a discussion of how iteration aids in text processing.

LEARNING OBJECTIVES

By the end of this lesson, you will be able to:

- Create a Python script that uses a `for` loop to repeat an activity until a specific criterion is met.
- Create a Python script that uses a `while` loop to repeat an activity as long as a specific criterion holds true.
- Using string operations to manipulate text.

ITERATIONS OVERVIEW

Lesson 5 introduced control structures. These structures are used to "control" the flow of data through an application. Python supports various structures through control statements of sequence, iteration, and selection. In Lesson 5 selection and progression were discussed. The sequence control structure (executed in a sequence statement) is completed one statement after the other. The selection control structure (implemented in a selection statement) executes only after a particular condition is met. Although these types of code statements allow applications to run, in most cases, using only sequence and selection statements would make for very long program code.

In this lesson, a third control structure is introduced: iteration. Iteration, along with iterative code statements, provides efficiency in the program design and development of Python applications. Further, in this lesson, iteration statements will be created using two specific types of iteration structures (definite and indefinite loops) that each serve a distinct purpose.

Simply stated, iteration control structures, also known as loops, repeat actions. There are two primary types of loops: loops that repeat actions a predetermined number of times (definite loops) and loops that act until the algorithm determines that the execution of the loop should stop (indefinite loops).

As you work through this lesson, there are a number of key terms you will see. These include the following:

- **Sequence control structures** are sequential line-by-line executions of program code within a program.

- **Selection control structures** allow programmers to ask questions, and then, based on the result, perform different actions.

- **Iteration control structures** allow programmers to execute code repeatedly. Examples of these iteration structures are definite loops and indefinite loops.

THE ANATOMY OF A LOOP

Every morning at 4:00 a.m., my device screams, "Wake Up! Wake Up! Wake Up!" A computer can easily output these exclamations, not just three times but literally hundreds of times. As a developer, you would not need to write hundreds of output statements to accomplish this.

Let's look at how a loop can be used to output such statements. In this case, we will use the `for` loop to output (print) the statements three times:

```
for eachPass in range(3):
    print("Wake Up!", end = " ")
```

In this example, the loop repeatedly calls the `print` function. The constant 3 on the first line tells the loop the number of times to call this function. The result is that when this code is executed, the following is displayed to the user:

```
Wake Up! Wake Up! Wake Up!
```

To print 10 or 1000 exclamations, you would simply change the 3 to 10 or to 1000. This type of loop is called a `for` loop.

This is a **definite iteration**, as the loop executes a definite number of times based on the number stated in the range, which is defined as 3 in our example and as is shown in Figure 7.1.

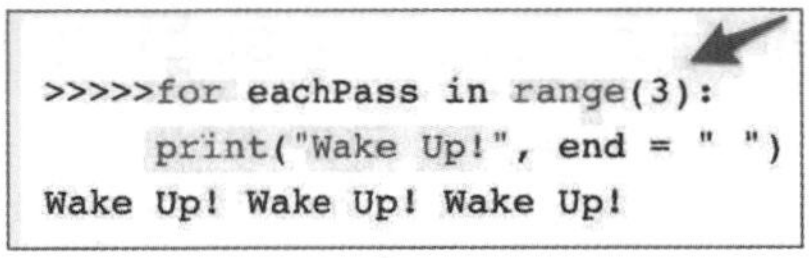

```
>>>>>for eachPass in range(3):
        print("Wake Up!", end = " ")
Wake Up! Wake Up! Wake Up!
```

Figure 7.1: A definite iteration

It is worth looking more closely at the statements that make up a loop using the `for` loop:

```
for <variable> in range (<an integer expression>):
    <statement -1>




    <statement -n>
```

The first line of code in a loop is referred to as the **loop header**. You can see in the first line of code that the most relevant information in our loop is the integer expression showing the number of iterations that the loop is executing. The colon (`:`) terminates the loop header.

The **loop body** is made up of the statements within the remaining lines of code located below the header.

Statements in the loop body are executed in sequence on each pass-through. In Python, these statements must be indented and aligned within the same column.

NOTE Your integrated development environment (IDE) should automatically indent the lines under the loop header. Best practice dictates a four-space indentation if your IDE does not provide this automatic feature.

THE FOR LOOP

Python's `for` loop is the control statement that easily supports definite **iteration**, where we know exactly how many times the loop should execute. The format of a `for` loop was shown before, but let's look at it again:

```
for <var> in <iterable>:
    <statement(s)>
```

A `for` loop is traditionally used when a developer wants to repeat a block of code a fixed number of times. As you can see in the code in Listing 7.1, we know the number of "passes" that the loop will take based on the number defined in the loop header.

LISTING 7.1

A for loop in action

```
for eachPass in range(3):
    print("Wake Up!")
```

When this listing is executed, the following output is displayed:

```
Wake Up!
Wake Up!
Wake Up!
```

As you can see, the loop happened three times. More specifically, the `range(3)` sets a sequence of three item numbers starting at 0 and ending before reaching that value included, which is 3. The Python `for` statement iterates (repeats) the members of the sequence in order, executing the block statements each time. If you changed the range to a different number, then the `for` statement would iterate that many times.

> **NOTE** If you've used other programming languages such as C, C++, or Java, then you might notice that the `for` loop in Python doesn't use braces ({}) to mark the beginning and end of the code block that will be iterated with the loop. Rather, Python uses indenting to determine what code to run.

THE WHILE LOOP

An `if` statement evaluates a condition, performs specific activities based on that condition, and then moves on to the next set of instructions in the code. Although similar in execution, a `while` loop repeats a specific set of instructions as many times as needed as long as a condition is True. We use the term **iteration** to refer to each time a set of instructions runs.

The basic syntax for a `while` loop is:

```
while (condition == True):
    ⟨statement(s)⟩
```

In order to iterate through a loop a given number of times, we use a counter variable to increment the variable by a constant measure. For example, we might increase the counter variable by 1, or we may double it. We often refer to that counter variable as an "incrementer."

This changing of the counter variable used in the condition is extremely important as it ensures that the condition will eventually stop being `True`. Without such a condition, we would end up with an endless loop that would run forever, commonly referred to as an infinite loop.

In the example of using a `while` statement presented in Listing 7.2, we simply display the integers 0 through 9.

LISTING 7.2

Using a while statement

```
i = 0
while ((i < 10) == True):
    print(i)
    i = i + 1
```

This listing goes through the following steps:

1. It starts by setting a variable `i` to 0.

2. It then uses a `while` loop that will run as long as `i` is less than 10. We can see that the `while` statement checks to see if `i` is less than 10. If so, then it executes the indented statements.

3. Inside the loop, the `while` statement prints the value of `i` and then increments `i` by 1.

The result is that the loop iterates until the value of `i` is equal to 10 or higher. In this case, when the value of `i` is 10, the loop stops. When you execute this code, you see the following output:

```
0
1
2
3
4
5
6
7
8
9
```

Listing 7.3 is a second example that displays integers backward from 100 to 0. Both 100 and 0 are included in the results.

LISTING 7.3

Iterating backward

```
i = 100
while ((i >= 0) == True):
    print(i)
    i = i - 1
```

In this listing, the variable i is set to 100. Then a while loop is executed as long as the value of i is greater than or equal to 0. As long as this is true, the value of i is printed, then the value is decremented by 1. The while condition is then checked again to see if the value of i is still greater than or equal to 0. The end result is that this loop will print the values from 100 down to 0.

Considering our banking application, in order to make it as efficient as possible and to address the needs of our customers, we want to make sure the program always works. We do not want our customers to encounter a situation where the program either continuously processes, or just stops and waits on their input, ignoring their input once it is received.

When dealing with a while loop, we must make sure there is an action present at the beginning of the execution. For example, if a customer enters an incorrect account number and the system does not recognize the account number, the application may not execute. Or if we have constructed our code to work *while the account numbers are valid*, and then the systems encounter an account number that is not valid, we may have a problem. It is important that our banking application has an escape route so that when the program encounters a condition that does not pass the condition of the loop, the program knows how to handle this situation.

Unexecutable while Loop

Because a while loop starts with a condition and executes the instructions in the loop only if that condition is met, there is a possibility that the instructions in the while loop may not execute if the condition is met at the start of the loop. Take a look at Listing 7.4 and consider what will happen when it is executed.

LISTING 7.4

An Unexecutable while loop

```
i = 1
while (i < 0):
    print("This message will never be displayed.")
```

You can see that in this listing, we start with a value 1. In the `while` loop, we check to see if that value of `i` is less than 0. Because 1 is not less than 0, the condition for the `while` evaluates to `False` and thus the instructions in the `while` loop's body do not execute.

In Listing 7.5 we see a second example of a `while` loop that won't have its body executed.

LISTING 7.5

Prompting until we get a match

```
input_value = input("Enter the phrase – Hello, World!: ")
while input_value != "Hello, World!":
  print("Please enter only – Hello, World!")
  input_value = input("Enter the phrase – Hello, World!: ")
```

When this listing is run it prompts the user to enter a specific value to input. If the user enters the correct value, the program stops. If the user does not enter the correct value, the program prompts the user to enter the value again and stops *only* when the user enters the correct value.

The listing uses a `while` loop to continue to prompt the user to enter the right phrase. The program won't end until the correct phrase is entered with the exact punctuation and case requested:

```
Enter the phrase – Hello, World!: Hello
Please enter only – Hello, World!
Enter the phrase – Hello, World!: Hello World
Please enter only – Hello, World!
Enter the phrase – Hello, World!: Hello, World!
```

> **TIP** Remember that Python is always case-sensitive by default.

FOR VS. WHILE LOOPS

The `for` and `while` operations are similar in that each function can iterate through items in a dataset. However, there are significant differences.

- for
  - Automatically determines the start point and the end point based on the number of items in the dataset or using a defined range
  - Uses inherent index values, so we do not have to define the values in the script

- `while`
  - Requires that the developer define an initial condition
  - Uses values defined by the developer rather than values that are inherent to the dataset
  - Requires an incrementer or other instruction that changes the value used in the initial condition to avoid an infinite loop
  - May not run at all if the initial condition is not met

These differences do not mean that one function is better than the other. Instead, we have to take the differences into account to determine which loop is most efficient in processing the data.

In Listing 7.6, we are asking for a user's name and adding the name to the program. Eventually, these names will become a part of our users for our ERP application.

LISTING 7.6

Collecting usernames

```
names = []
uContinue = ""

while uContinue != "N":
  name = input("What's your name? ")
  print("You entered: "+name)
  names.append(name)
  uContinue = input("Continue (Y or N) ")

print(names)
```

The code is structured so that it prompts the user for a name. Each name that is entered is appended to names. After receiving a name, the code asks the user to enter "**Y**" if they want to continue or to enter "**N**" if they want to stop. Once the user indicates they don't want to continue, the list of names is printed.

The following shows the program running and three names being added:

```
What's your name? John Smith
You entered: John Smith
Continue (Y or N) Y
What's your name? Fred Flintstone
You entered: Fred Flintstone
Continue (Y or N) Y
What's your name? Barney Rubble
You entered: Barney Rubble
Continue (Y or N) N
['John Smith', 'Fred Flintstone', 'Barney Rubble']
```

What would the changes be to Listing 7.6 if we wanted to limit the number of names entered? In Listing 7.7, the program has been modified to hold a maximum of five names.

LISTING 7.7

Collecting a limited number of usernames

```
names = []
uContinue = ""
count = 0

while count < 5 and uContinue != "N":
  name = input("What's your name? ")
  print("You entered: "+name)
  count += 1
  names.append(name)
  uContinue = input("Continue (Y or N) ")

print(names)
```

You can see that a new variable called count has been added to the listing. This variable is used to keep track of the number of names that have been entered. The while loop's condition has also been changed. In addition to the continue needing not be equal to "N," the count of names also has to be less than 5. Within the while body, count is incremented each time a name is added. Now when the program is executed, the loop will end after five names whether or not the user entered an "N."

STRINGS AND STRING OPERATIONS

Python uses the string (str) data class for values that consist of individual characters, as opposed to numeric values, Booleans, and other integer values. In Python, string values are always presented inside quotation marks.

We've created string variables before; however, Listing 7.8 shows another example of how to create a string variable, using name = "John".

LISTING 7.8

Creating a string variable

```
name="John"
print(name)
print(type(name))
```

The output from running this listing presents the name that was entered as well as confirms the type of the name variable:

```
John
<class 'str'>
```

Determining the Length of a String

Once you've created a string, there are a number of special operations that can be done with or on them. For example, we can use the len( ) method to calculate the number of characters in a string, including not only letters but also spaces and punctuation. The syntax of the len( ) method is:

```
len(variable)
```

In Listing 7.9 we use len( ) to calculate the number of characters in the string. Note that the comma, space, and exclamation point are included in the count.

LISTING 7.9

Finding the length of a string

```
message = "Hello, World!"
print(len(message)) #prints the length (number of characters) in a string
```

When you run this short listing, you see the output is simply the count of characters:

```
13
```

> **NOTE** You can change the text in the string assigned to message in Listing 7.9 to see the different results that are displayed.

Listing 7.10 presents a second example of using len( ). This listing prompts for a name and presents the length.

LISTING 7.10

Checking the length of a name

```
firstname = input("Please enter your first name: ")
lastname = input("Please enter your last name: ")
print(firstname, lastname)
print(len(firstname) + len(lastname))
```

Looking at the code, we can see that the user is prompted for their first name, which is stored in the firstname variable. They are then prompted for their last name, which is stored in lastname. The program then prints the values of firstname and lastname before printing the sum of the length of both names. The following is an example of running this listing:

```
Please enter your first name: John
Please enter your last name: Smith
John Smith
9
```

Note that the sum being printed is of the two individual names and doesn't include the space between them. The space isn't part of either string.

Now we can put these strings into the scenario of the banking application that we've used before. First, in our banking application, we could use strings to track a number of details that might not change throughout the application. This could be the name of our application, the version, and more:

```
string1 = "Our Banking Application"
string2 = "version 1.0"
string3 = "beta"
```

In addition to general information, name accuracy is extremely important for our banking customers. Not only should our banking portal accurately match names to account numbers, but we would like to demonstrate good customer service by addressing our customers by their preferred name. We can design our application so that users are presented with one input: "Please enter your first and last name. This allows us to personalize the user experience."

Splitting a String

A typical task in text analysis is to identify the individual words in a string. This allows calculations related to word frequency and the creation of a set of distinct words in a string. The split() method is used to separate the words in a string. While we can define other delimiters in cases where we need to, Python assumes by default that words are separated by whitespace (such as spaces and tabs).

In Listing 7.11, we split the "Hello, World!" phrase into separate words. Because Python uses whitespace to delineate words by default, it considers the punctuation characters to be part of the adjacent words. In more complex analysis, we can use a separate step to remove these characters from the original string before splitting the string into individual words.

LISTING 7.11

Splitting a string

```
message = "Hello, World!"

print(message.split())
```

When you run this listing, `split()` will break the strings within `message` apart based on the whitespace and store them in a list of strings. As a result, the following will be displayed:

```
['Hello,', 'World!']
```

Our ERP banking application may at times need to break up a user or customer's name for a form or perhaps a mailing address. Hence, it is valuable to understand how Python can aid in handling the names within strings so that you may slice and control the order for efficiency. For example, Listing 7.12 shows a simple example where a name is split.

LISTING 7.12

Splitting a name

```
fullname = input("Please enter your full name (last name, first name): ")
print(fullname.split())
```

This listing is not perfect, but it illustrates the `split()` method again in a scenario that you are more likely to see. In this case, a name is entered and then split into pieces:

```
Please enter your full name (last name, first name): Smith, John
['Smith,', 'John']
```

You'll see that the last name still includes the comma from the original user input. This is okay for now.

Storing Characters

While we can use index values to retrieve a specific character from a string, we can also store that value in its own variable in case we want to use it elsewhere in the code. Note that we can use either definite loops or indefinite loops to support the efficiency of the process.

Using the example of "John Smith," we can create variables that store specific characters in the string as shown in Listing 7.13.

LISTING 7.13

Pulling and storing characters from a string

```
name = "John Smith"
print(name)

char1 = name[0] # stores the first character as char1
print(char1)

char6 = name[5] # stores the fifth character
print(char6)

char_last = name[-1] # stores the last character
print(char_last)
```

This listing creates a new string called name and puts the value "John Smith" into it. After printing the name, various characters are pulled from the string using an index value. These characters are then printed. Remember that the first index value is 0, not 1, so name[0] pulls the first character and name[1] pulls the second. The output when this listing is executed is:

```
John Smith
J
S
h
```

Our ERP banking application could automatically create usernames for uniformity and ease of use. Specifically, it could select the first few and the last few characters of the user's first and last name, which can be accomplished by specifying the index values of a string within Python. This can be done uniformly across various lengths of names and makes it simpler to select the characters.

Comparison Operators in Strings

Suppose that a developer needs to create code that would quickly process a large data list containing customer banking information. The script should look for customers whose checking account balances had fallen below a certain threshold. The script should perform this "look" until it reaches the end of the file. The developer could harness the power of the iteration statement along with conditional statements and comparison operators to test for equality.

Strings, when used in Python, support the comparison operators == (equality) and != (inequality); however, as we have stated before, it is important to remember that string comparisons in Python are case-sensitive. "Hello" is not equal to "hello."

Listing 7.14 compares the same name using different casing.

- The == operator will output True if the strings are the same and False if they are different.

- The != operator will output True if the strings are different and False if they are the same.

LISTING 7.14

Comparing strings

```
fname_1 = "john"
fname_2 = "john"
fname_3 = "John"

#This will display True if the two strings are equal
#and False if they aren't equal
print(fname_1, "==", fname_2)
print(fname_1 == fname_2)

#This will display True if the two strings are equal
#and False if they aren't equal
print(fname_1, "==", fname_3)
print(fname_1 == fname_3)

#This will display False if the two strings are equal
#and True if they aren't equal
print(fname_1, "!=", fname_3)
print(fname_1 != fname_3)
```

You can see that this listing sets up three strings that will be used in the comparisons. Three different comparisons are then done and the results of True or False are printed. Before each comparison, the information being compared is also printed to make it easier to see from the output what is happening:

```
john == john
True
john == John
False
john != John
True
```

One common problem we might run into with our ERP banking application is that when we ask users to enter data, some users prefer to key only in lowercase. Others will use mixed case, while others will sometimes have the caps lock key on (on purpose or not).

Passwords and other security strings are typically case-sensitive, whereas other values like web addresses and usernames are normally not sensitive to case, even though the system that manages those values (like a web server OS or a programming language) may be case-sensitive. While we can always ask that a user use only uppercase or lowercase, there is no guarantee that they will do so. We can instead use a script to normalize the characters to work within the system similar to what is illustrated in Listing 7.15.

LISTING 7.15

Ignoring character case

```
value1 = "username"
value2 = input("Enter your username: ")
print(value1 == value2.lower())
```

This is a short listing, but it shows how to ignore case when comparing two strings. The program does assume the original username, value1, is already in lowercase format. The program prompts the user to enter a username (value2), which is compared against the saved username (value1). The method lower() is used on the string to force what the user entered into all lowercase. This means that if the user enters "**username**," then it will match regardless of the case. The following shows the program being run multiple times:

```
Enter your username: username
True
Enter your username: USERNAME
True
Enter your username: Fred
False
Enter your username: UserName
True
Enter your username: User Name
False
```

As you can see, it accepts the user input in any case. If the two strings match, then True was returned. If they do not, then False is returned.

> **NOTE** Run the program yourself and test it using lowercase input, uppercase input, and mixed-case input, as well as misspelled input. In the code, "username" is the preexisting value, but you can change this to a different value if you wish.

In our ERP banking application, we want to ensure that the strings are handled properly, and we can employ several checks to make sure the strings are in a proper format. Comparison operators are often involved to help with this.

Concatenating Strings

Concatenation is the process of combining two or more strings into a new string. We use the + operator to concatenate strings in Python. Similarly, the ∗ operator repeats the items in a list a given number of times.

Use caution when attempting to add different types together. Python does not understand how to concatenate different data types. If attempting to add a string to a list such as:

```
['first'] + "second"
```

the interpreter will return an error. The correct way to accomplish this task would be to make the two objects the same type. In this case, we would put the string into its own list and then add the two together like so:

```
['first'] + ["second"]
```

Listing 7.16 presents the use of concatenation.

LISTING 7.16

Concatenating strings

```
first_name = "John"
last_name = "Smith"

print(first_name)
print(last_name)

full_name = first_name + last_name
print(full_name)

full_name_upper = first_name.upper() + last_name.upper()
print(full_name_upper)
```

This listing starts by creating two strings to hold a name. These are first_name and last_name. These are then printed so their values can be seen. The two strings are then concatenated using the + operator and the resulting string, full_name, is displayed. Finally, the two strings have the upper() method called upon them and the results are concatenated together. Again, the final result is displayed. The resulting output is:

```
John
Smith
JohnSmith
JOHNSMITH
```

In the ERP banking application, it could be that the customer's name needs to be used in a pamphlet that is being mailed. The format could be a last name then first name format all in uppercase. Listing 7.17 presents this along with additional formatting.

LISTING 7.17

Formatting names for a pamphlet

```
first_name = "John"
last_name = "Smith"
full_name_upper = last_name.upper() + ", " + first_name.upper()
print (full_name_upper)
```

This listing takes a single name and formats it. It uses the same process that we used in the previous listing of converting the name to uppercase by using the `upper()` method. The difference is that a literal string (`", "`) is also concatenated along with the last name and first name. The literal string adds the command and space resulting in the following output:

```
SMITH, JOHN
```

In this listing, only a single name is being formatted. For our ERP banking application, it could be that each name is formatted within a loop and printed as part of a pamphlet or mailing labels for all the customers.

Slicing Strings

While it's good to be able to retrieve individual values from a string based on their index values, we sometimes need to retrieve multiple characters at the same time. We use the term *slicing* to refer to the process of retrieving a range of characters from a string, rather than retrieving individual characters.

In Python, we use the syntax `variable[range]` to retrieve a range of characters from a string. The options include:

- `variable[x:y]` retrieves a string starting with index x and ending with the character *before* index y. If y is equal to the length of the string, the range will include the last character in the string.

- `variable[:y]` retrieves the characters from index 0 through the character *before* index y. This is equivalent to using `[0:y]`.

- `variable[x:]` retrieves a string that starts with the character at index x and includes all characters to the right of that character. This is equivalent to using `[x:(length)]`.

Listing 7.18 illustrates slicing a basic "Hello, World!" string, and then retrieving slices of that string. Look at the code in the listing and try to predict what the output will look like for each `print` statement. Then look at the output to check your predictions.

LISTING 7.18

Slicing a string

```
message = "Hello, World!"

print(message)
print(len(message))

# extract the substring from message starting from the first character (index 0)
# through the character whose index value is 4.
message_1 = message[0:5]

print("message_1 is " + message_1)

# Extract the substring from message starting from the first character (index 0)
# through the character whose index value is 4. The lower bound is not specified,
# so Python uses 0.
message_2 = message[:5]

print("message_2 is " + message_2)

# Extract the substring from message starting from the eighth character (index 7)
# through the character whose index value is 9 (one less than 10)..
message_3 = message[7:10]

print("message_3 is " + message_3)

# Extract the substring from message starting from the eighth character (index 7)
# through the last character. Index 14 is past the end of the string.
message_4 = message[7:14]

print("message_4 is " + message_4)

# Extract the substring from message starting from the eighth character (index 7)
# all the way to the last character, regardless of index value.
message_5 = message[7:]

print("message_5 is " + message_5)
```

This listing starts by creating a string variable called message and placing "Hello, World!" into it. The value of message is then printed along with its length. After this, sections of the string are extracted and displayed.

Throughout this listing, comments are used to describe what is happening. You can see that the first slicing occurs using message[0:5]. This slices off starting at the first character (position 0) and takes up to the character o, which is just before position 5. The result is:

```
Hello
```

The next slicing uses message[:5] to store a value in the message_2 variable. In this case, the slicing starts at the beginning of the string and goes to the character just before the index of 5 (so index of 4). Again, the result is the same as doing message[0:5]:

```
Hello
```

The third slicing uses message[7:10]. You can see from this that the slice is taken starting at the character with the index position of 7 (which would be the 8th character) and goes to the character just before the index position of 10. The result is that message_3 equals the characters in positions 7, 8, and 9, which are:

```
Wor
```

The fourth slice is similar to the third, except that the value starts at the index position of 7 and goes to the index position of 13 (one less than 14). Because 14 is past the end of the string, the characters are printed from index position 7 to the end:

```
World!
```

In general, you should avoid reading past the end of a string. The last slicing shows the alternative way to read to the end of the string using message[7:]. This starts at index position 7 and goes to the end:

```
World!
```

The full output from running this listing is:

```
Hello, World!
13
message_1 is Hello
message_2 is Hello
message_4 is Wor
message_4 is World!
message_5 is World!
```

Breaking "Hello, World!" apart is not overly practical. In our ERP banking application, however, there is an example where slicing makes a lot more sense. Taking a customer or username and breaking it into parts would be something that might need to happen. For example, if you do a single prompt to ask the customer for their name, you could then use Python to break the full name into separate strings for first name and last. Listing 7.19 takes a hard-coded full name and breaks it into two parts, a first name and a last name.

LISTING 7.19

Splitting a name

```
name="John Smith"
first_name = name[0:4]
last_name = name[5:10]
print(first_name)
print(last_name)
print(first_name.upper())
print(last_name.upper())

print(name[0:1] + name[5:6])
print(first_name[0:1] + last_name[0:1])

print(name[0:1] + ". " + last_name)
```

> **NOTE** You might have noticed that we are using a specific name. This code would have to be rewritten with different values for names that are different lengths. Don't worry about this for now!

You can see that the listing starts with a name of "John Smith." Then, using the slicing methods you just learned, the first name is pulled by slicing the first through fourth characters (index positions 0 to 3) from name. This value is put into the first_name variable. Similarly, the sixth (index position 5) character through the 11th character (index position 10) are sliced and placed into the variable last_name.

The listing then prints the first and last names as they were stored followed by printing them in uppercase as you've seen before. The next two print statements, however, are more interesting and produce the same results. They both display the initials for John Smith, JS. First, using the name variable, the first letter of the first name and last name are sliced and printed. The second uses the first_name and last_name variables that were sliced from name, and then slices the first character off of each to print. In the output, you can see that they both produce the same result of printing JS.

The last `print` statement combines the slicing to print the initial from the first name and the full last name. To make it more presentable, a literal string is concatenated in the middle to put a period and space after the first name initial. The full output from this listing is:

```
John
Smith
JOHN
SMITH
JS
JS
J. Smith
```

> **NOTE** To verify you understand the index positions and slicing, try modifying Listing 7.19 to include a middle name. Include the middle initial when printing the initials.

Searching Strings

Python supports search operations on strings, using the `in` operator to check if a substring exists in a string. This will perform an operation similar to searching a web page or other electronic document for a specific word or phrase.

It is important to note that searches are case-sensitive by default, so a search for "He" is not the same as a search for "he." Normalizing the case means that the user can search for a string using any case, regardless of the case that matching substrings are in.

As you will see in Listing 7.20, the `in` operator returns `True` if the first operand is contained within the second, and `False` otherwise. In this situation, the output is Boolean: either the substring exists in the message or it does not. The output does not tell us where the substring is located inside the message, nor does it tell us how many times the substring appears in the message.

LISTING 7.20

Searching within a string

```python
message = "Hello, World!"

print("He" in message)    # we use the in operator to check if the
                          # string "He" exists in "Hello World"

print("he" in message)    #everything is case sensitive

print("he" in message.lower())

print("ch" in message)
```

In this listing, we are again using the string "Hello, World!" We are also using the `print` function to display the result of our checks. In the first check, using the `in` keyword, we are seeing if "He" is in the value contained within the `message` variable. "He" is in "Hello, World!" so the result is `True`, which is displayed in the first line of the output:

```
True
False
True
False
```

The second check searches for "he" in the "Hello, World!" string stored in `message`. Because the search is case-sensitive, "he" is not found and thus `False` is displayed. The third check compares "he" to a lowercased version of the string in `message`, which would be `True`. Finally, a check to see if "ch" is in our `message` string, which returns `False` because it is not.

ITERATING THROUGH STRINGS

As you have learned, Python uses the string (`str`) data class for values that consist of individual characters, as opposed to numeric values, Booleans, and other integer values. In Python, string values are always presented inside quotation marks. Python treats strings as though they are a group of individual characters rather than as a single value. The `for` loop can be used to iterate (or move through) the characters in a string. This allows us to look for specific characters in the same way we might want to find a name in a list.

In Listing 7.21, we iterate through a "Hello, World!" string and extract each character individually.

LISTING 7.21

Iterating through a string

```
# create a string variable
message = "Hello, World!"

# use a for loop to iterate through the list character by character
for ctr in message:
    print(ctr)
```

As you can see, "Hello, World!" is again used as our string stored in the variable message. Using a for loop, we can iterate through each letter of message. A variable, ctr, is used to step through each item (each character) in the string. The repetition automatically stops when it reaches the last character of the string. The resulting output is:

```
H
e
l
l
o
,

W
o
r
l
d
!
```

It is worth looking at a slightly more complicated example as shown in Listing 7.22. In this scenario, we will again use a for loop, but this time we will iterate through a list of names. These could be the names of the employees of our banking application.

In this case, we will use the first names of some of our employees. We will print each employee name, and then list each letter of their name.

LISTING 7.22

Iterating through employees

```
employees = ["Billy", "Jayden", "Magda", "Luis"]
for ctr in employees:     # iterate through the list of employees
  print(ctr)
  for ctr2 in ctr:        # iterate through each employee
    print(ctr2.upper())
  print("----")
```

Looking at the listing, you see that we place each name into the variable employee. This variable contains four strings, each of which is an employee's name. A for loop is used to iterate through the list of employees with a counter called ctr being used to select each name.

Within each iteration of the for loop, the current name will be held within the ctr variable. Once we have each name, we print it using print(ctr). We can also then iterate through the individual name using a second for loop embedded within the first:

```
    for ctr2 in ctr:
      print(ctr2.upper())
```

This loop should look just like the loop used in Listing 7.21, except we are using `ctr` instead of `message`. The variable `ctr` will have the current name from the outer loop. Once the code has iterated through the individual name, another call to `print` is done to display a few dashes to separate the current name from the next name. The resulting output looks like the following:

```
Billy
B
I
L
L
Y
----
Jayden
J
A
Y
D
E
N
----
Magda
M
A
G
D
A
----
Luis
L
U
I
S
----
```

Being able to iterate and select specific characters within a string can be useful to control user or customer names in forms and data structures. In our banking application, there are instances where we would need to slice a name or address for mailing purposes. Other times, there may be a need to reduce a name length or select either the first few or last few characters.

> **NOTE** Remember that how you name variables is important. In Listing 7.22, the variables `ctr` and `ctr2` were used. The following is the same listing with variables that are more appropriately named. Consider this version of the listing and compare it to Listing 7.22 and consider which is more descriptive of what is being done.

```
employees = ["Billy", "Jayden", "Magda", "Luis"]
for name in employees:
  print(name)
  for letter in name:
    print(letter.upper())
print("----")
```

SUMMARY

Python supports a variety of control structures that determine how content in a program will work and interact. This lesson continued the exploration including additional control structures that make creating algorithms possible. The lesson concluded with a discussion of how iteration aids in text processing.

Now that you have completed Lesson 7, you should be able to

- Create a Python script that uses a for loop to repeat an activity until a specific criterion is met.

- Create a Python script that uses a while loop to repeat an activity as long as a specific criterion holds true.

- Use string operations to manipulate string variables.

EXERCISES

The following exercises will allow you to demonstrate that you have achieved the objectives for this lesson.

You should complete each exercise and make sure that the code runs without errors. The exercises here include:

Exercise 1: Separating Your Fruits

Exercise 2: Keeping It Short

Exercise 3: Fruit Finder

Exercise 4: It's Divisible

Exercise 5: Identify the Numbers

Exercise 6: And the Total Is...

Exercise 7: Multiplication Tables

Exercise 8: Sum of Prime Numbers

Exercise 9: One Letter at a Time

Exercise 10: Length without `len()`

Exercise 11: Count the Numbers

Exercise 12: Fizz Buzz

Exercise 1: Separating Your Fruits

Given the list `fruit_list`, write a script that iterates through the list and prints each item on a separate line:

```
fruit_list = ["apple", "banana", "cherry", "gooseberry", "kumquat", "orange",
"pineapple"]

# your code here
```

Exercise 2: Keeping It Short

Create a program that takes an input list of strings, identifies all the strings with two or more characters, and stores the results in another list. For example, the following list

```
a = ["a", "bc", "rye", "hello", "c", ""]
```

would produce the following output:

```
["bc", "rye", "hello"]
```

Exercise 3: Fruit Finder

Starting with the defined `fruit_list` in the following code block, update the script to perform the following tasks:

- Prompt the user to enter the name of a fruit.
- If the fruit is in `fruit_list`, display an appropriate message to tell the user its index value in the list.
- If the fruit is not in `fruit_list`, display an appropriate message to the user and prompt them to try again.
- The script should repeat itself until the user enters a stop word at the prompt.

```
fruit_list = ["apple", "banana", "cherry", "gooseberry", "kumquat", "orange",
"pineapple"]

# your code here
```

> **TIP** It's always a good idea to tell the user how to end a loop!

Exercise 4: It's Divisible

Write two scripts, each of which displays all numbers divisible by 50 between 100 and 1000 (inclusive).

- Use the `range()` function with `for` in one script.
- Use `while` without `range()` in the other script.

Both scripts should have identical outputs.

```
# script 1: range
# your code here
# script 2: while
# your code here
```

Exercise 5: Identify the Numbers

Write two scripts. The first should identify all prime numbers between 0 and 100, and the second should compute the sum of all numbers between 0 and 100.

Exercise 6: And the Total Is...

Create a script that asks the user for a variable number of values and displays the sum of those values to the user. The program should prompt the user for values until the user enters the word "quit" (uppercase or lowercase), display the values used in the calculation, and then display the total of those values.

Exercise 7: Multiplication Tables

Write a script that asks the user for an integer value and then displays the multiplication table of that input number from 1 through the integer squared.

Exercise 8: Sum of Prime Numbers

Write a Python script that determines if an input number can be expressed as the sum of two prime numbers. For example, the number 10 can be expressed as the sum of two prime numbers:

- 10 = 3 + 7 : both prime numbers
- 10 = 5 + 5 : both prime numbers

However, the number 11 cannot be:

- 11 = 1 + 10 : neither 1 nor 10 are prime numbers
- 11 = 2 + 9 : 9 is not a prime number
- 11 = 3 + 8 : 8 is not a prime number
- 11 = 4 + 7 : 4 is not a prime number
- 11 = 5 + 6 : 6 is not a prime number

Exercise 9: One Letter at a Time

Write a Python script that asks the user for a string and displays the characters of the string to the user, with each character on a new line. For example, if the input is **Hello**, the output should be:

```
H
e
l
l
o
```

Exercise 10: Length without len()

Write a Python script that computes the length of a string without using the `len()` function.

Exercise 11: Count the Numbers

Write a Python script that computes the frequency of each digit in a given integer.
For example, if the input number is 334, the output should be:

```
3 occurs 2 times
4 occurs 1 time
```

Exercise 12: Fizz Buzz

Write a program that performs the following steps:

1. Ask the user for a number.
2. Output a count starting with 0.
   - Display the count number if it is not divisible by 3 or 5.
   - Replace every multiple of 3 with the word "fizz."
   - Replace every multiple of 5 with the word "buzz."
   - Replace multiples of both 3 and 5 with "fizz buzz."

3. Continue counting until the number of integers replaced with "fizz," "buzz," or "fizz buzz" reaches the input number.

4. The last output line should read "TRADITION!!"

The following is an example of output if 7 is entered:

```
How many fizzing and buzzing units do you need in your life? 7
0
1
2
fizz
4
buzz
fizz
7
8
fizz
buzz
11
fizz
13
14
fizz buzz
TRADITION!!
```

Lesson 8

Understanding Basic Data Structures: Lists

In addition to storing a single value in a variable, Python supports data structures that allow us to store multiple elements in a single variable. In this lesson, we will introduce several such structures and then take a closer look at lists. Python uses lists and these other structures as basic data types with specific features associated with each.

LEARNING OBJECTIVES

By the end of this lesson, you will be able to:

- Explain several data structures available to Python developers.
- Use lists to store data collections and retrieve specific values from a collection.
- Add, remove, or change items in a list.
- Slice, copy, sort, combine, and manipulate lists.

DATA STRUCTURE OVERVIEW—PART 1

In Lesson 5 we discussed several specific types of control structures that are used to control the flow of data through an application. As business problems have become more complex, developers have created data structures to help solve them. In Python, we use data structures to combine several values into a single unit. We do this so that each combination can be processed as one entity. As we have learned, a string is a specific data structure that organizes text as a sequence of characters. Similarly, *lists, tuples, dictionaries*, and *sets* organize data values. In this lesson, we will cover lists. In the subsequent three lessons, we will cover each of the others: tuples, dictionaries, and sets.

Variables were introduced in Lesson 2. *Variables* are areas set aside in memory that are used to store data. Variables represent the values needed for the program. They are called variables because the exact value can vary each time we run the program, and their values can change between the start of a program and the end of a program.

But what would we do if a need arises to store a list of information, and that list does not change? For example, what if you needed to store data that doesn't rapidly change over time in an employee directory? Python uses lists, tuples, dictionaries, and sets for this. These data structures, like strings, organize data but extend the capabilities of programmers to use any data type. Table 8.1 introduces a simple explanation for each of these structures. This lesson and the next three will expand and clarify the explanations in the table.

> **NOTE** Strings can only accept text, so they are limited in what they can store.

As we go through the next few lessons, there are several terms that will be covered related to data structures. These are:

- **List:** A list is a sequence of data values called items or elements. It allows duplicate members.
- **Tuple:** A tuple is a collection that is ordered and immutable (which means unchangeable). It allows duplicate members.
- **Dictionary:** A dictionary organizes data values by association with other data values rather than by sequential positions. It does not allow duplicate members.
- **Set:** A set is a collection that is unordered and unindexed. A set does not allow duplicate members.
- **Index:** An index returns the position of a target element in a list. The element must be in the list, otherwise an error is raised.
- **Variable:** A variable is a value set aside in memory that can change value over time.

Table 8.1 Types of Data Structures

Structure	Syntax	Definition
List	Lists are enclosed in brackets: `l = [1, 2, "a"]`	Lists are ordered and changeable.
Tuple	Tuples are enclosed in parentheses: `t = (1, 2, "a")`	A tuple is ordered and is immutable (cannot be changed).
Dictionary	Dictionaries are built with curly brackets: `d = {"a":1, "b":2}`	A dictionary is unordered, changeable, and indexed. Dictionaries have keys and values.
Set	Sets are written with curly brackets: `s = {1, 2, 3}`	A set is an unordered collection of items. Every set element is unique and must be immutable (cannot be changed). However, a set itself is mutable. We can add or remove items from it.

CREATING LISTS

A Python list is a sequence of data values called items (or elements). The list of items is ordered, but it can also be changed. The list is considered a basic data type in Python and can be used to store a collection of items. Following is a real-world example of a list, a class roster:

- Amir
- Lena
- Maya
- Roberta

The length of a list is equal to the number of items within the list. We create lists by placing all the items or elements within square brackets and separated by commas. The basic syntax of a list is:

```
name_of_list = ['element 1', 'element 2', 'element 3', … ]
```

If you were to create a list for the class roster, it would be:

```
students = ['Amir', 'Lena', 'Maya', 'Roberta']
```

Let's create a few lists, including a list of numbers, a list of strings, and a list that contains both strings and numbers. Note that Python treats each collection as a list, regardless of what kind of data is included in the collection. Listing 8.1 creates three lists.

LISTING 8.1

Creating lists

```
list_of_numbers = [1, 2, 4, 6]
print(list_of_numbers)
print(type(list_of_numbers))

list_of_strings = ["Kate", "Jennifer", "Mike"]
print(list_of_strings)
print(type(list_of_strings))

list_of_items = ["Kate", "124 W Main Street Boston", 24, 4.0]
print(list_of_items)
print(type(list_of_items))
```

Listing 8.1 is straightforward in that it does the same thing three times. It creates a list, prints the items in the list, and then prints the type of the list. When you run this listing, you see the following output:

```
[1, 2, 4, 6]
<class 'list'>
['Kate', 'Jennifer', 'Mike']
<class 'list'>
['Kate', '124 W Main Street Boston', 24, 4.0]
<class 'list'>
```

> **NOTE** You might have noticed that in our listing we used double quotes ("), but in the output there are single quotes ('). Python treats single and double quotes similarly so you can use either in your code. The only stringent rule is that you need to use them in pairs when creating a string. You can create a string as "my string" or 'my string', but you cannot do "my string'.

As you can see, the first list, list_of_numbers, is assigned four numbers using the syntax that was shown earlier. Each element that will be assigned to the list is placed within square brackets separated by a comma. Notice that we are not using a keyword to define the list. Python knows that list_of_numbers is a list because it is being assigned the values from the right that are listed within square brackets.

The entire list is then printed by passing the list variable to the print method. This is followed by printing the list_of_numbers by using type(). Notice that the type is indeed a list. After printing the numbers, the same process is done for a list of strings, and then a mixed list of strings and numbers.

Listing 8.2 presents a second example. In this case, the list is being created and then several items are being added to it. Specifically, the following items are being added (in this specific order):

- First name
- Last name
- Position
- Employee number

LISTING 8.2

A list of employees

```
list1 = []

num = input ("Enter number: ")
print(num)

for num in range(0,int(num)):
  firstname = input("Enter first name: ")
  lastname = input("Enter last name: ")
  position = input("Enter position: ")
  empnum = input("Enter employee number: ")
  list_of_items = [firstname, lastname, position, empnum]
  list1.append(list_of_items)

for ctr in list1:
  print(*ctr, sep = ", ")
```

In this example, we start with an empty list variable named list1. We know it is an empty list because it is assigned open and close square brackets with nothing between them. This is the list to which we will be adding each of our employees.

Next the user is asked to enter a number that corresponds to the number of employees for which we will gather information. We save this number in the variable num. The listing prints the value out as confirmation.

Next, the num variable is used in a for loop. Using a range of 0 to the number of employees (num converted to an integer), we will loop, and the for statement block of code will be executed. Within the for loop, the user is prompted to enter a first name, last name, position, and employee number. Each of these values is stored in its own variable and the variables are then added to a new list variable called list_of_items. You can see this list is created using the syntax shown earlier:

```
list_of_items = [firstname, lastname, position, empnum]
```

Once we've created this second list, we append it to the original list we created in the first line of the listing:

```
list1.append(list_of_items)
```

After appending, the `for` loop iterates and the prompts are given for the next employee until we reach the number originally entered by the user.

Once all the employees have been entered, a final `for` loop iterates through the list of employees, `list1`, and prints each item (identified by `ctr`). The `print` statement includes something new as well, which is the `sep` parameter. This is a value that is placed between each item being printed in each list being displayed: in this case, a comma and space.

Listing 8.2 covers a lot. Enter it and run the listing to see the output. The following output shows three employees being entered:

```
Enter number: 3
3
Enter first name: Kate
Enter last name: Adams
Enter position: CEO
Enter employee number: 111
Enter first name: Jennifer
Enter last name: Brown
Enter position: VP Development
Enter employee number: 222
Enter first name: Mike
Enter last name: Carson
Enter position: CTO
Enter employee number: 333
Kate, Adams, CEO, 111
Jennifer, Brown, VP Development, 222
Mike, Carson, CTO, 333
```

NOTE Don't fret if you didn't follow everything in Listing 8.2. We'll be covering similar code again in this lesson.

When it comes to our ERP banking application, we will find that lists are also valuable because we can use them to process sets of information and data points. This can be used to collect information, such as names or employee numbers, and store them in variables. In an application situation, this might be used to push information to a database or other collection.

DETERMINING LIST LENGTH

Now that we have learned how to create lists, let's apply the concept. If we want to know the number of elements within a list, we can use the `len()` function, which returns the length of the list. The `len()` function will compute the number of elements in the list, using the following syntax:

```
len(list)
```

Listing 8.3 creates a simple list of names and then uses the `len()` method to return the number of elements.

LISTING 8.3

Determining the number of names

```
list_of_strings = ['Kate', 'Jennifer', 'Mike']
howMany = len(list_of_strings)
print(howMany)
```

This is a simple listing that creates three names in a list called `list_of_strings`. The number of elements in the `list_of_strings` is determined by passing it to the `len()` method. The result of running Listing 8.3 is that 3 is printed. You could add additional names to the first line of code and see how the number changes when the program is executed. You could also have simplified the listing by simply combining the last two lines into one:

```
print(len(list_of_strings))
```

In our ERP banking application, we could store information on customers who access our application throughout the day. We could then use the `len()` method with this list to determine the number of customers who used the application.

WORKING WITH LIST INDEXES

Python uses indexes to identify items in a list, and we can retrieve specific items using those index values. Each item in the list has a value and an index (its position in the list). Python uses zero-based indexing, meaning the first item in a list has the index value of 0 and the last item in a list has an index value equal to the length of the list minus 1. Python will report an error if we try to retrieve a value from a list using a nonexistent index.

For example, remember our class roster:

- Amir
- Lena
- Maya
- Roberta

We defined our roster using a simple list called `students`:

```
students = ['Amir', 'Lena', 'Maya', 'Roberta']
```

Each item in a list, in this case, each name, is treated as a separate value in the collection. The logical structure of a list resembles the structure in a string. Similar to each character in a string, each item in a list has a unique index that specifies its position. For example, as shown in Figure 8.1, the first position (or index) in the list is 0 (in our example, Amir), and the index of the last item in the list (Roberta) is the length of the list minus 1 (so Roberta is in position 3).

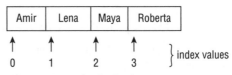

Figure 8.1: List indexing

In Listing 8.4, we present a list of three names and then access each one using an index.

LISTING 8.4

Accessing names by index

```
list_of_strings = ["Kate", "Jennifer", "Mike"]
print(list_of_strings)

#access the first element in the list using the [] and
#the index starting from zero for the first element
person_1 = list_of_strings[0] #access the first element of the list
print(person_1)

person_2 = list_of_strings[1] #access the second element of the list
print(person_2)

person_3 = list_of_strings[2] #access the third (and last) element of the list
print(person_3)

#this will cause an error because there are only three items in the list
person_4 = list_of_strings[3]
```

Note that this listing contains comments indicating what is happening. When you run this listing, you will get the following output, which includes an error:

```
['Kate', 'Jennifer', 'Mike']
Kate
Jennifer
Mike
----------------------------------------------------------------
IndexError                            Traceback (most recent call last)

<ipython-input-5-c7ee4853e173> in <module>
     14
     15 #this will cause an error because there are only three items in the list
---> 16 person_4 = list_of_strings[3]

IndexError: list index out of range
```

You can see that a list of three names is created. Because index numbering starts at zero, these are indexed from 0 to 2. After creating `list_of_strings`, the `print` method is called to show that, indeed, the list was created, and the three names were added. Each element is accessed by using the name of the list followed by square brackets and the index number. The element is saved to a new variable, which is then printed. The first element, `list_of_strings[0]`, is assigned to `person_1`, which is then printed. You can see that it was successful, because the name Kate is displayed. The same is done with the second and third elements as well.

The error occurs when the program attempts to assign `list_of_strings[3]` to `person_4`. The use of index 3 is attempting to find a name that is beyond the end of our list as shown in Figure 8.2. As such, Python displays an error. If we look at the error, it even states, "`list index out of range`."

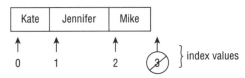

Figure 8.2: Accessing beyond the list

NOTE It is a common mistake to try to access the last item of a list by using the length of the list instead of the length minus 1. This will give an error because this would be trying to access an element that is past the end of the list. Remember, index counting starts with 0.

For our ERP application to make efficient use of strings and lists, it is critical that it be able to select specific items within the list for analysis or manipulation. When we are taking input from a customer regarding their account details or from a bank employee who is looking into an issue with a customer account, we want to ensure that the right information is selected.

Our ERP can handle and manipulate items in the list via the list index. Listing 8.5 shows a very simple example of how banking customer information could be used within a list.

LISTING 8.5

Customer details in a list

```
customer_details = ["Ava McDougle", "ava@email.com", "123-456-7890"]

name = customer_details[0]  # access the first element of the list
print(name)

email = customer_details[1] # access the second element of the list
print(email)

phonenumber = customer_details[2] # access third/ last element
print(phonenumber)
```

This code simply shows an example of using customer information in a list. You can see that the first element in the list is the name, the second is the email address, and the third is the phone number. The code copies each of these items out of the list and then prints them.

> **NOTE** In Listing 8.5, each list element is a string. We could also create a list that contained a list of customers by creating a list that contained several `customer_detail` lists. It would be a list of lists.

NEGATIVE INDEXING IN LISTS

Using indexing, we can easily get any element by its position within the list. Attempting to retrieve an element by position is simple if we use a position from the start (also called the head) of a list.

But what if we want to take the last element of a list? How is that accomplished?

Python supports negative indexing, which counts from the end of the list, as shown in Figure 8.3. It is important to remember that the index value −1 always references the last item in a list, regardless of how many items there are. Sequential negative values count backward from there, so −2 is the next-to-last item, −3 is the third-to-last item, and so on. Python will report an error if the negative index value references an item that does not exist. In Listing 8.6, we explore negative indexing.

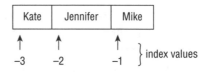

Figure 8.3: Negative indexing

LISTING 8.6

Accessing the end of a list

```
list_of_strings = ["Kate", "Jennifer", "Mike"]
person_1 = list_of_strings[-1] #-1 refers to the last element in the list
print(person_1)

person_2 = list_of_strings[-2] #-2 refers to second-to-last element in list
print(person_2)

person_3 = list_of_strings[-3] #-3 refers to third-to-last element in list
print(person_3)

# this will report an error because there are only three items in the list
person_4 = list_of_strings[-4]
```

Listing 8.6 is very similar to Listing 8.4, except the elements are being accessed from the end of the list and with each change of the negative index number, we work toward the beginning as indicated by the comments in the listing. Similar to Listing 8.4, when the indexing reaches a point beyond the list, in this case −4, an error is displayed. In the following output, we see that the names are presented in reverse order before the error is finally displayed:

```
Mike
Jennifer
Kate
---------------------------------------------------------------------
IndexError                              Traceback (most recent call last)

<ipython-input-8-a726a73b85c5> in <module>
     10
     11 # this will report an error because there are only three items in the list
---> 12 person_4 = list_of_strings[-4]

IndexError: list index out of range
```

The ERP banking application is almost always handling data for analysis and manipulation to provide the most efficient and effective information for the organization. For instance, we may be interested in the last few transactions performed by our customers to understand their recent account activity. Gathering information at the end of an index can be complex if the length has to be calculated and then we have to subtract the expected characters, but Python makes that much easier with negative indexing.

With negative indexing, we can quickly read from the end of the list or string without needing to calculate any length at all. By simply using negative values, Python automatically understands you want to move to the end of the string and then step back the appropriate elements. Listing 8.7 again shows a simple example. This time, we have a list that contains a customer's recent account activity. From that list, we can easily display the last three transactions performed by the customer.

LISTING 8.7

Accessing a customer's last transactions

```
transactions = [
  "1AB23456C0011523D,+$25.00",
  "1AB23456C5541225D,-$56.00",
  "1AB23456C8613005D,-$393.00",
  "1AB23456C3542215D,+$544.23",
  "1AB23456C0145125D,-$5.55",
  "1AB23456C3485125D,-$8.76"]

print("Last transaction: " + transactions[-1])
print("2nd from last transaction: " + transactions[-2])
print("3rd from last transaction: " + transactions[-3])
```

When this listing is executed, the following is displayed:

```
Last transaction: 1AB23456C3485125D,-$8.76
2nd from last transaction: 1AB23456C0145125D,-$5.55
3rd from last transaction: 1AB23456C3542215D,+$544.23
```

Note that each transaction in this listing is presented as a string. Each of these strings could be manipulated to pull out the transaction IDs from the amounts.

SLICING LISTS

Indexing allows us to access or update only a single cell in a list; however, there may be a need to get a subset of data from the list. In Lesson 7, we saw that a string could be sliced to pull out a subset of the characters. In the same manner, a slice can also be done to obtain a subset of a list elements. When pulling a single slice from a list, it will always be of contiguous elements.

You can specify where to start the slicing and where to end:

```
slice[start:end]
```

You can also specify the step, which allows you to slice certain multiples, e.g., only every third item:

```
slice[start:end:step]
```

Python supports slicing in lists, allowing us to retrieve multiple elements from the list with a single command. Table 8.2 summarizes the parameters used when slicing.

Table 8.2 Slicing parameters

Parameter	Description
start	This specifies the starting integer whose position would note where the slice would begin. This value is optional.
end	An integer that denotes the position at which to end the slicing.
step	An integer that indicates the "step" of the slicing or the number of positions it will skip between grabbing values. The default is 1. This value is also optional.

Let's take a look at the example of how we can slice an actual list. We have the list mySlicedList, which includes the letters a through i in alphabetical order. We want to make a copy of the list that includes data in positions 1 through 5. Figure 8.4 shows the indexing on mySlicedList.

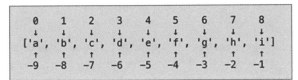

Figure 8.4: mySlicedList indexing

Following the syntax shown earlier (my_SlicedList[*start*:*end*]), we use:

```
my_SlicedList [1:5]
```

With this example, **start** is the index of the first element to include, and **end** is the index of the item to stop at *without including it in the slice*. So, my_SlicedList [1:5] returns ['b', 'c', 'd', 'e']. This is confirmed by running Listing 8.8.

LISTING 8.8

Slicing a list of characters

```
my_SlicedList = ['a', 'b', 'c', 'd', 'e', 'f', 'g', 'h', 'i']
print(my_SlicedList)
print(my_SlicedList[1:5])
```

The output generated is:

```
['a', 'b', 'c', 'd', 'e', 'f', 'g', 'h', 'i']
['b', 'c', 'd', 'e']
```

We can also use numbers instead of strings as values. For example, the code in Listing 8.9 will create a list named myList that includes sequential numbers starting with 1 and ending at 11.

LISTING 8.9

Slicing a list of numbers

```
myList = list(range(1, 11))

print(myList)

mySlicedList = myList[2:6]
print(mySlicedList)
```

We have used the range() method before. As you may recall, it generates a list of numbers. In this case, a list of numbers from 1 to 10 (one less than 11) is generated. You can see this in the output when myList is printed:

```
[1, 2, 3, 4, 5, 6, 7, 8, 9, 10]
[3, 4, 5, 6]
```

You also can see in the output that our slice is taken as [2:6] and assigned to mySlicedList. When we print mySlicedList, you get the value starting in the index position 2 (which has a value of 3) and all those that follow, up to, but not including the value in index position 6. Remember indexes start at 0.

Listing 8.10 presents another example, where a set of lists can be sliced to create groups of information from two corresponding lists, one containing transaction date and the other containing transaction amounts. This list is more complicated.

LISTING 8.10

Slicing a set of lists with corresponding data

```
trans_date=['2021-04-03','2021-12-03',
            '2021-13-03','2021-15-03','2021-22-03',
            '2021-25-03','21-30-03','2021-03-04']
trans_amt=[2.45,4.50,5.75,10.00,12.30,4.25,15.25,16.20]
print(trans_date)

input_to_date = input("What end date would you like to see all the transaction \
amounts from? (format: YYYY-DD-MM): ")

trans_date_to = trans_date.index(input_to_date)
#print(trans_date_to)

print(trans_amt[0: int(trans_date_to)+1])
```

In this code, there are transaction dates in the first list (trans_dates) and there are transaction amounts that correspond to those dates in a second list (trans_amt). The date at index 0 in `trans_dates` corresponds to the amount at index 0 in the `trans_amt` list. So, on `2021-04-03` there was an amount of `2.45`. You can see these two lists are created at the beginning of the listing.

The listing then prints all the transaction dates using `print(trans_date)` followed by a prompt asking the user to enter one of the dates. The program will then do some calculations and print all the amounts up to and including that date's calculation. Running the listing and entering the third date, 2021-13-03, will print the first three amounts:

```
['2021-04-03', '2021-12-03', '2021-13-03', '2021-15-03', '2021-22-03', '2021-25-03',
'2021-30-03', '2021-03-04']
What end date would you like to see all the transaction amounts from?
(format:YYY-DD-MM): 2021-13-03
[2.45, 4.5, 5.75]
```

Looking closer at the code, you'll see that one `print` function is commented out. If you uncomment that line by removing the # symbol, then the value of `trans_date_to` will also be printed. This value was determined in the previous line where the `index()` function is used to search the `trans_date list` to try to match an element equal to the value entered by the user (`input_to_date`). The call to `trans_date.index()` will return the index number for the first element it finds that is equal to the value entered by the user. In the case of entering 2021-13-03, this would be `2`.

The next line in the program:

```
trans_amt[0: int(trans_date_to)+1]
```

uses the index value and slices the `trans_amt` list to pull the items from the beginning up to and through the same index value of the date entered. Because the value in `trans_date_to` is the index value, we need to add 1 to it.

Using the Slice Object

A slice object is used to specify how to slice a sequence. You get this subset of items using `slice()`. In contrast to `range()`, which is used to create data, list slicing is used on an existing list.

> **NOTE** `Slice()` is essentially a function. In Python, a function is simply a block of code that only runs when the function is called. When using functions, we pass data, called parameters, into the function, and then allow the function to return data as a result. We will cover functions in a lot more detail in Lesson 13. This will include learning how to create our own functions.

The `slice()` function will return a slice object that can be used to then slice a list. Listing 8.11 is a modified version of Listing 8.10 that uses a call to the `slice()` function to create the slice object that will then be used on the `trans_amt` list.

LISTING 8.11

Using slice()

```
trans_date=['2021-04-03', '2021-12-03',
    '2021-13-03', '2021-15-03', '2021-22-03',
    '2021-25-03', '2021-30-03', '2021-03-04']
trans_amt=[2.45,4.50,5.75,10.00,12.30,4.25,15.25,16.20]

print(trans_date)

input_to_date = input("What end date would you like to see all the transaction \
amounts from? (format: YYYY-DD-MM): ")

trans_date_to = trans_date.index(input_to_date)
#print(trans_date_to)

slicenum = slice(0, int(trans_date_to)+1)
slicelist = trans_amt[slicenum]

print(slicelist)
```

In this case, two lines were added:

```
slicenum = slice(0, int(trans_date_to)+1)
slicelist = trans_amt[slicenum]
```

In the first line, a slice object called `slicenum` is created that indicates the index range we want to slice. This is from 0 to the element one past `trans_date_to`. Since `trans_date_to` was 2, this would be from 0 to 3. This slice object, `slicenum`, is then used as the value between the square brackets to slice the `trans_amt` list and create a sliced list called `slicelist`:

```
slicenum = slice(0, int(trans_date_to)+1)
slicelist = trans_amt[slicenum]
```

The output from Listing 8.11 is the exact same as that of Listing 8.10. We simply have two ways to get to the same result.

When working with our banking application, there are also multiple ways to do things. Large datasets containing demographic data are common within an organization. A banking application could conceivably handle several hundred if not thousands of customers at any given time, and using elements such as slicing lists is not uncommon.

The slice() function allows us to return a specified subset of data from a larger dataset. For instance, we may want to create a sublist of the first 56 customers of the day. We can use the slice function along with the index of the list to return that data:

```
y = ("customer 1", "customer 2", "customer 2",.........."customer 100", )
x = slice(0, 56)
print(y[x]) # print the names of the first 56 customers
```

ADDING ITEMS TO A LIST

Lists are mutable; in other words, we can change the size of a list we have already defined by adding new values or removing existing values. We use the append() method to add items to an existing list. Each new item is added at the end of the existing list. The append() method is called by simply passing the value we want added:

```
list.append(value)
```

In Listing 8.12, we start with an empty list and then add three names to the list, one at a time.

LISTING 8.12

Appending names to a list

```
list_of_names = [] #create an empty list
print(list_of_names)

list_of_names.append("Greg")
print(list_of_names)

list_of_names.append("Mario")
print(list_of_names)

list_of_names.append("Maria")
print(list_of_names)
```

This listing should be easy to follow. The empty list, list_of_names, is created and printed. This is followed by calling the append() method three times with a call to the print function after each. You can see from the output that after each append, a new item is added to our list:

```
[]
['Greg']
['Greg', 'Mario']
['Greg', 'Mario', 'Maria']
```

If we needed to add customer information to our ERP banking application, we could prompt the user to enter the data and then use the append() method to add it as shown in Listing 8.13.

LISTING 8.13

Capturing customer information into a list

```
info = [] #the info list is initially empty
info.append(input("Please enter the customer's first name: "))
info.append(input("Please enter the customer's last name: "))
info.append(input("Please enter the customer's account number: "))
info.append(input("Please enter the customer's account balance: "))

print(info)
```

In this listing, we add the following customer information items:

- Customer's first name

- Customer's last name

- Customer account number

- Account balance

Each item is added one at a time in the order we want them added to our list. Once the user has entered all four items, the information is printed:

```
Please enter the customer's first name: John
Please enter the customer's last name: Adams
Please enter the customer's account number: 11-11111-1
Please enter the customer's account balance: 340.59
['John', 'Adams', '11-11111-1', '340.59']
```

INSERTING LIST ITEMS

The list type includes several methods for inserting and removing elements. Another method is insert(), which has the following syntax:

```
list.insert(index, obj)
```

The method insert() expects an integer index and the new element as arguments as shown in the preceding syntax. The index is the index value (position) where the object (obj) needs to be inserted.

In Listing 8.14, to illustrate insert( ), we start with a list of two items. We then add a new item as the first item in the list (index 0), and a fourth item in the third position in the list (index 2).

LISTING 8.14

Inserting items into lists

```
list_of_names = ["John", "Mike"]
print(list_of_names)

list_of_names.insert(0,"Amy")   #insert Amy as the first item, at index 0
print(list_of_names)

list_of_names.insert(2,"Mario") #insert Mario as the third item, at index 2
print(list_of_names)
```

When you run this listing, you see that the list is initially printed, and then it is reprinted after each insertion:

```
['John', 'Mike']
['Amy', 'John', 'Mike']
['Amy', 'John', 'Mario', 'Mike']
```

As can be seen, Amy was added at the beginning of the list (index 0) and then Mario was added into the third position, which was index position 2.

For our banking scenario, as the bank gets new customers or as existing customers add new information or make new transactions, we need to update our records. Therefore, the bank's ERP application needs the ability to add new information to customer records as it is acquired. The ERP application can effectively add new data elements without deleting or re-creating the entire list via insert( ). This updated information could be captured about employees or customers and then pushed into a database for long-term storage.

Listing 8.15 adds more information such as an address and phone number to our customer records.

LISTING 8.15

Inserting additional customer information

```
info = ["John", "Smith", "Boston", "Junior Software Developer"]
info.insert(2, input("Please enter an address: "))
info.insert(3, input("Please enter a phone number: "))

#this code should be executed last
print("First name: " + info[0])
print("Last name: " + info[1])
print("Address: " + info[2])
print("Phone number: " + info[3])
print("City: " + info[4])
print("Profession: " + info[5])
```

In this listing, you can see that our customer information (info) is stored in a list and contains first name, last name, city, and profession. To this list, we will add an address and phone number. The user is prompted for this information, which is then added between the last name and city using insert().

The input() method is included within the insert() method to make the code more compact. The value insert() will use the value returned from the input statement as its second parameter. This is more efficient and just as clear as doing this in multiple steps:

```
address = input("Please enter an address: ")
info.insert(2,address)
phonenumber = input("Please enter a phone number: ")
info.insert(3,phonenumber)
```

When this listing is run, something similar to the following will be displayed:

```
Please enter an address: 123 Some Street
Please enter a phone number: 317-555-1212
First name: John
Last name: Smith
Address: 123 Some Street
Phone number: 317-555-1212
City: Boston
Profession: Junior Software Developer
```

REMOVING LIST ITEMS

We can use the remove() method to remove items from a list. The syntax of the remove() method is:

```
remove(value)
```

The `remove()` method takes the value (not the index) as its parameter. In cases where the value occurs more than once in the list, the `remove()` method deletes only the first occurrence of the value. For example, we might start with a list of names, with one name included twice in the list. When we use `remove()` to remove that value from the list, only the first instance is affected and the second one remains in the list. Listing 8.16 illustrates this point, using the name "Layla David."

LISTING 8.16

Removing a name from a list

```
list_of_names = ["John Smith", "Layla David", "Maria Smith", "Layla David"]
print(list_of_names)
list_of_names.remove("Layla David")
print(list_of_names)
```

This listing creates a list of names (`list_of_names`) that is then printed. Using the `remove()` method, one name ("Layla David") is removed. The list is then printed a second time. As can be seen in the final output, only the first instance of the name was removed:

```
['John Smith', 'Layla David', 'Maria Smith', 'Layla David']
['John Smith', 'Maria Smith', 'Layla David']
```

We can imagine a scenario in which our ERP banking application captures some incorrect information from either user error or imported data. We can add functions that use the `remove()` method to ensure that we have control over this information and can remove incorrect elements. This is used in error correction. Listing 8.17 presents an extremely simplified example of removing a number of items from a list to get rid of the duplicates.

LISTING 8.17

Cleaning up a list

```
input_list = ["Haythem", "Mike", 1, "Layla",
 "Livia", "Layla", 2, 1, 2, 3, "Mike",
 "Jesse", "Haythem"]
input_list.remove(1)
input_list.remove(2)
input_list.remove("Layla")
input_list.remove("Mike")
input_list.remove("Haythem")
print(input_list)
```

After running this listing, we can see that the duplicates have been removed:

```
['Livia', 'Layla', 1, 2, 3, 'Mike', 'Jesse', 'Haythem']
```

Deleting versus Removing Items

It is worth noting that remove() requires that you pass a value. If you want to remove an item from a list based on its index position, then you can use the del keyword to delete that item. The syntax of using the del keyword is:

```
del list[index]
```

Note that the del keyword can also remove the entire list if you don't include the index. For example, the following deletes the item in the second index position of a list called input_list:

```
del input_list[2]
```

However, the following deletes the entire input_list:

```
del input_list
```

Listing 8.18 illustrates the use of del using a list of fruits. The list is presented and then two items are removed.

LISTING 8.18

Deleting produce

```python
produce_list = ["Apple", "Banana", "Cherry",
 "Date", "Eggplant", "Fig", "Apple", "Grape "]

print(produce_list)

del produce_list[6]

print(produce_list)
```

When this listing is executed, it prints the original list that is created. It then removes the item at index position 6 before printing the list again. The output shows that the second instance of "Apple" was removed:

```
['Apple', 'Banana', 'Cherry', 'Date', 'Eggplant', 'Fig', 'Apple', 'Grape ']
['Apple', 'Banana', 'Cherry', 'Date', 'Eggplant', 'Fig', 'Grape ']
```

Popping Instead of Removing

While we are learning about removing items from a list, it is helpful to discuss the pop( ) method. This method is like a cross between the remove( ) method and the del keyword. The pop( ) method has the following syntax:

```
pop(index)
```

Additionally, the pop( ) method returns the item value that is removed from the list. Listing 8.19 is a rewrite of Listing 8.18 using pop( ) instead of the del keyword. The value returned from calling pop( ) is also captured in a variable called val and then displayed at the end of the listing.

LISTING 8.19

Popping produce off the list

```
produce_list = ["Apple", "Banana", "Cherry",
 "Date", "Eggplant", "Fig", "Apple", "Grape "]

print(produce_list)

val = produce_list.pop(6)

print(produce_list)
print(val)
```

The output from the produce_list is the same. We can see that the second Apple in index position 6 was removed and returned to the variable val:

```
['Apple', 'Banana', 'Cherry', 'Date', 'Eggplant', 'Fig', 'Apple', 'Grape ']
['Apple', 'Banana', 'Cherry', 'Date', 'Eggplant', 'Fig', 'Grape ']
Apple
```

You've now seen three ways to remove items from a list. Table 8.3 summarizes the differences.

Table 8.3 Comparison of the ways for removing items from a list

remove()	pop()	del
Method	Method	Keyword
Uses a value	Uses an index	Uses an index
Single item removed	Single item removed	Single item or entire list removed
No return value	Removed value returned	No return value

CONCATENATING LISTS

We can use the + operator to concatenate two or more lists in Python. The result is a new list that includes all items in the original lists. The syntax for concatenating items is:

```
list1 + list2 + list3
```

Listing 8.20 presents an example where we start with two lists, each of which includes two names. We then concatenate the lists into a new third list that contains all items in the original two lists.

LISTING 8.20

Concatenating lists

```
list_of_names_1 = ["Haythem", "Mike"]
print(list_of_names_1)

list_of_names_2 = ["Jesse", "Layla"]
print(list_of_names_2)

list_of_names = list_of_names_1 + list_of_names_2
print(list_of_names)
```

When this program is executed, the two lists that are created are each printed so that we can see the values. Then, a new list called list_of_names is created by concatenating the original two lists using +. This combined list is then displayed to confirm that the concatenation occurred:

```
['Haythem', 'Mike']
['Jesse', 'Layla']
['Haythem', 'Mike', 'Jesse', 'Layla']
```

How might the concatenation operator and lists be used in our ERP banking operation? As new users sign up for our bank's service, we will need to collect different kinds of information from them at various stages of the sign-up process. For instance, we may need their username, password, formal name, address, date of birth, Social Security number, etc., all collected at different stages in the sign-up process. However, at the end of the process, we will want to combine all the collected information for the customer and save it as a single list referencing the customer's account number. Python allows us to achieve this easily by using the + operator to combine multiple lists into one.

LIST COMPREHENSION

Another option for creating a list based on existing lists is list comprehension, which is a short way to create a list using existing values. For example, suppose we want to create a list that includes the digits 1–10. One option is to use a for loop to build the list, as shown in Listing 8.21.

LISTING 8.21

List generation

```
numbers = list()

for i in range(0,11):
    numbers.append(i)

print(numbers)
```

In this script, we start with an empty list called numbers. We then use for with range() to loop through the values in the range function and append each value individually to the list, resulting in the following output:

```
[0, 1, 2, 3, 4, 5, 6, 7, 8, 9, 10]
```

We can use list comprehension to generate the same list but with less code, using the syntax presented in Listing 8.22.

LISTING 8.22

List comprehension with range

```
numbers = [i for i in range(0,11)]
print(numbers)
```

In this listing, the `for` loop is embedded within the list definition, using the same `range()` function to generate the values that we want to include in the list.

We can expand this to generate a new list based on an existing list using syntax like the following, where `transform()` can be any function applied to an element in an existing list to generate a new value for the new list:

```
New_list = [transform(element) for element in old_list]
```

For example, you might have a list of names and you want to create a new list with uppercase equivalents of the existing names. We can do that using list comprehension as shown in Listing 8.23.

LISTING 8.23

List comprehension with an existing list

```
names = ["Miriam","Mary","Dave","Nick"]

names_upper = [name.upper() for name in names]
print(names_upper)
```

This creates a new list called `names_upper` with the following values:

```
['MIRIAM', 'MARY', 'DAVE', 'NICK']
```

Without the list comprehension approach, the code would be much longer, as shown in Listing 8.24.

LISTING 8.24

New uppercase list without list comprehension

```
names = ["Miriam","Mary","Dave","Nick"]
names_upper= []

for name in names:
    names_upper.append(name.upper())

print(names_upper)
```

List comprehension also permits the use of conditional statements to identify the values that should be included in the new list. In Listing 8.25, we start with a list that includes both positive and negative numbers, before we create empty lists `positive` and `negative`. We then include a conditional statement using both `for` and `in` to identify which values from the `numbers` list should be added to our each of our new lists.

LISTING 8.25

List comprehension with conditional statements

```
numbers = [1,2,-1,6,-5,-2]

positive = []
negative = []

positive = [number for number in numbers if number>=0]
negative = [number for number in numbers if number<0]

print(positive)
print(negative)
```

The output shows that the numbers were added to the correct lists:

```
[1, 2, 6]
[-1, -5, -2]
```

As shown in Listing 8.26, we can also include an if-else statement in a list comprehension operation, allowing us to use a single statement to evaluate each value in the original list and apply a transformation based on that value.

LISTING 8.26

List comprehension with if-else

```
numbers = [1,2,-1,6,-5,-2]
label = ["positive" if number>=0 else "negative" for number in numbers]
print(label)
```

In this case, Python examines each value in the numbers list and replaces the value with the label "positive" or "negative," depending on the number's value. The new label list includes the output of the operation:

```
['positive', 'positive', 'negative', 'positive', 'negative', 'negative']
```

SORTING LISTS

Python includes the sort method that allows us to sort the values of a list or to copy a list. By default, the sort method will sort the values in a list alphabetically (for text values as shown in Listing 8.27) or in ascending order (for numbers).

LISTING 8.27

Sort values in a list

```
names = ["Miriam","Mary","Dave","Nick"]
print(names)
names.sort()
print(names)
```

This script presents a simple list of names and then calls the `sort()` method on it. The result is a list that includes the same names but in alphabetical order:

```
['Miriam', 'Mary', 'Dave', 'Nick']
['Dave', 'Mary', 'Miriam', 'Nick']
```

An important point here, though, is that this replaces the original list, so the order in which the items originally appear is lost in the transformation.

COPYING LISTS

If we want to copy a list, one option is to assign the list to a new variable:

```
a = [1,2,3]
b = a
```

This approach means that the lists remain synchronized, so if we change one of the lists, the other list will reflect those changes automatically as shown in Listing 8.28.

LISTING 8.28

Update a copied list

```
a = [1,2,3]
b = a

a.append(4)

print(a)
print(b)
```

Even though the code in Listing 8.28 does not append a value to list b, the new value 4 appears in both lists:

```
[1, 2, 3, 4]
[1, 2, 3, 4]
```

If we want the lists to remain separate (so that b is truly a copy of a that does not update when a updates), we have two options. The longer one shown in Listing 8.29 uses a for loop to append each value in list a to list b.

LISTING 8.29

Copy a list

```
a = [1,2,3]
b = []

for i in a:
    b.append(i)

print(a)
print(b)

a[0]=0

print(a)
print(b)
```

The output shows that while b was originally identical to a, the first item in list b did not change when we changed the first item in list a:

```
[1, 2, 3]
[1, 2, 3]
[0, 2, 3]
[1, 2, 3]
```

A more efficient way to perform a copy operation like this is to use the copy() function as shown in Listing 8.30, which creates a new, independent copy of an existing list.

LISTING 8.30

The copy method

```
a = [1,2,3]
b = a.copy()
print(a)
print(b)

a[0]=0

print(a)
print(b)
```

As with the approach in Listing 8.29, the output from Listing 8.30 shows that list b is independent of list a in that we can change a value in one list without changing the other list:

```
[1, 2, 3]
[1, 2, 3]
[0, 2, 3]
[1, 2, 3]
```

SUMMARY

This lesson introduced several data structures used in the Python programming language before diving into the list data structure. These data structures are used to treat collections as a single entity, which is a shortcoming of the single variable.

In this lesson, we used lists to store data collections and retrieve specific values from a collection. Germane to this lesson was the introduction of the index value. An index value refers to a position within an ordered list.

Now that you have completed this lesson, you should be able to

- Explain several data structures available to Python developers.

- Use lists to store data collections and retrieve specific values from a collection.

- Add, remove, or change items in a list.

- Slice, copy, sort, combine, and manipulate lists.

In the next lesson, you'll learn about a similar data structure, the tuple, and see how it differs from lists.

EXERCISES

The following exercises allow you to demonstrate the objectives for this lesson. You should complete each exercise and make sure that the code runs without errors. These exercises are designed to test your understanding of the current lesson topics.

Complete each exercise as described and run the code to make sure it works as expected before starting the next exercise. The exercises in this lesson are:

Exercise 1: All About You

Exercise 2: Shopping List

Exercise 3: List Deletion

Exercise 4: List Modification

Exercise 5: A Complete List Program

Exercise 1: All About You

Prompt the user to answer a series of 3–5 questions about themselves (such as their name, their age, their birthday, or where they live) and save the answers in a list. Display the results to the user.

Exercise 2: Shopping List

Present the user with an existing list of items (such as a shopping list for the grocery store) and prompt the user for 2–4 more items to add to the list. Update the list with the new items and display the updated list.

Exercise 3: List Deletion

Present the user with a list of 7–9 items (such as the lists created in the previous exercises). Prompt the user to enter one item to delete from the list. Delete the named item from the list and display the updated list.

Exercise 4: List Modification

Present the user with a list of 7–9 items (such as the lists created in the previous exercises). Prompt the user to select one item from the list to update, along with the new value for that item. Change the item's value and display the new list to the user.

Exercise 5: A Complete List Program

This exercise checks your knowledge and readiness by having you pull together everything you've learned into a complete program. Create a new program that does all of the following:

- Create a list with at least five elements.
- Ask the user for their first name.
- Ask the user for their last name.
- Ask the user for a value.
- Ask the user for an operation ("add" or "remove").
- If the operation is "remove":
  - If the value exists in the set, remove the value from the list, and display the updated list to the user.
  - If the value does not exist in the list, display a user-friendly error message.

- If the operation is "add":
  - If the value exists in the list, display a user-friendly error message.
  - If the value does not exist in the list, add the value to the list, and display the updated set to the user.
- Repeat until the user enters "quit."
- When the user enters "quit," display the original set, the final version of the updated list, and the difference between the two lists, along with their first name and last name concatenated.

Lesson 9

Understanding Basic Data Structures: Tuples

In this lesson, we continue to look at understanding basic data types in Python; however, we shift from lists to tuples. In the previous lesson, you learned about lists, which store a sequence of data values. You learned that these values stored in a list did not have to be unique and that you could add and remove them. In this lesson, the focus shifts to tuples, which are a collection of values, which will still allow you to have duplicates; however, the values are ordered and unchangeable.

LEARNING OBJECTIVES

By the end of this lesson, you will be able to:

- Use tuples to store data collections
- Use tuples to retrieve values
- Work with indexes and tuples

- Slice and combine tuples
- Understand immutability
- Search tuples.

TUPLES AND TUPLE OPERATIONS

A tuple is another way to save a group of related pieces of data in Python. The biggest difference between a tuple and a list is that a tuple is *immutable*, which means that we cannot add or remove items from a tuple after we have defined it. However, as with lists, we can:

- Store values of any data type, including different data types in the same tuple
- Compute the length of a tuple
- Use index values to retrieve specific items from a tuple
- Slice tuples to retrieve multiple items at the same time

The basic syntax of a tuple is:

```
thisTuple = ("element1", "element2", "element3")
```

Syntax of Tuples vs. Syntax of Lists

Like lists, tuples are a basic data structure type in Python, and the process of creating a tuple is nearly the same as creating a list. The only differences are that, for tuples, we use parentheses to group the values instead of the square brackets used to create a list. We also must create a tuple in its entirety when we first define it. As with a list, we can use any data type in a tuple, and we can mix data types in a single tuple.

To create a simple tuple to hold information on a person, we would do:

```
info = ("Maria", "Smith", 31, "123 Main Street", "000-00-0000")
```

This should look remarkably similar to the methods we used in Lesson 8 for lists, except that we use parentheses instead of square brackets ([]) to group the items. Listing 9.1 uses the info tuple that was just shown.

LISTING 9.1

Creating a tuple

```
age_range = (18,120)
#tuple containing only numbers
```

```
print(age_range)
print(type(age_range))

#tuple containing strings and numbers
info = ("Maria", "Smith", 31, "123 Main Street", "000-00-0000")
print(info)
print(type(info))
```

In this example, one tuple is created that includes only numbers, and a second tuple (our `info` tuple) is created that contains strings and numbers. In addition to creating the tuples, the listing prints the values stored as well as each of the tuples' type:

```
(18, 120)
<class 'tuple'>
('Maria', 'Smith', 31, '123 Main Street', '000-00-0000')
<class 'tuple'>
```

When programming our ERP banking application, it's important to know when we should use a tuple instead of a list. Generally, tuples are faster than lists. Further, tuples are used when the data should not be changed and needs to be immutable. A tuple could be used to hold customer information similar to what is shown in Listing 9.2.

LISTING 9.2

A tuple with banking customer information

```
Customer = ("John", "Smith", 1005162, 34455.45)
print(Customer)
```

While Listing 9.2 is very simple, you can see that it contains a tuple with the following information:

- A customer's first name
- A customer's last name
- An account number
- An account balance

Running the listing prints the results:

```
('John', 'Smith', 1005162, 34455.45)
```

Tuple Length

Just like lists, we can use the `len()` method to compute the number of elements in a tuple. The syntax is:

```
len(tuple)
```

Listing 9.3 starts with the same tuples used in Listing 9.1. In addition to printing the tuples, it returns the number of items in each.

LISTING 9.3

Checking tuple length

```
age_range = (18,120)
print(age_range)
print(len(age_range))

info = ("Maria", "Smith", 31, "123 Main Street", "000-00-0000")
print(info)
print(len(info))
```

The output from this listing is:

```
(18, 120)
2
('Maria', 'Smith', 31, '123 Main Street', '000-00-0000')
5
```

As with lists, there are times we want to ensure that tuple lengths do not exceed certain limits as it can impact other downstream functionalities such as directory records or databases. Similarly, this could be used on strings to ensure that password lengths are sufficient to be secure or usernames are not too long. Listing 9.4 creates a simple example of a program that checks the length of a password to make sure it meets the requirement of being at least 8 characters.

LISTING 9.4

Password length

```
password = ('P', 'a', 's', 's', 'w', 'o', 'r', 'd')

if len(password) >= 8:
  print("Your password meets the requirements and the length is", len(password))
else:
  print("Your password length does not meet the requirements.")
```

In this program, a variable called password is used to hold what could be considered a password value for an application (note that you should never hard-code a password into an application). In this case, the values placed into the password variable spell "password." When this program executes, it checks the length of the password variable (which is a tuple) and ensures that it meets a minimum length of 8 characters. Since it does, a message is displayed along with the length of the password tuple:

```
Your password meets the requirements and the length is 8
```

If a couple of the characters are removed from the first line and we rerun the program, a different message is displayed indicating that the tuple does not meet the requirements. Specifically, changing the first line to:

```
password = ('P', 'a', 's', 's')
```

results in the following output:

```
Your password length does not meet the requirements.
```

TUPLE INDEX VALUES

Just like with lists, Python assigns an index value to each item in a tuple, starting with the value 0 for the first item and continuing with sequential values for the remaining items. The last item has an index value equal to the length of the tuple minus 1. We can then use these values to retrieve specific items from the list, using the following syntax:

```
tuple[index_value]
```

If we attempt to retrieve an item using a nonexistent index, Python will report an error.

The example in Listing 9.5 starts with an info tuple and retrieves each of the values in the tuple sequentially.

LISTING 9.5

Accessing tuple values with an index

```
info = ("Maria", "Smith", 31, "123 Main Street", "000-00-0000")
print(info)
print(len(info))
print(info[0]) #retrieves the first item in the tuple
print(info[1])
print(info[2])
print(info[3])
print(info[4])
print(info[5]) #this statement reports an error because there are only five items
in the tuple
```

This program creates an `info` tuple that contains what appears to be information on a person. The information is printed along with the length, which is 5 for the five items in the tuple. Following this, a call to `print` is made, with a different index used for each, starting at 0 and going to 5. Because the index value starts at 0, when the code tries to call `info[5]`, an error occurs. The output from running this listing follows along with the error that is displayed. Note that the error indicates that the index was out of range for the tuple:

```
('Maria', 'Smith', 31, '123 Main Street', '000-00-0000')
5
Maria
Smith
31
123 Main Street
000-00-0000

--------------------------------------------------------------------
IndexError                              Traceback (most recent call last)
<ipython-input-8-69a91fe85df5> in <module>
      7 print(info[3])
      8 print(info[4])
----> 9 print(info[5]) #this statement reports an error because there are only
five items in the tuple

IndexError: tuple index out of range
```

NEGATIVE INDEXING IN TUPLES

Tuples in Python support negative indexing, which counts from the end of the list. In the example shown in Listing 9.6, the index value **–1** always references the last item in a list, regardless of how many items there are. Sequential negative values count backward from there, so **–2** is the next-to-last item, **–3** is the third-to-last item, and so on. Python will report an error if the negative index value references an item that does not exist.

Look at the code in Listing 9.6 and predict which value each variable references in the list. Confirm your answers with the associated output.

LISTING 9.6

Using negative index values with tuples

```
info = ("Maria", "Smith", 31, "123 Main Street",
  "000-00-0000", "Boston", "Software Developer")
print(info[-1]) #last item in the tuple
print(info[-2]) #second to last item in the tuple
print(info[-9]) #this will report an error because the tuple includes only eight items
```

You can run this to see what the different negative index values present. The call to info[-1] will display the last item in the tuple. info[-2] will display the second-to-last item in the tuple. The call to info[-9] will display an error because the tuple includes only eight items.

The developers of our ERP banking application prefer to use the simplest methods, especially those that are straightforward, so negative indexing is a great way for them to access elements at the end of the list. In Listing 9.7, our developers are looking for ways to access tuple information such as new customer names without having to determine the length.

The customer list in Listing 9.7 contains quite a few customers, and we need to select the three newest ones, who are the last in the list. The last three customers can be obtained using negative indexing.

LISTING 9.7

Getting the last three customers

```
info = ("Wendi, Garek","Pearline, Engdahl","Kellen, Tristram",
  "Latisha, Franza","Calla, Hedve","Janis, Boehike",
  "Fidelia, Schonfeld","Ottilie, Agle","Cristabel, Thad",
  "Althea, Truc","Tonia, Elvyn","Margalo, Barney","Jacenta, Joseph",
  "Merle, Gillan")
print(info[-1])
print(info[-2])
print(info[-3])
```

When this listing is executed, the last three customers on the list are indeed displayed:

```
Merle, Gillan
Jacenta, Joseph
Margalo, Barney
```

SLICING TUPLES

Python supports slicing in tuples, which allows us to retrieve a range of multiple elements from the tuple with a single command. We use the syntax `tuple[range]` to retrieve a range of items from a tuple. Options include:

- `tuple[x:y]`: Retrieves a range of values starting with index x and ending with the item **before** index y. If y is equal to the length of the list, the output includes the last item in the list.
- `tuple[:y]`: Retrieves the items from index 0 through the item **before** index y. This is equivalent to using `[0:y]`.
- `tuple[x:]`: Retrieves a string that starts with the item whose index is x and includes all items to the right of that character. This is equivalent to using `[x:(length)]`.

Listing 9.8 demonstrates slicing a tuple to retrieve a name and an address.

LISTING 9.8

Slicing a tuple

```
info = ("Jonathan", "Vance", "679 Birchpond Street","Merrillville", "IN", "46410")

# we extract only the first two elements from the tuple and
# store them in a new tuple
name = info[0:2]
print("The name is:")
print(name)

# we extract only the last four elements from the tuple and
# store them in a new tuple
address = info[2:6]
print("The address is:")
print(address)
```

As can be seen, the call to `info[0:2]` extracts only the first two elements in the tuple. These are placed in a new tuple called `name`. The call to `info[2:6]` extracts the last four elements from the tuple and assigns them to a new tuple called `address`. Both results can be seen in the output that is produced:

```
The name is:
('Jonathan', 'Vance')
The address is:
('679 Birchpond Street', 'Merrillville', 'IN', '46410')
```

Listing 9.9 presents a second example; however, this time the code has been updated from the previous listing so that each range references only one index value. We can see, however, that the output still matches the output from the previous listing.

LISTING 9.9

Slicing tuples again

```
info = ("Jonathan", "Vance", "679 Birchpond Street", "Merrillville", "IN", "46410")

# we extract only the first two elements from the tuple and
# store them in a new tuple
name = info[:2]
print("The name is:")
print(name)

# we extract only the last four elements from the tuple
# and store them in a new tuple
address = info[2:]
print("The address is:")
print(address)
```

The only difference in this listing from the previous one is how the tuples are sliced. You can see that the name is extracted from the beginning of the info tuple, up to but not including the value with an index of 2 (remember indexes start with 0). The call to split the address starts at index position 2 and goes to the end of the info tuple.

> **NOTE** As you can see from Listings 9.8 and 9.9, often the same results can be obtained using more than one approach.

IMMUTABILITY

Tuples are immutable, which means that we cannot add or remove items after we have defined the tuple. Attempts to append items at the end of a tuple, insert new items, or remove existing items will result in errors. Listings 9.10 through 9.14 are simple listings that show many of the methods that we used with lists that do not work with tuples because of this immutability. The output for each listing is shown after the code. You will see that each displays an error.

LISTING 9.10

Tuples do not support the append() method

```
info = ("Maria", "Smith", 31, "123 Main Street", "Boston")
print(info)

info.append("MA")
```

The output from Listing 9.10 shows an error when trying to do an append on a tuple as shown here:

```
('Maria', 'Smith', 31, '123 Main Street', 'Boston')
----------------------------------------------------------------------
AttributeError                          Traceback (most recent call last)


<ipython-input-15-841c199b975c> in <module>
      2 print(info)
      3
----> 4 info.append("MA")


AttributeError: 'tuple' object has no attribute 'append'
```

LISTING 9.11

Tuples do not support the insert() method

```
info = ("Maria", "Smith", 31, "123 Main Street","Boston")
print(info)

info.insert(5,"MA")
```

The output from Listing 9.11 shows an error when trying to do an insert on a tuple as shown here:

```
('Maria', 'Smith', 31, '123 Main Street', 'Boston')
Traceback (most recent call last):
  File "main.py", line 4, in <module>
    info.insert(5,"MA")
AttributeError: 'tuple' object has no attribute 'insert'
```

LISTING 9.12

Tuples do not support the remove() method

```
info = ("Maria","Smith",31,"123 Main Street","Boston")
print(info)

info.remove("Boston")
```

The output from Listing 9.12 shows an error when trying to do a remove on a tuple as shown here:

```
('Maria', 'Smith', 31, '123 Main Street', 'Boston')
Traceback (most recent call last):
  File "main.py", line 4, in <module>
    info.remove("Boston")
AttributeError: 'tuple' object has no attribute 'remove'
```

LISTING 9.13

Tuples do not support the pop() method

```
info = ("Maria","Smith",31,"123 Main Street","Boston")
print(info)

info.pop(1)
```

The output from Listing 9.13 shows an error when trying to do a pop on a tuple as shown here:

```
('Maria', 'Smith', 31, '123 Main Street', 'Boston')
Traceback (most recent call last):
  File "main.py", line 4, in <module>
    info.pop(1)
AttributeError: 'tuple' object has no attribute 'pop'
```

LISTING 9.14

Tuples do not support the del keyword on elements

```
info = ("Maria","Smith",31,"123 Main Street","Boston")
print(info)

del info[1]
```

The output from Listing 9.14 shows an error when trying to use the `del` keyword to delete an item from a tuple as shown here:

```
('Maria', 'Smith', 31, '123 Main Street', 'Boston')
Traceback (most recent call last):
  File "main.py", line 4, in <module>
    del info[1]
TypeError: 'tuple' object does not support item deletion
```

You should note, however, that you can use the `del` keyword to delete an entire tuple. The statement `del info` will remove the entire tuple.

While developing our ERP banking application, it's important to remember the distinction between the immutability of tuples and the mutability of lists. When our dataset should be read-only, we can implement tuples, while lists can be more beneficial when information, such as addresses or phone numbers, needs to be updated.

CONCATENATING TUPLES

We can use the + operator to concatenate two or more tuples in Python. The result is a new tuple that includes all items in the original tuples. The syntax for concatenating a tuple is the same as concatenating lists:

```
tuple1 + tuple2 + tuple3
```

In Listing 9.15, we start with two tuples, each of which includes two names. We then concatenate the tuples into a new third tuple that contains all items in the original two tuples.

LISTING 9.15

Concatenating tuples

```
tuple_of_names_1= ("Haythem","Mike",)
print(tuple_of_names_1)

tuple_of_names_2= ("Jesse","Layla",)
print(tuple_of_names_2)

tuple_of_names = tuple_of_names_1 + tuple_of_names_2
print(tuple_of_names)
```

The resulting output shows that our two tuples were indeed combined into a new one:

```
('Haythem', 'Mike')
('Jesse', 'Layla')
('Haythem', 'Mike', 'Jesse', 'Layla')
```

Just as with our lists, our ERP banking application will often concatenate tuples to bring in and blend various pieces of information so that we can provide a greater data-set for analysis or operation. In Listing 9.16, we see how customer data could be used within tuples.

LISTING 9.16

Combining banking customer data using tuple concatenation

```
name=("Layla","Bernstein",)
address=("123 Main Street, Leola, AR, 19987",)
contact=("474-887-9483","LBernstein@email.com",)
fullcontact = name + address + contact
print(fullcontact)
```

In the listing, there are tuples for a client's name and address as well as their contact information. These three separate pieces of information are combined into a new tuple to provide full contact information. We can confirm that the information was combined by printing the resulting tuple (fullcontact):

```
('Layla', 'Bernstein', '123 Main Street, Leola, AR, 19987', '474-887-9483',
'LBernstein@email.com')
```

SEARCHING TUPLES

The for and in operators work with tuples in the same way they work with lists:

- for iterates through the items in the tuple.
- in examines each item to determine its value.

As with lists, we can combine for and in to determine not only if an item is in a tuple or not, but also how many times that specific value appears. Listing 9.17 presents an example of searching through a tuple to find a name.

LISTING 9.17

Searching a tuple

```
# create a tuple
tuple_of_names = ("Kate","Jennifer","Mike","Pete","Alex","Mike")
search_term = "Mike"

# check that the search term occurs at least once in the tuple
if search_term in tuple_of_names:
    print (search_term + " appears at least once in the tuple.")

# iterate through tuple to see if search term can be found
for name in tuple_of_names:
    if name == search_term:
        print("We found " + search_term)
```

Like previous listings, this one starts by creating a new tuple. The tuple is called `tuple_of_names` and contains a number of names. We then define a variable, `search_term`, that contains a name that we will try to find within the `tuple_of_names`.

Next in our listing, we show how an `if` statement can be used to see if a value is within the tuple by using the simple format of:

```
if <item> in <tuple>
```

In this case, if our search term (`search_term`) is in our tuple (`tuple_of_names`), then the `if` statement evaluates to True and a message is printed. We know "Mike" is in the tuple, so our message is printed.

We then can see how a `for` statement can be used to iterate through our tuple to search for an item. In this case a variable called `name` is used to store each item in the tuple sequentially. The value in `name` is then compared to the search term. If they match, then a message is displayed saying the item was found. The final output from the listing is:

```
Mike appears at least once in the tuple.
We found Mike
We found Mike
```

SUMMARY

This lesson continued the exploration of basic data types in Python; however, we shifted from lists to tuples. You learned that tuples are a collection of values that will still allow you to have duplicates; however, the values are ordered and unchangeable.

Now that you have completed Lesson 9, you should be able to:

- Use tuples to store data collections and retrieve specific values from a collection.
- Work with indexes and tuples.
- Slice and combine tuples.
- Understand immutability and which methods don't work on tuples as a result of immutability.
- Search tuples.

EXERCISES

The following exercises are provided to allow you to demonstrate that you have achieved the objectives for this lesson. You should complete each exercise and make sure that the code runs without errors. These exercises are designed to test your understanding of the current lesson topics.

Complete each exercise as described and run the code to make sure it works as expected before starting the next exercise. The exercises in this lesson are:

Exercise 1: Creating Tuples

Exercise 2: Modifying Tuples

Exercise 3: Where's Waldo?

Exercise 4: A Complete Tuples Program

Exercise 1: Creating Tuples

Create four tuples:

- One tuple with a person's first name and last name
- A second tuple with the person's current profession
- A third tuple with the person's current address
- A fourth tuple with the person's previous address

Combine all tuples into a new, single tuple that contains all items from the original tuples.

Exercise 2: Modifying Tuples

Using the final tuple from the previous activity, write a program that performs the following steps:

- Display the tuple to the user.

- Prompt the user to enter a value that should be changed.
- Prompt the user to enter the updated value for that item.
- Update the value and display the updated tuple to the user.

> **TIP** You cannot update the contents of a tuple, but you can update the contents of a list.

Exercise 3: Where's Waldo?

Write a program to search the following tuple and find the instances of "Waldo." Have your resulting program indicate how many times Waldo is found.

```
Names = ( "John", "Fred", "Waldo", "Wally", "Waldorama", "Susan"
    "Nick", "Waldo", "Waldo", "Reese", "Haythem", "Kim", "Ned", "Ron")
```

Exercise 4: A Complete Tuple Program

This exercise checks your knowledge and readiness for the next lesson by having you pull together everything you've learned into a complete program. This exercise is the same as Exercise 5 in Lesson 8, except instead of using lists, you use tuples. Create a new program that does all the following:

- Creates a tuple with at least five elements.
- Asks the user for their first name.
- Asks the user for their last name.
- Asks the user for a value.
- Asks the user for an operation ("add" or "remove").
    - If the operation is "remove":
        - If the value exists in the set, remove the value from the tuple and display the updated tuple to the user.
        - If the value does not exist in the tuple, display a user-friendly error message.
    - If the operation is "add":
        - If the value exists in the tuple, display a user-friendly error message.
        - If the value does not exist in the tuple, add the value to the tuple, and display the updated set to the user.

- Repeat until the user enters "quit."
- When the user enters "quit," display the original set, the final version of the updated tuple, and the difference between the two tuples, along with their first name and last name concatenated.

TIP Because tuples are immutable, you might have trouble figuring out how to remove or add an item. You might need to create a new tuple and remove the original when you are done.

Lesson 10
Diving Deeper into Data Structures: Dictionaries

We've seen how to use lists and tuples to store data, where we can use automatically assigned index values to identify specific values in the collection. Python also supports the use of dictionaries, which give us the ability to define the index values ourselves, and sets, which are unorganized and unindexed. We will discuss dictionaries in this lesson and sets in Lesson 11.

LEARNING OBJECTIVES

By the end of this lesson, you will be able to:

- Store and retrieve a data collection using a dictionary with defined index values
- Learn how to iterate through a dictionary
- See if values exist in a dictionary
- Clear the items from a dictionary

DATA STRUCTURE OVERVIEW—PART 2

In the previous lessons, we introduced data structures in Python with the purpose of explaining, using, and differentiating between lists and tuples. As a quick review: Python supports several built-in data structures. These include strings, lists, tuples, dictionaries, and sets. Let's review these items prior to discussing the next data structure.

Lists, strings, and tuples are ordered sequences of objects. Unlike strings that contain only characters, lists and tuples can contain any type of objects. Lists and tuples are similar to arrays, which are found in other programming languages. Tuples, like strings, are immutable, meaning they cannot be changed. Lists are mutable, so they can be extended or reduced if the need arises.

In this lesson and the following lesson, we will further explore these built-in collections through the practice of storing, retrieving, and manipulating data within a dataset. Table 10.1 summarizes the four different data structures we will cover.

Table 10.1 Data Structures

Type of Data Structure	Syntax	Description
List	Lists are enclosed in brackets: `l = [1, 2, "a"]`	A list is ordered and mutable (changeable).
Tuple	Tuples are enclosed in parentheses: `t = (1, 2, "a")`	A tuple is ordered and immutable (cannot be changed).
Dictionary	Dictionaries are built with curly braces: `d = {"a":1, "b":2}`	A dictionary is unordered, mutable, and indexed, and can have keys and values.
Set	Sets are written with curly braces: `s = {1, 2, 3}`	A set is an unordered collection of items. Every set element is unique and must be immutable. However, a set itself is mutable. We can add or remove items from it.

GETTING STARTED WITH DICTIONARIES

A **dictionary** is a collection of items using defined keys. The key acts as a unique index, which does not have to be an integer, and each key maps to a specific value in the dictionary. Each item in a dictionary is a pair made of a key and a value. Dictionaries are not sorted. Dictionaries are written with curly braces {}.

Unlike other data types that store only a single value as an element, the dictionary holds **key: value** pairs as individual elements: we must define both the key and the value for each element in a dictionary. You can access the list of keys or values independently, allowing a more meaningful index that we can use to retrieve and manage the data stored in a collection.

We cannot have duplicate keys in a dictionary as each key must be unique. There is no defined order among elements within a dictionary. The basic syntax of a dictionary is:

```
MyFirstDict = {
    "key1": "value1",
    "key2": "value2",
    "key3": "value3"
}
```

The Python language includes several methods to work in dictionaries. A method is simply a function that can be used based on an object's type (we will further explore methods in Lesson 13). Table 10.2 contains a listing of various methods that we can use in our applications when working with dictionaries. We will explore most of these methods in this lesson.

Table 10.2 Common Dictionary Methods

Method	Description
keys()	Returns a list containing the dictionary's keys
items()	Returns a list containing a tuple for each key: value pair
values()	Returns a list of all the values in the dictionary
get()	Returns the value of the specified key
pop()	Removes the element with the specified key
update()	Updates the dictionary with the specified key: value pairs
copy()	Returns a copy of the dictionary
clear()	Removes all the elements from the dictionary

Let's create a quick dictionary for a collection of student names. As Listing 10.1 shows, we start by defining an empty dictionary named account_dict. We then add individual items to the dictionary, using a unique key for each entry along with the student's first name. Note that the items do not have to be added in a specific order, as long as each item has a unique key.

LISTING 10.1

Creating a dictionary

```
accounts_dict = dict()
accounts_dict['X10000'] = 'Anita'    #Assign key X10000 and value Anita
accounts_dict['X10002'] = 'Michael'  #Assign key X10002 and value Michael
accounts_dict['X10003'] = 'Nia'      #Assign key X10003 and value Nia
print(accounts_dict)
```

The output from calling `print` is a display of the dictionary and its three key: value pairs:

```
{'X10000': 'Anita', 'X10002': 'Michael', 'X10003': 'Nia'}
```

In the ERP banking application we've been discussing, creating sets of key: value pairs can be extremely useful in analysis or rapid development. Dictionaries enable the ERP application to quickly recall various pieces of information tied in the key: value pairs.

Listing 10.2 is another dictionary example that starts data pairs as Listing 10.1, but then adds another record with a key of `'X10003'` and a value of `'Kyra'`. Take a look at the code and predict what will happen.

LISTING 10.2

Adding another key value and name

```
accounts_dict = dict()
accounts_dict['X10000'] = 'Anita'    #Assign key X10000 and value Anita
accounts_dict['X10002'] = 'Michael'  #Assign key X10002 and value Michael
accounts_dict['X10003'] = 'Nia'      #Assign key X10003 and value Nia
accounts_dict['X10003'] = 'Kyra'     #Assign key X10003 and value Kyra

print(accounts_dict)
```

Keep in mind that a dictionary cannot include the same key in more than one record. As such, when this listing is executed, the fourth item does not get added as a new element. Instead, it updates the previous record that had the same key.

GENERATING A DICTIONARY

In the previous examples, we first created an empty dictionary, and then we added items to that dictionary. Another option is to create the dictionary and its key: value pairs in the same step. To create the dictionary and values in one step:

- The dictionary is named using a variable, just as we have done in earlier examples.
- The data collection is included in curly braces {}.
- Each item is defined using the syntax "key": value.
- Items are separated by commas.

Listing 10.3 illustrates the syntax for creating a dictionary in one step with an example.

LISTING 10.3

Creating a dictionary in one step

```
myFirstDict = {
  "brand": "Mercedes",
  "model": "GLE",
  "year": 2021
}
print(myFirstDict)
```

When this is run, the following data is presented:

```
{'brand': 'Mercedes', 'model': 'GLE', 'year': 2021}
```

Dictionaries allow us to combine two lists of information that are related to key: value pairs. This is helpful when we want to take customer IDs and pair them with usernames, or when we have one list of states and another list of their associated population information and need to combine them into dictionaries.

Consider when new users sign up and select an abbreviation for their state. Then, whenever the full state name is required, it could be found based on the abbreviation. In doing an association of state abbreviations to state names, two lists could be created with the state information in the same order:

```
states_abbrev = ["AL", "AK", "AZ", "AR", "CA", "CO", "CT", "DE",
  "FL", "GA", "HI", "ID", "IL", "IN", "IA", "KS", "KY", "LA",
  "ME", "MD", "MA", "MI", "MN", "MS", "MO", "MT", "NE", "NV",
  "NH", "NJ", "NM", "NY", "NC", "ND", "OH", "OK", "OR", "PA", "RI",
  "SC","SD", "TN","TX","UT","VT","VA","WA","WV","WI","WY"]
states_full = ["Alabama", "Alaska", "Arizona", "Arkansas", "California", "Colorado",
```

```
"Connecticut", "Delaware", "Florida", "Georgia", "Hawaii", "Idaho", "Illinois",
"Indiana", "Iowa", "Kansas", "Kentucky", "Louisiana", "Maine", "Maryland",
"Massachusetts", "Michigan", "Minnesota", "Mississippi", "Missouri", "Montana",
"Nebraska", "Nevada", "New Hampshire", "New Jersey", "New Mexico", "New York",
"North Carolina", "North Dakota", "Ohio", "Oklahoma", "Oregon", "Pennsylvania",
"Rhode Island", "South Carolina", "South Dakota", "Tennessee", "Texas", "Utah",
"Vermont", "Virginia", "Washington", "West Virginia", "Wisconsin", "Wyoming"]
```

The state name and abbreviation could then be pulled using searches and similar index values. This association, however, can be done more easily using a key: value pair from a dictionary that contains the state names as the values and their associated abbreviations as the keys, as illustrated in Listing 10.4, which transforms the two lists into a single dictionary of key: value pairs, in which

- The key is the state abbreviation, and
- The value is the full state name.

LISTING 10.4

Using a dictionary for state abbreviations

```
states = {
 "AL":    "Alabama",
 "AK":    "Alaska",
 "AZ":    "Arizona",
 "AR":    "Arkansas",
 "CA":    "California",
 "CO":    "Colorado",
 "CT":    "Connecticut",
 "DE":    "Delaware",
 "FL":    "Florida",
 "GA":    "Georgia",
 "HI":    "Hawaii",
 "ID":    "Idaho",
 "IL":    "Illinois",
 "IN":    "Indiana",
 "IA":    "Iowa",
 "KS":    "Kansas",
 "KY":    "Kentucky",
 "LA":    "Louisiana",
 "ME":    "Maine",
 "MD":    "Maryland",
```

```
    "MA":    "Massachusetts",
    "MI":    "Michigan",
    "MN":    "Minnesota",
    "MS":    "Mississippi",
    "MO":    "Missouri",
    "MT":    "Montana",
    "NE":    "Nebraska",
    "NV":    "Nevada",
    "NH":    "New Hampshire",
    "NJ":    "New Jersey",
    "NM":    "New Mexico",
    "NY":    "New York",
    "NC":    "North Carolina",
    "ND":    "North Dakota",
    "OH":    "Ohio",
    "OK":    "Oklahoma",
    "OR":    "Oregon",
    "PA":    "Pennsylvania",
    "RI":    "Rhode Island",
    "SC":    "South Carolina",
    "SD":    "South Dakota",
    "TN":    "Tennessee",
    "TX":    "Texas",
    "UT":    "Utah",
    "VT":    "Vermont",
    "VA":    "Virginia",
    "WA":    "Washington",
    "WV":    "West Virginia",
    "WI":    "Wisconsin",
    "WY":    "Wyoming"
}
print(states)
```

As you can see from the listing, the dictionary combines the two lists into a single dictionary with **abbreviation: name** pairs, and the resulting states dictionary is printed:

```
{'AL': 'Alabama', 'AK': 'Alaska', 'AZ': 'Arizona', 'AR': 'Arkansas', 'CA':
'California', 'CO': 'Colorado', 'CT': 'Connecticut', 'DE': 'Delaware', 'FL':
'Florida', 'GA': 'Georgia', 'HI': 'Hawaii', 'ID': 'Idaho', 'IL': 'Illinois', 'IN':
'Indiana', 'IA': 'Iowa', 'KS': 'Kansas', 'KY': 'Kentucky', 'LA': 'Louisiana', 'ME':
'Maine', 'MD': 'Maryland', 'MA': 'Massachusetts', 'MI': 'Michigan', 'MN': 'Minnesota',
'MS': 'Mississippi', 'MO': 'Missouri', 'MT': 'Montana', 'NE': 'Nebraska', 'NV':
'Nevada', 'NH': 'New Hampshire', 'NJ': 'New Jersey', 'NM': 'New Mexico', 'NY': 'New
York', 'NC': 'North Carolina', 'ND': 'North Dakota', 'OH': 'Ohio', 'OK': 'Oklahoma',
'OR': 'Oregon', 'PA': 'Pennsylvania', 'RI': 'Rhode Island', 'SC': 'South Carolina',
'SD': 'South Dakota', 'TN': 'Tennessee', 'TX': 'Texas', 'UT': 'Utah', 'VT': 'Vermont',
'VA': 'Virginia', 'WA': 'Washington', 'WV': 'West Virginia', 'WI': 'Wisconsin', 'WY':
'Wyoming'}
```

Another common example that could be used in our ERP banking application or elsewhere would be a dictionary that includes values for name, age, and address. Listing 10.5 shows this simple information dictionary.

LISTING 10.5

Customer information dictionary

```
info = {
  "name": "Robert",
  "age": 34,
  "address": "123 Main Street, Louisville, KY"
}

print(info)
```

The output from printing this dictionary is:

```
{'name': 'Robert', 'age': 34, 'address': '123 Main Street, Louisville, KY'}
```

> **NOTE** String values used in each pair should be enclosed in quotation marks. Quotation marks are not required for non-string types.

RETRIEVING ITEMS FROM A DICTIONARY

Dictionaries allow us to analyze data. Using dictionaries, we can find totals, averages, median, and more. We can access specific key: value pairs in a dictionary using the syntax *dict_name[key]*.

In Listing 10.6, we create a dictionary similar to the example in Listing 10.1, and then we retrieve one of the records. Note that we do not have to know the order of items in the dictionary, as we would with a list or tuple. We simply need to know what key is assigned to the value we want to retrieve.

LISTING 10.6

Retrieving a dictionary item

```
students_dict = dict()
students_dict['X10000'] = 'Michael' #Assign key X10000 and value Michael
students_dict['X10002'] = 'Nia'     #Assign key X10002 and value Nia
students_dict['X10003'] = 'Anita'   #Assign key X10003 and value Anita

print(students_dict['X10002'])
```

When Listing 10.6 is run, the program prints the value that is saved in the dictionary that has the key of X10002. The output is:

```
Nia
```

Let's look at another example. Consider the following two lists:

```
states = ['CA', 'NY', 'KY']
population  = [39557045,19542209,4468402]
```

In these lists, the state and population lists are in the same order, e.g., CA has a population of 39,557,045. We can use the information in these two lists to create a dictionary where the state abbreviations are used as keys and the values are the respective populations. This has been done in Listing 10.7.

LISTING 10.7

A dictionary with states and populations

```
state_pop = {
  'CA': 39557045,
  'NY': 19542209,
  'KY': 4468402
}

print(state_pop['CA'])
print(state_pop['NY'])
print(state_pop['KY'])
```

After creating the dictionary, we are able to retrieve the population of each state individually by using the state abbreviation. Each `print` statement accesses our `state_pop` dictionary with a different key. The result is that each state's population is displayed:

```
39557045
19542209
4468402
```

Let's build a dictionary that has the yearly revenue for the years 2017–2021. We can use a dictionary that contains a key for each year and a value of the amount of revenue for that year:

```
yearly_revenue = {
    2017 : 1000000,
    2018 : 1200000,
```

```
    2019 : 1250000,
    2020 : 1100000,
    2021 : 1300000,
  }
```

Using the access method we've learned, we can access each value to calculate the average income as well as output the sum of income for all the years. This is shown in Listing 10.8.

LISTING 10.8

Working with dictionary items

```
yearly_revenue = {
    2017 : 1000000,
    2018 : 1200000,
    2019 : 1250000,
    2020 : 1100000,
    2021 : 1300000,
  }

total_income = \
yearly_revenue[2017]+yearly_revenue[2018]+yearly_revenue[2019]
+yearly_revenue[2020]+\
yearly_revenue[2021]
average_income  = total_income/5

print(total_income)
print(average_income)
```

This listing accesses each item in the `yearly_revenue` dictionary using the year as the key value. The value from each year is accessed and added to a `total_income`, which is then printed. Additionally, the total income is then divided by the number of years to get the average, which is also printed. The end result is:

```
5850000
1170000.0
```

Note that because we were adding all the items in the dictionary, we could have also calculated the `average_income` using `total_income/len(yearly_revenue)`. Like with other data structures, the `len()` function will return the number of items in the dictionary, which we know in this case is 5.

USING THE KEYS() METHOD

We can use a `for` loop to iterate through a dictionary using the `keys()` method. The syntax of this is:

```
for id in dictionary.keys():
```

This will look at each key value in the dictionary and return the value associated with each key. As with other uses of `for` and `in`, the process stops after the last item in the dictionary. In the example in Listing 10.9, we use the `keys()` method to retrieve each student's name from the dictionary as an individual value.

LISTING 10.9

Retrieving student names by ID

```
students_dict = dict()
students_dict['X10000'] = 'Michael'
students_dict['X10002'] = 'Nia'
students_dict['X10001'] = 'Anita'

for student_id in students_dict.keys():
    print(students_dict[student_id])
```

You can see that student IDs are used as the keys for the dictionary and names are set as the values. Using the `for` loop, each student ID is iterated through and used as an index to print the value (the student's name in this case). The resulting output is:

```
Michael
Nia
Anita
```

If you wanted to see each ID also printed in the `for` loop, you could add the following line to the `for` loop's body:

```
print(student_id)
```

Dictionaries can vary in size, so it is important for our banking application to be able to handle differing numbers of values so that the analysis can be performed on the dictionary as a whole. Combining a `for` loop with the `keys()` method enables the application to iterate through the dictionary to apply the manipulation to each key or value, or both.

As an example, we could create a dictionary that contains yearly income for an account. A `for` loop could then be used to not only display the individual values in the dictionary, but also the total revenue, as shown in Listing 10.10.

LISTING 10.10

Printing and summing a variable number of items

```
yearly_revenue = {
    2017 : 1000000,
    2018 : 1200000,
    2019 : 1250000,
    2020 : 1100000,
    2021 : 1300000,
 }
total_income = 0
for year_id in yearly_revenue.keys():
  total_income+=yearly_revenue[year_id]
  print(year_id, yearly_revenue[year_id])

print(total_income)
print(total_income/len(yearly_revenue))
```

This solution is much better than the one presented earlier in Listing 10.8 because it can adapt to a different number of items in the `yearly_revenue` dictionary. You'll notice in the following output that the total income and average income balance with what was seen in Listing 10.8:

```
2017 1000000
2018 1200000
2019 1250000
2020 1100000
2021 1300000
5850000
1170000.0
```

USING THE ITEMS() METHOD

We can also use a `for` loop to iterate through a dictionary using the `items()` method. While the `keys()` method works to retrieve values from a dictionary, we can use the `items()` method to retrieve either keys or values.

In Listing 10.11 we will again use the `students_dict` dictionary. This time we will retrieve the individual keys as well as the individual values.

LISTING 10.11

Retrieving keys and values

```
students_dict = dict()
students_dict['X10000'] = 'Michael'
students_dict['X10002'] = 'Nia'
students_dict['X10001'] = 'Anita'

for key,value in students_dict.items():
    print(key)
    print(value)
```

When this listing is executed, you can see that the values (student names) and keys (student IDs) are printed:

```
X10000
Michael
X10002
Nia
X10001
Anita
```

Now that we have the ability to extract the keys, we also want to be able to recall the values of the key: value pairs. For example, if our ERP banking application were tracking loan accounts, it might be beneficial to extract the values from the key: value pairs and perform a sum to determine how much is loaned out or perform interest calculations to determine how much the bank is earning each month.

Listing 10.12 presents a program that asks the user for five loan account numbers and their corresponding balances in key: value pairs and assigns each pair to the same dictionary. It then displays the contents of the dictionary in the last step, in the format "key: value," with each key: value pair on a separate line.

LISTING 10.12

Loan account balances

```
loans = dict()
ctr = 1
while ctr <= 5:
    loan_id = input("Please enter the loan ID for loan "+str(ctr)+": ")
    loan_amt = input("Please enter the loan amount for loan "+str(ctr)+": ")
    loans[loan_id]=loan_amt
    ctr+=1
```

```
for key,value in loans.items():
    print(key,": ", value)
```

Looking closer at this listing, you can see that we've created a new dictionary called loans to hold our loan IDs and amounts. Using a counter called ctr and a while loop, the user is prompted five times to enter the information. Each key: value pair is then added with the line:

```
loans[loan_id]=loan_amt
```

Once added, the counter is incremented, and the next set of information is requested from the user. Once all five entries are entered, a for loop is used to print the results.

When this listing is executed, the output should reflect the information the user enters:

```
Please enter the loan ID for loan 1: aaa
Please enter the loan amount for loan 1: 100
Please enter the loan ID for loan 2: bbb
Please enter the loan amount for loan 2: 200
Please enter the loan ID for loan 3: ccc
Please enter the loan amount for loan 3: 300
Please enter the loan ID for loan 4: ddd
Please enter the loan amount for loan 4: 400
Please enter the loan ID for loan 5: eee
Please enter the loan amount for loan 5: 500
aaa :  100
bbb :  200
ccc :  300
ddd :  400
eee :  500
```

REVIEWING THE KEYS(), VALUES(), AND ITEMS() METHODS

We can use the keys() or values() method in the dictionary class to retrieve the keys or values stored in a dictionary. We can use items() to display both the keys and values.

Listing 10.13 demonstrates the use of all three methods—keys(), values(), and items()—on the same dictionary so that you can see how the results differ.

LISTING 10.13

Seeing the different method output

```
students_dict = dict()
students_dict['X10000'] = 'Michael'
students_dict['X10002'] = 'Nia'
students_dict['X10001'] = 'Anita'

print(students_dict.keys())
print(students_dict.values())
print(students_dict.items())
```

This listing again uses a simple `student_dict` dictionary. This is followed by three `print` statements that use each of the three methods that have been shown in this lesson. The `print` statement shows you the collection that is returned by each method. In the output, you'll see that:

- `keys()` returns a collection of each individual key in the dictionary.

- `values()` returns a collection of each of the values in the dictionary.

- `items()` returns a collection with each of the key: value pairs in the dictionary.

You see the results clearly in the output that is displayed:

```
dict_keys(['X10000', 'X10002', 'X10001'])
dict_values(['Michael', 'Nia', 'Anita'])
dict_items([('X10000', 'Michael'), ('X10002', 'Nia'), ('X10001', 'Anita')])
```

Now that we have the ability to extract elements from the dictionaries, we would also want to ensure that our ERP banking application has the correct elements selected and manipulated. In instances where we may want to control certain elements, we could copy or duplicate lists with `keys()`, `values()`, and `items()`. There could be a scenario similar to what is shown in Listing 10.14 where we have a list of accounts and we need to separate the account IDs and account names into separate lists.

LISTING 10.14

Separating a dictionary

```
acct_list = {
    "100001" : "Federica, Yolane",
    "100002" : "Celestine, Kirbee",
    "100003" : "Paton, Riannon",
    "100004" : "Abbot, Gilligan",
```

```
    "100005" : "Dorine, Chandra",
    "100006" : "Natica, Ginnie",
    "100007" : "Sperling, Lucille",
    "100008" : "Kermit, Iseabal",
    "100009" : "Kat, Tori",
    "100010" : "Estella, Cristine",
    "100011" : "Pauly, Genovera",
    "100012" : "Idelia, Beverley",
    "100013" : "Nickola, Nessie",
    "100014" : "Baudin, Jasmina",
    "100015" : "Bates, Lily",
    "100016" : "Martguerita, Keelia",
    "100017" : "Kirbee, Katharina",
    "100018" : "Camden, Eadie",
    "100019" : "Iphlgenia, Roberta",
    "100020" : "Saint, Joelly",
    "100021" : "Lowry, Eadie",
    "100022" : "Keelia, Tani",
    "100023" : "Philoo, Darlleen",
    "100024" : "Artie, Ginnie",
    "100025" : "Ajay, Roseline",
    "100026" : "Frodi, Brandise",
    "100027" : "Daveta, Dorene",
    "100028" : "Liebermann, Paulita",
    "100029" : "Zola, Wynne",
    "100030" : "Heisel, Sue",
    "100031" : "Sigfrid, Jsandye",
    "100032" : "Kimmie, Jean",
    "100033" : "Muriel, Merle",
    "100034" : "Viddah, Nelle",
    "100035" : "Lewes, Selia",
    "100036" : "Lemuela, Marita",
    "100037" : "Kalinda, Tatiania",
    "100038" : "Firmin, Desirae",
    "100039" : "Casimir, Nita",
    "100040" : "Pillsbury, Stevana",
    "100041" : "Willie, Ira",
    "100042" : "Connelly, Etta",
    "100043" : "Cookie, Joleen",
    "100044" : "Himelman, Belva",
    "100045" : "Annabella, Ketti",
    "100046" : "Wandie, Brynna",
    "100047" : "Gaynor, Emelina",
    "100048" : "Christal, Tonia",
    "100049" : "Lowry, Wilma",
    "100050" : "Sholley, Corene"
}
```

```
acct_IDs = acct_list.keys()

acct_names = acct_list.values()

print(acct_IDs)
print("=======================")
print(acct_names)
```

Whereas we've combined lists in past examples, in this program, we are separating the account IDs from the account names. This is done by pulling the keys into the `acct_IDs` list using `keys()`, and by pulling the values (the names) into `acct_names` list using `values()`. The result is that the information from the dictionary is transformed into two separate lists. After the split, these lists were printed:

```
dict_keys(['100001', '100002', '100003', '100004', '100005', '100006', '100007',
'100008', '100009', '100010', '100011', '100012', '100013', '100014', '100015',
'100016', '100017', '100018', '100019', '100020', '100021', '100022', '100023',
'100024', '100025', '100026', '100027', '100028', '100029', '100030', '100031',
'100032', '100033', '100034', '100035', '100036', '100037', '100038', '100039',
'100040', '100041', '100042', '100043', '100044', '100045', '100046', '100047',
'100048', '100049', '100050'])


=======================
dict_values(['Federica, Yolane', 'Celestine, Kirbee', 'Paton, Riannon', 'Abbot,
Gilligan', 'Dorine, Chandra', 'Natica, Ginnie', 'Sperling, Lucille', 'Kermit,
Iscabal', 'Kat, Tori', 'Estella, Cristine', 'Pauly, Cenovera', 'Idelia, Beverley',
'Nickola, Nessie', 'Baudin, Jasmina', 'Bates, Lily', 'Martguerita, Keelia', 'Kirbee,
Katharina', 'Camden, Eadie', 'Iphlgenia, Roberta', 'Saint, Joelly', 'Lowry, Eadie',
'Keelia, Tani', 'Philoo, Darlleen', 'Artie, Ginnie', 'Ajay, Roseline', 'Frodi,
Brandise', 'Daveta, Dorene', 'Liebermann, Paulita', 'Zola, Wynne', 'Heisel, Sue',
'Sigfrid, Jsandye', 'Kimmie, Jean', 'Muriel, Merle', 'Viddah, Nelle', 'Lewes, Selia',
'Lemuela, Marita', 'Kalinda, Tatiania', 'Firmin, Desirae', 'Casimir, Nita',
'Pillsbury, Stevana', 'Willie, Ira', 'Connelly, Etta', 'Cookie, Joleen', 'Himelman,
Belva', 'Annabella, Ketti', 'Wandie, Brynna', 'Gaynor, Emelina', 'Christal, Tonia',
'Lowry, Wilma', 'Sholley, Corene'])
```

USING THE GET() METHOD

We can use the `get()` method to access a specific key: value pair in a dictionary by referencing the index for that pair. This is an alternative to using `dict_name[key]`.

In Listing 10.15, we create a dictionary with name, age, and address data. We then use `get()` to retrieve the "name" value from the dictionary.

LISTING 10.15

Retrieving by the value of the key

```
info = {
  "name": "Robert",
  "age": 34,
  "address": "123 Main Street, Louisville, KY"
}

name = info.get("name") # access the value of the key name directly.
print(name)
```

The output from running this list is:

Robert

Our ERP banking application might need to select pieces of information based on the account ID or username entered. This could be accomplished with the get() method to store information about the customer and recall it as needed. We might want to verify that the user is a customer and has an account, or perhaps we want to bring up verification information when the customer is making a transaction.

In Listing 10.16, we show a simple program that asks the user for an account number. This is then used to access and display the full name of the account owner if it exists in the dictionary. If the name isn't found, then an error message is displayed.

LISTING 10.16

Searching for an account holder

```
accounts = {
        '001': 'Daniel Atkins',
        '002': 'Rachael Ingram',
        '003': 'Caiden McKee',
        '004': 'Tiara Johns',
        '005': 'Dawson Drake',
        '006': 'Lisa Short',
        '007': 'Karlee Richard',
        '008': 'Kaden Knox',
        '009': 'Kendrick Galvan',
        '010': 'Aidyn Herrera'
}
```

```
account = accounts.get(input("Please enter an account number (e.g. 001): "))
if account == None:
  print("Account not found.")
else:
  print(account)
```

As you can see, a call to the get() method is used to see if an account number entered by the user is within the accounts dictionary. If it is, the value is stored in the account variable. If not, the value None will be returned and stored in account. An if statement is then used to print the name or an error. The following shows the output from running the program twice:

```
Please enter an account number (e.g. 001): 007
Karlee Richard

Please enter an account number (e.g. 001): 999
Account not found.
```

USING THE POP() METHOD

We can use the pop() method to remove and return an element from a dictionary given an input key. Unlike the get() method, pop() removes the key: value pair from the dictionary. We can also choose to store the removed value (without the key) in a separate variable for reuse.

Listing 10.17 presents an example of using pop().

LISTING 10.17

Using pop()

```
students_dict = dict()
students_dict['X10000'] = 'Michael'
students_dict['X10001'] = 'Nia'
students_dict['X10002'] = 'Anita'

print(students_dict)          #print original dictionary

students_dict.pop("X10000")   #we remove the first entry
print(students_dict)          #print modified dictionary

person = students_dict.pop("X10001") #remove and store an entry
print(person)          #we display the element returned from the pop method
print(students_dict) #print the final dictionary to see changes
```

In this example, we again create a dictionary with three student names. We then pop() the first entry with key "X10000", which removes it from the dictionary. When we view the dictionary again, we see that the entry is gone as can be seen in the first two lines of the output:

```
{'X10000': 'Michael', 'X10001': 'Nia', 'X10002': 'Anita'}
{'X10001': 'Nia', 'X10002': 'Anita'}
Nia
{'X10002': 'Anita'}
```

You also can see in the final step that we pop() another entry using the key value "X10001" and store it in a variable called person. We can then display the value from that entry separately from the dictionary. The last line prints the students_dict dictionary one more time so that we can see what remains, which is only one entry at this point.

When it comes to our ERP banking application, if incorrect data is entered, there are several ways that Python allows us to remove it. We can program our application to use the pop() method to remove the value. This could be tied to a specific request or coded to be performed automatically for duplicates or errors. For our current scenario, we need to grab the account numbers past a certain number to perform maintenance.

Listing 10.18 shows an example of how we can move all accounts after 100025 in our acct_list dictionary to a new dictionary.

LISTING 10.18

Removing items with calls to pop()

```
acct_list = {
    "100001" : "Federica, Yolane",
    "100002" : "Celestine, Kirbee",
    "100003" : "Paton, Riannon",
    "100004" : "Abbot, Gilligan",
    "100005" : "Dorine, Chandra",
    "100006" : "Natica, Ginnie",
    "100007" : "Sperling, Lucille",
    "100008" : "Kermit, Iseabal",
    "100009" : "Kat, Tori",
    "100010" : "Estella, Cristine",
    "100011" : "Pauly, Genovera",
    "100012" : "Idelia, Beverley",
    "100013" : "Nickola, Nessie",
    "100014" : "Baudin, Jasmina",
    "100015" : "Bates, Lily",
    "100016" : "Martguerita, Keelia",
    "100017" : "Kirbee, Katharina",
```

```
        "100018" : "Camden, Eadie",
        "100019" : "Iphlgenia, Roberta",
        "100020" : "Saint, Joelly",
        "100021" : "Lowry, Eadie",
        "100022" : "Keelia, Tani",
        "100023" : "Philoo, Darlleen",
        "100024" : "Artie, Ginnie",
        "100025" : "Ajay, Roseline",
        "100026" : "Frodi, Brandise",
        "100027" : "Daveta, Dorene",
        "100028" : "Liebermann, Paulita",
        "100029" : "Zola, Wynne",
        "100030" : "Heisel, Sue",
        "100031" : "Sigfrid, Jsandye",
        "100032" : "Kimmie, Jean",
        "100033" : "Muriel, Merle",
        "100034" : "Viddah, Nelle",
        "100035" : "Lewes, Selia",
        "100036" : "Lemuela, Marita",
        "100037" : "Kalinda, Tatiania",
        "100038" : "Firmin, Desirae",
        "100039" : "Casimir, Nita",
        "100040" : "Pillsbury, Stevana",
        "100041" : "Willie, Ira",
        "100042" : "Connelly, Etta",
        "100043" : "Cookie, Joleen",
        "100044" : "Himelman, Belva",
        "100045" : "Annabella, Ketti",
        "100046" : "Wandie, Brynna",
        "100047" : "Gaynor, Emelina",
        "100048" : "Christal, Tonia",
        "100049" : "Lowry, Wilma",
        "100050" : "Sholley, Corene"
}

newlist = dict()

for key,value in list(acct_list.items()):
  if int(key) > 100025:
    newlist[key] = value
    acct_list.pop(key)

print("List after 100025", newlist)
print("=======================")
print("List before 100025", acct_list)
```

```
#acct_IDs = acct_list.keys()
#acct_names = acct_list.values()
#print(acct_IDs)
#print(acct_names)
```

In this listing, we have created a rather long dictionary called acct_list that contains many account ID keys and the name of the person associated with the account as the value for the dictionary item.

The objective of the program is to move the items from the acct_list dictionary to a new dictionary if the account ID is greater than 100025. These records will be removed from the acct_list dictionary and be added to a new dictionary called newlist.

Once we've defined newlist as a dictionary, a for loop is used to cycle through each key: value using a call to item(). The function list() is used to create a copy of the dictionary so the values can be removed during iteration through the loop. In each iteration of the loop, the key is converted to an integer and then checked to see if it is greater than 100025. If it is, then a new element is added to newlist based on the key and value pulled from acct_list. A call to pop() using the key value then removes the item from acct_list. When the acct_list and newlist are printed, you can see that the records have been shifted from one dictionary to the other:

```
List after 100025 {'100026': 'Frodi, Brandise', '100027': 'Daveta, Dorene', '100028':
'Liebermann, Paulita', '100029': 'Zola, Wynne', '100030': 'Heisel, Sue', '100031':
'Sigfrid, Jsandye', '100032': 'Kimmie, Jean', '100033': 'Muriel, Merle', '100034':
'Viddah, Nelle', '100035': 'Lewes, Selia', '100036': 'Lemuela, Marita', '100037':
'Kalinda, Tatiania', '100038': 'Firmin, Desirae', '100039': 'Casimir, Nita', '100040':
'Pillsbury, Stevana', '100041': 'Willie, Ira', '100042': 'Connelly, Etta', '100043':
'Cookie, Joleen', '100044': 'Himelman, Belva', '100045': 'Annabella, Ketti', '100046':
'Wandie, Brynna', '100047': 'Gaynor, Emelina', '100048': 'Christal, Tonia', '100049':
'Lowry, Wilma', '100050': 'Sholley, Corene'}


========================
List before 100025 {'100001': 'Federica, Yolane', '100002': 'Celestine, Kirbee',
'100003': 'Paton, Riannon', '100004': 'Abbot, Gilligan', '100005': 'Dorine, Chandra',
'100006': 'Natica, Ginnie', '100007': 'Sperling, Lucille', '100008': 'Kermit,
Iseabal', '100009': 'Kat, Tori', '100010': 'Estella, Cristine', '100011': 'Pauly,
Genovera', '100012': 'Idelia, Beverley', '100013': 'Nickola, Nessie', '100014':
'Baudin, Jasmina', '100015': 'Bates, Lily', '100016': 'Martguerita, Keelia', '100017':
'Kirbee, Katharina', '100018': 'Camden, Eadie', '100019': 'Iphlgenia, Roberta',
'100020': 'Saint, Joelly', '100021': 'Lowry, Eadie', '100022': 'Keelia, Tani',
'100023': 'Philoo, Darlleen', '100024': 'Artie, Ginnie', '100025': 'Ajay, Roseline'}
```

The last four lines of the listing are commented out. They can be uncommented and the program can be run again to see lists containing the keys and values that remain in the acct_list.

WORKING WITH THE IN OPERATOR

We can use the `in` operator to check if a key exists in a dictionary. Listing 10.19 jumps right into an example of using the `in` keyword to do this check.

LISTING 10.19

Checking for the existence of a key

```
info = {
  "name": "Robert",
  "hobbies": ['fishing','dancing'],
  "address": "123 Main Street, Louisville, KY"
}

key1 = "ssn"
if  key1 in info.keys(): # we use the in operator to check if
                         # the key1 exists in the list of keys
    print(key1 + " exists in the dictionary.")
    print("The value stored in the dictionary is: " + info[key1])
else:    # display an error message if the key does not exist
    print(key1 + " does not exist in the dictionary.")

print("*********************************************************")

key2 = "name"
if  key2 in info.keys(): # we use the in operator to check if
                         # the key2 exists in the list of keys
    print(key2 + " exists in the dictionary.")
    print("The value stored in the dictionary is: " + info[key2])

else:
    print(key2 + " does not exist in the dictionary.")
```

In this listing, a dictionary called `info` has been created using the keys `"name"`, `"hobbies"`, and `"address"` with various values. We then search for the string "ssn" within the keys. If it is found, then a message is displayed along with the value stored in the dictionary with the key. In this case, "ssn" is not part of the keys. A second check is done to see if "name" is within the keys as well. It is found as can be seen in the output:

```
ssn does not exist in the dictionary.
*********************************************************
name exists in the dictionary.
The value stored in the dictionary is: Robert
```

Our ERP banking application can handle the many pieces of information from a customer, but how would we go about determining if the necessary information is available? Using the `in` operator can enable our application to check for specific keys for that customer record. Listing 10.20 walks through a sample process where we can determine if the key exists.

LISTING 10.20

ERP app to check for ssn key

```
account_info = {
  "owner": "Violet Duffy",
  "accounts": ['checking','savings'],
  "address": "123 Main Street, Louisville, KY"
}

user_input = input("Please enter a key to search: ")
if user_input in account_info.keys():
  print(user_input + " exists in the account. The value is set to ", account_
info[user_input])
else:
  print(user_input + " does not exist in the user account.")
```

This listing prompts the user to enter the key they want to find in the account information (dictionary). The following shows the output from running the program with a key that exists:

```
Please enter a key to search: owner
owner exists in the account. The value is set to  Violet Duffy
```

If we run the program again with a key that doesn't exist, we see a different result:

```
Please enter a key to search: ssn
ssn does not exist in the user account.
```

UPDATING A DICTIONARY

We can use the `update()` method to change the values in a dictionary. When using `update()`, the new entry must include the key for the entry that you are updating. Python will replace the current entry with the new one if the key already exists. If there is no entry with that key, Python will add a new entry to the dictionary.

In the example shown in Listing 10.21,

1. We create a new dictionary with three student names and print it.

2. We update the name in the first entry using the update() method and print the updated dictionary.

3. We use update() to add a new record to the dictionary, using a key that does not already exist.

LISTING 10.21

Updating a dictionary

```
students_dict = dict()
students_dict['X10000'] = 'Michael'
students_dict['X10001'] = 'Nia'
students_dict['X10002'] = 'Anita'

print(students_dict)

new_person = {'X10000':'Jeffrey'} # create a new entry (key: value pair)
students_dict.update(new_person) # use the update method to update the value
                                 # for key 'X10000'
print(students_dict)

new_person = {'X10003':'Erin'}
students_dict.update(new_person)
print(students_dict)
```

In this listing, we create a new students_dict dictionary with three student IDs (keys) and their names (values). We then print the students_dict to show the values it contains:

```
{'X10000': 'Michael', 'X10001': 'Nia', 'X10002': 'Anita'}
```

We then create a new student that contains the update we would like applied to students_dict. You can see that the update is placed in a variable called new_person. It contains the key of X10000 and the new name of Jeffrey. In the next line, the update() method is called to update students_dict with the new_person. Because the key of X10000 already exists in the dictionary, this update is applied, and Michael is updated to Jeffrey. The next line calls to again print the dictionary so we can see that the update happened:

```
{'X10000': 'Jeffrey', 'X10001': 'Nia', 'X10002': 'Anita'}
```

We then assign new information to new_person to be used to update the students_dict dictionary. This time we use a key of X10003 which will be updated to *Erin*. Because the key doesn't exist, the update() method does an addition instead of an update. The following shows all the output from running the listing, including the last line with the addition:

```
{'X10000': 'Michael', 'X10001': 'Nia', 'X10002': 'Anita'}
{'X10000': 'Jeffrey', 'X10001': 'Nia', 'X10002': 'Anita'}
{'X10000': 'Jeffrey', 'X10001': 'Nia', 'X10002': 'Anita', 'X10003': 'Erin'}
```

We can use the update() method in various ways in our ERP banking application. For example, suppose a banking customer moves or changes last names. The banking application needs to be able to adjust the records in the dictionary in order to keep it accurate.

Listing 10.22 changes the customer information in a fictional bank account. The code updates the account holder's full name, the accounts, and the address.

LISTING 10.22

Updating a dictionary

```
info = {
    "name": "Enzo",
    "accounts":"",
    "address":"",
}

print(info)
print("====================")

new_name = {'name' : "Enzo Stephens"}
new_accounts = {'accounts': ['Checking', 'Savings','Auto Loan']}
new_address = {'address':'321 Smithfield Lane, New Town, PA, 11876'}
info.update(new_name)
info.update(new_accounts)
info.update(new_address)
print(info)
```

When this is run, you can see the values that are in the dictionary before and then after the update:

```
{'name': 'Enzo', 'accounts': '', 'address': ''}
====================
{'name': 'Enzo Stephens', 'accounts': ['Checking', 'Savings', 'Auto Loan'], 'address':
'321 Smithfield Lane, New Town, PA, 11876'}
```

It is worth noting that you can also use `update()` all on one line, using a comma after each key: value pair that you want to update. Listing 10.23 rewrites Listing 10.22 to do a single call to `update()`.

LISTING 10.23

Updating a dictionary in a single call

```
info = {
    "name": "Enzo",
    "accounts":"",
    "address":"",
}


print(info)
print("====================")


new_info = {'name' : "Enzo Stephens", 'accounts': ['Checking', 'Savings','Auto Loan'],
'address':'321 Smithfield Lane, New Town, PA, 11876' }


info.update(new_info)


print(info)
```

The output from running this is the same as the previous listing:

```
{'name': 'Enzo', 'accounts': '', 'address': ''}
====================
{'name': 'Enzo Stephens', 'accounts': ['Checking', 'Savings', 'Auto Loan'], 'address':
'321 Smithfield Lane, New Town, PA, 11876'}
```

DUPLICATING A DICTIONARY

We have two options for duplicating a dictionary. The first option is to simply reference the dictionary through another variable. For example, in Listing 10.24, we copy a dictionary by assigning it to another variable named `students_dict2`.

LISTING 10.24

Duplicating a dictionary

```
students_dict = dict()
students_dict['X10000'] = 'Michael'
students_dict['X10001'] = 'Nia'
students_dict['X10002'] = 'Anita'

students_dict2 = students_dict

print(students_dict)
print(students_dict2)
```

The output shows us that the two dictionaries are identical:

```
{'X10000': 'Michael', 'X10001': 'Nia', 'X10002': 'Anita'}
{'X10000': 'Michael', 'X10001': 'Nia', 'X10002': 'Anita'}
```

This method also ensures that the new dictionary will always have the same values as the original dictionary. In Listing 10.25, we change one of the existing values and add a new value.

LISTING 10.25

Updating a referenced dictionary

```
students_dict = dict()
students_dict['X10000'] = 'Michael'
students_dict['X10001'] = 'Nia'
students_dict['X10002'] = 'Anita'

students_dict2 = students_dict

print(students_dict)
print(students_dict2)

update_person = {'X10002':'Beth'}
new_person = {'X10003':'George'}

students_dict.update(update_person)
students_dict.update(new_person)

print(students_dict)
print(students_dict2)
```

The output shows that both dictionaries contain the same entries, both before and after the updates:

```
{'X10000': 'Michael', 'X10001': 'Nia', 'X10002': 'Anita'}
{'X10000': 'Michael', 'X10001': 'Nia', 'X10002': 'Anita'}
{'X10000': 'Michael', 'X10001': 'Nia', 'X10002': 'Beth', 'X10003': 'George'}
{'X10000': 'Michael', 'X10001': 'Nia', 'X10002': 'Beth', 'X10003': 'George'}
```

Another option is to use the copy() method to create a true copy of a dictionary. Listing 10.26 creates a short dictionary of student names and duplicates the dictionary.

LISTING 10.26

Copying a dictionary

```
students_dict = dict()
students_dict['X10000'] = 'Michael'
students_dict['X10001'] = 'Nia'
students_dict['X10002'] = 'Anita'

another_dictionary = students_dict.copy()

print(another_dictionary)
```

Again, the students_dict is used. By calling the copy() method on the students_dict dictionary, a copy is returned and assigned to a new dictionary called another_dictionary. When printed, we can see that another_dictionary is indeed a copy:

```
{'X10000': 'Michael', 'X10001': 'Nia', 'X10002': 'Anita'}
```

In this case, however, the two dictionaries remain independent of each other, so changes to the first dictionary do not affect the copy made using the copy() method, as shown in Listing 10.27.

LISTING 10.27

Updating a copied dictionary

```
students_dict = dict()
students_dict['X10000'] = 'Michael'
students_dict['X10001'] = 'Nia'
students_dict['X10002'] = 'Anita'

print(students_dict)
```

```
another_dictionary = students_dict.copy()

update_person = {'X10002':'Beth'}
new_person = {'X10003':'George'}

students_dict.update(update_person)
students_dict.update(new_person)

print(students_dict)
print(another_dictionary)
```

The output shows that the original dictionary includes the requested updates, but the new copy does not:

```
{'X10000': 'Michael', 'X10001': 'Nia', 'X10002': 'Anita'}
{'X10000': 'Michael', 'X10001': 'Nia', 'X10002': 'Beth', 'X10003': 'George'}
{'X10000': 'Michael', 'X10001': 'Nia', 'X10002': 'Anita'}
```

In certain situations, our ERP banking application may need to make copies of the customer records or transaction data in order to perform analysis or error detection without making any changes to the original set. Using the copy() method allows the original to be left intact. Furthermore, selecting specific records to copy from a dictionary could be useful for the banking application for selecting specific transactions or accounts that match the criteria for review.

In Listing 10.28 we want to determine the high wealth accounts in our ERP banking application. This listing does this and prints the accounts that have balances over 10,000.

LISTING 10.28

Determing the high wealth accounts in our bank

```
acct_bals = {
    100000 : 48213,
    100001 : 51734,
    100002 : 57182,
    100003 : 80223,
    100004 : 126407,
    100005 : 6906,
    100006 : 31751,
    100007 : 103604,
    100008 : 56302,
    100009 : 102858,
    100010 : 62231,
    100011 : 74452,
    100012 : 114445,
```

```
    100013 : 116356,
    100014 : 93835,
    100015 : 117400,
    100016 : 86871,
    100017 : 110701,
    100018 : 140843,
    100019 : 70847,
    100020 : 121284,
    100021 : 65575,
    100022 : 58480,
    100023 : 91149,
    100024 : 16864,
    100025 : 95236,
    100026 : 112596,
    100027 : 13542,
    100028 : 149743,
    100029 : 64281,
    100030 : 112104,
    100031 : 148971,
    100032 : 22793,
    100033 : 111465,
    100034 : 16781,
    100035 : 36179,
    100036 : 108157,
    100037 : 40644,
    100038 : 20916,
    100039 : 9413,
    100040 : 20919,
    100041 : 147567,
    100042 : 111814,
    100043 : 54442,
    100044 : 7364,
    100045 : 90014,
    100046 : 18668,
    100047 : 125017,
    100048 : 8983,
    100049 : 109160
}

highwealth_list = acct_bals.copy()

for key,value in list(highwealth_list.items()):
  if value < 10000:
    highwealth_list.pop(key)

print(highwealth_list)
```

Our listing starts by creating a dictionary of our accounts called acct_bals. This contains the data we will be using. We then copy this dictionary of balances to a new dictionary called highwealth_list. By creating a new dictionary, we are able to manipulate and remove items without impacting the original data in the acct_bals dictionary.

A for loop is then used along with the pop() method to remove any balances that are less than $10,000. Once the for loop has completed the check, the resulting highwealth_list dictionary is printed to confirm that the lower balance accounts were removed:

```
{100000: 48213, 100001: 51734, 100002: 57182, 100003: 80223, 100004: 126407, 100006:
31751, 100007: 103604, 100008: 56302, 100009: 102858, 100010: 62231, 100011: 74452,
100012: 114445, 100013: 116356, 100014: 93835, 100015: 117400, 100016: 86871, 100017:
110701, 100018: 140843, 100019: 70847, 100020: 121284, 100021: 65575, 100022: 58480,
100023: 91149, 100024: 16864, 100025: 95236, 100026: 112596, 100027: 13542, 100028:
149743, 100029: 64281, 100030: 112104, 100031: 148971, 100032: 22793, 100033: 111465,
100034: 16781, 100035: 36179, 100036: 108157, 100037: 40644, 100038: 20916, 100040:
20919, 100041: 147567, 100042: 111814, 100043: 54442, 100045: 90014, 100046: 18668,
100047: 125017, 100049: 109160}
```

CLEARING A DICTIONARY

We can use the clear() method to delete all key: value pairs from a dictionary. This does not delete the dictionary variable. It simply removes all data from the dictionary. This function is particularly useful if you want to reset and rebuild a dictionary to update its contents quickly. Listing 10.29 is a straightforward example that shows how to use clear() to empty a dictionary.

LISTING 10.29

Clear a dictionary

```
info = {
  "name": "Robert",
  "age": 34,
  "address": "123 Main Street, Louisville, KY"
}

print(info) #display the dictionary
info.clear() #apply the clear method to remove all key: value pairs from the
dictionary
print(info) #display the (empty) dictionary
```

A simple dictionary is created, and its contents are displayed. A call to `clear()` then empties the dictionary as can be seen by another call to `print`. The output is:

```
{'name': 'Robert', 'age': 34, 'address': '123 Main Street, Louisville, KY'}
{}
```

Note that the `print()` command at the end displays an empty dictionary. If the dictionary did not exist, Python would report an error because it would not recognize the variable.

The `clear()` method might also be used in our ERP banking application. During repeatable reviews or audits, we might use the `clear()` method to delete all key: value pairs from a dictionary so that it can perform repeated analysis without creating a new data variable each time.

SUMMARY

We have already learned how to use lists and tuples to store data, where we can use automatically assigned index values to identify specific values in the collection. In this lesson, we learned that Python also supports the use of dictionaries, which give us the ability to define the index values ourselves.

Now that you have completed Lesson 10, you should be able to:

- Store, retrieve, and manipulate a data collection using a dictionary with defined index values.
- Store and retrieve a data collection using a dictionary with defined index values.
- Iterate through the items in a dictionary.
- See if values exist in a dictionary.
- Clear the items from a dictionary.

EXERCISES

The following exercises are provided to allow you to demonstrate that you have achieved the objectives for this lesson. You should complete each exercise and make sure that the code runs without errors. The exercises in this lesson are:

Exercise 1: Working with Text

Exercise 2: Separating the High from the Low

Exercise 3: High and Low All in One

Exercise 4: Self-Assessment

Exercise 1: Working with Text

Write a program that inputs a text file. The program should print the unique words in the file in the form of a dictionary in alphabetical order.

Exercise 2: Separating the High from the Low

Using the following dictionary of account balances, write the code to create two new dictionaries that pull data from `acct_bals` called `low_balances` and `high_balances`. The `low_balances` dictionary should contain all accounts with a balance under 100,000. The `high_balances` should contain all accounts with a balance of 100,000 or higher.

Once you've created the two new dictionaries, print out the number of entries and the average balance of each:

```
acct_bals = {
    100000 : 48213,
    100001 : 51734,
    100002 : 57182,
    100003 : 80223,
    100004 : 126407,
    100005 : 6906,
    100006 : 31751,
    100007 : 103604,
    100008 : 56302,
    100009 : 102858,
    100010 : 62231,
    100011 : 74452,
    100012 : 114445,
    100013 : 116356,
    100014 : 93835,
    100015 : 117400,
    100016 : 86871,
    100017 : 110701,
    100018 : 140843,
    100019 : 70847,
    100020 : 121284,
    100021 : 65575,
    100022 : 58480,
    100023 : 91149,
    100024 : 16864,
    100025 : 95236,
    100026 : 112596,
    100027 : 13542,
    100028 : 149743,
```

```
    100029 : 64281,
    100030 : 112104,
    100031 : 148971,
    100032 : 22793,
    100033 : 111465,
    100034 : 16781,
    100035 : 36179,
    100036 : 108157,
    100037 : 40644,
    100038 : 20916,
    100039 : 9413,
    100040 : 20919,
    100041 : 147567,
    100042 : 111814,
    100043 : 54442,
    100044 : 7364,
    100045 : 90014,
    100046 : 18668,
    100047 : 125017,
    100048 : 8983,
    100049 : 109160
}
```

Exercise 3: High and Low All in One

Rewrite your code in Exercise 3 so that you create only one new dictionary to determine the number of low and high balances and their averages. Hint: you can use the `clear()` method.

Exercise 4: Self-Assessment

This exercise is a bit more complicated and provided as a self-assessment, allowing you to check your knowledge and readiness for the next lesson.

Create a program that does the following. You will notice this is similar to what you've done with lists and tuples:

- Define a dictionary with at least five elements.
- Ask the user to enter a key.
    - If the key already exists, ask the user for an operation ("update" or "remove").
        - If the operation is "remove":
            - Remove the entry from the dictionary and display the updated dictionary to the user.

- If the operation is "update":
  - Ask the user to enter a value to be added with the key.
  - Update the value in the dictionary for the key.
  - Display the updated dictionary to the user.
- If the entered key does not exist, display a message saying it is a new key and ask the user to enter the value to be added. When the user enters the value, display the new list.
- Repeat until the user enters "quit."
- When the user enters "quit," display the original dictionary, the final version of the updated dictionary, and the differences between the two.

TIP Test each option for the user input to make sure that each operation works as expected. You may find it useful to create a flowchart or similar diagram to plan the program before starting to write the code.

Lesson 11

Diving Deeper into Data Structures: Sets

We've seen how to use lists, tuples, and dictionaries to store data. In this lesson, we tackle one final basic data structure: sets. A set is an unordered collection of items in which every set element is unique and must be immutable (cannot be changed). A set itself, however, is mutable. We can add or remove items from it.

LEARNING OBJECTIVES

By the end of this lesson, you will be able to:

- Store, retrieve, and manipulate data in a set.
- Iterate through a set.
- Determine if values exist in a set.
- Clear or remove items from a set.
- Work with multiple sets to determine differences including intersections and unions.

SETS

As mentioned, a **set** is an unordered and unindexed collection of unique items. Specifically:

- The values stored in a set are not indexed in any way. To retrieve an item from a set, you use the value itself, rather than an index.

- Each item in a set must be unique. You cannot include multiple items with the same value in the same set.

- The contents of a set are not ordered. You can add the items in any order you wish, and Python will typically retrieve them in a different, random order.

The steps to create a set are similar to those used to create other data collections, such as lists and tuples. The main difference is the use of curly braces ({ }) to define the collection as a set.

It is important that we differentiate dictionaries from sets. *Dictionaries* and *sets* are almost identical, except that *sets* do not actually contain values: a set is simply a collection of unique keys. In Listing 11.1 a set of names is created and then the values are retrieved from the set.

LISTING 11.1

Creating a set

```
names = {"Robert", "Mark", "Nancy"}

print(names)
```

When this listing is executed, the output should be similar to:

```
{'Robert', 'Nancy', 'Mark'}
```

It is important to note that the order of the items in a set is random, so the names may appear in a different order than the order in which they were added. We cannot assume they will be returned in the same order in which they were added.

> **NOTE** If you look at Listing 11.1, you will see that it is similar to the listings you've seen for sets and tuples. The easy way to differentiate the three is that lists are enclosed in brackets, tuples are enclosed in parentheses, and sets are enclosed in braces.

Our ERP banking application might be coded to perform trend and demographic analysis, in which it might make use of a set to ensure that the values contained are unique. For example, the application can look for data points such as how many unique first names their customers have, which distinct locations are being flagged for fraudulent transactions, which unique vendors the customers use for partnerships and rewards, and more.

In Listing 11.2, we create a simple set that contains a collection of various terms such as bank account types or terminology that could be used within an ERP banking application.

LISTING 11.2

Banking terms in a set

```
banking  = {"Checking","Savings","Loans","Dividends"}
print(banking)
```

This is again a straightforward example that creates a set of four unique banking terms that we can later use. The output that is printed contains the four terms:

```
{'Checking', 'Savings', 'Dividends', 'Loans'}
```

> **NOTE** If you run Listing 11.2 multiple times, the output might be displayed in a different order each time.

RETRIEVING ITEMS FROM A SET

While storing the unique items in the set is valuable, having the ability to retrieve information from the set is equally important. We can use a `for` loop with `in` to iterate through a set. Again, because the set is not ordered, the items may appear in a different order than how they were added to the set. In Listing 11.3, we show using a `for` loop to retrieve the names individually from the same set we used in Listing 11.1.

LISTING 11.3

Looping through a set

```
names = {"Robert", "Mark", "Nancy"}

for name in names:
    print(name)
```

When this listing is executed, each of the names in the set is displayed:

```
Robert
Nancy
Mark
```

ADDING ITEMS TO A SET

Sets, much like dictionaries, are not very useful when they contain no values. In order to be effective, the add( ) method can be used to add new items to a new or existing set so that the data can be recalled later when required. In Listing 11.4, additional names are added to an existing set.

LISTING 11.4

Adding to a set

```
names = {"Robert", "Mark", "Mohamed"}
print(names)

names.add("Demetrius")
names.add("Alice")
names.add("Rita")

print(names)
```

In this listing, we start with a set of three names called names. To confirm what is in the list, we print the values. The add( ) method is then used three times. In each call, a new name is passed to the method and added to the list. Once the three calls to add( ) are completed our new list is printed. We can see in the output that Demetrius, Alice, and Rita have in fact been added:

```
{'Robert', 'Mohamed', 'Mark'}
{'Mark', 'Alice', 'Demetrius', 'Rita', 'Robert', 'Mohamed'}
```

CREATING AN EMPTY SET

In the previous examples, we created a set by assigning values that were contained within curly braces. Python knows because there are curly braces and the values are not in key:value pairs that a set is being created. We can also create an empty set by using the set( ) method. This can be useful if we need to stage an empty set that we intend to add data to at a later time. Listing 11.5 illustrates the creation of an empty set.

LISTING 11.5

Creating an empty set and then using it

```
names_set = set()

print(names_set)

names_set.add("Morgan")
names_set.add("Alice")
names_set.add("Gilbert")

print(names_set)
```

In this listing, a variable called `names_set` is created and assigned the return value of `set()`. This result is that `names_set` is an empty set that can be used. To confirm that it is empty, we print `names_set`, which outputs:

```
set()
```

The program then continues by adding three names to the set using the `add()` method that was covered in the previous section. Now when `names_set` is printed, we see that the three values are displayed:

```
{'Alice', 'Gilbert', 'Morgan'}
```

The full output is:

```
set()
{'Alice', 'Gilbert', 'Morgan'}
```

In order to receive user input into a set, our ERP banking application would declare the empty set first before requesting user input. This can make the set have a variable length when coupled with a loop so our application could intake several pieces of data such as account numbers or transaction keys and insert them into the single set.

UNDERSTANDING SET UNIQUENESS

Each item in a set must be unique within that set. Duplicate items will be ignored. We can see this happen with an example such as the one shown in Listing 11.6. In this example, we create another set of names, with some of the names duplicated during input.

LISTING 11.6

Adding duplicates to a set

```
names = {"Robert", "Mark", "Nancy", "Robert", "Mark", "Jenny", "Robert"}

print(names)
```

When we print the names set, we see that only distinct values are stored in the set:

```
{'Nancy', 'Jenny', 'Robert', 'Mark'}
```

The duplicate copies of "Robert" and "Mark" were not included. Similarly, Listing 11.7 shows that if we try to add a duplicate value to a set using the add() method, then again, the addition of the new element will be ignored.

LISTING 11.7

Uniqueness in sets

```
names = ["Trystan", "Clarence", "Nancy", "Trystan", "Clarence", "Jenny", "Trystan"]
print(names)

names_set = set(names)
print(names_set)

names_set.add('Jenny')
print(names_set)
```

In this listing, we start by creating a list of names. We know this is a list because square brackets are used when initializing the values. When the names list is printed, we can see in the first line of output that all the names are included, even the duplicates:

```
['Trystan', 'Clarence', 'Nancy', 'Trystan', 'Clarence', 'Jenny', 'Trystan']
{'Jenny', 'Trystan', 'Clarence', 'Nancy'}
{'Jenny', 'Trystan', 'Clarence', 'Nancy'}
```

We then create a set called names_set and by using the set() method, we assign the names that are stored in the names list. We print the names_set to show the values that were stored. You can see in the second line of output that because names_set is a set, all the duplicates are gone. Finally, we call the add() method to add "Jenny" to our set. When we print the set a second time, we see that nothing changed, because "Jenny" already exists, and sets can't have duplicates.

Regarding our ERP banking application, the feature of forcing uniqueness can be valuable. If one considers how the transaction record IDs or account IDs should be unique, it is useful to be able to ensure that duplicate values are not populated into the set at all. Quite literally, the set would ignore any duplicates and not store the values.

SEARCHING ITEMS IN A SET

We can use the `in` operator to check whether an element exists in a set. This operation returns the Boolean value `True` if the value exists in the set and `False` if it does not. In Listing 11.8 we show this in action by searching for a specific state in a set of state abbreviations.

LISTING 11.8

Searching for a specific state

```
states_abbrev = {"AL", "AK", "AZ", "AR", "CA", "CO", "CT", "DE", "FL", "GA",
"HI", "ID", "IL", "IN", "IA", "KS", "KY", "LA", "ME", "MD",
"MA", "MI", "MN", "MS", "MO", "MT", "NE", "NV", "NH", "NJ",
"NM", "NY", "NC", "ND", "OH", "OK", "OR", "PA", "RI", "SC",
"SD", "TN", "TX", "UT", "VT", "VA", "WA", "WV", "WI", "WY"}

print("DC" in states_abbrev)

print("PR" in states_abbrev)

print("CA" in states_abbrev)
```

The output from each call to `print` in this listing will be either `True` or `False`. The listing starts with a set of state abbreviations called `states_abbrev`. Using the `in` keyword, the set is checked to see if three different abbreviations exist, and the return value of the check is printed. This will return `True` if the item is in the set and `False` otherwise. As we can see from the output, DC and PR were not in `states_abbrev`, and CA is:

```
False
False
True
```

While one of the main advantages of a set is that it contains unique values, our ERP banking application would be even better with the ability to verify whether a value exists in a set and provide an error back to the user if it does. If the application implements unique usernames or account IDs, a function like the `in` operator is useful to ensure that the value is in fact unique and not already contained within the set. In Listing 11.9, we see a scenario where we check to see if a customer name is in our list of customers.

LISTING 11.9

Searching items in a set

```python
cust_list = {"Wolf Inc",
    "Acme Inc",
    "Murray Ltd",
    "BankCorps",
    "PierBank",
    "BankRoad",
    "Cashop",
    "Welch-Mann",
    "Oberbrunner, Hamill and Marvin",
    "Faust Inc.",
    "Watera",
    "Jacobson LLC",
    "Micron Computers",
}

print(cust_list)
lower_list = [x.lower() for x in cust_list]
if input("Enter a customer name: ").lower() in lower_list:
  print("The customer name you entered matches an existing customer.")
else:
  print("That name did not match any in our customer list.")
```

This program prompts the user to enter a customer name and then determines if it is within the list of existing customers. More importantly, the program ignores the case of the customer, so that "piersbank" equals "PiersBank".

Breaking down the code, you can see that we start by creating a set of customer names called cust_list. We print this set of names so that it is easier to see. The next line:

```python
lower_list = [x.lower() for x in cust_list]
```

uses a for loop to iterate through our customer list. Using the lower() method, each value in the list is converted to lowercase and added to a list called lower_list. For example, "PiersBank" is changed to "piersbank". The result of this line of code is the creation of a list called lower_list that contains all the values from cust_list saved in lowercase.

The next line of code does even more. We then prompt the user to enter a customer name, which is converted to lowercase again using the lower() method. The entered name is checked using the in keyword to see if it is contained within the lower_list that we just created. If the name is found in the list, then a message is displayed saying it was found, otherwise a message is displayed saying it was not. The following code shows the results of running the program twice, once with a name that is found and once with a name that is not. Notice that the name that was found was not capitalized the same as the value in our set, but we still found it.

```
{'Acme Inc', 'Cashop', 'PierBank', 'Oberbrunner, Hamill and Marvin', 'Murray Ltd',
'Welch-Mann', 'BankRoad', 'Jacobson LLC', 'Micron Computers', 'BankCorps',
'Watera', 'Wolf Inc', 'Faust Inc.'}
Enter a customer name: BANKRoad
The customer name you entered matches an existing customer.

{'Wolf Inc', 'Acme Inc', 'BankRoad', 'Oberbrunner, Hamill and Marvin', 'Jacobson LLC',
'Murray Ltd', 'Micron Computers', 'Cashop', 'BankCorps', 'Faust Inc.', 'PierBank',
'Watera', 'Welch-Mann'}
Enter a customer name: Piers Bank, Inc.
That name did not match any in our customer list.
```

CALCULATING THE LENGTH OF A SET

We can use the len() method to compute the number of elements in a set. We create a new set and then use len() to display the number of items in the set as shown in Listing 11.10.

LISTING 11.10

Getting the number of items in a set

```
food = {"pasta", "burger", "hot dog", "pizza"}
print(food)
print(len(food))
```

The output from running this listing shows the items in the set followed by the number of items:

```
{'hot dog', 'pasta', 'pizza', 'burger'}
4
```

If our ERP banking application is expecting a certain number of elements in a set, it might be worth using the len() method to ensure that the set has the required number of elements. We also need to make sure that the datasets that are being analyzed match the number the user is expecting. We could also use this for ensuring that there is a matching number of elements, especially if we're combining two or more data points in a union.

Listing 11.11 uses len() to confirm the number of usernames being added to our ERP banking application. For example, if the user enters 5, the program will ask the user for 5 different usernames that it will store in a set.

> **NOTE** Remember that Python lists and sets are zero indexed.

LISTING 11.11

Checking the length of a set

```
user_names = set()
integer = int(input("Please enter an integer for the number of usernames you would /
like to enter: "))
while len(user_names) < integer:
  username = {input("Please enter a username: ")}
  user_names.update(username)
print(user_names)
```

This program creates a new set called `user_names`. It then prompts the user to enter a number that is converted to an integer. The user is then prompted to enter new names until we have a total number of usernames equal to the number they entered. Once the stated number of names is entered, the set of words provided by the user is displayed. The following shows one possible outcome from running the program:

```
Please enter an integer for the number of usernames you would like to enter: 5
Please enter a username: JohnDoe
Please enter a username: JohnDoe
Please enter a username: SueSmith
Please enter a username: FredMercury
Please enter a username: HaythemBalti
Please enter a username: RoyRogers
{'FredMercury', 'RoyRogers', 'HaythemBalti', 'JohnDoe', 'SueSmith'}
```

In looking at the output, you might notice that six names were entered instead of five. Remember, because we are using a set, there must be uniqueness in the values stored. When the second "JohnDoe" is entered, it is seen as a duplicate and thus is not added. Because our `while` loop is based on the length of the set, the user will be prompted until there are five unique usernames added.

DELETING ITEMS FROM A SET

We can use the `discard()` or `remove()` method to delete elements from a set. These methods behave differently:

- `discard()` will **not** raise an error if the item to remove does not exist.
- `remove()` will raise an error if the item to remove does not exist.

Listing 11.12 illustrates the use of these two methods as well as highlights the difference.

LISTING 11.12

Deleting items from a set

```
food = {"pasta", "burger", "hot dog", "pizza"}
print(food)

food.discard("pasta")
print(food)

food.remove("burger")
print(food)

# The next two lines try to remove an item that isn't in the set!
food.discard("pasta")  # this will not report an error
food.remove("pasta")   # this will report an error
```

In this listing, we start by creating a set of food items, which are then printed. We then use discard() to delete one item, *pasta*. Then *burger* is deleted using remove(). We then repeat the discard() and remove() steps and try to remove an item that is not in the set (*pasta*) with each. We see from the output that the call to discard() says nothing about the missing item, but the final remove() step reports an error because that item no longer exists in the set:

```
{'hot dog', 'pasta', 'pizza', 'burger'}
{'hot dog', 'pizza', 'burger'}
{'hot dog', 'pizza'}
------------------------------------------------------------------------
KeyError                                 Traceback (most recent call last)

<ipython-input-35-753fa67537fd> in <module>
     12

     13 #this WILL report an error because pasta doesn't exist in the set anymore.

---> 14 food.remove("pasta")


KeyError: 'pasta
```

We can take an element out of a set in our ERP banking application, such as an invalid account number ID or name, using the discard() or remove() method as well. If we need to alert the user that the value does not exist, we can use the remove() method. If the ERP banking application does not need to alert the user, it could be programmed to use discard() so that we can ensure that the value is not contained within the set.

In Listing 11.13, the `in` operator and the `remove()` method are used in a script that will remove items from a set based on user input. The user will be asked for a name. If the name exists, it is removed from the current set and displayed. If the name does not exist, then a user-friendly message is displayed along with a list of the names currently in the set.

LISTING 11.13

Deleting items from a set

```
names = {"Savion", "Amiah", "Niko", "Jackson"}
print(names)
user_input = input("Please enter a name to remove: ")
if user_input in names:
  names.remove(user_input)
  print(names)
else:
  print("You did not enter a name in the set. Currently the names in the set are " +
str(names))
```

You can see that the user input is captured in a variable called `user_input`. The `if` statement checks to see if it is in the `names` set. If it is, then it is removed like we want:

```
{'Jackson', 'Savion', 'Niko', 'Amiah'}
Please enter a name to remove: Niko
{'Jackson', 'Savion', 'Amiah'}
```

If the name does not exist, then the user-friendly message is indeed displayed:

```
{'Amiah', 'Jackson', 'Niko', 'Savion'}
Please enter a name to remove: Aubrey
You did not enter a name in the set. Currently the names in the set are
{'Amiah', 'Jackson', 'Niko', 'Savion'}
```

CLEARING A SET

We can use the `clear()` method to empty a set. This is useful if we want to completely update an existing set with new data. In Listing 11.14, we create a set of food items, clear the set, and then update the set with new items.

LISTING 11.14

Clearing a set

```
food = {"pasta", "burger", "hot dog", "pizza"}
print(food)

food.clear() # this will empty the food set
print(food)
```

When this is executed, we see the initial values in the list followed by confirmation that the list was cleared:

```
{'hot dog', 'pasta', 'pizza', 'burger'}
set()
```

Imagine that our ERP banking application has finished processing the most recent audit and needs to import data into the same set structure. We could program the application to use the `clear()` method such as for clearing member names from audits. This can enable the application to be more dynamic through reusing sets when they are no longer needed rather than creating new sets. In Listing 11.15, we can see such a dynamic process in action. In the program, the set that is cleared is based on a name that the user enters.

LISTING 11.15

Clearing a set solution

```
names_1 = {"Ben", "Gary", "Jaiden"}
names_2 = {"Sandra", "Rudy", "Marc"}
names_3 = {"Brittany", "Hope", "Jaylen"}

print("names_1", names_1)
print("names_2", names_2)
print("names_3", names_3)
user_input = input("Please enter a name that corresponds to a name in the list: ")
if user_input in names_1:
  names_1.clear()
  print("names_1 set cleared")
elif user_input in names_2:
  names_2.clear()
  print("names_2 set cleared")
elif user_input in names_3:
  names_3.clear()
  print("names_3 set cleared")
else:
  print("The input does not exist as a variable in any of the sets.")
```

This listing creates three sets of names, which are then printed so that you can see them. The user is then prompted to enter a name from one of the lists. Using an if–elif–else structure, the program dynamically determines which list should be cleared and then clears it. The following shows the output from entering a name from the names_2 set:

```
names_1 {'Jaiden', 'Ben', 'Gary'}
names_2 {'Marc', 'Sandra', 'Rudy'}
names_3 {'Jaylen', 'Hope', 'Brittany'}
Please enter a variable name that corresponds to a name in the list: Rudy
names_2 set cleared
```

POPPING ITEMS IN A SET

We can use the pop() method to return and remove the last element in a set. Because sets are unordered, the item returned by the pop() method is random. The pop() method does not take an argument, which means that you cannot use it to remove a specific item from the set.

In Listing 11.16, we create a set of four food items and use pop() to identify and remove one of those items. Note that while "pizza" is the last item added to the new set, it may not correspond to the popped item, because sets are unordered.

LISTING 11.16

Popping items from a set

```
food = {"pasta", "burger", "hot dog", "pizza"}

item = food.pop() #item is not necessarily "pizza" because sets are unordered.

print(item)
print(food)
```

In the second line of code in this listing, the pop() method is called on the food set that was created. The item removed from the food set is returned and stored in the item variable. You can see the results of this action in the two print lines that follow, which show the final values of both item and the food set:

```
hot dog
{'pasta', 'pizza', 'burger'}
```

Again, what is popped off the food set can vary. You might see a different result than *hot dog* as shown here. If the listing is executed multiple times, then different results might be seen.

DELETING A SET

We can use the `del` method to completely delete a set and its contents. In Listing 11.17, we create a set of food items, print it out, and then delete it. Printing a nonexistent set will throw an error.

LISTING 11.17

Deleting a set

```
food = {"pasta", "burger", "hot dog", "pizza"}

print(food)    # This will print

del food       # Delete the set
print(food)    # This will report an error because
               # the set doesn't exist anymore
```

The following is the output from running this listing. As you can see, it includes an error because the `food` set no longer exists when we try to print it the second time:

```
{'burger', 'pizza', 'pasta', 'hot dog'}
------------------------------------------------------------------------
NameError                             Traceback (most recent call last)

<ipython-input-38-36e6a08655fd> in <module>
      3
      4 del food #delete the set
----> 5 print(food) #this will report an error because the set doesn't exist
anymore

NameError: name 'food' is not defined
```

With any type of processing or work being completed, it can be useful to relinquish the resources back to the machine when it is no longer required. Our ERP banking application could be programmed so that after the audit or analysis is complete, it releases the resources for the processes to be run again or powered down.

In Listing 11.18, we have sets of names associated with various accounts. The program prompts the user for a name and then deletes the set that contains that name.

LISTING 11.18

Deleting a set of account names

```python
acct_names_1 = {"Hayden", "Rishi", "Jane"}
acct_names_2 = {"Hailee", "Kasen", "Dylan"}
acct_names_3 = {"Leah", "Maxwell", "Rory"}

print("acct_names_1", acct_names_1, "acct_names_2", acct_names_2, "acct_names_3",
acct_names_3)
user_input = input("Please enter a name: ").capitalize()
if user_input in acct_names_1:
  del acct_names_1
  print("Deleted acct_names_1")
elif user_input in acct_names_2:
  del acct_names_2
  print("Deleted acct_names_2")
elif user_input in acct_names_3:
  del acct_names_3
  print("Deleted acct_names_3")
else:
  print("The name you entered is not in any of the sets.")
```

Much of this listing should look familiar, but there is a new concept presented. The listing starts by creating and displaying the contents of three sets. This is followed by requesting the input of a name from the user. In the past, we've used the lower() method to force the input to be lowercase. In this example, we are using a new method called capitalize(), which will capitalize the first letter of the text that is entered and make the remaining text lowercase. This means that if the user enters Hayden, hayden, HAYDEN, HaYdEn, or any other case format, the result will be Hayden.

Once the account name is entered, an if–elif–else statement is used to determine if the name exists in one of the account name sets. If so, that set of names is removed using del. If there is no set with that name, an error message is displayed.

DETERMINING THE DIFFERENCE BETWEEN SETS

Sometimes it is important to know what has changed, or what the differences are between two things. This is true of sets as well. We can use the difference() method to compare two sets and return a set containing the items that appear in the first set but do not appear in the second set.

In Listing 11.19, we have two sets that include one item that is not in the other set. The `difference()` method only looks for items in the first set that do not appear in the second set, and it ignores other items in the second set.

LISTING 11.19

Determing the difference

```
shake_1 = {"kiwi", "banana", "peanut butter"}
shake_2 = {"banana" "kiwi", "spinach"}
shake_3 = shake_1.difference(shake_2) #this set will contain the
                                      #difference of shake_1 and shake_2

print(shake_1)
print(shake_2)
print(shake_3)
```

You should look at this listing closely. The `difference()` does not return all the differences between the two lists, but rather tells you what is in your original list that is not in the second list. In the output you can see the results of comparing the differences of `shake_2` to the original list of `shake_1`:

```
{'kiwi', 'banana', 'peanut butter'}
{'spinach', 'banana', 'kiwi'}
{'peanut butter'}
```

If you wanted to see the difference of what is in the second set, `shake_2`, from the first list, `shake_1`, you could add the following line:

```
shake_4 = shake_2.difference(shake_1)
```

Printing `shake_4` would display:

```
{'spinach'}
```

The `difference()` method is a valuable analysis tool for our ERP banking application because it can be used to find results without matching values. Perhaps we want to compare the user's location to all the bank branch locations to ensure there's a local one in the state.

In Listing 11.20, the user is prompted for the abbreviations of the states that are local to them. After the user enters the states by them, a list of abbreviations for the states that the user does not have access to yet are displayed.

LISTING 11.20

States where the user doesn't have access

```
states_abbrev = {"AL", "AK", "AZ", "AR", "CA", "CO", "CT", "DE", "FL", "GA", "HI",
"ID", "IL", "IN", "IA", "KS", "KY", "LA", "ME", "MD", "MA", "MI", "MN", "MS",
"MO", "MT", "NE", "NV", "NH", "NJ", "NM", "NY", "NC", "ND", "OH", "OK", "OR",
"PA", "RI", "SC", "SD", "TN", "TX", "UT", "VT", "VA", "WA", "WV", "WI", "WY"}

user_input = input("Please enter the abbreviation of a state that is local to
you [type 'done' to quit]: ").upper()

local_states = set()

while user_input != 'DONE':
  local_states.update({user_input})
    user_input = input("Please enter another abbreviation of a state near you [type /
'done' to quit]: ").upper()

print(states_abbrev.difference(local_states))
```

This listing prompts the user to enter state abbreviations. The user can enter "done" to indicate when they are done entering states. At that time, the difference() method will be used to determine the states they didn't enter. Those states are then displayed to the user. The following is an example of several states being entered:

```
Please enter the abbreviation of a state that is local to you [type 'done' to
quit]: OH
Please enter another abbreviation of a state near you [type 'done' to quit]: IN
Please enter another abbreviation of a state near you [type 'done' to quit]: IL
Please enter another abbreviation of a state near you [type 'done' to quit]: ky
Please enter another abbreviation of a state near you [type 'done' to quit]: tn
Please enter another abbreviation of a state near you [type 'done' to quit]: MI
Please enter another abbreviation of a state near you [type 'done' to quit]: xx
Please enter another abbreviation of a state near you [type 'done' to quit]: done
{'MN', 'AL', 'VT', 'SD', 'LA', 'WI', 'ID', 'WY', 'AK', 'MA', 'CT', 'IA', 'OK',
'VA', 'UT', 'ME', 'GA', 'WA', 'ND', 'DE', 'CO', 'MD', 'NY', 'AR', 'NM', 'NV',
'PA', 'TX', 'OR', 'MT', 'NE', 'MO', 'NJ', 'NC', 'CA', 'HI', 'AZ', 'WV', 'RI',
'NH', 'MS', 'SC', 'FL', 'KS'}
```

> **TIP** It's always a good idea to tell the user how to get out of a loop!

INTERSECTING SETS

We can use the `intersection()` method to compute the intersection of two or more sets. The result includes only the values that both sets have in common. In Listing 11.21, notice that there is at least one item that appears in both sets. We use `intersection()` to identify the shared items.

LISTING 11.21

Finding common items in sets

```
shake_1 = {"kiwi", "banana", "peanut butter"}
shake_2 = {"banana", "kiwi", "spinach"}

# The shake_3 set will contain the intersection of shake_1 and shake_2
shake_3 = shake_1.intersection(shake_2)

print(shake_1)
print(shake_2)
print(shake_3)
```

When you run this listing, the `shake_1` and `shake_2` sets are displayed followed by the contents of `shake_3`, which contains their intersection:

```
{'kiwi', 'banana', 'peanut butter'}
{'banana', 'kiwi', 'spinach'}
{'banana', 'kiwi'}
```

In contrast to the `difference()` method, the `intersection()` method enables our ERP banking application to find the same values in different lists. This is useful in analysis to determine relevant data points and begin to match on key values to create joins and unions (a type of data connection) in data science. We can use this in Listing 11.22 to determine if the customer has a local bank branch.

LISTING 11.22

Determining a local bank branch

```
branch_states = {"AZ", "CA", "FL", "GA", "IN", "KY", "MA", "NV", "NY", "NC",
"PA", "SC", "TN"}

local_states = set()
```

```
user_input = input("Please enter the abbreviation of a state that is local to you \
[type 'done' to quit]: ").upper()
while user_input != 'DONE':
  local_states.update({user_input})
  user_input = input("Please enter another abbreviation of a state that is local \
to you [type 'done' to quit]: ").upper()

local_branches = branch_states.intersection(local_states)
if not local_branches:
  print("You are not local to any bank branches.")
else:
  print(branch_states.intersection(local_states))
```

The code includes a set of state abbreviations representing states that have bank branches. Like previous listings, the user is prompted for the abbreviation of a state that is local to them. This value is stored in the new set called `local_states` after being adjusted to uppercase. This is repeated until the user enters "done" (in uppercase or lowercase).

Once the user completes the input, a list of the states that both the user has access to (`local_states`) and the bank has branches in (`branch_states`) is displayed. If there are no similar (intersecting) states, then a meaningful message is displayed to the user that they are not local to any bank branches.

COMBINING SETS

We can use the `union()` method to compute the union of two or more sets. The result is a new set of items that exist in at least one of the sets. In Listing 11.23 we create three sets of food items and then combine all three sets into a new set.

LISTING 11.23

Combining sets

```
shake_1 = {"kiwi", "banana", "peanut butter"}
shake_2 = {"banana", "kiwi", "spinach"}
shake_3 = {"orange", "apple", "almonds"}

#the union method combines two or more sets. We can add as many sets as needed.

shake_4 = shake_1.union(shake_2,shake_3)

print(shake_4)
```

Notice that "kiwi" and "banana" appear in two sets, but each of those values appears only once in the results:

```
{'banana', 'spinach', 'peanut butter', 'almonds', 'kiwi', 'orange', 'apple'}
```

The `union()` method provides the functionality to our ERP banking application to effectively combine multiple lists, without creating new sets and while also leaving the individual sets for future reference. At times, the analysis may call for datasets to be combined such as demographics and area information that may be used in mortgage pre-approval or loan underwriting.

SUMMARY

Prior to this lesson, we saw how to use lists and tuples to store data, where we can use automatically assigned index values to identify specific values in the collection. We also learned about dictionaries, which give us the ability to define the index values ourselves. In this lesson, we learned about a fourth basic data structure, sets, which are unorganized and unindexed.

Now that you have completed Lesson 11, you should be able to:

- Store, retrieve, and manipulate data in a set.

- Iterate through a set.

- Determine if values exist in a set.

- Clear or remove items from a set.

- Work with multiple sets to determine differences including intersections and unions.

EXERCISES

The following exercises are provided to allow you to demonstrate the objectives for this lesson. You should complete each exercise and make sure that the code runs without errors. The exercises include:

Exercise 1: Line by Line

Exercise 2: Adding New Names

Exercise 3: Popping Accounts

Exercise 4: Everywhere That Mary Went...

Exercise 5: Self-Assessment

Exercise 1: Line by Line

Our ERP banking application has a requirement to splice out the unique records contained within a set to make individual rows in a database. Use a `for` loop to retrieve items from the following set and print each item on its own line:

```
banking  = {"Checking","Savings","Loans","Dividends","IRAs"}
```

Exercise 2: Adding New Names

Create a set with at least three customer names in it and print it. Then add at least three more items to the set and print the updated set.

Exercise 3: Popping Accounts

The functionality of using `pop()` can be used in the ERP banking application for extracting and removing a specific erroneous value. Create a script that performs the following steps:

- Display the set to the user along with the number of items in the set.
- Ask the user if they want to remove an item from the set.
- If the user says yes:
  - Verify that there is at least one item in the set.
  - Remove a random item from the set.
  - Display the updated set to the user.
  - Prompt the user to remove another item.
- If there are no items in the set, display an output message to that effect and end the script.
- If the user says no, end the script.

Don't use the `clear()`, `remove()`, or `discard()` methods in your solution. Here is the first line of code to get you started:

```
account_numbers = {"L000012","L000023","S0001243","C122399" }
# your code here
```

Exercise 4: Everywhere That Mary Went...

The following code includes a set of the states that Mary has visited:

```
mary_states = {"AZ", "CA", "FL", "GA", "IN", "KY", "MA", "NV", "NY", "NC",
"PA", "SC", "TN", "WA", "WV", "WI", "WY", "OR"}

# your code here
```

Update the code to perform the following steps:

- Prompt the user for the abbreviation of a state they have visited and store the value in a new set.
- Repeat the prompt and continue storing values in the same set until the user enters "done" (in uppercase or lowercase).
- Display a list of the states that either the user or Mary has visited.
- Display a list of states that neither the user nor Mary has visited.

Exercise 5: Self-Assessment

This exercise is provided as a self-assessment, allowing you to check your knowledge and readiness for the next lesson. This assessment combines concepts presented in the lesson in a single program without the guidance provided in the lesson activities. You'll notice this is similar to Exercise 4 in Lesson 10, but this time sets are used. Use your program to do the following:

- Define a set with at least five elements.
- Ask the user for a value.
- Ask the user for an operation ("add" or "remove").
  - If the operation is "remove":
    - If the value exists in the set, remove the value from the set, and display the updated set to the user.
    - If the value does not exist in the set, display "Sorry, the value does not exist."
  - If the operation is "add":
    - If the value exists in the set, display "your item exists."
    - If the value does not exist in the set, add the value to the set, and display the updated set to the user.
- Repeat until the user enters "quit."
- When the user enters "quit," display the original set, the final version of the updated set, and the difference between the two sets.

Pulling It All Together: Prompting for an Address

In this lesson, we'll put everything we've learned in the book so far into a single program, including declaring variables, storing values into variables, accepting user input, and displaying input values to the user. We will also, of course, use proper Python syntax along the way as well as take advantage of data types we've seen.

This is a code-along, rather than a lesson, like the other chapters. We will start with a completely empty program and add code to it a little at a time to build out a complete program. You should start at the beginning of the lesson and complete the steps in the order given. Verify that your code runs as expected and without error before continuing to the next step.

One step includes a challenge activity. This is optional and the code for the challenge activity is not included in the steps that follow it. But you are encouraged to try it on your own before going to the next step. We will provide all code for the program at the end of the activity, including the solution for the challenge activity.

LEARNING OBJECTIVES

By the end of this lesson, you will be able to:

- Add comments to a Python script.
- Declare a variable in Python.
- Accept user input and store the input value in a variable.
- Display a user-friendly output statement.
- Use the `split` method to divide a string into separate words.
- Retrieve individual values from a list.

STEP 1: GETTING STARTED

For this activity, you will need an IDE that supports Python. Because this is a basic application, you can use Replit if you wish, but we recommend using a computer-based IDE rather than a web-based IDE. Good examples include Jupyter Notebook, IDLE, or Visual Studio Code.

> **NOTE** Most developers use computer-based IDEs to write code because they are typically more robust than web-based IDEs like Replit (`https://replit.com/`). It's good to get in the habit of using them for larger programs, although Replit is a great tool if you just want to test a small block of code.

Open your selected IDE and create a new file named `project_1`. If you are using Jupyter Notebook, it will automatically add the filename extension `.ipynb` to the filename. Otherwise, make sure that the filename ends in `.py` (e.g., `project_1.py`). This tells your IDE that the file is in Python so that it can use the correct compiler when you run the code.

You should also **document** any program you write. While the exact details in the documentation can vary from one developer (or organization) to the next, document comments should include your name, the date the program was written, and a short comment about why the program was created. Before adding any code to the new file, add the following information at the top of the file as comments:

```
# Name: Firstname Lastname
# Date created: Current date
# Purpose: Code-along for Python course
```

Comments can also include information like the most recent revision to the program, the organization the program was created for, and even contact information (like an email address or website) for the person or organization that created the program. You are welcome to add additional comments to the current file if you wish.

Save the changes to the file. You can run it now if you wish (and it's good to run a program after significant changes to check for errors), but it won't output anything because we only have comments at this point, with no executable statements.

STEP 2: ACCEPT USER INPUT

The first thing we want the program to do is prompt the user for a value and store that value for future use. Because we want to store the input, we start by defining a variable. Remember that declaring a variable creates a named memory space that the program can use not only to store the value, but also to retrieve the value later in the program.

Python also allows us to prompt the user for the information we want to store in the variable in the same instruction we use to declare the variable. In this case, we want to ask the user for their street address. Add the code in Listing 12.1 to your program.

LISTING 12.1

Prompting for input

```
# Name: Firstname Lastname
# Date created: Current date
# Purpose: Code-along for Python course

user_address = input("Enter an address (e.g., 123 Main Street): ")
```

Note a couple of things in this code:

- We create a variable named `user_address`. Python will store whatever the user enters into this named memory space.

- We use the `input` function to tell Python to prompt the user for a value, and we assign that value to the `user_address` variable using the equals sign (=).

- We include a specific prompt to tell the user what kind of information we want them to enter. In this case, we also provide examples to make it more likely that the user will enter data in the format we expect the information to be in.

NOTE UX (or *user experience*) is a term used to describe how user-friendly an application is. It refers not only to how the application looks and how easy it is to use, but also to the process of guiding users to use the app appropriately, to reduce the chance of errors that can be caused by bad user input. In this case, we give examples to help make sure the user enters the street address in the correct format for this application. In addition, to help ensure a great user experience, all text that will display to the user should use correct spelling and grammar.

If you run the command now, the program will prompt you for an address:

```
Enter an address (e.g., 123 Main Street):
```

Enter an address of your choice and hit Enter. Depending on the IDE you are using, you may see the input following the prompt, like:

```
Enter an address (e.g., 123 Main Street): 789 Bradford Street
```

In other IDEs, you may not see anything at all after you hit the Enter key. Remember that we are declaring a variable and storing the input value in that variable. The process of storing a value may not produce output unless there is an error in how the value is stored.

Once you are sure you can enter a value without problems, save the program and continue to the next step.

STEP 3: DISPLAY THE INPUT VALUE

In Python, we use the `print` command to display values to the user. While you can `print` a real value, in most cases, we tell Python to `print` a variable, in which case it retrieves the value stored in the named variable and displays the retrieved value to the user.

Here, we want to display the address entered by the user. Add the additional commands shown in Listing 12.2 to your code.

LISTING 12.2

Displaying the address back to the user

```
# Name: Firstname Lastname
# Date created: Current date
# Purpose: Code-along for Python course

user_address = input("Enter an address (e.g., 123 Main Street): ")
if user_address.strip(): #check that string is not empty (after removing leading
                         #and trailing spaces)
    print(user_address)
```

Run the script to test that it works. It should prompt you for a value and then display that value to you on a separate line. Enter any address you want, but in our examples, we will use **789 Bradford Street**:

```
#Enter an address (e.g., 123 Main Street): 789 Bradford Street
789 Bradford Street
```

This is a great way to allow the user to see what they entered and verify they entered the correct information. But because it only displays the value, there is no context for that value. Let's add that in the next step.

STEP 4: MODIFY THE OUTPUT

Let's add the phrase "Your address is" at the beginning of the output. We do this by including the phrase with the variable in the print command, using a plus sign to *concatenate* them. Remember that text phrases like this also have to be in parentheses. Listing 12.3 shows our updated script with the modified output.

LISTING 12.3

The modified output

```
# Name: Firstname Lastname
# Date created: Current date
# Purpose: Code-along for Python course
```

```
user_address = input("Enter an address (e.g., 123 Main Street): ")
if user_address.strip(): #check that string is not empty (after removing leading
                         #and trailing spaces)
    print("Your address is " + user_address)
```

Run the program again. You should see the new output phrase with the value entered:

```
Enter an address (e.g., 123 Main Street): 789 Bradford Street
Your address is 789 Bradford Street
```

NOTE Challenge

This output phrase is in the form of a complete sentence, so we might want to add a period at the end. Can you work out how to do this on your own?

STEP 5: SPLIT A TEXT VALUE

A complete street address includes (at least) two discrete values: the street name and the building or house number. Remember that any text value is technically a **string**. While we humans see words and phrases, Python (and most other programming languages) only sees a string of individual characters rather than individual or meaningful words. We can use that to our advantage if we want to reuse only part of a string value.

In this case, we can use the split function to split the full address string into individual parts, using the space character as the defined separator in the string. We can then store each of those individual values in a list and then use those values separately from the rest of the original string. Update your code as shown in Listing 12.4.

LISTING 12.4

Splitting the address into pieces

```
# Name: Firstname Lastname
# Date created: Current date
# Purpose: Code-along for Python course

user_address = input("Enter an address (e.g., 123 Main Street): ")
if user_address.strip(): #check that string is not empty (after removing leading
                         #and trailing spaces)
    print("Your address is " + user_address)
    split_address = user_address.split()
```

When we run this code, Python will split the string into separate strings, using the space character as the default separator. Those individual strings will be stored as separate values in a list named `split_address`.

If you run the code at this point, you can't really see this happening. But you can include a temporary `print` instruction to see the list itself, as shown in Listing 12.5.

LISTING 12.5

Displaying split information with a simple print

```
# Name: Firstname Lastname
# Date created: Current date
# Purpose: Code-along for Python course

user_address = input("Enter an address (e.g., 123 Main Street): ")
if user_address.strip(): #check that string is not empty (after removing leading
                         #and trailing spaces)
    print("Your address is " + user_address)
    split_address = user_address.split()
    print(split_address)   # temporary instruction to verify the list
```

The output should look like:

```
Enter an address (e.g., 123 Main Street): 789 Bradford Street
Your address is 789 Bradford Street
['789', 'Bradford', 'Street']
```

We don't need this `print` statement in the full program, so we can comment it out after using it to test the `split` function, as shown in Listing 12.6.

LISTING 12.6

Commenting out unneeded code

```
# Name: Firstname Lastname
# Date created: Current date
# Purpose: Code-along for Python course

user_address = input("Enter an address (e.g., 123 Main Street): ")
```

```
if user_address.strip(): #check that string is not empty (after removing leading
                         #and trailing spaces)
    print("Your address is " + user_address)
    split_address = user_address.split()
    #print(split_address)  # temporary instruction to verify the list
```

> **NOTE** Why Not Delete It?
>
> If you add temporary code to test the working code, you can certainly
> delete it when you are done testing. However, commenting it out allows
> you to reuse the code if you need to later without having to type it out. It
> also provides a certain level of documentation so that you can see what
> you've already tested to avoid running the same tests multiple times.
> Note that we also added a comment so that we could remember why we
> included the code in the first place.

STEP 6: DISPLAY ONLY THE HOUSE NUMBER

Now that we have split the address string, we can use each value independently of the
others. For example, suppose that we only want to print the house or building number,
without the street name. Because that value is stored as the first element in the `split_`
`address` list, we can retrieve it using the index value *0* (keeping in mind that when you
have a collection of data, like a list, the first value always has index 0). Listing 12.7 provides
the updated code that shows the house number.

LISTING 12.7

Displaying the house number

```
# Name: Firstname Lastname
# Date created: Current date
# Purpose: Code-along for Python course

user_address = input("Enter an address (e.g., 123 Main Street): ")
if user_address.strip(): #check that string is not empty (after removing leading
                         #and trailing spaces)
    print("Your address is " + user_address)
    split_address = user_address.split()
    #print(split_address)  # temporary instruction to verify the list
    print(split_address[0])
```

This produces output that displays the house number, but without any context:

```
Enter an address (e.g., 123 Main Street): 789 Bradford Street
Your address is 789 Bradford Street
789
```

Now let's make that output more meaningful by updating the print statement as shown in Listing 12.8.

LISTING 12.8

Improving the output

```
# Name: Firstname Lastname
# Date created: Current date
# Purpose: Code-along for Python course

user_address = input("Enter an address (e.g., 123 Main Street):")
if user_address.strip(): #check that string is not empty (after removing leading
                         #and trailing spaces)
    print("Your address is " + user_address)
    split_address = user_address.split()
    #print(split_address)  # temporary instruction to verify the list
    print("Your house number is " + split_address[0])
```

This gives us output like:

```
Enter an address (e.g., 123 Main Street): 789 Bradford Street
Your address is 789 Bradford Street
Your house number is 789
```

STEP 7: DISPLAY THE STREET NAME

Now let's set up our program to display only the full street name, without the house number. In this case, we need to combine the rest of the elements in the list and display them in a user-friendly message. Update the code with a new print statement as shown in Listing 12.9.

LISTING 12.9

Displaying the street name

```
# Name: Firstname Lastname
# Date created: Current date
# Purpose: Code-along for Python course

user_address = input("Enter an address (e.g., 123 Main Street): ")
print("Your address is " + user_address)

split_address = user_address.split()
#print(split_address)  # temporary instruction to verify the list

print("Your house number is " + split_address[0])
print("Your street is " + " ".join(split_address[1:]))
```

When you run the code, though, you'll see that it doesn't display the output exactly right. In our example address, the output looks like this:

```
Enter an address (e.g., 123 Main Street): 789 Bradford Street
Your address is 789 Bradford Street
Your house number is 789
Your street is Bradford Street
```

STEP 8: ADD THE PERIOD

Now we can look at the challenge from an earlier step: how to add a period at the end of the output statements. This is actually as easy as adding the space between the street name and street type in the previous step: just add + " . " to the end of each output statement as shown in Listing 12.10.

LISTING 12.10

Adding the periods

```
# Name: Firstname Lastname
# Date created: Current date
# Purpose: Code-along for Python course
```

```
user_address = input("Enter an address (e.g., 123 Main Street): ")
if user_address.strip(): #check that string is not empty (after removing leading
                          #and trailing spaces)
    print("Your address is " + user_address+".")
    split_address = user_address.split()
    #print(split_address)  # temporary instruction to verify the list
    print("Your house number is " + split_address[0]+".")
    print("Your street is " + " ".join(split_address[1:])+".")
```

The output will now include the periods, which improves the UX for the application:

```
Enter an address (e.g., 123 Main Streete): 789 Bradford Street
Your address is 789 Bradford Street.
Your house number is 789.
Your street is Bradford Street.
```

SUMMARY

In our example here, we are looking at a very basic address, but in reality, addresses can be much more complex, including directional indicators (N, S, E, W, for example) and apartment or unit numbers. Experiment with using a more complex address in this application.

Later in the book, we will look at creating an application that can produce specific outcomes based on conditional values that can change from one run to the next. You may find it useful to come back to this exercise when you can include code that tells the program to do one thing if there are only three elements in the address or to do different things if the address is more complex.

Lesson 13
Organizing with Functions

A function is a block of code that is executed only when it's called. While Python includes many built-in functions, we can also write new, custom functions to create reusable components that we can use every time we need them.

LEARNING OBJECTIVES

By the end of this lesson, you will be able to:

- Explain the syntax required to define a customized function.
- Demonstrate the use of function parameters, including the use of default values.
- Demonstrate the use of indefinite or arbitrary parameters in a function.
- Use keywords to define parameters in a function.

FUNCTIONS OVERVIEW

A *function* is a block of organized, reusable code that uses one or more Python statements to complete a single, related action. We use functions to help with code reusability, increased readability, and redundancy checking (making sure that we do not use the same lines over and over within an application).

Python provides many built-in functions, such as the `print()` function that we've been using throughout this book; however, we are also allowed to create or define our own functions. A function that you define yourself in a Python program is known as a *user-defined function*. You are free to assign nearly any name to a user-defined function, but you cannot use the Python reserved words as function names.

As you progress through this lesson, here are a few key terms you should know:

- **Functions** are blocks of organized, reusable code.

- **Function code blocks** are groups of Python program code executed as a unit, such as a module, a class definition, or a function body. A colon (`:`) is used to start a function code block.

- **User-defined functions** are functions defined by the user. These functions use the `def` keyword to define them.

- **Built-in functions** are functions that are built into Python.

- **Redundancy checking** is used to check that the same code lines are not unnecessarily repeated within an application.

- **Docstrings** (short for *Python documentation*) are used to organize functions, modules, classes, and methods. Docstrings are similar to comments, but docstrings describe what the function does rather than how.

- **Parameters** are the variables listed inside the parentheses in the function definition. You can think of parameters as variables that we define as part of defining a function. Their purpose is to store the values provided by our function arguments.

- **Arguments** are pieces of information passed into functions. An argument is the value sent to the function when called upon.

DEFINING FUNCTIONS IN PYTHON

As we stated earlier, a function in Python is a block of organized, reusable code. A function performs a single, related action. A function in Python can take any number of parameters. When defining functions within Python, we must adhere to the following rules:

- Python function blocks begin with the keyword `def` followed by the function name and parentheses `()`.

- Input arguments should be placed within these parentheses.

- The first statement of a function can be an optional statement—the documentation string of the function, or docstring.

- We exit a function using the statement `return [expression]`. The `exit` function may optionally pass back an expression to the caller of the function. The action of

Return None would essentially provide an indication that the function completed successfully, while no return function leaves the function to operate with no return as if it was completed.

- The colon (:) delineates the start of the function code block, which should be indented.

When working with functions, we must remember that functions must be declared and then called. Let's take a look at the syntax to do both.

A user-defined function is declared by using the def keyword, followed by the function name and any parameters, which are included in parentheses. This is followed by a colon. The function block then begins after this, as the basic syntax shows here:

```
def function_name(function_parameters):

    function_body   # Set of Python statements
    return          # optional return statement
```

The syntax of calling a function that doesn't return anything is:

```
function_name(parameters)
```

Whereas the syntax for calling a function when the function returns something is:

```
Myvariable = function_name(parameters)
```

In this case, the value returned from the function is stored in Myvariable.

Let's take a look at a Python function in action. Listing 13.1 presents a user-defined function for adding two numbers and returning the result.

LISTING 13.1

A user-defined function for adding numbers

```
def add(num1, num2):
    return num1 + num2

sum1 = add(100, 200)
sum2 = add(8, 9)

print(sum1)
print(sum2)
```

In this case, we have declared a function named add() in the first line. In the function body, two numbers (num1, num2) will be added together, and the result will be returned. You can see that when the function is defined in line 1 that num1 and num2 are passed as parameters. Together, the first two lines contain our entire user-defined function.

After we declare the function, we call the function twice to perform the addition. We then print the output in the final two lines of the listing. The results of running the program and using our new function are:

```
300
17
```

In our second example in Listing 13.2, we define a function named find_greater with two parameters:

- **numbers:** A list of numbers

- **threshold:** An integer used as a threshold

The function iterates through the list of numbers, comparing each number to the threshold value, and prints the numbers that are greater than the threshold number.

LISTING 13.2

The find_greater function

```
def find_greater(numbers,threshold):
    for num in numbers:
        # we only display the numbers that are above the input threshold
        if (num > threshold):
            print(num)

numbers = [1,5,5,7,10,1]
find_greater(numbers,0) # find all numbers greater than 0
print("----")
find_greater(numbers,5) # find all numbers greater than 5
```

In this listing, we again start by defining a function using the def keyword followed by the function name, find_greater, and then the two parameters that will be used by our function. The first line then ends with the colon to indicate the function body starts next. The next several lines are indented, indicating they are our function body. In this case, we use a for loop to iterate through each number in the list that is passed into the function in the numbers parameter. We use this to see if the individual list elements are greater than the threshold number that is also passed in. If so, the number is printed.

Our listing then defines a list called numbers that will be used. We know this is not part of the function because our code is no longer indented as part of the function body. The list of numbers is then passed to our newly defined function along with a threshold value of 0. Some dashes are printed and then our newly defined function is called a second time with the same list of numbers, but this time with a threshold of 5. The resulting output is:

```
1
5
5
7
10
1
----
7
10
```

Listing 13.3 is a similar example. In this case, we define and implement the function called find_div, which finds all the elements in a list of numbers that are divisible by a given value.

LISTING 13.3

Creating a function to find numbers divisible by a factor

```
def find_div(transactions,factor):
    for num in transactions:
      if (num % factor == 0):
        print(num)

transactions = [1,5,5,7,10,1,9,12]
print("Factor of 3:")
find_div(transactions,3) # find all transactions divisible by 3
print("Factor of 2:")
find_div(transactions,2) # find all transactions divisible by 2
```

Listing 13.3 is very similar to Listing 13.2, except the mathematical check in our new function is different. Additionally, instead of simply printing a dashed line between the two calls to our newly defined function, a print statement is done before each call to help identify the output, which can be seen in the following:

```
Factor of 3:
9
12
Factor of 2:
10
12
```

As customers make transactions in our banking ERP application, we may also want to perform some analysis. Perhaps we are interested in learning about the average amount of the last 5 or 10 transactions made by our customers. We may also want to display this information to them. The customer information may be stored in a separate database. We can use a function in Python that takes the customer account number and their recent transactions to calculate and provide the average transaction amount, or perhaps certain elements, such as whether they are divisible by a certain number. We can perform this for all our customers by simply defining a function at one place in our ERP application.

FUNCTION SYNTAX

To reiterate, when creating user-defined functions in Python, we use the keyword `def` followed by the function name and required parameters in parentheses. In this syntax, the `function_name` should use the same naming conventions we use for variables: all lowercase letters, with underscores to separate individual words.

The parameters in parentheses are input values that the function will use for calculations and other operations within the function. A function can include any number of parameters.

In our ERP banking application, there will be certain tasks that we need to perform regularly. One such task could be checking whether a specific account number exists in our customer database, or perhaps the ERP application needs to check whether a value violates a maximum allowable limit to trigger an audit. We can write a few lines of code to check this. However, common tasks like these are performed fairly regularly throughout our ERP application. Instead of duplicating code at multiple places within our application, we can create a function that implements our task, such as searching for a specific account number, and uses the function throughout the application. Designing our ERP application in such a way is highly beneficial because if our implementation for the specific task changes at any point, we only have to modify our code at one location.

In the example in Listing 13.4, we define a function named `check_transaction_limit`, which takes one parameter, `amount`, as input and checks if it is above or within the transaction limit.

LISTING 13.4

Function to check a transaction limit

```
def check_transaction_limit(amount):
    # checks if the transaction exceeds the limit
    if amount > 10000:
```

```
        print("Above maximum transaction limit!")
    else:
        print("Transaction is within the limit.")

# using the above defined function, we can now check the transaction limits
check_transaction_limit(5000)
check_transaction_limit(13000)
```

There are two points worth noting in this example. The first is that the function allows us to avoid repeating the same code more than once. More importantly, with the function in place, our code that uses the function becomes very streamlined. Calling a function called `check_transaction_limit` with a value passed is much more readable. When the preceding listing is executed, we see the results:

```
Transaction is within the limit.
Above maximum transaction limit!
```

DEFAULT INPUT VALUES

We can assign default values to function parameters so that we do not have to provide parameter values each time we call a function. When we run a function that includes a default value for at least one parameter, we can optionally provide a different value to use when the function runs. If we do not provide a value, Python will use the defined default value instead.

The way we define a default value for a parameter is by setting the value equal to the default value. In the example in Listing 13.5, we define a function named `display` that takes `message` as its only parameter, with the default value "Hello Customer."

When we run the function, we can choose to provide a different parameter value. If no value is provided, the function prints the default message.

LISTING 13.5

Using defaulted parameter values

```
def display(message="Hello Customer"):
  print(str(message))

# we can use the display method to print several messages.
display("Hello World")
display()      #Default value will be used
display(True)
```

In this listing, we create a function called `display` in the first two lines of code. This function is used to display several messages. The message that will be displayed is passed to the function and a call to `print()` will display it.

After defining the function, we then call it three times. The first time it is called with the string "Hello World" passed. You can see in the output that the passed string is displayed. The second time the function is called, nothing is passed. As a result, the default value that was set in the first line of code when we defined the function is used and "Hello Customer" is displayed. In the third call to the function, the value of `True` is passed, and thus is also displayed. The full output is:

```
Hello Customer
Hello Customer
True
```

In Listing 13.6 we again define a `find_greater` function; however, this time we can see that it uses the default of `0` as the `threshold` value. As such, if we don't pass or specify a different value for `threshold`, then it will be defaulted to `0`.

LISTING 13.6

Using a default value

```
def find_greater(transactions,threshold=0):
    for trans in transactions:
        # we only display the transactions that are above the input threshold
        if (trans > threshold):
            print(trans)

transactions = [10,15,15,27,100,10]
find_greater(transactions)     # find all numbers greater than 0
find_greater(transactions,15) # find all numbers greater than 15
```

You can see that the threshold is set equal to zero, thus making zero a default value. When the `find_greater` function is called with just the transaction list being passed, the default value for `threshold` (0) is used. When a value is passed for the threshold, such as the 15 passed in the second call to `find_greater`, then the default value is overwritten.

Our banking ERP application can perform multiple tasks that provide value to our customers as well as to our employees. One such task that can be informative is knowing all the transactions that the customer performed in a specific month; another might be providing the largest transaction in a given period. For a given customer account, we can search through the different months in the year and get the transaction data for the month in question. We may even want to provide a default value to the month selection, such as the current month. We can achieve this using the default input value in Python functions.

PARAMETER SYNTAX

When defining a function, parameters with default values must follow parameters without default values in the function header. The example in Listing 13.7 shows two versions of a `display` function.

LISTING 13.7

Order matters with default parameters

```
def display(message1, message2 = "Hello World"):
    print(str(message1) + str(message2))

# this will throw an error because the parameter with the default
# value precedes the parameter that does not have a default value

def display2(message1 = "Hello World", message2):
    print(str(message1) + str(message2))
```

In this listing, the first function (`display`) includes two parameters. The first parameter (`message1`) requires a value when the function runs, but the second (`message2`) has the default value `"Hello World"`. This function runs without error.

The second function (`display2`) reverses the parameters, which Python does not allow. This function throws an error when we try to run it:

```
------------------------------------------------------------
File "main.py", line 1
  def display2(message = "Hello World", message2):

SyntaxError: non-default argument follows default argument.
```

In our previous ERP banking application scenario, we discussed looking at transaction data for a specific month. We may want to further generalize our approach to increase the utility of our transaction history function. We may also be interested in the transaction history for other customers. We can achieve this by passing the customer account number as one of the parameters and passing month with a default value of the current month as another parameter, if the user doesn't specify another date or account. We can now use our transaction history function for any customer in our database.

ARBITRARY ARGUMENTS

By default, functions must be called with the correct number of arguments. If a function expects two arguments, then the code must call the function with two arguments. For example, the following function expects two arguments and gets two arguments when called:

```
def the_function(fname, lname):
  print(fname + " " + lname)

the_function("LaChone", "McMillan")
```

In situations where we do not know exactly how many arguments are passed into a function, we can add an asterisk (*) before the parameter name within the function definition. Adding the asterisk in front of the name of the parameter in the definition allows for an arbitrary and unlimited number of inputs. The function then receives a tuple for this parameter. This tuple contains a number of arguments that the function can then access accordingly.

In Listing 13.8, we define a function called display_customer_input that allows an indefinite number of inputs using a parameter called *argv.

LISTING 13.8

Variable amount of information passed to a function

```
def display_customer_input(*argv):
    for arg in argv:
        print(arg)

customer_1 = ["John", "Doe", "Programmer", "80000"]
customer_2 = ["Jane", "Doe", "Scientist", "80000"]
customer_3 = ["Charles", "Painter"]

display_customer_input(*customer_1)
print("----")
display_customer_input(*customer_2)
print("----")
display_customer_input(*customer_3)
```

The display_customer_input function includes a for loop that evaluates each input value at runtime. The program then creates three separate lists of customers that will provide a variable amount of information. customer_1 and customer_2 provide all the details, but customer_3 only provided first name and profession. You see that regardless of the variable number of parameters, the call to the `display_customer_input` function works for each of them:

```
John
Doe
Programmer
80000
----
Jane
Doe
Scientist
80000
----
Charles
Painter
```

As new customers join our company, our ERP application should be able to collect their information to save in our database. We can have these inputs as optional. However, in doing so, we may not know beforehand how many inputs the customer has filled in. We can handle such variable inputs in our ERP application by using the Python function's indefinite number of parameters.

In the example in Listing 13.9, we create a function called `compute_sum` that takes as input an indefinite number of integers and returns the sum of those numbers.

LISTING 13.9

Function to compute the sum of a variable number of items

```
def compute_sum(*numbers):
    total = 0
    for n in numbers:
        total += n
    return total

numbers = 1,5,5,7,10,1
summation = compute_sum(*numbers)
print(summation)
```

You can see that `compute_sum` can accept a variable amount of information being passed because of the asterisk in front of the number parameter. The function uses a `for` loop to calculate the total of all the numbers it receives. That total number is then returned. In Listing 13.9, the `compute_sum` is called with six different numbers and the total is returned. The output from this listing based on the values assigned to `numbers` is 29. We could change the quantity of numbers passed and our function would continue to work.

KEYWORD ARGUMENTS

In arbitrary arguments, we access the arguments passed into our functions by accessing a tuple of them. However, we can also use keyword arguments using the key: value method. By using the key: value method, the user creates an indefinite number of arguments for a function, in which each argument includes both a variable name and a value as shown in Listing 13.10.

LISTING 13.10

Using keyword arguments

```
def my_function(fam1, fam2, fam3):
  print("The youngest family member is "+fam3)

my_function(fam1="Ezekiel",fam2="Sherry",fam3="Louis")
print("----")
my_function(fam2="Homer",fam3="Lisa",fam1="Bart")
```

This listing creates a function called `my_function` that takes three parameters named `fam1`, `fam2`, and `fam3`. The listing assumes `fam3` is the youngest family member and prints a message saying so.

When calling `my_function` the first time, each value provided is assigned to an argument. Thus "Ezekial" is assigned to `fam1`. The function then uses these values when displaying the output. The second time the function is called, we see that the order of the assigned arguments does not match the order they were declared in the function. This is okay as long as all of the required arguments are assigned. You see that in both cases, the `fam3` value was displayed as part of the output:

```
The youngest family member is Louis
The youngest family member is Lisa
```

ARBITRARY KEYWORD ARGUMENTS

If we do not know the number of keyword arguments passed to our function, Python supports the use of arbitrary keyword arguments. With arbitrary keyword arguments, the order of the arguments does not matter.

To address this, we simply add two asterisks (∗∗) before the parameter name in the function definition as shown in Listing 13.11. By adding two asterisks before the parameter name, the function now receives a dictionary of arguments and can access them.

LISTING 13.11

Accepting arbitrary arguments

```
def my_function(**family):
  print("Her last name is " + family["lname"])

my_function(fname = "Emery", lname = "McMillan")
```

In this listing, `family` is defined to accept arbitrary keywords, which means it will receive an indefinite number of arguments that include both a keyword and value. When called, the keywords used are `fname` and `lname` and the values assigned to them are "Emery" and "McMillan." In the method definition of `my_function`, you can see that the value stored in the `lname` keyword is displayed within a `print` statement resulting in the following output:

```
Her last name is McMillan
```

In Listing 13.12, we do an example where we use ∗∗kwargs to create an indefinite number of arguments that include both a keyword and a value. We do not have to define the exact keywords in the function itself. Instead, we can define different keywords (and different values) each time we run the function.

LISTING 13.12

The display function

```
def display(**kwargs):
    # iterate through the list…
    for keyword,value in kwargs.items():
        print(keyword + ": " + value)

display(first_name = 'Robert', last_name = 'Johnson')
print("----")
display(first_name = 'Mary', age = "32", location = "Dallas")
```

The `display` function is declared using ∗∗kwargs, which means it can accept an indefinite number of keywords. Keyword/argument pairs are gained within a dictionary (kwargs). Again, these are keyword arguments, which means each argument has a variable name and a value. In the `display` function, we use a `for` loop to iterate through the list and display each argument.

We call the `display` function twice. The first time we call the `display` function, we provide a person's first and last name. In the second example, we provide a first name, an age, and a location. The resulting output is:

```
first_name: Robert
last_name: Johnson
----
first_name: Mary
age: 32
location: Dallas
```

In our ERP application, occasionally we may want to conduct customer surveys. As part of these surveys, we may also want to provide the customer with the opportunity to add additional feedback. Our survey may contain several sections and each section may have its own additional feedback option. As we work to analyze and curate the survey results, we will want the ability to process this additional feedback. We can achieve this using the keyword arguments in Python functions.

SUMMARY

Prior to this lesson, we've seen how to store, retrieve, and manipulate a data collection using a dictionary with defined index values. We have also learned how to manipulate data in a set. This lesson built upon many of the objectives learned in the previous lessons in order to present the use of functions within Python.

Remember, a function is an independent block of code that is executed only when it's called by using its name. While Python includes many built-in functions, we can also write new, custom functions to create reusable components that we can use every time we need them. A function can be built in, or users can define a function. A function that you define yourself in a Python program is known as a user-defined function. You are free to assign any name to a user-defined function, but you cannot use the Python reserved words as function names.

Functions take on arguments and parameters. These can easily be confused. Remember, a parameter is the variable listed inside the parentheses in the function. An argument, however, is the value sent to the function when called upon.

Now that you have completed Lesson 13, you should be able to:

- Explain the syntax required to define a customized function.

- Demonstrate the use of function parameters, including the use of default values.

- Demonstrate the use of indefinite or arbitrary parameters in a function.

- Use keywords to define parameters in a function.

> **NOTE** It is important to differentiate functions from methods in Python programming. You will learn more about methods in Lesson 14 on object-oriented programming, including classes and objects.

EXERCISES

The following activities are based on tools and concepts presented in this lesson. Completing them will demonstrate your understanding of using Python to create reusable functions. The exercises include:

Exercise 1: Lower Numbers

Exercise 2: This Will Be

Exercise 3: Finding the Largest

Exercise 4: Simple Calculator

Exercise 5: Which Is Greater?

Exercise 1: Lower Numbers

Write a program that performs the following tasks:

1. Accept at least five and no more than ten integers from the user and store the values in a list.
   - Give the user the option to stop input after receiving five numbers.
   - Stop accepting input when the user chooses to stop or when there are ten numbers in the list.
2. Calculate the average value of the input numbers and use this value as a threshold.
3. Create a `find_lower` function that accepts the list of numbers and the threshold value as parameters and then calculates and displays the values from the list that are lower than the threshold value.

Exercise 2: This Will Be

Create a function that searches a string for an input group of characters and replaces each instance of the group with a new group of characters. For example, the function might be used to replace all occurrences of the phrase "this is" with "this will be."

Exercise 3: Finding the Largest

Define the `find_largest` function used in the following code snippet. The function should compute the largest value from an input list of numbers and print the result:

```
# Put your function code here

# do not change this code below
transactions = [1000,55322,511000,700,1050,1200]
find_largest(transactions)
```

Exercise 4: Simple Calculator

Design a function called `simple_calculator` that performs basic math operations (addition, subtraction, multiplication, division) on two operands. Use the function to create a program that allows the user to perform simple calculations on two numbers. For example, the program should allow the user to input two numbers of their choice, perform the selected operation on the numbers, and display the result.

Exercise 5: Which Is Greater?

Create a function that takes as input a variable number of keyword arguments using the following pattern:

```
word_1=value, word_2=value,...,word_n = value
```

The function should return the word with the highest corresponding value, with the word and value in a tuple. Using the example data included in the following code, the result would be `word_3 6`.

```
def compute_max_value(**kwargs):
    #remove pass and place your code here
    pass

(word,freq) = compute_max_value(word_1 = 1,word_2 = 3,word_3 = 6,word_4 = 5)
print(word,freq) # should return word_3 6
```

PART III

Object-Oriented Programming in Python

Lesson 14: Incorporating Object-Oriented Programming

Lesson 15: Including Inheritance

Lesson 16: Pulling It All Together: Building a Burger Shop

Lesson 14

Incorporating Object-Oriented Programming

This lesson looks at tools that help us use Python as an object-oriented language, which allows us to create classes, objects, and methods that we can reuse in other parts of our code.

LEARNING OBJECTIVES

By the end of this lesson, you will be able to:

- Explain classes in object-oriented programming.
- Create a class that includes at least three attributes appropriate for that class.
- Use a class to create two or more separate objects.
- Define and use a constructor in a class.
- Create one or more methods that describe a behavior associated with a class and implement those methods in a program.
- Include static and class methods in your classes.

OBJECT-ORIENTED PROGRAMMING OVERVIEW

Object-oriented programming (OOP) is a programming paradigm based on objects. OOP solves problems by carrying out all computations on objects. We use *objects* in code to represent real-world concepts that our code will interact with, such as employee IDs or employee types. Objects allow us to streamline development by reducing redundant code.

There are four principles that define and differentiate object-oriented programming. These principles are *encapsulation*, *abstraction*, *polymorphism*, and *inheritance*. We will discuss inheritance in detail in the next lesson.

The basic object in this approach is the *class*, which represents primary things or concepts we want to reuse in the overall solution. We create one class per object and include properties (or *attributes*) of the class to define what it can do and how we can use it in our code. As you progress through this lesson, the following are a few key terms to be aware of:

- **Classes** are a type of object with a state and behavior. (Example: the vehicle class)

- **Objects** is an instance of a class. (Examples: Honda Accord, Toyota Camry, midsize vehicle, luxury vehicle)

- **Attributes** define a property of an object. (Example: vehicles have four wheels)

- **Encapsulation** is the formation of a digital barrier around a class that keeps the information hidden from the rest of the code in the program.

- **Abstraction** is an extension of encapsulation; abstraction keeps object-oriented programming simple in that certain properties and methods from the outside code are hidden.

- **Polymorphism** is the ability of an object within the object-oriented programming paradigm to take on many forms.

- **Instantiation** is the process of allocating memory for an object after its constructor has been run.

- **Constructors** are a unique method that Python calls for instantiations (creations) of object definitions found within a class.

DEFINING CLASSES

When using an object-oriented approach to software development, classes represent or describe real-world entities. To define a class, we use the keyword `class` followed by the name of the class. Within the class, we define its attributes, which describe its state. The following shows the basic syntax for creating a class in Python named `VehicleClass`:

```
class VehicleClass:
    pass
```

> **NOTE** In general, you shouldn't add the word "class" to the names of your classes. We've done it here simply to make it clear what is happening in the example. In a script we'd name the class `Vehicle`. Additionally, in this snippet of code the word pass is being included as a placeholder for future code that will go into the class. Python will recognize the word pass and allow the class to function until you add the actual code.

We also use specific naming conventions (sometimes referred to as style guides) to make the code easier to read, especially when multiple developers are working on the same project. For now, our class called `VehicleClass` is empty.

We use PascalCasing for class names that we create, wherein each word in the class name is capitalized (including the first word). For example: `ClassName`, `Person`, `Product`. We use lowercase characters for attributes, with underscores to separate words as necessary. For example: `first_name`, `last_name`.

> **NOTE** Because Python can be a little inconsistent with naming guidelines, always refer to the official style guide found at `https://www.python.org/dev/peps/pep-0008/#naming-conventions`.

A class is a definition, like the blueprint of a house. A blueprint is a detailed model of a building. It may show you how to build your house, but you can't live in a blueprint. Instead, you must build the house, following the plan in the blueprint before you can move in. Similarly, in some cases, you must instantiate an object, based on the definition contained in the class before you can use it.

Another way to approach this is to think of a class as an idea and an object as the instantiation of that idea. For example, a class is like the idea of a German shepherd, whereas an object is my German shepherd named Buster.

There are several parts to a class. Two core parts are attributes and methods.

Attributes

As mentioned, classes represent real-world entities such as a vehicle or person. Attributes within a class define the properties of that class. For instance, a vehicle class might have attributes such as make, model, color, and VIN. These properties define what's unique about each vehicle. There are two types of attributes that Python supports that we will cover in this lesson: instance attributes and class attributes.

Methods

Another important aspect of classes is methods. Methods are functions within classes that allow us to perform a certain behavior or task. Python offers three types of methods within a class:

- Instance methods
- Static methods
- Class methods

> **NOTE** More details on attributes and methods are covered throughout the rest of this lesson.

CREATING OBJECTS

We use classes as a blueprint for creating objects. For example, we know in the real world what represents a car (a vehicle with four wheels, doors, engine, and so on). If we wanted to create a certain type of car, we would use the basic prototype of a car (the class) along with the attributes associated with that class (four wheels, doors, engines) and create various instances or copies of that class (a midsize car, a truck, an SUV). In making these copies, we call the class to instantiate objects, which represent concrete realizations of the class.

Once we have defined a class, we can use it to create instances of the class (called objects). We do this by setting the name of our instance variable equal to the name of the class followed by parentheses. For example, if we have a class for a person called Person, we can create an instance called p of that class with the following snippet:

```
p = Person()
```

> **NOTE** Attributes of an object are represented as instance variables. Each object comes with its individual set of instance variables. We use these variables as storage for the object's state.

Of course, the class will need to exist. Let's dive deeper into some code to understand all of these concepts in action. Consider the following class:

```
class Person:
    # init method or constructor
    def __init__(self, name):
        self.name = name #name is an instance attribute.
```

In this code, a class called Person is created by using the keyword class. Within the class Person, we created a method called __init__ using the keyword def. The __init__ method takes as input two variables, self and name. As mentioned previously, a method is a function within a class that performs a certain task.

Let's first look at the __init__ method and understand what it does. Most classes include a specific method __init__. This is a special method that is called when an object is created from a class. It allows the class to define and *initialize* the instance attributes of the class. This method is often called a constructor in other programming languages.

A *constructor* is a special method within a class called while creating an instance of an object using definitions found within the class. Constructors initialize instance variables that objects rely upon to work. The __init__ method is called when we instantiate a class to define and initialize instance variables. In the preceding code, the __init__ method is used to instantiate the Person object.

> **NOTE** Instance variables represent the data attributes found within the __init__ method.

Second, let's look at the self keyword that we include in the parameters of the __init__ method. The keyword self is a reference to the current Person object and can be used to define and access the instance attributes within the class. In the Person class defined earlier we only define a single instance attribute called name, which we use to access the self variable:

```
self.name = name #name is an instance attribute
```

In this case, we take the value passed when creating the class and apply it to the name attribute of the class.

The Person class we created is very simple. It only contained one single instance attribute called name and an __init__ method used to create objects. Even though it is simple, we can use the Person class to create an object as shown in Listing 14.1.

LISTING 14.1

Creating a Person object

```
class Person:
    # init method or constructor
    def __init__(self, name):
        self.name = name #name is an instance attribute.

p = Person("Karl Johnson")
print(p.name)
```

When this script is executed, the output is the name that was passed to the Person class when it was created. In this case:

```
Karl Johnson
```

In the code, we included the Person class that was presented before along with two additional instructions. The first instruction is

```
p = Person("Karl Johnson")
```

This instruction simply creates an object called p derived from the class Person. When this line of code is executed, the value of "Karl Johnson" is passed. This value is passed to the __init__ method, which is executed to construct our Person object.

In the second instruction, we simply print the value of the name attribute of the object:

```
print(p.name)
```

In general, we can access attributes and methods of an object by calling the object followed by a period, then the name of the attribute or method:

```
object_name.attribute_name
```

In Listing 14.1, the Person class has one attribute called name. We can use multiple attributes within a class, as shown in the newer version of the Person class in Listing 14.2.

LISTING 14.2

Person class with multiple attributes

```
class Person:

    def __init__(self, fname, lname):
        self.first_name = fname
        self.last_name = lname

person_1 = Person("Lewis", "Montes")
print(person_1.first_name)
print(person_1.last_name)

person_2 = Person("Robin", "Durham")
print(person_2.first_name)
print(person_2.last_name)
```

In this listing, we simply changed the Person class to include two instance attributes. Instead of name, we now have first_name and last_name. As can be seen, we also changed the __init__ method to accept two inputs, fname and lname, which will be assigned to first_name and last_name, respectively, during the object creation (i.e., during the execution of the __init__ method).

You can also see that when we created the Person objects, person_1 and person_2, we included the first name and last name as parameters. Creating person_1, we passed "Lewis" and "Montes":

```
person_1 = Person("Lewis", "Montes")
```

In this case, if we did not include the parameters, the object attributes couldn't be created, so we'd get an error. Later in this lesson, you'll see how to initialize objects even if the parameters aren't provided.

Finally, in the listing you see that we can access the attributes of the objects using the dot operator:

```
print(person_1.first_name)
```

When the listing is executed, the print functions display the names that are contained in our Person objects:

```
Lewis
Montes
Robin
Durham
```

WORKING WITH METHODS

Python classes allow data and functionality to be bundled together. When we create new classes, we create a new type of object. This allows new instances of that type. Each class instance has attributes attached to it for maintaining the class state; however, class instances can also have methods for modifying its state. This is defined by its class.

A *method* is a function defined within a class. While attributes normally refer to properties associated with the class (like a person's name or the number of legs an animal has), methods normally describe what the class can do. A class can have any number of methods.

Methods that allow users to simply observe but not change the state of an object are called *accessor methods*. Methods that allow for the modification of an object are called *mutators*.

In Listing 14.3, we create a method named display_info that is designed to display the attributes associated with the Person class—in this case, their first and last name—with a user-friendly statement. Using this method, we will be able to display a person's name.

LISTING 14.3

Adding a method to our Person class

```
class Person:
    def __init__(self, fname, lname):
        self.first_name = fname
        self.last_name = lname
    def display_info(self):
        print("Person First Name: " + self.first_name)
        print("Person Last Name: " + self.last_name)

person_1 = Person("Lewis","Montes")
person_1.display_info()

person_2 = Person("Robin","Durham")
person_2.display_info()
```

Much of this listing is similar to the previous listing. What is unique is that we have now defined a method called `display_info` in the `Person` class. This definition is like what we've done for functions. The difference is that we included the method within the class. Note that the code for the method is indented to show that it is within our class.

The method within our class can access the attribute variables through the use of `self`. We do not need to pass `self` to our method because Python automatically does this for us. In short, `self` is a reference to the object that is being created and can be used by the method to access the attributes within the class. When accessing the attributes, we can use `self` followed by the dot operator and then the class attribute we want. You can see that first name is accessed in our class method using `self.first_name`.

You can see that we access our newly defined method after declaring objects and assigning values to their attributes. We call the class method the same way we call an attribute. We use the object instance name, the dot operator, and then the name of the method. You see that for `person_1` this is:

```
person_1.display_info()
```

This runs the method accessing the `person_1` attributes. Later in the listing, the same is done for `person_2`. The resulting output is:

```
Person First Name: Lewis
Person Last Name: Montes
Person First Name: Robin
Person Last Name: Durham
```

> **NOTE** We mentioned the use of `self` to access the attributes within the current object. This parameter can actually be called anything you want; however, `self` is what is considered standard and thus what is recommended to be used in your programs.

In our ERP banking application, we may be interested in accessing specific information about our customers or employees and performing some tasks related to that data. Perhaps we want to find out the employee's or customer's joining date, our customer's transaction history, or the average amount of their most recent transactions—or even output a complete listing of all their information. We can use methods associated with `Employee` and `Customer` class objects to achieve this in Python.

Another example of the use of methods is in Listing 14.4. In the listing, we create the `BankCustomer` and `BankAccount` classes. These classes contain basic attributes along with a method for displaying the attributes.

LISTING 14.4

Using methods in our banking app

```
class BankCustomer:
    def __init__(self,c_id,fname,lname):
        self.first_Name=fname
        self.customer_ID=c_id
        self.last_Name=lname

    def display_info(self):
      print("Customer's first name is " + self.first_Name)
      print("Customer's last name is " +    self.last_Name)
      print("Customer's ID is " + str(self.customer_ID))

class BankAccount:
    def __init__(self,a_id,name,type):
        self.account_ID = a_id
        self.account_Name=name
        self.account_Type= type
    def display_info(self):
      print("The account name is " + self.account_Name)
      print("The account type is " +    self.account_Type)
      print("Account ID is " + str(self.account_ID))

# Set up customer1
customer1 = BankCustomer(100004,"Layla","Brennan")
```

```
# Set up customer2
customer2 = BankCustomer(100005,"Moises","Cardenas")

# Set up customer3
customer3 = BankCustomer(100006,"Maria","Pierce")

# Set up account1
account1 = BankAccount(1004,"Layla's Account","Checking")

customer1.display_info()
customer2.display_info()
customer3.display_info()
account1.display_info()
```

The code in this listing is a bit longer, but overall straightforward. Two classes are created, each with their own attributes and __init__ methods. Each class has its own display_info() method defined that uses print functions to display the class attributes to the user. You should again note the use of self that allows the method to access the attributes that are locally available within the current object.

It is also worth noting that both the BankCustomer and BankAccount class have a method with the name display_info(). These are independent methods associated to their respective classes, so the identical names are not an issue.

On the other end of our banking application, we use separate classes to represent Managers, Tellers, and Customer Service Representatives. Each of these employee types can be a class that is customized to the role, as shown in Listing 14.5. Each of these classes can also have __init__ methods and display methods to construct and present their specific information as well.

LISTING 14.5

Classes to represent employees in our banking app

```
class Manager():
    def __init__(self, n, i, t):
        self.name = n
        self.id = i
        self.team = t

    def display(self):
        print("Manager name is: " + self.name)
        print("Manager ID is: " + self.id)
```

```
        print("Manager's team is: ")
        for member in self.team:
            print(member)


class Teller():
    def __init__(self, n, i, b):
        self.name = n
        self.id = i
        self.bank_branch = b

    def display(self):
        print("Teller's employee ID is:" + self.id)
        print("Teller's name is: " + self.name)
        print("Teller's bank branch is: " + self.bank_branch)


class CustomerServRep():
    def __init__(self, n, i, c):
        self.name = n
        self.id = i
        self.call_center = c

    def display(self):
        print("Customer Service Rep's employee ID is:" + self.id)
        print("Customer Service Rep's name is: " + self.name)
        print("Customer Service Rep's call center is: " + self.call_center)


# Create managers
m1 = Manager("Julia Juarez", "A1152254", ["Robert A", "LaTerrance S"])
m2 = Manager("Whitney Solomon", "A1155626",["Lilyana J", "Angeline P"])
m1.display()
m2.display()

# Create tellers
t1 = Teller("Lamar Mercer", "A1152278", "Columbia Ave.")
t2 = Teller("Karly Robinson", "A1152278", "Constitution Dr.")
t1.display()
t2.display()

# Create Customer Service Reps
cs1 = CustomerServRep("Clayton Ryan", "A1152211", "Headquarters")
cs2 = CustomerServRep("Gage Barnett", "A1152212", "Headquarters")
cs1.display()
cs2.display()
```

This listing creates the three classes that were mentioned and then uses each to create two examples using the constructor. Each of the examples is then printed. The resulting output is:

```
Manager name is: Julia Juarez
Manager ID is: A1152254
Manager's team is:
Robert A
LaTerrance S
Manager name is: Whitney Solomon
Manager ID is: A1155626
Manager's team is:
Lilyana J
Angeline P
Teller's employee ID is:A1152278
Teller's name is: Lamar Mercer
Teller's bank branch is: Columbia Ave.
Teller's employee ID is:A1152278
Teller's name is: Karly Robinson
Teller's bank branch is: Constitution Dr.
Customer Service Rep's employee ID is:A1152211
Customer Service Rep's name is: Clayton Ryan
Customer Service Rep's call center is: Headquarters
Customer Service Rep's employee ID is:A1152212
Customer Service Rep's name is: Gage Barnett
Customer Service Rep's call center is: Headquarters
```

You might notice that each of the classes in Listing 14.5 has attributes in common. Managers, tellers, and customer service representatives are all employees of our bank, and just like all roles in our bank, each employee will have a name and an ID. In Lesson 15, we will show another OOP construct, inheritance, that can be used to better organize these similarities among our classes.

CLASS ATTRIBUTES

As mentioned before, there are two types of attributes within classes in Python: class attributes and instance attributes. So far, we have only dealt with instance attributes, but it is very important to understand class attributes and when to use one over the other.

With instance attributes, which you've seen, each object created with the class has its own copy of the attribute. You saw that these were defined within the `__init__` method.

There are times when we will want all the objects created by a class to share an attribute. These attributes are associated with the class as a whole instead of being associated with each instance. These are thus appropriately called class attributes. Class and instance attributes differ in the following ways:

- Class attributes are shared among all instances of a class.
- Instance attributes are specific to the underlying object derived from the class.
- Class attributes are defined outside of the __init__ method.
- Instance attributes are defined inside the __init__ method.

To understand the difference between both, let's consider the example in Listing 14.6 where we create a Manager class.

LISTING 14.6

A manager class with a class attribute

```
class Manager:
    level = "L1" # this is a class attribute shared among all objects

    def __init__(self,fname,lname):
        self.fname = fname # instance attribute tied to the object
        self.lname = lname # instance attribute tied to the object

p1 = Manager("Haythem","Balti")
print(p1.fname)
print(p1.level)
p2 = Manager("Kim","Weiss")
print(p2.fname)
print(p2.level)
```

The Manager class includes a class attribute named level and is assigned the value L1. That means that any object instantiated from this class will have a class attribute level, and it will have the value L1.

Next, in the __init__ method, we initialize two instance attributes for first name (fname) and last name (lname). These two variables will be specific and unique to each object.

After declaring the class, we create two objects. We then display the fname and level attributes of both objects. As can be seen in the following output, both objects share the same value for the level attributes:

```
Haythem
L1
Kim
L1
```

Using class attributes can also be useful in our ERP banking application. Listing 14.7 presents another example of using class attributes versus instance attributes that might be seen in a banking application.

LISTING 14.7

Using a class attribute in our account class

```
class CheckingAccount:
    type = "checking"
    def __init__(self,id,balance):
        self.account_id = id
        self.balance = balance


ch1 = CheckingAccount("ID13434",120000)
ch2 = CheckingAccount("ID13435",180000)

print(ch1.type)
print(ch2.type)
```

In this code we created a class CheckingAccount with instance attributes id and balance and one class attribute called type, which is assigned the value "checking." That means that all objects created from the CheckingAccount class will have the same value for type.

Working with Static Methods

You may notice that the methods we created so far within a class have had an input value of self, which refers to the underlying object executing the method. These instance methods can only execute after the class has been instantiated (after an object has been created). After we instantiate the class, we can call the instance methods.

There are times when we might want to run a class method without creating an object. What if our method doesn't require an object to run? Consider the script in Listing 14.8.

LISTING 14.8

A math method

```
class MathFormula:
    def pow(self,x,y):
        return x**y;

m = MathFormula()
print(m.pow(3,3))
```

If you run this listing, you'll see that the output of 27 is displayed. In this script, we created a `MathFormula` class that contains a method called `pow`. The method `pow` takes as input x and y and simply computes x to the power of y, or x^y.

If we look closely, the `MathFormula` does not have any attributes and the `pow` method doesn't perform any operation on an attribute of the class. In other words, this method should run directly through the class without having to instantiate an object since we aren't operating on any class attribute/method.

This can be done with the concept of static methods.

Static methods are methods within a class that can be executed through the class instead of being executed after the class is instantiated. To see why static methods are useful, let's consider the changes made to Listing 14.8 that are shown in Listing 14.9.

LISTING 14.9

A static math method

```
class MathFormula:
    @staticmethod
    def pow(x,y):
        return x**y;

print(MathFormula.pow(3,3))
```

Two things have changed in the code. First, we introduced a new instruction before the definition of the `pow` method. The instruction simply includes `@staticmethod`. This is called a decorator in Python, and it is instructing Python to consider the following method to be a static method, which is able to execute without the class being instantiated. Once a method is created as static, you cannot use it to call the instance attributes/methods of the underlying class.

The second change (which is triggered by the first change) is that we removed the self-reference in the `pow` method arguments. Now the method simply accepts as input the x and y values.

Because the method is now static, we can execute it directly through the class as was shown in the listing:

```
print(MathFormula.pow(3,3))
```

Static methods are contained in some way since they cannot access instance attributes or methods. Typically, static methods can be used within a single class to perform unrelated tasks. For instance, in Listing 14.10, we added two more static methods to our `MathFormula` class.

LISTING 14.10

A more robust math class

```
class MathFormula:
    @staticmethod
    def display(message):
        print(message)
    @staticmethod
    def pow(x,y):
        return x**y
    @staticmethod
    def isEven(x):
        if x%2==0:
            return True
        return False


MathFormula.display("hello")
MathFormula.display("world")
MathFormula.display (MathFormula.pow(3,2))
```

As can be seen, the `MathFormula` class now almost acts like a library where we can include a set of static methods that are reusable and that perform various tasks. Each method is self-contained and performs its task without being able to refer to any instance attribute or method. The output from running this listing is:

```
hello
world
9
```

Working with Class Methods

As mentioned previously, static methods cannot access instance attributes, but what if we want the static methods within a class to access class attributes? In this case, we are referring to class methods. Class methods are similar to static methods in the sense that they can also be called without instantiating the class. A class method, however, allows access to the class attributes. To understand the concept of class methods, consider the example in Listing 14.11.

LISTING 14.11

A sales class

```python
class Sales:
    @staticmethod
    def applySalesTax(amount):
        sales_tax = 0.06
        return amount*(1+sales_tax)
    @staticmethod
    def applySalesTaxMany(amounts):
        out = list()
        sales_tax = 0.06
        out = [amount*(1+sales_tax) for amount in amounts]
        return out
```

Here we created a class called `Sales` where we perform sales and tax-related activities. In the first static method (`applySalesTax`), we apply the `sales_tax` to the input amount and we return the result. In the second method, we use the same logic to apply the sales tax to a list of amounts (in this case, it could be the prices of several items within an order).

As can be seen, both methods use the `sales_tax` variable. It would be better to be able to have the sales tax as an attribute of the class so that it is not confused with an instance attribute. That means that all methods within the class can share that attribute. In order to do that, we can use the concept of *class methods*. In this case, both methods will need to be converted into class methods, as shown in Listing 14.12.

LISTING 14.12

Using a class method

```python
class Sales:
    sales_tax = 0.06
    @classmethod
    def applySalesTax(cls,amount):

        return amount*(1+cls.sales_tax)
    @classmethod
    def applySalesTaxMany(cls,amounts):
        out = list()
        sales_tax = 0.06
        out = [amount*(1+cls.sales_tax) for amount in amounts]
        return out

print(Sales.applySalesTax(20))
print(Sales.applySalesTaxMany([10,20,30]))
```

As can be seen, the `sales_tax` attribute was moved out of the methods and placed at the base level of the class so that each method can access it. Additionally, the `@classmethod` decorator was added to each of the classes to indicate they are class methods. The output of this listing should look similar to the following:

```
21.200000000000003
[10.600000000000001, 21.200000000000003, 31.8]
```

It is important to notice that similar to static methods, class methods cannot access any instance attributes (attributes defined in the `__init__` method).

SUMMARY

In this lesson, we were introduced to the object-oriented programming paradigm. We reviewed the foundations of object-oriented design and applied those concepts.

Now that you have completed Lesson 14, you should be able to:

- Explain classes in object-oriented programming.

- Create a class that includes at least three attributes appropriate for that class.

- Use a class to create two or more separate objects.

- Define and use a constructor in a class.

- Create one or more methods that describe a behavior associated with a class and implement those methods in a program.

- Include static and class methods in your classes.

EXERCISES

The following exercises are provided to allow you to demonstrate the objectives for this lesson. You should complete each exercise and make sure that the code runs without errors. The exercises include:

Exercise 1: Create Your Own Class

Exercise 2: Classy Vehicles

Exercise 3: Streamlined Banking

Exercise 4: Using a Calculator in Class

Exercise 1: Create Your Own Class

Create a class that describes something other than a person, vehicle, or animal. The class can be anything you wish as long as it meets the following criteria:

- Do not use people, vehicles, or animals.
- The category must be broad enough to include different examples of the category.
- It must represent a real-life object.

Include at least three attributes that are common to most (if not all) instances of the class. Use appropriate naming conventions.

Implement the appropriate __init__ method and display function to create and display objects, respectively.

Exercise 2: Classy Vehicles

Create a class that describes vehicles. Include the following in your class:

- Attributes for the vehicle type, year, color, and number of doors.
- A constructor.
- An instance method to your class that displays formatted information about the vehicle.
- A method called has_wheels() that returns True if the vehicle has wheels and False if it does not.

Once you've defined your class, create several objects for different vehicles including a boat with zero wheels. For each vehicle you create, call your display method as well as the has_wheels method.

Include at least three attributes that are common to most (if not all) instances of the class. Use appropriate naming conventions.

Exercise 3: Streamlined Banking

Rewrite Listing 14.5 to use constructors for the BankCustomer and BankAccount classes.

Exercise 4: Using a Calculator in Class

Practice designing and implementing a program that has more than one class. To that end, build a basic calculator that allows the user to input two values and an operator and then outputs the results. Criteria include the following:

- Design a class called `SimpleCalculator` that performs basic math operations (addition, subtraction, multiplication, division) on two operands. Create a separate method for each operation in the class.

- The program should accept two values and an operator from the user, perform the selected operation using those two values, and display the result to the user in a meaningful way.

- The user should be able to exit the program at any time, using a keyword like "Quit" or "Exit" in any letter case. If the user chooses to exit, the program should end with an appropriate output message thanking the user.

Lesson 15

Including Inheritance

As we learned in the previous lesson, object-oriented programming uses objects, classes, and methods to solve problems. Developers who work in this programming paradigm must also be familiar with polymorphism and inheritance. Inheritance allows us to inherit attributes and methods from other classes. Polymorphism uses those inherited methods to perform different tasks. This lesson focuses on inheritance.

LEARNING OBJECTIVES

By the end of this lesson, you will be able to:

- Define inherited classes that have different properties than their parent classes.
- Use overriding to replace a property in a parent class with a property in an inherited class.

Inheritance is one of the most important concepts of object-oriented programming because it allows us to derive new classes that automatically reuse and extend the code of similar but more general classes. Inheritance streamlines our coding processes and makes it easier to reuse existing code. Here are some of the key terms from this lesson:

- **Inheritance** allows the definition of classes to inherit methods and properties from other classes.
- **Parent class** or **base class** is the original class that is being inherited from. This can be any standard class.
- **Child class** or **derived class** is a class that inherits the functionality of the parent class.

UNDERSTANDING INHERITANCE

In object-oriented programming, we can create new classes based on an existing class, and the new classes *inherit* the attributes and methods we have already defined for the original class. It is imperative that we understand that we are able to differentiate the parent class from the child class.

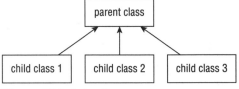

Figure 15.1: Inheritance

The *parent class* is the class being inherited from, also called a *base class*. The *child class* is the class that inherits from another class, also called a *derived class*. Figure 15.1 helps to illustrate this.

As an example, we can create a Person class that includes attributes that are appropriate for any person, such as first name and last name.

We can then create additional classes that refer to people, such as Employee, Manager, and Customer. If we create these classes independently, we have to include an attribute, such as name, within each of the classes.

Instead, as a shortcut, we can create a child class that inherits the properties of the parent class, meaning that we only have to specify additional attributes that are important for that specific class. Figure 15.2 illustrates a Person parent class that is inherited by three child classes.

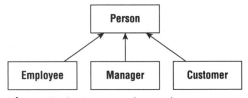

Figure 15.2: A Person base class

An employee is a person. An Employee class contains all the attributes from the Person class, and it can contain additional attributes that are unique to being an employee. We might need to know the employee's department, when they were hired, what their pay rate is, and so on, which would all be captured in the Employee class.

> **NOTE** It is worth repeating: We use the terms **base class** or **parent class** to reference the original class (in this case, the **Person** class), and the term **child class** to refer to the derived class (e.g., **Employee**).

CREATING A PARENT CLASS

Any class can be a parent class. The syntax is the same when creating a parent class as it is when creating a standard class, as we learned in the previous lesson. Listing 15.1 presents an example of creating a class for a person. Inheritance will allow us to use this class.

LISTING 15.1

Creating a base class

```
class Person:
    def __init__(self,fname,lname):
        self.first_name = fname
        self.last_name = lname
    def display(self):
        print(self.first_name + " " + self.last_name)

x = Person("Asia", "Roberson")
x.display()
```

You should already be familiar with everything in this code. A simple class called Person is created that contains two attributes (first_name and last_name), a constructor, and a method called display that prints the first and last names. The Person class is then used to instantiate an object called x that is used to execute the display method. The result is a printed name:

```
Asia Roberson
```

CREATING A CHILD CLASS

We have created a class called Person that we can use as a parent class. Now let's use it to create a child class. The child class will inherit the functionality from a parent class. This happens by sending the parent class as a parameter for the child class:

```
class childClass(ParentClass)
```

We can create a class named Employee, which will inherit the properties and methods from the Person class by passing Person to Employee in the class definition:

```
class Employee(Person):
    pass
```

This makes Employee a *child* or *derived* class of Person. Similarly, Person is the *parent* or *base* class of Employee.

> **NOTE** We use the pass statement as a placeholder for future code.

The Employee class has the same properties and methods as the Person class. When we instantiate an object using the Employee class, because it is a child of Person, we will be able to use the Person attributes and methods. This means we could execute the display method from the Person class as well as use its constructor:

```
x = Employee("Jason", "Jones")
x.display()
```

This prints the name of our first employee: Jason Jones.

Let's look at this in action using Listing 15.2 where we create the same Person class that includes first name and last name as attributes and a display method that we did in Listing 15.1.

LISTING 15.2

Creating an Employee class that inherits from Person

```
# Create Person class
class Person:        # This is a parent or base class
    def __init__(self,fname,lname):
        self.first_name = fname
        self.last_name = lname
    def display(self):
        print(self.first_name + " " + self.last_name)

# Create employee class that inherits from person class.
class Employee(Person):      # Employee is a child class
    pass

e = Employee("Haythem","Balti")
e.display()
```

The first half of this listing is the same as Listing 15.1 where a Person class is defined. Where we see new code is after the Person class is defined.

In this case, we define a new `Employee` class that automatically inherits everything we included in the `Person` class, because `Person` passed in the parentheses:

```
class Employee(person):
```

The body of the new `Employee` class only contains `pass`, which is a placeholder for future code that causes nothing to happen. As a result, there is nothing in our `Employee` class other than what it inherits from `Person`.

Since `Employee` inherits the methods of our `Person` class, we can use the `__init__` method to create `Employee` objects. This means we can pass a first and last name and they will be used with the call to `__init__` that was defined. Additionally, because `Employee` inherits the methods of the `Person` class, we can also reuse the `display` method to display the content of the `Employee` object. The result is that our `Employee` was initialized with the name passed into it, and the result is displayed:

```
Haythem Balti
```

Let's consider our ERP banking application. Assume we will need to manage internal employee data as well as external customer data, and also assume these different groups of data share certain similarities. For instance, any employee or customer data that we create will have a first name, last name, and address. Different employees within our company also share similar types of attributes, such as employee ID, department, and salary. To link such common data across different objects and make our ERP application more manageable as well as more extensible, we can use class inheritance. This reduces the amount of code and time required to create an effective solution. Listing 15.3 helps to illustrate using inheritance in a snippet of a banking application.

LISTING 15.3

Using inheritance with tellers who are employees

```
class Employee:
  def __init__(self,name_in,loc):
    self.name = name_in
    self.location = loc
  def display(self):
    print("Employee name: " + self.name)
    print("Employee location: " + self.location)

class Teller(Employee):
  pass

t1 = Teller("Regina Hayden","Baltimore")
t2 = Teller("Sonny Gutierrez","Philadelphia")
t1.display()
t2.display()
```

In this code, we create an Employee class that includes two string attributes: name and location. We implement appropriate __init__ and display methods to create and display objects, respectively.

We then use inheritance to create another class called Teller that inherits from the Employee class. To illustrate the Teller class, two Teller objects are created and used to display each object's information using the display method that was inherited from Employee. The output is:

```
Employee name: Regina Hayden
Employee location: Baltimore
Employee name: Sonny Gutierrez
Employee location: Philadelphia
```

INHERITING AT MULTIPLE LEVELS

In a previous example, we used Person as a generic class for any person, and then we created Employee as a person who is employed. A manager or director is both a person and an employee, so as shown in Listing 15.4, we can use inheritance to use Employee as a parent class, and we can create a Director class that is a child class of the parent class Employee, as illustrated in Figure 15.3. The Director class inherits the attributes and methods of both the Employee and Person classes. A Director is an Employee and a Person.

Figure 15.3: Multi-level inheritance

LISTING 15.4

Multiple levels of inheritance

```
class Person:
    def __init__(self,fname,lname):
        self.first_name = fname
        self.last_name = lname
    def display(self):
        print("First Name: " + self.first_name)
        print("Last Name: " + self.last_name)

class Employee(Person):
    def __init__(self,emp_id,fname,lname):
        Person.__init__(self,fname,lname)
        self.employee_id =emp_id
```

```
class Director(Employee):
    def __init__(self,emp_id,fname,lname,d_level):
        Employee.__init__(self,emp_id,fname,lname)
        self.director_level = d_level

d1 = Director("E24523525","Haythem","Balti","D-LEVEL-1")
d1.display()
print("Employee ID: " + d1.employee_id)
print("Director Level: " + str(d1.director_level))

print("----")

d2 = Director("E425345324534","Haythem","Balti","D-LEVEL-5")
d2.display()
print("Employee ID: " + d2.employee_id)
print("Director Level: " + str(d2.director_level))
```

This listing creates a Person base class similar to what was in previous listings. It contains a first and last name attribute as well as the __init__ method and a display method. It should look familiar.

The Employee class is defined to inherit from Person. This time we've added an additional attribute called employee_id to the class. When Employee objects are created, they will have all the attributes of the Person class as well as the added employee_id attribute.

We also defined an __init__ method as a constructor for the Employee class. This constructor receives the employee ID as well as the first and last name of the person. The net line of the __init__ method calls the constructor (__init__ method) of the base class, Employee, and passes along the first and last name (fname and lname). This executes the code in the Employee __init__ method. The level (d_level) is then assigned to the attribute as well.

The Director class operates in nearly the same way, except it uses the Employee class as its parent class. The Director class adds yet another attribute, director level (d_level) that can be used.

The Director class also has a constructor defined that takes the values needed to initialize all our class attributes. This time it calls the Employee __init__ method and then sets the value of the director level. Note that the Director __init__ method calls the Employee __init__ method. The Employee __init__ method then in turn calls the Person __init__ method.

With the classes defined, the listing then creates and displays two `Director` objects called d1 and d2. The values placed in these objects are then displayed to the screen:

```
Person First Name: Haythem
Person Last Name: Balti
Employee ID: E24523525
Director Level: D-LEVEL-1
----
Person First Name: Haythem
Person Last Name: Balti
Employee ID: E425345324534
Director Level: D-LEVEL-5
```

> **NOTE** In Listing 15.4, we are calling the `Person` `display` method. When displaying information about an employee or manager, we likely would want to include additional information. We'll learn how to do this in the next section.

OVERRIDING METHODS

We can redefine methods inherited from the parent class in the child class. This process is called *overriding* because a method added to the child class will override a method with the same name in the parent class. We've actually already used this in Listing 15.4 where we overrode the `__init__` methods. We can overload other methods as well.

When we add the `__init__` method to the child class, the child class will no longer inherit the parent's `__init__` method. We say that the child's `__init__` method *overrides* the inheritance of the parent's `__init__` method.

In Listing 15.5, we again create a `Person` class and an `Employee` class. However, we redefine the `display` method for the employee to provide more detailed output.

LISTING 15.5

Overriding the display method

```python
class Person:
    def __init__(self, fname, lname):
        self.first_name = fname
        self.last_name = lname
    def display(self):
        print("Person First Name: " + self.first_name)
        print("Person Last Name: " + self.last_name)
```

```
class Employee(Person):
    def display(self):
        print("Employee ID: " + self.employee_id)
        print("Employee First Name: " + self.first_name)
        print("Employee Last Name: " + self.last_name)

ourEmployee = Employee("Haythem","Balti")
ourEmployee.employee_id = "E15454513"

ourEmployee.display()
```

This listing defines a Person class similar to what was in earlier listings. The new code is within the Employee class. Within Employee, we now have a display method that prints information relevant to an employee instead of using what was in Person. When this listing is executed, we see that the output from calling the display method on an Employee object (ourEmployee) is:

```
Employee ID: E15454513
Employee First Name: Haythem
Employee Last Name: Balti
```

In our ERP application, we may want to provide certain access and modification privileges to a selected group of employees. This could be the higher administration in our company or senior managers in a specific department. We can achieve this in Python by overriding or redefining the specific methods that control access rights from our general employee class.

We might also want to present information differently depending on the various roles that employees serve within our bank. In Listing 15.6, we expand our banking application's classes to include employees, managers, tellers, and customer service representatives. We then create objects from these classes and show how each can display relevant information.

LISTING 15.6

Classes with overriding in our banking application

```
class Employee:
    def __init__(self,n,i):
        self.name=n
        self.id=i
    def display(self):
        print("Employee name is: " + self.name)
        print("Employee ID is: " + self.id)
```

```
class Manager(Employee):
  def __init__(self,t,n,i):
    Employee.__init__(self,n,i)
    self.team=t
    self.id=i
  def display(self):
    print("Manager's employee ID is: " + self.id)
    print("Manager's name is: " + self.name)
    print("Manager's team is: " + self.team)

m1=Manager("Robert A, LaTerrance S","Julia Juarez","A1152254")
m2=Manager("Lilyana J, Angeline P","Whitney Solomon","A1155626")
m1.display()
m2.display()

class Teller(Employee):
  def __init__(self,b,n,i):
    Employee.__init__(self,n,i)
    self.bank_branch=b
  def display(self):
    print("Teller's employee ID is: " + self.id)
    print("Teller's name is: " + self.name)
    print("Teller's bank branch is: " + self.bank_branch)

t1=Teller("Columbia Ave.","Lamar Mercer","A1152278")
t2=Teller("Constitution Dr.","Karly Robinson","A1152278")
t1.display()
t2.display()

class CustomerServRep(Employee):
  def __init__(self,c,n,i):
    Employee.__init__(self,n,i)
    self.call_center=c
  def display(self):
    print("Customer Service Rep's employee ID is: " + self.id)
    print("Customer Service Rep's name is: " + self.name)
    print("Customer Service Rep's call center is: " + self.call_center)

cs1=CustomerServRep("Headquarters","Clayton Ryan","A1152211")
cs2=CustomerServRep("Headquarters","Gage Barnett","A1152212")
cs1.display()
cs2.display()
```

While this listing is longer than those we've been working with, there is nothing new being presented. Rather, we are simply defining classes and then using them to create objects and display information.

We start with our base Employee class that includes two string attributes: name and id, and we also implement the appropriate __init__ and display methods to create and display objects.

We then use inheritance to create another class called Manager that inherits from the Employee class. This contains an additional attribute specific to the Manager class named team. We include a constructor as well as display method that overrides the Employee display method. Our new method includes displaying the newly added team attribute of the Manager class.

We also create two other classes that also inherit from the Employee class: one class called Teller and another class called CustomerServRep. The Teller class includes an attribute that is specific to the Teller class named bank_branch. The CustomerServRep contains an attribute named call_center. Both override the __init__ and display methods once again.

When the listing is run, each of the derived classes is used to create two objects. The display method is called on each. From the output, we can see that each class called its own display method to present the appropriate information:

```
Manager's employee ID is: A1152254
Manager's name is: Julia Juarez
Manager's team is: Robert A, LaTerrance S
Manager's employee ID is: A1155626
Manager's name is: Whitney Solomon
Manager's team is: Lilyana J, Angeline P
Teller's employee ID is: A1152278
Teller's name is: Lamar Mercer
Teller's bank branch is: Columbia Ave.
Teller's employee ID is: A1152278
Teller's name is: Karly Robinson
Teller's bank branch is: Constitution Dr.
Customer Service Rep's employee ID is: A1152211
Customer Service Rep's name is: Clayton Ryan
Customer Service Rep's call center is: Headquarters
Customer Service Rep's employee ID is: A1152212
Customer Service Rep's name is: Gage Barnett
Customer Service Rep's call center is: Headquarters .
```

SUMMARY

This lesson continued the introduction of the object-oriented programming paradigm in Python. We have now seen the fundamental concepts of the paradigm, which are polymorphism, abstraction, encapsulation, and inheritance. In this lesson we explored the concept of inheritance, offering you hands-on experience in the definition of new classes that use this property.

Now that you have completed Lesson 15, you should be able to:

- Define inherited classes that have different properties than their parent classes.
- Use overriding to replace the property in a parent class with a property in an inherited class.

EXERCISES

Object-oriented programming and inheritance are powerful constructs for you to use in your Python programs. The following exercises will help reinforce what you learned in this lesson. The exercises include:

Exercise 1: Basic Inheritance

Exercise 2: Adding Attributes

Exercise 3: Creating More Children

Exercise 4: Dogs and Cats

Exercise 5: Hourly Employees

Exercise 6: File System

Exercise 1: Basic Inheritance

Create a base class that is based on a noun topic. This "*Noun*" class could be something such as animal or vehicle. Don't use a noun based on the examples used within this lesson, such as person or employee. Create your base class with an at least one attribute and include a constructor and `display` method.

Use inheritance to create a class that will inherit from the *Noun* class. Create two objects using the new class and display each object's information using the `display` method.

As an example, we could start with an `Animal` class, create a `Mammal` class that inherits from `Animal`, and then create two `Mammal` objects. You will need to identify an appropriate class based on your own *Noun* class as well as appropriate objects that represent the inherited class.

Exercise 2: Adding Attributes

Add at least two attributes to the new class you created in the previous activity. These attributes should be different from the attributes in the original *Noun* class and specific to the new class.

As an example, an `Animal` class might include the attributes of name and place. The `Mammal` class that inherits from the `Animal` class could include mammal-specific attributes, such as gender and fur length.

Override the `__init__` and `display` methods to display the new attributes, and then create at least two new objects based on the inherited class and display them with the class attributes.

Exercise 3: Creating More Children

Create a second and a third class that inherit from the *Noun* class you started with.

- Include at least three class-specific attributes for each class.
- For each of the new classes, override the `__init__` and `display` methods to display the new attributes.
- Create at least two new objects based on the inherited class and display them with the class attributes.

Exercise 4: Dogs and Cats

Create a class that inherits from your initial inherited class from the previous exercises. Include at least one attribute specific to this class. Create two objects based on this class and display all attributes for each object.

As an example, if we started with an `Animal` class and then created a `Mammal` class that inherits from `Animal`, we could have also created additional classes that inherit from `Mammal`, such as `Dog` and `Cat`, which would have their own class-specific attributes.

Exercise 5: Hourly Employees

Change the code in Listing 15.7 as follows:

- Add an attribute to the `Director` class called `team`. The team represents the employees that the director manages. The `team` attribute should be a list of `Employee` objects.
  - Implement the `add_employee` method, which takes as input an `Employee` object and adds it to the `team` attribute.
  - Implement the `display` method of the `Director` class to display the information about the director and the list of the employees that the director manages.
- Create another class called `HourlyEmployee` that inherits from `Employee`.
  - Add one attribute to the `HourlyEmployee` class called `hourly_rate`, which represents the hourly pay rate for the hourly employee.
  - Implement the `__init__` method and `display` methods for the `HourlyEmployee` class.

After you make these changes, verify that the code works by making sure it can display the attributes of `Director` using the `display` method.

LISTING 15.7

Exercise 5

```python
class Person:
    def __init__(self,fname,lname):
        self.first_name = fname
        self.last_name = lname
    def display(self):
        print("Person First Name: " + self.first_name)
        print("Person Last Name: " + self.last_name)

class Employee(Person):
    def __init__(self,emp_id,fname,lname):
        Person.__init__(self,fname,lname)
        self.employee_id =emp_id
    def display(self):
        print("Employee ID: " + self.employee_id)
        print("Employee First Name: " + self.first_name)
        print("Employee Last Name: " + self.last_name)

class Director(Employee):
    def __init__(self,emp_id,fname,lname,d_level):
        # do not change this code
        Employee.__init__(self,emp_id,fname,lname)
        self.director_level = d_level
        self.team = list()
    def display(self):
        # a method that displays all the attributes of a director object
        pass
    def add_employee(self,emp):
        # a method to add an employee object to the team attribute
        pass

class HourlyEmployee(Employee):
    # implement this  class
    pass


# DO NOT CHANGE THIS CODE
d1 = Director("E24523525","Haythem","Balti","D-LEVEL-1")
```

```
# create first employee object
e1 = Employee("E4746456456","Mark","Smith")
# add employee e1 to the team attribute of the Director class
d1.add_employee(e1)
# create second hourlyemployee object
e2 = HourlyEmployee("E47464578978","Mary","Lang")
# add hourly employee e2 to the team attribute of the Director class
d1.add_employee(e2)

d1.display()
```

Exercise 6: File System

This exercise is provided as a self-assessment, allowing you to check your knowledge and readiness for the next lesson. This assessment combines concepts presented in the module in a single program without the guidance provided in the lesson activities.

Use Python to model a computer's file system.

1. Create a class called FileItem that represents any file in an operating system.

   • Research and identify attributes that are common to all files in an OS, such as permissions, owner, size, and so on.

2. Create a class called CSVFile that inherits from FileItem and that represents a CSV file in an operating system.

   • Include attributes that are specific to a CSV file.

3. Create a class JPGFile that inherits from FileItem and that represents a JPG file in an operating system.

   • Include attributes that are specific to a JPG file.

4. Create a class MP3File that inherits from FileItem and that represents an MP3 file in an operating system.

   • Include attributes that are specific to an MP3 file.

Pulling It All Together: Building a Burger Shop

In this lesson, we will build an application to pull together many of the concepts we've learned up to this point related to object-oriented programming using Python. Specifically, we'll focus on building an application that accepts a customer's order at a burger shop.

LEARNING OBJECTIVES

By the end of this lesson, you will be able to:

- Design classes for the burger application using object-oriented concepts.
- Create objects using the classes you've created.
- Use your objects within a Python application.
- Display output that includes data from your class objects.

REQUIREMENTS FOR OUR APPLICATION

Our burger shop application allows customers to place custom orders for hamburgers and other items. Within the ordering process, we will want the customer to be able to specify what kind of food or drink they want, then we'll need to calculate the cost of the order and display the completed order to the user. More specifically, the completed application must be able to perform the following steps:

- Ask the customer if they want a burger, a side, a drink, or a combo.
  - A combo must include a burger, a side, and a drink.
- Prompt them for details about their selection, such as condiments for a burger, what kind and size of drink, and so on.
- Create the item based on their selections.
- Add the item to the order.
- Repeat these steps until the customer doesn't want to order anything else.
- Display the order details including the price.
- Thank the customer for their business.
- Give the customer the option to cancel their order at any point in the ordering process.

PLAN THE CODE

As a first step in any development process, we start by planning what needs to be coded in our application. This step of planning can include flowcharts or other diagrams to help visualize how the program will be structured and what it will do. We'll start with the big picture here and then focus on smaller parts of the program as we work through the steps.

The main program itself must include the following steps:

1. Greet the customer and ask their name.
2. Ask the customer what they want to order (one item at a time!).
3. Ask the customer for customizations, such as burger toppings or drink size.
4. Add each item to the order as it is requested.
5. Ask the customer to continue or complete their order after each item.
6. When the customer completes the order, the program will display the order and the total price for the order.

The customer should be able to order any combination of the following items:

- Burger

- Drink
- Side

We also want to allow them to order a combo that includes a burger, a drink, and a side at a discount.

> **NOTE** You'll notice that the planning and design of our application includes a lot of information that seems redundant with the requirements that were mentioned. This should make sense because the objectives of the application are to meet the requirements. If your planning includes items that were not a part of the requirements, then you should consider whether they should be included, or whether they are beyond the scope of your current application.

CREATE THE CLASSES

Looking at this from an object-oriented programming approach, we can identify multiple objects in this scenario. These include:

- The order itself
- The items the customer can order, which we know to be:
  - Burger
  - Drink
  - Side
  - Combo

We can define the order itself as a class. We can also define each of the items that can be ordered as a class. We can then use these classes in the main program to streamline the code.

We can start with the classes themselves, including the classes we've already identified:

- order
- burger
- drink
- side
- combo

To keep our code organized, we'll create a separate class file that will hold all of our classes. Later we'll create the code file that references the classes. Let's start by creating a new file named menu.py. This file should be created in the same folder where you plan to create the rest of your burger application.

> **NOTE** In most Python editors, you can simply name the file using the .py extension. If you are using Jupyter Notebook, create a new text file (which will have the extension .txt) and rename it to have the extension .py.

CREATE THE FOOD ITEM CLASS

All the items on our burger shop menu have two properties in common: the name of the item and a price. This means that we can create a parent class that references those properties first, and then create child classes for the individual menu items and their specific properties.

Add a new food_item class to the menu.py file as shown in Listing 16.1.

LISTING 16.1

The food_item class

```
class food_item:
    def __init__(self,name,price):
        self.name = name
        self.price = price
    def __str__(self):
        return "Item: " + self.name + "\n" + "Price: $" + str(self.price) + "\n"
    def get_price(self):
        return self.price
```

The food_item class includes three methods:

- The __init__ method, which initializes the values of our food item.
- The __str__ method, which creates the string representation of an object derived from the food_item class. In our case, we want to simply return the following representation:

```
Item: Item Name
Price: Item Price
```

- The get_price method, which simply returns the price of the food item.

> **NOTE** Because our file contains only a class file, it cannot run independently. We will use this class in the main code, which we will create later in this lesson to run the program.

Create a Burger Class

We can reuse the `food_item` class to derive the `burger` class using inheritance. In our case, we will also track the condiments of the burger. To do that, we will add another attribute to the burger (besides `name` and `price` inherited from `food_item`), which we will call `condiments`. This attribute will track the list of condiments we want in the burger.

For our case, we can use a simple list to store the condiments. The `burger` class is presented in Listing 16.2. You can add this into your `menu.py` file that already contains the `food_item` class.

LISTING 16.2

The burger class

```
class burger(food_item):
    def __init__(self,name,price):
        super(burger, self).__init__(name,price)
        self.condiments = []
    def add_condiment(self,condiment):
        if condiment not in self.condiments:
            self.condiments.append(condiment)
    def __str__(self):
        s = super(burger, self).__str__()
        s = s + "Condiments:" + ", ".join(self.condiments)
        return s
```

The `__init__` method in our `burger` class calls the `super()` method to initialize the name and price from the parent class of `food_item`. It then simply initializes the `condiments` list to empty.

Additionally, within the `burger` class, a method `add_condiment` is included, which simply adds a `condiment` to the `condiments` list. Note that the `add_condiment` method checks first to determine if the provided condiment exists in the list of condiments, and if it doesn't, it will add it to the list.

Finally, we override the `__str__` method to generate the string representation of a burger object. In our case, we will first want to display the name and price, which we can do by calling the `__init__` method of the parent class, `food_item`. We do this by using super function. Finally, we concatenate the string generated by the parent class and the list of the condiments in the burger class and return the string. When this method is executed, a burger object will have the following string representation:

```
Item: Item Name
Price: Item Price
Condiments: [Condiment1,Condiment2]
```

Create a Drink Class

Drinks will have sizes associated with them, in addition to the name and price. As with the burger class, in Listing 16.3 we'll create this as a subclass of food_item and customize it to include sizes. This listing should also be added into your menu.py file.

LISTING 16.3

The drink class

```
class drink(food_item):
    def __init__(self,name,size,price):
        super(drink, self).__init__(name,price)
        self.size= size
    def __str__(self):
        s = super(drink, self).__str__()
        s = s + "Size: " + str(self.size) + "oz"
        return s
```

Similar to the burger class, we have overridden the __init__ method and the __str__ method. This time, we added the size attribute to the drink class. Note that the addition of the size attribute in the drink class must also be updated in the __str__ class. With this update, a drink object will have the following string representation:

```
Item: Item Name
Price: Item Price
Size: "Size in oz"
```

Create a Side Class

All the sides on our menu have the same price, so we can create a subclass based on food_item without adding anything extra. Listing 16.4 presents the class to hold our side objects. As with the previous classes, add this into your menu.py file.

LISTING 16.4

The side class

```
class side(food_item):
    def __init__(self,name,price):
        super(side, self).__init__(name, price)
```

Create a Combo

A combo is much more complicated than the other food items. While it does include both a name and a price, a combo includes multiple items as well as a discounted price based on the price of the individual items. Listing 16.5 presents a combo class, which again, should be added to your menu.py file.

LISTING 16.5

The combo class

```
class combo(food_item):
    def __init__(self,name,b,d,s,discount):
        self.name = name
        self.burger = b
        self.drink = d
        self.side = s
        self.discount = discount
        self.price = self.burger.get_price() + self.drink.get_price() +
self.side.get_price() - self.discount
    def __str__(self):
        s = ""
        s = s + "Combo: " + self.name + "\n"
        s = s + str(self.burger) + "\n" + str(self.drink)+ "\n" + str(self.side)+ "\n"
        s = s + "Combo Price Before Discount: $" +
str(self.burger.get_price()+self.drink.get_price()+self.side.get_price())+ "\n"

        s = s + "Discount: $" + str(self.discount)+ "\n"
        s = s + "Combo Price After Discount: $" + str(self.price)+ "\n"

        return s
```

Here, we include a burger, a drink, and a side, add together the separate prices of each item, and apply a discount. The result is the list of items in the combo and the final price of the combo.

Create the Order Class

The last class we need to create is the order itself. Create the `order` class shown in Listing 16.6 in the new file. We have named this file `order.py`.

LISTING 16.6

The order class

```
class order:
    def __init__(self,name):
        self.name = name
        self.items = []
    def add_item(self,item):
        self.items.append(item)
    def get_price(self):
        price = 0.0
        for item in self.items:
            price = price + item.get_price()
        return price
    def __str__(self):
        s = [str(item) for item in self.items]
        return "\n".join(s)
    def display(self):
        print("==========================================")
        print("Here is a summary of your order")
        print("Order for " + self.name)
        print("Here is a list of items in the order")

        for item in self.items:
            print("------------")
            print(str(item))
        print("------------")
        print("Total Order Amount :$" + str(self.get_price()))
        print("==========================================")
```

This class sets up a new order with the following properties:

- It includes a `name` property that identifies (or names) the order.

- It creates a new empty list named `items` that will hold the items in the order.

- It gets the price for each item and adds that price to the total price for the order.

- It joins the individual items in the `item` list into a new string that it can display to the customer.
- We also define a series of output statements to the customer, including their name, a complete list of the items ordered, and the total price.

CREATE THE MAIN FILE

We now have classes for all the items we need for our burger shop. Next, we can create the main file that will use the classes we just created to prompt the customer for the items they want to order and add up the title.

Create a new file named `main.py` in the same folder as the `menu.py` file we just created. We'll start with the code that greets the customer and sets up the order as shown in Listing 16.7.

> **NOTE** If you are using Jupyter Notebook, you can create and use a `main.ipynb` file that will run from Jupyter Notebook, as long as it is in the same folder as `menu.py`.

LISTING 16.7

Creating an order

```python
def order_many():
    print("Welcome to Mary's Burger Shop!")
    q1 = input("May I have your name for the order? ")
    o = order(q1)
    print("Let's get your order in!")
    done = False
    while done == False:
        item = order_once()
        o.add_item(item)
        q1= input("Do you need more items? (Enter n to stop.) ")
        if q1.lower()=="n":
            done = True
    return o
```

Here we create the main order function, which will perform the following steps:

- It greets the customer and asks for their name. That name is stored in the variable o as part of `order`.

- It creates a loop that allows the customer to request one item at a time until they complete the order. Each item is stored in an item list using the `add_item` function.

- It returns the complete order.

Create order_once

Next, we need to create the function that will accept individual items and add them to the order. Add the function in Listing 16.8 above the `order_many` function in your `main.py` file.

LISTING 16.8

Creating an order once

```
def order_once():
    possible_options = [1,2,3,4]
    print("Type 1 for a Burger.")
    print("Type 2 for a Drink.")
    print("Type 3 for a Side.")
    print("Type 4 for a Combo.")
    choice = None
    while choice == None:
        q1 = input("Please enter your choice:")
        if int(q1) in possible_options:
            choice = int(q1)
    item = None
    if choice == 1:
        item = get_burger_order()
    elif choice == 2:
        item = get_drink_order()
    elif choice == 3:
        item = get_side_order()
    elif choice == 4:
        item = get_combo_order()
    return item
```

Here, we present the customer with a list of items that they can choose from by entering a number to represent the item they want to order. The list `possible_options` is used to assign a value to each of the menu items. We reference it later to verify that the customer has entered an appropriate value.

The customer is presented options in a user-friendly format, so that the customer knows what they are expected to enter. We initialize `choice` and `item` as empty variables so that we can add values to those variables as we look through the choices.

We then include a `while` loop that prompts the customer for an item as long as no valid choice has been entered. The customer's choice determines where the program will go next based on a series of `elif` clauses. In the case of a burger (1), the program will run a `get_burger_order` that will collect details about the burger. For each other choice, the program runs the corresponding function to get that item. The value returned from the appropriate function is placed in `item`, which in turn is returned from our `order_once` function.

We can see that the function calls different methods based on the item being ordered, such as calling `get_burger_order`. We need to write the code for each of these methods.

Order a Burger

Let's start with the code to order a burger. We'll start by defining some of the values we want to use—specifically, the price of a burger and the available condiments. Start by adding the following constants to the top of the `main.py` file:

```
BURGER_PRICE = 6.00
BURGER_CONDIMENTS = ["tomato","lettuce","onion","cheese"]
```

> **NOTE** In real life, we would likely want to use variables that are defined elsewhere in the program—probably through a database of some sort. But for now, we'll create constants instead.

The next step is to define the `get_burger_order` function that includes specific steps related to ordering a burger, including adding condiments. Add the function presented in Listing 16.9 above the `order_once` function.

LISTING 16.9

Getting a burger order

```
def get_burger_order():
    b = burger("Burger",BURGER_PRICE)
    q1 = input("Do you want any condiments on your burger? (y for yes) ")
    if q1.lower() =="y":
        for condiment in BURGER_CONDIMENTS:
            q = input("Do you want " + str(condiment)+"? (y/n): ")
            if q.lower() == "y":
                b.add_condiment(condiment)
    return b
```

This code creates a burger along with its initial price. It then prompts the customer for condiments, using the list we defined earlier. It loops through each item in the list, adding the condiment only if the customer enters "y" at the prompt. Note that this is a strict "y or nothing" option. If the customer enters anything other than "y" (even nothing), the program will not add the condiment to the burger. Once the condiments are selected, the function returns the burger along with its selected condiments.

Now we have a series of steps that the program will perform:

- order_many: Greets the customer and creates the order. It also creates an item list that will store the output from order_once.

- order_once: Identifies a single item for the customer's order. If the customer orders a burger (as in our code so far), it triggers the get_burger_order function.

- get_burger_order: Asks the customer what condiments they want on their burger. It returns the burger order and passes it to order_once, which in turn passes the item to the item list maintained by order_many.

Add a Drink

Note that order_once allows the customer to order anything on the menu, but before that code will work, we must create the other functions it references. For the drink order, we need to start by defining the relevant constants. You should update the top of your menu.py file with the new constants included in Listing 16.10.

LISTING 16.10

Defining drink constants

```
BURGER_PRICE = 6.00
BURGER_CONDIMENTS = ["tomato","lettuce","onion","cheese"]

DRINK_TYPES = ["fanta", "coca cola", "sprite"]
DRINK_SIZES = [12, 16, 20]
DRINK_PRICES = [1.00,2.00,3.00]
```

Next, we'll create the function as shown in Listing 16.11 that prompts the customer for the drink and adds it to the order. This code should be added in your main.py file after the get_burger_order function.

LISTING 16.11

Adding a drink

```python
def get_drink_order():
    print("These are the available drinks:")
    print(DRINK_TYPES)
    print("These are the available sizes:")
    print(DRINK_SIZES)
    choice = False
    drink_name = None
    drink_size = None
    drink_price = None
    while choice == False:
        q1 = input("What drink do you want? ")
        if q1.lower() in DRINK_TYPES:
            choice = True
            drink_name = q1.lower()
        else:
            print("Please enter a valid drink.")
    choice = False
    while choice  == False:
        q1 = input("What size do you want? " + str(DRINK_SIZES) + ": ")
        if int(q1) in DRINK_SIZES:
            choice = True
            drink_size = int(q1)
        else:
            print("please enter a valid size")
    #locate the price of the drink based on the index of the size:
    drink_price = DRINK_PRICES[DRINK_SIZES.index(drink_size)]
    d = drink(drink_name,drink_size,drink_price)
    return d
```

This code shows the customer the available drink options and sizes and then prompts the customer to enter their choices.

- Note the use of if/else to identify that the customer has entered an appropriate value. If they enter something different (even misspelled), it prompts them to try again until a valid option is entered.

- After getting the drink and the size, it compares the size list to the price list and uses the index value of the selected size to find the appropriate price.

- It collects all three values (name, size, and price) into a `drink` class and returns the value from that class.
- As with the `get_burger_order` function, the result is passed back to `order_once`, which in turn passes that information back to `order_many` to add to the total order.

Add Sides

The side order function is similar to the drink order: We present the customer with a list of choices, accept the choice, and pass the value to `order_once`. First add the appropriate side constants into your `main.py` file. Listing 16.12 shows the updated list of constants.

LISTING 16.12

Defining side constants

```
BURGER_PRICE = 6.00
BURGER_CONDIMENTS = ["tomato","lettuce","onion","cheese"]

DRINK_TYPES = ["fanta", "coca cola", "sprite"]
DRINK_SIZES = [12, 16, 20]
DRINK_PRICES = [1.00,2.00,3.00]

SIDE_PRICE = 3.00
SIDES = ["fries","coleslaw","salad"]
```

With the constants in place, create the code that will prompt the customer for their choice of side and return the value with its price. Add the `get_side_order` function's code from Listing 16.13 into your `main.py` file after the `get_drink_order` function.

LISTING 16.13

Adding a side order

```
def get_side_order():
    print("These are the available sides:")
    print(SIDES)
    choice = False
    side_name = None
    while choice == False:
        q1 = input("What side do you want? ")
        if q1.lower() in SIDES:
```

```
            choice = True
            side_name = q1.lower()
        else:
            print("Please enter a valid side.")
    s = side(side_name,SIDE_PRICE)
    return s
```

Note here that all sides have the same price, unlike the drinks, so we simply need to include that value in the function's output. As with the drink order, if the customer does not input an expected value, the function tells them to try again.

Order a Combo

A combo includes a burger, a side, and a drink, with the advantage of giving the customer a discount on their order. For our burger shop, the price of a combo is $2 less than if the customer orders each of the items individually, so we need to define that in the constants. Listing 16.14 again shows an updated list of constant values that should be at the top of your main.py file.

LISTING 16.14

Defining combo constants

```
BURGER_PRICE = 6.00
BURGER_CONDIMENTS = ["tomato","lettuce","onion","cheese"]

DRINK_TYPES = ["fanta", "coca cola", "sprite"]
DRINK_SIZES = [12, 16, 20]
DRINK_PRICES = [1.00,2.00,3.00]

SIDE_PRICE = 3.00
SIDES = ["fries","coleslaw","salad"]

COMBO_DISCOUNT = 2.00
```

The function for the combo shown in Listing 16.15 will reuse the functions we've already created. You should place this in your main.py file after all those functions.

LISTING 16.15

Getting a combo

```python
def get_combo_order():
    print("Let's get you a combo meal!")
    print("First, let's order the burger for your combo.")
    b = get_burger_order()
    print("Now, let's order the drink for your combo.")
    d = get_drink_order()
    print("Finally, let's order the side for your combo.")
    s = get_side_order()
    c = combo("Combo",b,d,s,COMBO_DISCOUNT)
    #print(str(c))
    return c
```

Because the process of ordering a burger, a drink, or a side as part of a combo is exactly the same as ordering the items individually, this code is relatively straightforward. The final result includes the COMBO_DISCOUNT constant so that the customer gets the discount, and it passes the result to order_once, which passes it to order_many to add to the order total.

DISPLAY THE OUTPUT

Finally, we want our program to print out what the customer ordered, along with the total price. Right now, this is all stored in the order_many function (including the initial greeting to the customer), so we want to take the output from that function and display it to the customer.

Add the following code at the end of the main file:

```python
client_order = order_many()
client_order.display()
```

We now have our active code written, but we can't run it yet because the main file references classes that are located in another file. The final step is to tie them together.

TIE THE CODE FILES TOGETHER

When we want our program to run code that exists somewhere other than the same file, we must use the import function and tell Python exactly what we want to import. Assuming that both the main file and the menu file are in the same location, we add an import statement for each of the classes we defined in the menu file. Add the following code at the very top of the `main.py` file:

```
from menu import burger
from menu import drink
from menu import side
from menu import combo
from order import order
```

Listing 16.16 contains all the code that we've added to the `main.py` file.

LISTING 16.16

The complete `main.py`

```
from menu import burger
from menu import drink
from menu import side
from menu import combo
from order import order

BURGER_PRICE = 6.00
BURGER_CONDIMENTS = ["tomato","lettuce","onion","cheese"]

DRINK_TYPES = ["fanta", "coca cola", "sprite"]
DRINK_SIZES = [12, 16, 20]
DRINK_PRICES = [1.00,2.00,3.00]

SIDE_PRICE = 3.00
SIDES = ["fries","coleslaw","salad"]

COMBO_DISCOUNT = 2.00

def get_burger_order():
    b = burger("Burger",BURGER_PRICE)
    q1 = input("Do you want any condiments on your burger? (y for yes) ")
    if q1.lower() =="y":
        for condiment in BURGER_CONDIMENTS:
            q = input("Do you want " + str(condiment)+"? (y/n): ")
            if q.lower() == "y":
                b.add_condiment(condiment)
    return b
```

```python
def get_drink_order():
    print ("These are the available drinks:")
    print (DRINK_TYPES)
    print ("These are the available sizes:")
    print (DRINK_SIZES)
    choice = False
    drink_name = None
    drink_size = None
    drink_price = None
    while choice == False:
        q1 = input("What drink do you want? ")
        if q1.lower() in DRINK_TYPES:
            choice = True
            drink_name = q1.lower()
        else:
            print("Please enter a valid drink.")
    choice = False
    while choice  == False:
        q1 = input("What size do you want? " + str(DRINK_SIZES) + ": ")
        if int(q1) in DRINK_SIZES:
            choice = True
            drink_size = int(q1)
        else:
            print("please enter a valid size")
    #locate the price of the drink based on the index of the size:
    drink_price = DRINK_PRICES[DRINK_SIZES.index(drink_size)]
    d = drink(drink_name,drink_size,drink_price)
    return d

def get_side_order():
    print("These are the available sides:")
    print(SIDES)
    choice = False
    side_name = None
    while choice == False:
        q1 = input("What side do you want? ")
        if q1.lower() in SIDES:
            choice = True
            side_name = q1.lower()
        else:
            print("Please enter a valid side.")
    s = side(side_name,SIDE_PRICE)
    return s

def get_combo_order():
    print("Let's get you a combo meal!")
    print("First, let's order the burger for your combo.")
```

```python
    b = get_burger_order()
    print("Now, let's order the drink for your combo.")
    d = get_drink_order()
    print("Finally, let's order the side for your combo.")
    s = get_side_order()
    c = combo("Combo",b,d,s,COMBO_DISCOUNT)
    #print(str(c))
    return c

def order_once():
    possible_options = [1,2,3,4]
    print("Type 1 for a Burger.")
    print("Type 2 for a Drink.")
    print("Type 3 for a Side.")
    print("Type 4 for a Combo.")
    choice = None
    while choice == None:
        q1 = input("Please enter your choice:")
        if int(q1) in possible_options:
            choice = int(q1)
    item = None
    if choice == 1:
        item = get_burger_order()
    elif choice == 2:
        item = get_drink_order()
    elif choice == 3:
        item = get_side_order()
    elif choice == 4:
        item = get_combo_order()
    return item

def order_many():
    print("Welcome to Mary's Burger Shop!")
    q1 = input("May I have your name for the order? ")
    o = order(q1)
    print("Let's get your order in!")
    done = False
    while done == False:
        item = order_once()
        o.add_item(item)
        q1= input("Do you need more items? (Enter n to stop.) ")
        if q1.lower()=="n":
            done = True
    return o

client_order = order_many()
client_order.display()
```

SUMMARY

At this point, the code should work to place a customized order. We've created all of the classes and other code needed to have a burger shop application that allows the customer to place orders. Run your program a few times to make sure it works as expected (including ordering everything possible).

Once the program works, try tweaking it a bit with the following ideas:

- How could you add more condiments to the burger (such as mustard or ketchup)?

- Can you add more drink or side options?

- Can you include water at no cost?

- Can you add options that change the cost of a burger? For example, adding cheese might add a dollar to the price of the burger, or the customer could order a burger with two patties for a higher price.

PART IV

Data Processing with Python

Lesson 17: Working with Dates and Times

Lesson 18: Processing Text Files

Lesson 19: Processing CSV Files

Lesson 20: Processing JSON Files

PART IV

Working with Dates and Times

In previous lessons, you learned object-oriented programming (OOP) concepts. Remember that OOP is a way of structuring a program that allows properties, as well as behaviors, to be combined and reused in objects. Now that you understand this programming paradigm, let's take a look at how we can use those concepts as we process numeric/date-type data in Python.

LEARNING OBJECTIVES

By the end of this lesson, you will be able to:

- Describe classes that Python includes in its datetime module, based on date, time, or both.
- Define a value as a date or as a time.
- Split a datetime value into individual values, such as year, month, day, and hour.
- Use time and date values in a variety of operations.

Date and time are important concepts for any kind of computer work. We frequently need to timestamp activities as they are performed, aggregate data like sales volume based on time spans (such as hour, day, month, or year), and identify what activities have happened before other activities.

While humans generally treat dates and times as separate values, computers tend to treat any given second as a specific point in time, including the date as part of the entire value. Therefore, when we reference dates and times, we often need to split the value stored by a computer to get the specific value we need in a program. A few of the key concepts and terms you will encounter in this lesson include:

- **Python's datetime module** supplies classes for manipulating dates and times.
- The `now()` **function** is used to display the current date and time.
- The `today()` **function** returns the current local date and time.

GETTING STARTED WITH DATES AND TIMES

Python includes many useful functions, organized in libraries of code called modules. The datetime module provides classes that allow us to manipulate date and time data types as objects within a Python application.

We can use the `import` statement to include the datetime module within our Python programs. The `import` statement combines two operations. First it searches for the named module, and then it binds the results of that search to a name in the local scope. Once included in our Python program, we have access to date and time features.

> **NOTE** You can find more information on the `import` statement at https://docs.python.org/3/reference/simple_stmts.html#import.

Creating a Variable for a Date

The datetime module includes a `datetime` class. To create a date, the `datetime` class requires three parameters to create a date: year, month, day. We can use the `datetime` class (constructor) of the datetime module to create a static date using the following:

```
datetime.date(year, month, day)
```

Each value for year, month, and day must be an integer. Listing 17.1 shows a simple example of generating a date.

LISTING 17.1

Creating a date

```
import datetime

ada_bday = datetime.date(1815, 12, 10)
print(ada_bday)
```

In this case, the date being generated is Ada Lovelace's birthday: December 10, 1815. You can see that the first line imports our datetime module to give us access to the datetime class. We then create a new variable called ada_bday, which we assign a new date to. To get the date, we call the date method of the datetime class using datetime.date() and passing in the integer values for the year (1815), month (12), and day (10). The result is that the birthdate is displayed:

1815–12–10

In Listing 17.2, we take creating a date a step further. In this example, we create a script to ask the user for a year, month, and day. We then use these to create a new datetime object that is then displayed.

LISTING 17.2

Prompting for a date

```
import datetime

year = input("Please enter a year from 1900 to 2100: ")
while True:
  if int(year) >= 1900 and int(year) <= 2100:
    break
  else:
    year = input("Please enter a VALID year from 1900 to 2100: ")

month = input("Please enter a month from 1 to 12: ")
while True:
  if int(month) >= 1 and int(month) <= 12:
    break
  else:
    month = input("Please enter a VALID month from 1 to 12: ")
```

```
day = input("Please enter a day from 1 to 31: ")
while True:
  if int(day) >= 1 and int(day) <= 31:
    break
  else:
    day = input("Please enter a VALID day from 1 to 31: ")

user_date = datetime.date(int(year),int(month),int(day))
print(user_date)
```

This listing uses `while` loops and `if` statements to validate the input we are requesting from the user. This checks for the following validations:

- The year must be from 1900 to 2100.

- The month must be a value from 1 to 12.

- The day must be a value from 1 to 31.

In the checks, all ranges are inclusive, and a user-friendly message is displayed if an input value is out of range. The listing starts by prompting for the year. Then in a `while` loop, a check is done to see if the year (converted to an integer) is greater than or equal to 1900 and less than or equal to 2100. If so, then we break out of the `while` loop using the `break` command. This directs the program flow to the line following the `while`'s block of code, which is the prompt for the month. If the value isn't within the checked range, then the user is prompted again. This loops until a valid value is entered.

The same flow of logic is used to obtain the month and the day. It is worth noting that this program has a flaw. The program does not check to determine if the number of days fits the given month.

> **NOTE** It is a challenge left for you to validate the day based on the month. For example, April 31 is not a valid date because April has only 30 days. With the current listing, if you enter values for an invalid date, such as April 31st, you will get an unfriendly Python error.

After obtaining the `year`, `month`, and `day` from the user, a new datetime variable called `user_date` is created. It is initialized to the values that were obtained by the user. Notice, however, that the values were converted to integers using `int()`:

```
user_date = datetime.date(int(year),int(month),int(day))
```

When this listing is executed, the output will depend on what the user enters. Following is one example of possible outcome:

```
Please enter a year from 1900 to 2100: 2300
Please enter a VALID year from 1900 to 2100: 2022
Please enter a month from 1 to 12: 0
Please enter a VALID month from 1 to 12: 12
Please enter a day from 1 to 31: 25
2022-12-25
```

Creating a Variable for Time

We can also create a variable to hold the time by using the `time()` method of the `datetime` class. To format a time, we pass the hour, minute, and second values as integers to the `time()` method:

```
datetime.time(hour, minute, second)
```

In Listing 17.3 we set the time and apply it to a variable called `appointment`.

LISTING 17.3

Creating a time

```
import datetime

appointment = datetime.time(10, 30, 00)
print("Appointment time: " + str(appointment))
```

This listing simply sets the appointment to 10:30 and then prints it with a bit of text:

```
Appointment time: 10:30:00
```

Creating a Variable for Both Date and Time

In addition to the `date()` and `time()` methods, there is a `datetime()` method within the `datetime` class that works with both at the same time. Listing 17.4 shows this method in action.

LISTING 17.4

Creating a datetime

```
import datetime

appointment = datetime.datetime(2022, 12, 10, 10, 30, 00)
print("Appointment time: " + str(appointment))
```

In this listing, we set our appointment again for 10:30, but this time on December 10, 2022. You can see that the format of the `datetime` combines the earlier formats that we saw:

```
datetime( year, month, day, hour, minutes, second)
```

In the listing we assign these values to our `appointment` variable and then print the result:

```
Appointment time: 2022-12-10 10:30:00
```

GETTING THE CURRENT DATE AND TIME

We can use the attributes `now()` or `today()` to reference the current system time and date:

- `now()` always includes both date and time.
- `today()` always includes date, but time is optional.

In the example in Listing 17.5 we want to display the current date and time. This includes the following steps:

1. Import the datetime module.
2. Use the `datetime.now` class from the datetime module to calculate the current time.
3. Display the value generated by `datetime.datetime.now()`.

LISTING 17.5

What time is it now?

```
import datetime

time_now = datetime.datetime.now()
print(time_now)
```

The call to `datetime.datetime.now()` assigns the current date and time to the variable `time_now`, which is then printed. Your output should look similar to the following format but should show the current date and time from your computer at the time you ran the program:

```
2021-03-17 14:22:03.223618
```

We can also display the current date and time using `today()` instead of `now()`.

SPLITTING A DATE STRING

We can use string functions to extract individual pieces of a datetime output. For example, in Listing 17.6 we can see that the date's year, month, and day are separated by a dash (–), and a space separates the date from the time.

To split the date, we first use the `split` function to separate the date and time, using the default space character. We then split the date into three separate values, specifying the dash as the separator.

LISTING 17.6

Splitting a date

```
d = "2022-07-23 11:26:26.047342"
(d,t) = d.split()
(year,month,day) = d.split("-")
print(year)
print(month)
print(day)
```

We start this listing by setting a variable, d, equal to a string that represents a datetime, containing both a date and time. We then use the `split()` function to break this into two pieces, a date (d) and a time (t). The date is then stored in d and split into three pieces (`year`, `month`, and `day`) based on the dash. Finally, these three pieces are printed:

```
2022
07
23
```

We could have done the same process to break apart the time, except we would have used t and split based on a colon as shown in Listing 17.7.

LISTING 17.7

Splitting the time

```
d = "2022-07-23 11:26:26.047342"
(d,t) = d.split()
(hour, minute,second) = t.split(":")
print(hour)
print(minute)
print(second)
```

When the listing is run, the following is displayed:

```
11
26
26.047342
```

In Listings 17.6 and 17.7, we started with a string representation of a datetime. If we wanted to start with a datetime value, we would need to change it to a string before doing the split as shown in Listing 17.8.

LISTING 17.8

Splitting the date and time

```
import datetime

d = datetime.datetime.now()
d = str(d)

(d,t) = d.split()
(year,month,day) = d.split("-")
(hour, minute, second) = t.split(":")

print(year)
print(month)
print(day)
print(hour)
print(minute)
print(second)
```

This listing combines the actions of the previous two. It also imports the datetime module before defining a datetime variable, d, equal to the current date and time, which is then converted to a string before splitting it apart. The output is:

```
2021
03
17
16
09
00.636453
```

USING DATETIME ATTRIBUTES

Although we just saw how to split a datetime string into its various components, there is an easier way to get the pieces. The datetime module has several attributes built in:

- year
- month
- day
- hour
- minute
- second
- microsecond
- time zone information (tzinfo)

We can use these attributes to extract specific values included in a datetime value. For example, the following statement will extract the current year from the current date:

```
datetime.datetime.now().year
```

In Listing 17.9, the current date and time is assigned to a variable called time_now, and then specific values are extracted.

LISTING 17.9

Extracting with datetime attributes

```
import datetime

time_now = datetime.datetime.now()
```

```
print(time_now)

print(time_now.year)
print(time_now.month)
print(time_now.day)
print(time_now.hour)
print(time_now.minute)
print(time_now.second)
print(time_now.microsecond)
print(time_now.tzinfo)
```

You can see from this listing that using the attributes is much easier than converting a datetime to a string and splitting it. The output will be a breakout of the current date and time (so your output will differ):

```
2021-03-17 17:32:10.511058
2021
3
17
17
32
10
511058
None
```

The datetime class is one that is especially useful in our ERP banking application. We often need to tag items with the date and time. Additionally, there are times when we will need the ability to perform analysis on the date and time–stamped data. For instance, we might want to group all the transactions performed by all our customers by year. Using Python datetime objects, we can access the attributes such as year, month, day, and so on to perform our analysis.

CREATING CUSTOM DATETIME OBJECTS

We can create custom datetime objects by providing keyword arguments to the datetime __init__ method for the day, month, and year. Using these keywords, we can create a static date. Listing 17.10 illustrates this in action. The listing also shows that we can provide the date elements in any order using this method.

LISTING 17.10

Creating a custom date with named parameters

```
import datetime

t1 = datetime.date(year=2013, day=4, month=12)
t2 = datetime.date(year=2013, month=12, day=4)
t3 = datetime.date(day=4, year=2013, month=12)
t4 = datetime.date(day=4, month=12, year=2013)
t5 = datetime.date(month=12, year=2013, day=4)
t6 = datetime.date(month=12, day=4, year=2013)

print(t1)
print(t2)
print(t3)
print(t4)
print(t5)
print(t6)
```

When executed, we see that all six ways of creating the date result in the same output:

```
2013-12-04
2013-12-04
2013-12-04
2013-12-04
2013-12-04
2013-12-04
```

Our ERP application users may want to perform various tasks that involve specific dates. For instance, our customers may want to look at their account activity from a certain date or they may want to enter their date of birth while setting up their account. We can accept user input and create custom datetime objects using the `datetime` class or the `date` class from the datetime module in Python.

COMPARE DATETIME VALUES

We can compare datetime objects in the same way we can compare numeric values. In Listing 17.11 we illustrate this by creating and comparing two different dates.

LISTING 17.11

Comparing dates

```
import datetime

d1 = datetime.datetime(year=2013,month=12,day=4)
d2 = datetime.datetime(year=2014,month=3,day=12)

print(d1 > d2) # check if d1 is more recent than d2
print(d1 < d2)
print(d1 == d2)
```

In this listing, we create two dates, d1 and d2. We then check to see if d1 is greater than d2, less than d2, and equal to d2. A date that is more recent will be larger, and a date that is older will be smaller. The resulting output for this is that d1 is less than d2:

```
False
True
False
```

> **NOTE** You can play around with the dates in Listing 17.11 and see how the results change.

We can use the comparison of dates to quickly determine if a date is in the future or the past. In Listing 17.12, we create a script that receives a date input from the user for a year, month, and day that is converted to a date. Unlike Listing 17.2 earlier, no validation is being done. The script then uses comparison operators to compare the user's date against the current date, and then display an appropriate message.

LISTING 17.12

Past, future, or present?

```
import datetime

year = int(input("Please enter a year: "))
month = int(input("Please enter a month: "))
day = int(input("Please enter a day: "))

d1 = datetime.date(year,month,day)
today = datetime.datetime.today().date()
```

```
if d1 > today:
    print("That date is in the future.")
elif d1 < today:
    print("That date is in the past.")
elif d1 == today:
    print("That date is today!")
```

When this listing is run, the user enters three values, which are then used to create the date d1. The value for today's date is then captured and stored in a variable called today. When the today() method of datetime is called, we also include .date() after it. This causes the today() method to return just the date without the time included.

Once we have both the entered date and the date for today, we can do simple comparisons to determine if the entered date was from the future, the past, or today:

```
Please enter a year: 1999
Please enter a month: 12
Please enter a day: 31
That date is in the past.
```

Date comparisons can be used within our ERP application as well. We may want to provide our users with options to select data such as transaction activity from a certain time period. In such a case, we will want to make sure that the lower-bound datetime value is in the past compared to the upper-bound datetime value. We can perform this check by comparing the datetime objects in Python.

WORKING WITH UTC FORMAT

We can use datetime.utcnow() to get the current time in Universal Time Coordinated (UTC) format. UTC presents the current time using a 24-hour clock based on the Greenwich meridian, regardless of current time zone. Developers often use UTC as a way of generating a single global time that is not dependent on the user's location.

Listing 17.13 shows how we can use utcnow() instead of now() to generate the current time and date in UTC format.

LISTING 17.13

Working with UTC dates

```
import datetime
time_utc_now = datetime.datetime.utcnow()
```

```
print(time_utc_now)
print("-----")
print(time_utc_now.year)
print(time_utc_now.month)
print(time_utc_now.day)
print(time_utc_now.hour)
print(time_utc_now.minute)
print(time_utc_now.second)
print(time_utc_now.microsecond)
print(time_utc_now.tzinfo)
```

The output should be shifted by the number of hours your current time zone is from
UTC. For example, if you are in U.S. Eastern Standard Time (without daylight saving time
in effect), your current time is five hours less than UTC. During Daylight Saving Time, the
difference is four hours rather than five. The following is an example of output when run
at 4:00 pm in the Eastern time zone during Daylight Saving Time:

```
2021-03-17 20:02:56.827604
-----
2021
3
17
20
2
56
827604
None
```

Storing datetime objects in local time can be helpful; however, this can get complicated easily as our ERP application scales and reaches a more global population. For example, a common
problem is storing time during the Daylight Saving Time change in certain parts of the world. To
avoid such problems, we can store our datetime objects in the location-agnostic UTC format.

APPLYING TIMESTAMPS

Python can store dates as timestamps, where a date's timestamp value is the number of
seconds since midnight UTC, January 1, 1970. We can convert a datetime object into a
timestamp value using the timestamp class in datetime:

```
value = datetime.datetime.timestamp(some_date)
```

Listing 17.14 shows how we convert the current date into a timestamp value.

LISTING 17.14

Using timestamps

```
import datetime
import math     #included for the math.floor() method

d_now = datetime.datetime.now()

tstamp = math.floor(datetime.datetime.timestamp(d_now))

print(d_now)
print(tstamp)
```

Here we are converting the current time (now()) to a timestamp. We first assign the date and time to d_now. We then use d_now as the parameter to timestamp, which returns the timestamp value, which we store in tstamp. When we print this, we see the current datetime and the timestamp value:

```
2021-03-17 21:41:06.077512
1616017266.077512
```

If we run Listing 17.14 a second time, we will see that time has progressed, so the value in d_now will be later. We will also see that the value placed in tstamp is also bigger because our newer datetime is farther from January 1st, 1970. In fact, if we subtract our new timestamp value from the old one, we'd see roughly how many seconds it was between the times the program was run. Listing 17.15 helps to illustrate this change in timestamp values.

LISTING 17.15

Checking multiple timestamps

```
import datetime

d_now = datetime.datetime.now()
now_stamp = datetime.datetime.timestamp(d_now)

print(d_now)
print(now_stamp)
print("-----")
```

```
for ctr in range(0, 10):
  for ctr2 in range(0, 1000000):
    x = 1          # doing something to take some time...
    x = x + 1
  print(".")

d_later = datetime.datetime.now()
later_stamp = datetime.datetime.timestamp(d_later)

print(d_later)
print(later_stamp)

print("-----")
print(later_stamp - now_stamp)
```

As a note, this listing illustrates the time gap between two timestamps. Its functionality is to loop through two `for` loops where it is simply assigning values to a variable, but otherwise doing nothing.

Before doing this processing, a date is created with the current time (d_now) and used to get a timestamp called now_stamp. These values are printed to the screen. Once this is done the `for` loops do their thing with a dot being printed to the screen after each iteration of the outer loop.

Once the `for` loops are done processing, we grab the current date and time again in a variable called d_later. We use d_later to get a second timestamp. We again print the values of these to the screen.

Finally, we print the difference between the later_stamp and the now_stamp to get the difference between now and later. The result is roughly the number of seconds it took to do the printing and looping. Our output from the listing was:

```
2021-03-17 22:08:49.683516
1616018929.683516
-----
.
.
.
.
.
.
.
.
.

2021-03-17 22:08:53.067935
1616018933.067935
-----
3.3844189643859863
```

When you run this, you should see similar results, although your time might be higher or lower than the roughly 3.4 seconds our output took.

In regard to our ERP program, it is important to be able to present dates and times to users so that they are recognizable, and it is equally important to be able to convert them to effectively store them into a database. Python enables us to use the datetime object to convert into the timestamp so that we can insert it into the proper collections in the dataset.

ARITHMETIC AND DATES

Python includes the timedelta class in the datetime module. We can use this to add or subtract weeks, days, minutes, seconds, microseconds, and milliseconds to or from an existing datetime object. The format of using timedelta to add to an existing date is:

```
new_date = starting_date + datetime.timedelta(days=0, seconds=0,
microseconds=0, milliseconds=0, minutes=0, hours=0, weeks=0)
```

All of the arguments are optional, so only the ones you are using need to be included. Additionally, the timedelta can be added or subtracted from the original date. To add 3 days to an existing date called myDate, the following would be done:

```
myDate = myDate + datetime.timedelta(days=3)
```

In our example in Listing 17.16, we perform several actions using timedelta. Each starts with the current datetime.

LISTING 17.16

Arithmetic and dates

```
import datetime

print(datetime.datetime.now())

# add one day to the current datetime
d1 = datetime.datetime.now() + datetime.timedelta(days = 1)
print(d1)

 # subtract 4 weeks from the current datetime
d2 = datetime.datetime.now() - datetime.timedelta(weeks = 4)
print(d2)

# add one hour to the current datetime
d3 = datetime.datetime.now() + datetime.timedelta(minutes = 60, hours=1)
print(d3)
```

As a reminder, `timedelta` needs the datetime module, so our listing starts with an import. After printing out the current date/time, three simple `timedelta` operations are done that provide changes from the current time. The first adds one day. The second goes back 4 weeks using subtraction. The third adds both 60 minutes and 1 hour (for a total of 2 hours). When you run the listing, you should see something similar to the following but starting with the current date for you:

```
2021-03-18 01:15:52.388967
2021-03-19 01:15:52.389840
2021-02-18 01:15:52.390711
2021-03-18 03:15:52.391450
```

CALCULATING THE DIFFERENCE IN DAYS

We can also subtract one date from another date to calculate the number of days between two datetime objects. The result of this subtraction will be a `datetime.timedelta` value. We can then get individual elements out of the `timedelta` value by passing the same attributes that were shown in the previous section as arguments. Listing 17.17 shows how to get the number of days between two dates.

LISTING 17.17

Calculating the number of days between two dates

```
import datetime

d_now = datetime.datetime.now()
d_other = datetime.datetime(2021,1,1)

print(d_now)
print(d_other)

days_passed = d_now - d_other
print(days_passed)
print(days_passed.days)
```

We again start with the current date and store it in a variable called d_now. We also create a second date that is January 1, 2021, and store it in d_other. We then subtract the current date (d_now) from our January 1st date (d_other) and get a `timedelta` value that is stored in days_passed. When we print days_passed, we can see that it contains quite a bit of information (your details will vary based on your current date):

```
76 days, 1:29:31.105512
```

Since we are interested in the number of days that have passed, we can add the days attribute to days_passed and get just the days, as can be seen in the last line of the listing. The full output is:

```
2021-03-18 01:29:31.105512
2021-01-01 00:00:00
76 days, 1:29:31.105512
76
```

Listing 17.18 provides an example that does a little more. In this example, the user is prompted to enter a year, month, and day. Using this, a calculation is done to determine how far that date is from today. If the number of days is a negative number, then we know the date entered was in the past. If it is positive, we know it is in the future. If the date is today's date, then the program tells what the date will be in six months (26 weeks).

LISTING 17.18

What's the date?

```python
import datetime

year = int(input("Please enter a year: "))
month = int(input("Please enter a month: "))
day = int(input("Please enter a day: "))

d1 = datetime.datetime(year,month,day)
dnow = datetime.datetime.now()

days_passed = dnow - d1

if days_passed.days < 0:
  past_date = dnow +  datetime.timedelta(days_passed.days)
  print("That date is " + str(abs(days_passed.days)) +
      " days in the future. " + str(abs(days_passed.days)) +
      " days ago, the date was " + str(past_date.date())+".")
elif days_passed.days > 0:
  future_date = dnow + datetime.timedelta(days_passed.days)
  print("That date was " + str(abs(days_passed.days)) +
      " days ago. In " + str(abs(days_passed.days)) +
      " days, the date will be " + str(future_date.date())+".")
```

```
elif days_passed.days == 0:
    future_date = dnow + datetime.timedelta(weeks=26)
    print("That's today! In six months, the date will be " +
        str(future_date.date())+".")
```

You should run this listing with a date in the past, a date in the future, and the current date to see how the if–else statement works with the dates. You should see outputs similar to the following when you run it each time:

```
Please enter a year: 2021
Please enter a month: 3
Please enter a day: 18
That's today! In six months, the date will be 2021-09-16.

Please enter a year: 2021
Please enter a month: 1
Please enter a day: 1
That date was 76 days ago. In 76 days, the date will be 2021-06-02.

Please enter a year: 2021
Please enter a month: 12
Please enter a day: 25
That date is 282 days in the future. 282 days ago, the date was 2020-06-09.
```

In our ERP application, often we may want to perform arithmetic with dates and times. For instance, we may want to provide the users with an account balance notification every seven days from the day they set up an alert. We can easily perform this task in Python using the timedelta class in the datetime module.

USING DATE WITHOUT TIME

We touched on this earlier in this lesson, but we will address it in more detail here. The datetime module includes a date class that represents the date without the time. Listing 17.19 shows using date instead of datetime, which shows the date without the time.

LISTING 17.19

Showing the date without the time

```
import datetime
time_today = datetime.date.today() # calculates the current date
print(time_today)
print(time_today.year)
```

```
print(time_today.month)
print(time_today.day)
```

In this listing `date` is used instead of `datetime` to get the current date. The date is then printed. What is worth noting are the three lines of code that then follow: print just the current year, just the current month, and just the current day by using the `year`, `month`, and `day` attributes on the `date` variable that was created. The following shows sample output:

```
2020-01-22
2020
1
22
```

As a more interesting example Listing 17.20 uses `datetime.date` to get the current date and then uses subtraction to get a `timedelta` that contains the number of days until Christmas.

LISTING 17.20

Days until Christmas

```
import datetime

dnow = datetime.date.today()
christmas = datetime.date(dnow.year,12,25)

days_until = christmas - dnow

print("Today is: ", dnow)
print("Christmas is just " + str(days_until.days) + " away!")
```

As you can see, the listing prints the current date, then uses subtraction to get the difference between now and Christmas. The result is printed using the `days` attribute:

```
Today is:  2021-03-18
Christmas is just 282 days away!
```

In our ERP application, sometimes we may only be interested in the date and not the time, such as when users are entering their date of birth or when they are looking up a specific date's transaction activity. In such cases, we can directly use the `date` class from the datetime module instead of the `datetime` class.

USING TIME WITHOUT DATE

As we saw earlier in this lesson, we can also use the `datetime.time` class to create time objects that are independent of date. As a review, in Listing 17.21 we'll use the `time` class to generate a time that is not date-specific. We then use `time` to extract a time object from a full `datetime` value. Note that both objects are `datetime.time` objects.

LISTING 17.21

Using only time without a date

```
import datetime
# we create a time object, for 1:45:30 pm, using 24-hour time format
t = datetime.time(13,45,30)
print(t)
print(type(t))

current_time = datetime.datetime.now().time()
print(current_time)
print(type(current_time))
```

We start by creating a time object for 1:45:30 pm using a 24-hour time format. We then print its value so it can be confirmed, along with its type, which can indeed be seen in the output to be `datetime.time`:

```
13:45:30
<class 'datetime.time'>
10:15:49.422992
<class 'datetime.time'>
```

We then create `current_time`, which is set to only the current time by using the `.time()` at the end of the call to get the `now()` using datetime. We again print the value and the type to confirm that it truly is a time type and not a datetime type.

In our ERP application, we may want to display greetings such as "Good morning" or "Good afternoon" to our customers depending on the time of the day. This is independent of the day of the year. We can, therefore, use the `time` class from the datetime module instead of the `datetime` class. In Listing 17.22 we create a script that greets the user based on the time of day.

LISTING 17.22

Time of day greeting

```python
import datetime

noon = datetime.time(12,00,00)
current_time = datetime.datetime.now().time()

if current_time >= noon:
  print("Good afternoon!")
elif current_time < noon:
  print("Good morning!")

while True:
  user_input = input("Would you like to enter a time? [Type quit to exit] ")
  if user_input.lower() == 'quit':
    break
  elif user_input.lower() == 'yes':
    user_input_time = input("Enter a time [HH:MM:SS format]: ")
    time_split = [int(i) for i in user_input_time.split(":")]
    user_time = datetime.time(time_split[0],time_split[1],time_split[2])
    if user_time >= noon:
      print(str(user_time) + " is in the afternoon.")
    elif user_time < noon:
      print(str(user_time) + " is in the morning.")
```

In this listing, we are doing two different things. First, we are determining if it is currently before or after noon and displaying a message to the user. This is done by grabbing the current time and comparing it to a time we set in a variable called noon, which is set to 12:00:00.

We then do the second part of the listing, which asks the user if they want to enter a date. If they respond with yes, then we prompt them for a date and check to see if it is before or after noon. When we run this listing, what we see is dependent on the time of day:

```
Good afternoon!
Would you like to enter a time? [Type quit to exit] yes
Enter a time [HH:MM:SS format]: 1:23:00
01:23:00 is in the morning.
Would you like to enter a time? [Type quit to exit] yes
Enter a time [HH:MM:SS format]: 12:40:00
12:40:00 is in the afternoon.
Would you like to enter a time? [Type quit to exit] quit
```

SUMMARY

In this lesson, we focused on how datetime functions within classes in Python. A date in Python is not a data type of its own; however, Python provides an import of a module named datetime to work with dates as date objects. We frequently need to timestamp activities as they are performed, aggregate data like sales volume based on time span (hour, day, month, or year), and identify what activities have happened before other activities.

Now that you have completed Lesson 17, you should be able to:

- Describe classes that Python includes in its datetime module, based on date, time, or both.

- Define a value as a date or as a time.

- Split a datetime value into individual values, such as year, month, day, and hour.

- Use time and date values in a variety of operations.

EXERCISES

The following exercises are provided to allow you to demonstrate the objectives for this lesson. You should complete each exercise and make sure that the code runs without errors.

Exercise 1: Displaying Dates

Exercise 2: Leap Years

Exercise 3: The Past

Exercise 4: Unix Dates

Exercise 5: Yesterday, Today, and Tomorrow

Exercise 6: Setting Future Days

Exercise 7: Five Seconds in the Future

Exercise 8: Date Calculators

Exercise 1: Displaying Dates

Write a program to display the following:

- Current date and time

- Current year

- Current month
- Week number of the year
- Weekday of the week
- Day of the year
- Day of the month
- Day of the week

Exercise 2: Leap Years

Write a function that prompts the user for a year and checks whether it is a leap year. The function should return `True` if the input is a leap year and `False` otherwise.

Make sure to test your code with various inputs.

Exercise 3: The Past

Write a function that prompts the user for a date (or uses the current date if the user does not input a date) and subtracts five days from that date. The function should return the new date.

Display the result to the user.

Exercise 4: Unix Dates

Write a program that converts a Unix timestamp string to a human-readable date.

Exercise 5: Yesterday, Today, and Tomorrow

Write a program that prints the dates for yesterday, today, and tomorrow.

Exercise 6: Setting Future Days

Write a program that prints the date for the next five days, starting from today.

Exercise 7: Five Seconds in the Future

Write a program that adds five seconds to the current time and displays the result.

Exercise 8: Date Calculators

Build several different datetime calculators, each of which performs a different calculation. Each calculator should accept appropriate user input for that calculator and perform the specified calculation using that input.

For each calculator:

- You may define the format that the user should use to enter the values, but that format should be very clear to the user.
    - If the user does not enter data in the expected format, the program should display an appropriate message and prompt the user to try again.
- Create appropriate functions, classes, and methods to simplify your code.
- The user must be able to clear all input at any time to start over again.
- The user must be able to exit the program at any time.

NOTE User input can be simplified by breaking it up into discrete values. For example, instead of asking the user to enter a complete date (which could have a variety of formats), the program can prompt for separate date, month, and year values. This creates more work on the backend because your program will have to be able to convert the distinct values into a date, but it can make the program less error prone.

Put all the following calculators in a single program and allow the user to choose the one they wish to use.

Calculator 1: Time Duration

Add or subtract two different lengths of time.

- The calculator must include days, hours, minutes, and seconds.
- The user must be able to specify addition or subtraction between the two different input times.
- The output must display the results in multiple ways:
    - the number of days, hours, minutes, and seconds
    - the number of days
    - the number of hours
    - the number of minutes
    - the number of seconds

For example, if the user enters one value of 3 days, 5 hours, 15 minutes, and 0 seconds, and adds a value of 7 days, 20 hours, 50 minutes, and 10 seconds, the result will be:

- 11 days 2 hours 2 minutes 10 seconds
- 11.084838 days
- 266.03611 hours
- 15,962.167 minutes
- 957,730 seconds

Calculator 2: Add or Subtract Time from a Date

Given a date and time, add or subtract an input length of time and display the date and time of the result.

- The calculator must include days, hours, minutes, and seconds, for input and output.
- The user must be able to choose between addition and subtraction.

For example, if the user enters December 1, 2021, 12:04:00 PM, and wants to subtract 5 days, 3 hours, and 30 minutes, the result would be November 25, 2021, 08:34:00 PM.
Challenge: Include the day of the week (Monday, Tuesday, etc.) in the output.

Calculator 3: Age Calculator

Given a start date and an end date, calculate the amount of time passed between the dates, displayed in years, months, days, hours, minutes, and seconds. For example, given the start date September 1, 1994 and the end date December 1, 2021, the results would be:

- 25 years 3 months 10 days
- 303 months 10 days
- 1318 weeks 6 days
- 9,232 days
- 221,568 hours
- 13,294,080 minutes
- 797,644,800 seconds

Challenge: Update the calculator to include a specific time with each date.

Lesson 18
Processing Text Files

In many cases, when we need to analyze the contents of text for a specific purpose, the text already exists in a file, so it can be efficient to have Python read the text directly from the source file. Not only is this faster than manually inputting the text at runtime, but it also means that Python can look at a file whose contents may change over time. This allows Python to automatically perform the analysis on the most recent version of the file.

In addition, we may want to save the output of a script to use in another script or elsewhere. Python allows us to save the output to a file easily.

In this and the next two lessons, we will look at three main text file types:

- In this lesson, we'll review plain text files (.txt), such as the text from a book, or reviews collected by an online retailer.

- In Lesson 19, we'll review CSV files (`.csv`), which include records organized into columns like a table and are often generated by structured datasets.

- In Lesson 20, we'll review JSON files (`.json`), which can represent unstructured datasets with key: value pairs

We can use Python scripts to read these files, add (or append) content to an existing file, and create new files. We'll start with this lesson that covers plain text files.

LEARNING OBJECTIVES

By the end of this lesson, you will be able to:

- Know common functions for doing file input and output.
- Open, read, and display text-based files in a `.txt` format.
- Append content to an existing file.
- Replace data in an existing file with new data.
- Use the Python `os` module to check for existing files.
- Create a new text file.
- Delete a text file.

> **NOTE** The data files used in this lesson are available in the data folder located in the `JobReadyPython.zip` file that you can download from `www.wiley.com/go/jobreadypython`.

You can download the *Flatland* (`www.gutenberg.org/ebooks/97`) and *Alice's Adventures in Wonderland* (`www.gutenberg.org/ebooks/11`) files used in this lesson from Project Gutenberg (`www.gutenberg.org/`) and distributed in the public domain. The versions used in the examples and practice activities are included in the Resource files provided for this lesson.

FILE PROCESSING OVERVIEW

When compared to keyboard input from a human user, the primary advantages of accepting input data from a file are:

- Size constraints are lifted
- Data can be input more quickly
- Data can be used with different applications

Python programs can output data to a text file. The text file can be viewed as characters, words, numbers, or lines of text, depending on its intended purpose. When getting data from a text file, or when writing data to a text file, you must use strings. Numbers must be converted to strings prior to output. Strings must be converted back to numbers after the data is inputted.

In Python (as in other I/O systems), we use a *path* to identify the location of the file we want to use. A complete path must include all directories and subdirectories that the code needs to find the file we want to use, including the filename and filename extension. As you go through this and the next two lessons, the following are key terms you should be aware of:

- **Path:** A path identifies the location of the file to be utilized. A path can be **absolute** or **relative**.
- **Absolute path:** A path that includes all information required to find the file, regardless of where the script is stored.
  - An absolute path starts with a forward slash in front of a topmost folder and includes all subfolders leading to the target file, such as `/Users/username/Documents/Python Scripts/fileio/data/testfile.txt`.
  - Absolute paths are useful if the Python scripts are not stored in the same parent folder as the target files, or if the Python scripts may be used in different places in a system.
- **Relative path:** A path that starts from the directory where the Python script is stored and includes instructions on how to get to the file using that directory as a starting point.
  - Building on the example of an absolute path, if the Python script file is stored in the `fileio` subdirectory, the relative address to the same file is `data/testfile.txt`.
  - Relative paths are shorter, but they depend on the location of the Python script to work. If the files and scripts are stored independently of each other or if the script file may be moved to a different directory at a later time, an absolute path may be a better option.

> **NOTE** Be aware that Windows uses a backslash (\) to separate folders in a path, whereas Python uses a forward slash (/). This means that if you copy a path from Windows File Manager, you will need to change the backslashes to forward slashes for Python to be able to interpret the path.

INTRODUCTION TO FILE INPUT/OUTPUT

The purpose of application development is to take input data, process the data, and output information. Python has several basic functions to support that task. A few of the built-in functions are listed here. However, it is advisable to refer to the official Python documentation (`https://docs.python.org/3/tutorial/inputoutput.html`) for all functions available.

The basic functions and methods listed here are:

- `input()`
- `open()`
- `read()`
- `write()`
- `close()`
- `print()`

Each of these is covered briefly in a general overview. The rest of this lesson will then go into more specific detail for processing text files. The following two lessons will do the same with these functions for CSV and JSON files.

The `input()` Function

Python uses the `input()` function to read data from standard input, which by default comes from the keyboard. The `input()` function assumes that the input is a valid Python expression. The syntax of using this function is:

`input(prompt)`

The *prompt* is a string that appears to the user.

The `open()` Function

Before we can read or write a file, we must open it. We open it using Python's built-in `open()` function. This is the main function for working with files in Python. The `open()` function takes two parameters: *filename* and *mode*.

The `read()` Method

The `read()` method reads a string from an open file. It is important to note that Python strings can have binary data apart from text data. The basic syntax of the `read()` method is:

```
fileObject.read([count]);
```

The `write()` Method

The `write()` method writes any string to an open file. It is important to note that Python strings can have binary data and not just text. The `write()` method does not add a newline character (\n) to the end of the string. The basic syntax of the `write()` method is:

```
fileObject.write(string);
```

The `close()` Method

The `close()` method of a file object flushes any unwritten information and closes the file object, after which no more writing can be done. The basic syntax of the `close()` method is:

```
fileObject.close();
```

Listing 18.1 is a generic illustration of using `close` after opening a file.

LISTING 18.1

Simple file I/O script

```
f = open("myfile.txt", "r")
print(f.readline())
f.close()
```

The `print()` Function

The simplest way to produce output is by using the `print()` function, which we've used throughout this book. Using the `print()` function, you pass 0 or other expressions separated by commas. The basic syntax of the `print()` function is:

```
print ("12345")
```

PROCESSING TEXT FILES

So far, we have reviewed applications that have taken input from a user's keyboard for processing. However, a more efficient way is taking input from a data (text) file. A text file includes unformatted text saved in a specific location that is automatically read into a computer application. We call this location the **filepath** or simply the **path**.

A basic text file is useful for unstructured documents, and these files normally have the filename extension .txt. However, we can also use Python to analyze structured text documents that contain a dataset formatted using comma-separated values (CSV) or JSON notation. These files include unformatted text, but they use punctuation symbols like commas and brackets to provide more structure to the content.

We'll look first at plain text files in this lesson and then dive into CSV in Lesson 19 and JSON files in Lesson 20.

OPENING A FILE

Python uses the keywords open and close to open a file and to close it, respectively. The basic syntax for opening a file is:

```
open("path to the file","r,a,w,x")
```

In this syntax, the *path to the file* should be a path that Python can use to find the text file you want to open, including the filename and extension. The second argument is one of the following letters:

- r: Open the file as read-only. Python throws an error if the file does not exist.

- a: Open the file for appending. The original content cannot be changed, but we can add new content to the file. If the file does not yet exist, Python will create it.

- w: Open the file with full editing options, including changing existing content or adding new content. Python will create the file if it does not already exist.

- x: Create a new file with the specified name. Python returns an error if a file with that name already exists.

To open a file for input, use "r". If a file with the same name is not accessible, Python raises an error. The code for opening thefile.txt for input is:

```
f = open ("thefile.txt", "r")
```

A script that opens a file should close the file as well, to remove the file from memory and free up resources:

```
f.close()
```

In Listing 18.2, we open a text file that contains the first three paragraphs of Edwin Abbott's book *Flatland*, as downloaded from Project Gutenberg. The file itself is stored in a subdirectory named data that is in the same directory as this Python file, so we use the relative path data/flatland01.txt to locate it.

> **NOTE** You can download the text file for *Flatland* from www.gutenberg.org/ files/97/97.txt.

LISTING 18.2

Opening a the flatland01.txt file

```
# Open our file in read mode
f = open("data/flatland01.txt", mode="r")

# Read and display text file
print(f.read())

# Close our file resource
f.close()
```

We open the file as a file object named f with the "r" option to open the book in read-only mode. We then use the read() method, which we will cover in more detail later, to read the entire contents from the file object (f) and display it with the print command. After finishing with the file object, the close() method is then used to close our file object and free up resources. The output from this listing is:

```
FLATLAND

PART 1

THIS WORLD

SECTION 1  Of the Nature of Flatland

I call our world Flatland, not because we call it so, but to make its
nature clearer to you, my happy readers, who are privileged to live in
Space.

Imagine a vast sheet of paper on which straight Lines, Triangles,
Squares, Pentagons, Hexagons, and other figures, instead of remaining
fixed in their places, move freely about, on or in the surface, but
without the power of rising above or sinking below it, very much like
shadows--only hard with luminous edges--and you will then have a pretty
correct notion of my country and countrymen.  Alas, a few years ago, I
```

should have said "my universe:" but now my mind has been opened to higher views of things.

In such a country, you will perceive at once that it is impossible that there should be anything of what you call a "solid" kind; but I dare say you will suppose that we could at least distinguish by sight the Triangles, Squares, and other figures, moving about as I have described them. On the contrary, we could see nothing of the kind, not at least so as to distinguish one figure from another. Nothing was visible, nor could be visible, to us, except Straight Lines; and the necessity of this I will speedily demonstrate.

In our ERP application, information may come in with large blocks of text. We may collect feedback from our customers, or perhaps we are describing issues within incidents and for reporting. We can store the customer responses locally in a text file that we can then read and analyze using Python for further analysis and usage.

READING TEXT FROM A FILE

There are several ways to read data from an input file. The simplest way is to use the method `read()` to input all contents of a file as a string. If the file contains several lines of text, newline characters will be embedded.

Listing 18.3 is an example using the `read()` method. As with the example provided for `open()` in Listing 18.2, we open a file stored in a subfolder named `data` and read the contents of the file into memory. We then use `print` to display the text.

LISTING 18.3

Reading the contents of a text file

```
f = open("data/flatland.txt", mode="r")
text = f.read()
print(text)
f.close()
```

This time, we return what is read into a variable called `text` and then use `print` to display the contents of that variable. The results are the same as those in Listing 18.2.

Use the `read()` Method to Limit the Content

In the previous examples, we opened and printed an entire file. In some cases, we only need part of the content of a file. We can limit the `read()` method to display a specific number of characters from the file.

In Listing 18.4, we open the same file, but we display only the first 100 characters from the file.

LISTING 18.4

Limiting the amount read

```
f = open("data/flatland01.txt", "r")
print(f.read(100)) # this will pull the first 100 characters
f.close()
```

Because we are passing 100 to the read() method, only the first 100 characters will be read. Note that this includes all characters including newlines, spaces, and standard characters. The output this time is:

```
FLATLAND

PART 1

THIS WORLD

SECTION 1  Of the Nature of Flatland

I call our world Flatland, not b
```

Let's look at a second example of using read() and limiting the number of characters read. In Listing 18.5, we use the IncidentTicket.txt file that is available in the downloadable zip file mentioned at the beginning of this lesson and also shown in Listing 18.6. Within this listing, we define a new function called head() that takes as input a file and a number of characters. The function then reads the file and returns that number of characters starting at the beginning of the file.

LISTING 18.5

Creating a function to read characters from a file

```
def head(filepath,num_char):
  f = open(filepath, mode="r")
  output = f.read(num_char)
  f.close()
  return output

# return the first 20 characters in the file data/text.txt
text = head("IncidentTicket.txt",20)
print(text)
```

You can see that our head() function does exactly what was described. It opens the file passed to it (filepath), then reads the number of characters indicated (num_char). Those characters are placed in a variable called output that is returned from the head() function. Notice that we also close the file that we had opened.

After defining the head() function, we use it. We call head with the IncidentTicket .txt file and ask for 20 characters to be returned. These characters are placed in the variable, text, which is then printed:

```
Incident_Number:0001
```

If we change the number passed to head() from 20 to 50, our output becomes:

```
Incident_Number:0001
Customer:Acme_Bank
Technician
```

LISTING 18.6

IncidentTicket.txt

```
Incident_Number: 0001
Customer: Acme_Bank
TechnicianID: 00034
Location: Headquarters
Date: 04/05/2019

Lorem ipsum dolor sit amet, consectetur adipiscing elit. Aliquam ac mauris
urna. Integer aliquet finibus ipsum vitae semper. Class aptent taciti sociosqu
ad litora torquent per conubia nostra, per inceptos himenaeos. Nulla vehicula
scelerisque tristique. Ut in gravida lacus. Fusce posuere ex non luctus
accumsan. Donec accumsan orci in leo vehicula tempus. Integer posuere fringilla
metus, a efficitur metus blandit ac. Etiam at erat urna. Integer imperdiet diam
quam, vel viverra lacus fermentum eget.
```

For our ERP banking application, we are likely to be working with exceptionally large files. When working with large data files, we may not need to read the entire contents of a file, and instead we only need to read a few characters from it. For example, perhaps we need to check the finalized date of an incident ticket to determine whether we need to add it to the processing cycle.

Reading Lines

We can use the readline() method to read a file line by line. In Listing 18.7, we read the first four lines of the IncidentTicket.txt file. Note that blank lines count as lines.

LISTING 18.7

Reading lines of a text file

```
f = open("IncidentTicket.txt", "r") # read file in read mode.
print(f.readline()) # read first line
print(f.readline()) # read second line
print(f.readline()) # read third line
print(f.readline()) # read fourth line

f.close()
```

When this program is run, the IncidentTicket.txt file is opened for reading. The file handle, f, is then used with the readline() method to read four lines one by one before the file is closed. The output is:

```
Incident_Number:0001

Customer: Acme_Bank

TechnicianID: 00034

Location: Headquarters
```

In Listing 18.8, we again create a head() function that takes the file, but this time with a number of lines. The function reads the file, returns the top number of specified lines in the file, and finally closes the file.

LISTING 18.8

Creating a function to read lines of a file

```
def head(filepath,num_lines):
    f = open(filepath, mode="r")
    lines = ""
    for x in range(num_lines):
      lines += f.readline()
    f.close()
    return lines

# return the first 3 lines in the file
text = head("IncidentTicket.txt",3)
print(text)
```

This time, we open our file in the same manner, but then we need to do a little more than simply pass a number to a reading method. We create a variable called lines to hold the information we are reading from the file. We then use a loop to iterate through reading the lines of the file using readline(). Once done, we close our file and return the information stored in lines. The output is the first three lines of the IncidentTicket.txt file:

```
Incident_Number: 0001
Customer: Acme_Bank
TechnicianID: 00034
```

The number passed to head() can be changed to get different results.

Our ERP banking application could formulate incidents and reports via text files. To provide an import and export functionality, the tool could look at the first few lines of the text file where the identifying information resides. Python easily enables that functionality using methods such as readline().

Iterating through a File

Once we read a file using open(), the file object is an object that can be iterated, and thus works with a for loop. This is different from how we used a for loop in Listing 18.8, as can be seen in Listing 18.9.

LISTING 18.9

Iterating through a file

```
f = open("IncidentTicket.txt", "r")

for line in f:  # the file object can be iterated on at the line level.
    print(line) # with each iteration, line contains the current line.

f.close()
```

In this example, we open the file and iterate through the lines of the file. You can see that the iteration happens at the line level, so for each line (called line) in our file, we are using the file object called f, and then we are doing something. In this case, what we are doing is printing the current line.

Because we are using a `for` loop, the loop ends automatically when it reaches the last line of the file. The output is our complete file being printed:

```
Incident_Number: 0001

Customer: Acme_Bank

TechnicianID: 00034

Location: Headquarters

Date: 04/05/2019
```

Lorem ipsum dolor sit amet, consectetur adipiscing elit. Aliquam ac mauris urna. Integer aliquet finibus ipsum vitae semper. Class aptent taciti sociosqu ad litora torquent per conubia nostra, per inceptos himenaeos. Nulla vehicula scelerisque tristique. Ut in gravida lacus. Fusce posuere ex non luctus accumsan. Donec accumsan orci in leo vehicula tempus. Integer posuere fringilla metus, a efficitur metus blandit ac. Etiam at erat urna. Integer imperdiet diam quam, vel viverra lacus fermentum eget.

In Listing 18.10, we look at a second example. In this case, we create a function called `line_starts_with()` that we use to only print lines within a text file that begin with a given character. The function will take a filename and the character to be used for filtering the lines. This listing illustrates how we can iterate through our file and at the same time work with the data that we are reading.

LISTING 18.10

Iterating and checking the start of the line

```python
def line_starts_with(file_path,fchar):
  f = open(file_path, mode="r")
  output = ""
  for line in f:
    if fchar == line[0]:
      output += line
  return output

# return all lines in the file data/text.txt that start with "I".
text = line_starts_with("IncidentTicket.txt","I")
print(text)
```

You can see that much of this listing is similar to previous listings. What is different is that for each line (called `line`) that we read in, we look at the first character and see if it matches the character (`fchar`) that was passed to `line_starts_with()`. As can be seen, each line read in is simply an array of characters, so we can compare the first character (`line[0]`) to see if it equals `fchar`. If there is a match, we add the line to our output. If there isn't a match, we iterate to the next line in the file. Once the iterating is completed, we return the output.

In this case, we pass the `IncidentTicket.txt` file we've been using along with the letter "I". The results are only one line from our file printing:

```
Incident_Number: 0001
```

> **NOTE** Note that Listing 18.10 does not take the case of the letter into account when checking for matches. Passing "i" will not get the same result as passing "I". You can add logic to fix this if you want.

As we analyze the customer data in our ERP application, we may want to find specific words, phrases, or characters from the customer responses stored in our local file. We can achieve this in Python by iterating through the file object using a `for` loop.

ADD CONTENT TO A FILE

If we open a file in append (`"a"`) mode, we can use the `write()` method to add data at the end of the file. If the file named in the `open()` method does not exist, Python will create the file automatically.

In Listing 18.11, we create and open a text file in append mode and write several lines of text. After running the script, check your computer to see if the file was created and what text appears in the file.

What happens if you run the script again?

LISTING 18.11

Writing to a file

```
f = open("data/test_file.txt", "a")

f.write("Hello World!")
f.write("Hello World!")
f.write("Hello World!")

f.close()
```

Assuming that the test_file.txt file did not exist before you ran the script, you should see three instances of "Hello World!" in a single line when you open the file from your computer:

```
Hello World!Hello World!Hello World!
```

Each time you run the script, Python will add "Hello World!" three more times, on the same line.

The write() function by itself appends the new text to the end of the existing text, without creating new lines for the new text. We can solve this problem by adding the new-line character \n at the beginning of each string that should start on a new line as shown in Listing 18.12.

LISTING 18.12

Writing transaction data to a file

```python
import datetime

f = open("ReportFile.txt", "a")

f.write("Acme Bank EBP")
f.write("\nDate:" + str(datetime.date.today()))
f.write("\nReport File 0001")

f.close()
```

This listing opens or creates a file called ReportFile.txt in the current folder or directory. It then writes a bit of banking information including the current date. The newline character (\n) was used when writing the second and third lines of code so that they would not be on the same line. After running this script, check that the file was created. Your file should contain information similar to the following, but with the date you ran the program:

```
Acme Bank EBP
Date:2021-03-26
Report File 0001
```

> **NOTE** If you run Listing 18.12 multiple times, you will see that the bank name doesn't end up on a new line. You can use an additional newline character to fix this. One way is to change the following line to include a newline at the end:
>
> ```python
> f.write("\nReport File 0001\n")
> ```

Listing 18.13 presents another example of adding to a file. This time the code creates a function called `write_list_2_file` that takes as input a list and appends each element in the list as a separate line in a file.

LISTING 18.13

Writing a list to a file

```
customers = ["Ax Lodevick", "Frank Prys", "Ania Hearle",
"Justus Bodker", "Clementius Druce", "Ganny Penwright",
"Alick Rens", "Gwen Drewitt", "Jessie Wychard",
"Brina Elliss", "Derril Damiral", "Jade Cutajar",
"Brannon Goldsmith", "Valentin Salmons", "Tull Rennix",
"Quintina Whanstall", "Lev Frunks", "Doris Heskin",
"Idalina Moro", "Gillie Ledram"
]

def write_list_2_file(input_list,input_file_path):
    f = open(input_file_path, "a")
    for name in input_list:
      name = "\n"+name
      f.write(name)
    f.close()


write_list_2_file(customers,"Customers.txt")
```

In this listing, we start by creating a list of customers. We then define our function that opens the file, and then for each name in the list, writes the name to the file along with a newline character. Once we've iterated through all the names, the file is closed. The last part of our listing is a call to the newly defined function that passes the list of customers and the name of the file to write them to.

After you have run this listing the first time, you should have a file called `Customers.txt` in the same folder as your script. The file should have each customer name on its own line as such:

```
Ax Lodevick
Frank Prys
Ania Hearle
Justus Bodker
Clementius Druce
Ganny Penwright
Alick Rens
```

```
Gwen Drewitt
Jessie Wychard
Brina Elliss
Derril Damiral
Jade Cutajar
Brannon Goldsmith
Valentin Salmons
Tull Rennix
Quintina Whanstall
Lev Frunks
Doris Heskin
Idalina Moro
Gillie Ledram
```

The ability to edit an existing file or create a new file is important for any data analysis task. For the ERP banking application we've discussed, we might need to edit and update our analyzed data as we acquire new data from customers. We can do this in Python using file objects and their corresponding methods.

OVERWRITING THE CONTENTS OF A FILE

We can use the write() method to create a new blank file or to overwrite data in an existing file using the option "w" as the access mode. If the named file already exists, Python will delete the existing file and create a new blank file with the same name. This means that opening an existing file in write() mode erases any existing content in the file, even if no additional content is added.

The script in Listing 18.14 opens the local test_file.txt file in write mode. We then use the write() method to overwrite the existing contents of the file. If the file did not already exist, Python would create it and add the text to the new file.

LISTING 18.14

Overwriting a file

```
f = open("data/test_file.txt", "w")

f.write("This will overwrite whatever existed in the file.")

f.close()
```

This listing is noticeably short but illustrates the point. The "w" option is being used when we open the test_file.txt file in the data folder. When we then write to the file, the existing content will be overwritten. After running this code, check that the file was created and what its contents are. They should be:

```
This will overwrite whatever existed in the file.
```

What happens if you run the script multiple times? What you should find is that each time you run the listing, only the newly written data is contained within the file. Each time the file is overwritten.

In Listing 18.15 we extend our script for overwriting a file. This time we create a script that asks the user for two inputs:

- A path and filename
- Text that will be stored in the filename that was provided.

LISTING 18.15

Prompting the user for a file to overwrite

```
input_1 = input("Please enter a file name: ")
input_2 = input("Enter the text you would like within the file: ")

f = open(input_1, mode="w")
f. write(input_2)
f.close()
```

The script prompts the user for input for the filename (input_1) and the text to be saved to the file (input_2). It then creates a file named with the value that is stored in input_1 (or overwrites an existing file with the same name) and adds the text stored in input_2 to that file. You can check the contents of the file after you run the listing to confirm that it matches what was entered at the prompt.

> **TIP** Be sure that the path defined for input_1 includes an appropriate filename and filename extension.

After you have run the code once, run the code again, specifying the same filename you just created, and then type in new text. Check the text file again to confirm that it has been overwritten.

There are many scenarios in which files are used as ephemeral (temporary) storage so that they can be manipulated, or handled, before being processed or handed to another system. There are also times where logs are meant to hold information for only a certain period of time before they're overwritten, so overwriting a file can be beneficial in multiple ways, especially for storage space requirements. Our ERP banking application keeps temporary daily logs and overwrites them the next day as the data is not required past that point.

CREATING A NEW FILE

We can use the "x" option to create a new file. This is different from the "w" option because the "x" option will report an error if the named file already exists. For this reason, "x" should be used only to create a new file and in situations where you do not want Python to overwrite an existing file.

In Listing 18.16, we open two files from the data subdirectory: The first is another_file.txt and the second is test_file.txt that was created earlier.

LISTING 18.16

Creating a new file

```
# This file should not exist...
f = open("data/another_file.txt", "x")
f.close()

# We created this file earlier...
f = open("data/test_file.txt", "x")
f.close()
```

When we attempt to open the file another_file.txt in the data folder, it will open without error because the file does not already exist. However, the second file is the same test_file.txt file that we used in earlier activities in this lesson. Python throws an error if the file already exists because we are opening the file with the "x" option. The output when running this where the first file does not exist and the second does is an error similar to the following:

```
--------------------------------------------------------------------------
Traceback (most recent call last):
    f = open("data/test_file.txt", "x")
FileExistsError: [Errno 17] File exists: 'data/test_file.txt'
```

In Listing 18.17, we update Listing 18.15 to add a third prompt to the user. This time we ask the user to enter a read/write mode for the file ("a", "x", "r", or "w"), and then open the file with that mode.

LISTING 18.17

Prompting the user to create a file

```
input_1 = input("Please enter a file name: ")
input_2 = input("Enter the text you would like within the file: ")
input_3 = input("Enter the read/write mode for the file [a,x,r,w]: ")

f = open(input_1, input_3)
f. write(input_2)
f.close()
```

This listing lets us test each of the modes in an interactive manner.

In creating Python applications, we may need to create a new file for data processing. In our ERP application, we may want to store our analyzed data in a file separate from our raw data, thereby introducing the need to create a new file. All these functions—creating, editing, and saving a file—can be performed in Python using file objects and their corresponding methods.

USING THE OS MODULE

The os module in Python provides built-in functions for interacting with the operating system. The os module abstracts the functionalities of the platform, providing functions to navigate, create, delete, and modify files and folders. The os module allows us to perform several operations on files, including reading the contents of a directory and deleting existing files. We must import the os module before we can use it.

There may be a time where we want to create the existence of a particular directory or path. We can use the os module to assist with this. In the example in Listing 18.18, we import the os module and use exists to see if the file exists or not. This command produces a Boolean output, so we can use it in conditional statements.

LISTING 18.18

Checking for a file's existence

```
import os

if os.path.exists("data/missing_file.txt"):
    print("The file exists.")
else:
    print("The file doesn't exist.")
```

In this example, we check to see if a file with the pathname `data/missing_file.txt` exists. If it does, we print a message saying, "The file exists." If it does not, then we print a different message stating, "The file doesn't exist." To make the determination, we simply pass the path and file name to the `exists()` method within the `path` class of the `os` module.

Listing 18.19 is more functional. This script prompts the user for the name of a file and then checks to see if that file exists in the `data` subdirectory, relative to the Python script file.

LISTING 18.19

Checking for the entered file's existence

```
import os

file_name = input("Please enter a file name to check for: ")
if os.path.exists("data/"+file_name):
    print("The file exists.")
else:
    print("The file doesn't exist.")
```

The script operates much like the previous listing, with the only real difference being that the user is prompted to enter the filename.

DELETING A FILE

The `os` module includes the `remove()` function that can delete an existing file. If the named file does not exist, Python will report an error.

In Listing 18.20 we use `os.remove()` to delete a file that should exist and attempt to delete another file that should not exist. When we run the script, the first file is deleted successfully, but Python reports an error when we attempt to delete the second file.

LISTING 18.20

Deleting a file

```
import os

os.remove("data/test_file.txt") # Deleting file from previous example.
print("The file test_file.txt deleted successfully.")

# The following file doesn't exist, so will cause error!
os.remove("data/missing_file.txt")
print("The file missing_file.txt deleted successfully.")
```

If you ran Listing 18.11, then you should have a `data/test_file.txt` file on your system. As such, the call to `os.remove("data/test_file.txt")` should find a file and remove it, thus printing the message:

```
The file test_file.txt deleted successfully.
```

It is assumed you don't have a file called `data/missing_file.txt`, so the second call to `os.remove()` will fail. The result is an error message will be displayed by Python because it was unable to find the file:

```
FileNotFoundError: [WinError 2] The system cannot find the file specified:
'data/missing_file.txt'
```

> **NOTE** In Lesson 23, you'll learn how to handle errors more gracefully so that something such as a missing file doesn't crash your program.

Of course, we can check to see if the file exists before trying to delete it. That will also help avoid getting the error we saw from the previous listing. In Listing 18.21, the user is asked to enter a filename. If the filename is found, then the file is removed.

LISTING 18.21

Prompting to remove a file

```python
import os

file_name = input("Please enter a file name to check for: ")
directory = "data/"
if os.path.exists(directory+file_name):
    print("The file exists.")
    user_input = input("Would you like to delete the file? [yes/no]")
    if user_input.lower() == 'yes':
      os.remove(directory+file_name)
      print("The file "+directory+file_name+" was deleted successfully.")
else:
    print("The file doesn't exist.")
```

After prompting the user for a filename, this listing uses the `os.path.exists()` function we saw earlier in this lesson. If the file exists in the `data` directory below the current directory, then a message is displayed, and the user is asked if they would like to delete the file. If they say yes, then the file is removed. In the cases where there isn't a file by the entered name, a message is displayed saying the file doesn't exist.

The following is the output when a file exists, but the user says no to deleting:

```
Please enter a file name to check for: myFile.txt
The file exists.
Would you like to delete the file? [yes/no]no
```

The following is the output when the file exists, and the user says yes to delete:

```
Please enter a file name to check for: myFile.txt
The file exists.
Would you like to delete the file? [yes/no]yes
The file data/myFile.txt was deleted successfully.
```

And finally, the following is the result for a file that doesn't exist (because in this case, we just deleted it):

```
Please enter a file name to check for: myFile.txt
The file doesn't exist.
```

SUMMARY

In many cases, when we need to analyze the contents of a text for a specific purpose, the text already exists in a file, so it can be efficient to have Python read the text directly from the source file. Not only is this faster than manually inputting the text at runtime, but it also means that Python can look at a file whose contents may change over time. This allows Python to automatically perform the analysis on the most recent version of the file. This module focused on the input, processing, and output of data within Python.

Now that you have completed this lesson, you should be able to:

- Know common functions for doing file input and output.
- Open, read, and display text-based files in a *.txt* format.
- Append content to an existing file.
- Replace data in an existing file with new data.
- Use the Python os module to check for existing files.
- Create a new text file.
- Delete a text file.

EXERCISES

The following exercises will allow you to demonstrate your ability to achieve the objectives of the chapter. Unless otherwise specified, you may use any of the files provided in the book to complete these activities, create your own files, or find files that are available online. You should complete each exercise and make sure that the code runs without errors. The exercises include:

Exercise 1: Reading Lines

Exercise 2: Combination of the Two

Exercise 3: Combination of Them All

Exercise 4: Listing Lines

Exercise 5: Longest Word

Exercise 6: Listing Text

Exercise 7: Text in Reverse

Exercise 1: Reading Lines

Write a function that prompts the reader for an integer n and reads the first n lines of a file. Include a creative way to handle cases where n is greater than the number of lines available in the file.

Exercise 2: Combination of the Two

Write a function that takes as input the path to two text files and concatenates the files into a single new file.

Exercise 3: Combination of Them All

Write a function that takes a variable number of text files and concatenates them into a single new file.

Exercise 4: Listing Lines

Write a function that reads a text file line by line, stores each line in a list, and then returns the list.

Exercise 5: Longest Word

Write a function that takes as input the path to a text file and returns the longest word in the text file.

Exercise 6: Listing Text

Write a function that takes as input a list of strings and writes the list to a text file. Each element in the list should be a separate line in the new text file.

Exercise 7: Text in Reverse

Write a function that takes as input a text file and a new filename, and then copies the contents of the input text file to another file using the new filename. As a challenge, update the code so that the lines in the new file are in the reverse order of the lines in the original file.

Lesson 19
Processing CSV Files

In the previous lesson, we covered working with basic text files. In this lesson, we continue learning about working with files but transition to working with CSV files (.csv), which include records organized into columns like tables and are often generated by structured databases. We can use Python scripts to read these files, add (or append) content to an existing CSV file, and create new CSV files.

LEARNING OBJECTIVES

By the end of this lesson, you will be able to:

- Open, read, and display information from files in a .csv format.
- Append content to an existing .csv file.
- Replace data in an existing .csv file with new data.

READING CSV FILES

CSV stands for *comma-separated values*. A CSV file is a structured, text-only file that we use to organize data into rows and columns. CSV files use commas or other characters to separate individual column values within each row of the data. Because a CSV file is plain text, this format is often used to transfer data from one database system to another. Virtually all database management systems and spreadsheet applications have the ability to read and write raw data in CSV format.

Python includes a csv module that contains various classes and functions to handle CSV files. We can use the reader class within the csv library to read a CSV file and return the contents of the file in a list.

In Listing 19.1, we use the open() function to open an existing CSV file as a file object named f, and then we use the csv.reader function to read lines from the file.

LISTING 19.1

Reading a CSV file

```
import csv

# Use open function to read the CSV file and create
# a file object f:

with open('data/stocks_short.csv') as f:

    # Use the reader class under the csv module to
    # read the file using comma as the delimiter

    csv_file = csv.reader(f, delimiter=',')
    row = f.readline() # Read the firstline of the .csv
    print(row)
    row = f.readline() # Read the firstline of the .csv
    print(row)
```

This listing contains comments that explain what is happening. Because we are opening a CSV file, we start by importing the csv module. We then open the `stocks_short.csv` file, which needs to be located in the data folder below our current folder.

You might have noticed that we opened the CSV file differently from how we opened the text file in Lesson 18. In Lesson 18, we had opened the file in the following format:

```
f = open('data/stocks_short.csv')
```

or for reading, we could have used the following format:

```
f = open('data/stocks_short.csv', "r")
```

Using the with statement allows us to open a file in a manner that lets Python do more of the background work for us. For example, it will take care of closing the file. Once opened, we can do the processing in the code that is indented under the with statement. In this case, we create a reader that we call csv_file that we can use to read rows from our CSV file. We pass the reader the file handle we created, f, as well as what character is used to separate values in our rows. In this case, the delimiter is a comma.

With our reader created, we can call the readline() method to read a line of the file. We do this twice and then print the output from each read:

```
Date,Open,High,Low,Close,Volume
```

```
2018-10-02,20,20.1,17.6,18.5,2799073
```

While reading a single line at a time is nice, generally we want to read all the content within a file. A CSV file is an iterable object, so we can use a for loop to display the contents. Because of how a CSV file is structured, the column or field names appear on the first row of the output, and the data in each of the other rows includes values for each of those columns. Listing 19.2 expands on what was done in the previous listing.

LISTING 19.2

Iterating through a CSV file

```
import csv

with open('data/stocks_short.csv') as f:

    csv_file = csv.reader(f, delimiter=',')
    f.readline()

    # csv_file is an iterable object that we can iterate on using a for loop
    for row in csv_file:
        print(row)    # print entire row
```

We can see that we use a call to `readline()` to read the headings. We then use the `for` loop to iterate using our reader object (`csv_file`) to read each row. The result is that all the rows in our file are then printed:

```
['2018-10-02', '20', '20.1', '17.6', '18.5', '2799073']
['2018-10-03', '18.2', '18.75', '18.05', '18.65', '155562']
['2018-10-06', '18.48', '19.58', '18.48', '19.24', '188229']
['2018-10-07', '19.25', '19.48', '18.93', '19.24', '176606']
['2018-10-08', '19.17', '19.48', '18.9', '19.13', '37046']
['2018-10-09', '19.16', '19.55', '19', '19.25', '114523']
['2018-10-10', '19.25', '19.36', '18.77', '19', '34775']
['2018-10-13', '18.92', '19.1', '18.64', '19', '52514'']
['2018-10-14', '19.03', '19.03', '17.91', '18.1', '126457']
['2018-10-15', '18.07', '19.5', '18', '19.43', '46156']
```

In Listing 19.2, we print each entire row. We could also have printed individual items from each row as shown in Listing 19.3.

LISTING 19.3

Iterating through a CSV file and printing individual items

```
import csv

with open('data/stocks_short.csv') as f:
    csv_file = csv.reader(f, delimiter=',')

    for row in csv_file:
        print(row[0], " - ", row[1] )
```

This listing doesn't remove the header before iterating through the file, so you see that the heading items are displayed. The listing then displays the first and second value in each row with a dash between them:

```
Date  -  Open
2018-10-02  -  20
2018-10-03  -  18.2
2018-10-06  -  18.48
2018-10-07  -  19.25
2018-10-08  -  19.17
2018-10-09  -  19.16
2018-10-10  -  19.25
```

```
2018-10-13  -  18.92
2018-10-14  -  19.03
2018-10-15  -  18.07
```

Iterating through data and displaying it is nice, but generally we want to do more than that. For example, using the stock data, we could compute and display the average opening price for all stock items. In our `stocks_short.csv` file, each row of data includes values for a specific stock item, including:

- **Date:** The date of the following data
- **Open:** The opening price on that date
- **High:** The highest price on that date
- **Low:** The lowest price on that date
- **Close:** The closing price on that date
- **Volume:** The number of shares traded on that date

In Listing 19.4, we iterate through the file to compute and display the average opening price for all stock items.

LISTING 19.4

Calculating the average opening price

```
import csv

with open('data/stocks_short.csv') as f:

    csv_file = csv.reader(f, delimiter=',')
    f.readline()

    sum = 0
    count = 0

    for row in csv_file:
        sum += float(row[1])
        count += 1

    print(sum/count)
```

Most of this listing is similar to the previous listings. What is new is that we define sum and count variables and initialize them to zero. We then iterate through the rows of data and add the opening value from row[1] to our sum and increment our counter. Once we have looped through the entire file, we then print the sum divided by the count, which would be the average:

```
18.953
```

The examples so far have used the `stocks_short.csv` file. This is a shortened version of a much longer file named `stocks.csv` that was also in the downloadable zip file. We can change the `open` statement to use the `stocks.csv` file instead:

```
with open('data/stocks.csv') as f:
```

We can then see that the new average of the much larger set of data is:

```
19.51039885350318
```

We've been using our banking ERP application to tie together what we've been learning. Often, the data collected by our ERP application—such as customer transactions tagged with the transaction date—will be stored locally as a CSV file. Python allows us to easily read the CSV file using the built-in `csv` module and perform further analysis on the data.

USING THE DICTREADER CLASS

We can use the `DictReader` class within the `csv` package to read a CSV file and return a dictionary of key: value pairs, where each key is a column name and the value is the corresponding value for each row in the original CSV file.

In Listing 19.5, we iterate through the data in the CSV file and create a dictionary for each row. The column names from the first row are used as the keys, and values from the data in each row are paired with the keys.

LISTING 19.5

Creating a dictionary for each row in a CSV file

```
import csv

with open('data/stocks_short.csv') as f:

    csv_file = csv.DictReader(f, delimiter=',')

    # csv_file is an iterable object that we can iterate on using a for loop
    for row in csv_file:
        print(row)
```

You can see that we use the `DictReader` class under the `csv` module to read the file using a comma as the delimiter. We then iterate through each row and print the entire row. The output is:

```
{'Date': '2018-10-02', 'Open': '20', 'High': '20.1', 'Low': '17.6', 'Close': '18.5',
'Volume': '2799073'}
{'Date': '2018-10-03', 'Open': '18.2', 'High': '18.75', 'Low': '18.05', 'Close': '18.65',
'Volume': '155562'}
{'Date': '2018-10-06', 'Open': '18.48', 'High': '19.58', 'Low': '18.48', 'Close': '19.24',
'Volume': '188229'}
{'Date': '2018-10-07', 'Open': '19.25', 'High': '19.48', 'Low': '18.93', 'Close': '19.24',
'Volume': '176606'}
{'Date': '2018-10-08', 'Open': '19.17', 'High': '19.48', 'Low': '18.9', 'Close': '19.13',
'Volume': '37046'}
{'Date': '2018-10-09', 'Open': '19.16', 'High': '19.55', 'Low': '19', 'Close': '19.25',
'Volume': '114523'}
{'Date': '2018-10-10', 'Open': '19.25', 'High': '19.36', 'Low': '18.77', 'Close': '19',
'Volume': '34775'}
{'Date': '2018-10-13', 'Open': '18.92', 'High': '19.1', 'Low': '18.64', 'Close': '19',
'Volume': '52514'}
{'Date': '2018-10-14', 'Open': '19.03', 'High': '19.03', 'Low': '17.91', 'Close': '18.1',
'Volume': '126457'}
{'Date': '2018-10-15', 'Open': '18.07', 'High': '19.5', 'Low': '18', 'Close': '19.43',
'Volume': '46156'}
```

In Listing 19.6, we again use a `DictReader`. This time, we determine the largest volume of sales in the `stocks.csv` dataset.

LISTING 19.6

Using a DictReader

```
import csv
with open('data/stocks.csv') as f:

    csv_file = csv.DictReader(f, delimiter=',')
    vol = None
    max_vol = None

    for row in csv_file:
      vol = int(row["Volume"])
      if max_vol == None or max_vol < vol:
        max_vol = vol

    print(max_vol)
```

The output from running this listing is 8182600.

CREATING A DATASET LIST

We can read an entire CSV file and store the data in a list for later use. In Listing 19.7, we start with the short version of the CSV data, create a new list named dataset, use DictReader to convert each line of the data into a new row, and append each row to the dataset list.

LISTING 19.7

Creating a list from our dataset

```
def read_csv(filepath,delimiter=","):
    import csv
    dataset = list()
    with open(filepath) as f:

        # use the DictReader function of the csv module to
        # read the file using the same delimiter
        csv_file = csv.DictReader(f, delimiter=delimiter)

        # csv_file is an iterable object that we can iterate on using a for loop
        for row in csv_file:
            dataset.append(row)

    return dataset

dataset = read_csv("data/stocks_short.csv")
print(len(dataset)) # number of rows in the dataset
print("----")
print(dataset[0])   # print first row in the dataset
print("----")
print(dataset)
```

Note that we define the delimiter in the read_csv function and then reference the same delimiter when we call DictReader. In the output, we display the number of rows as the length of the dataset, the first row only, and then the entire dataset:

```
10
----
OrderedDict([('Date', '7/7/2006'), ('Open', '492.7'), ('High', '495.9'), ('Low',
'490.0999'), ('Close', '490.8'), ('Volume', '807950')])
----
[OrderedDict([('Date', '7/7/2006'), ('Open', '492.7'), ('High', '495.9'), ('Low',
'490.0999'), ('Close', '490.8'), ('Volume', '807950')]), OrderedDict([('Date',
'7/10/2006'), ('Open', '493.3'), ('High', '496.4'), ('Low', '491.0001'), ('Close',
```

```
'493.4'), ('Volume', '838869')]), OrderedDict([('Date', '7/11/2006'), ('Open', '493.4'),
('High', '496.7999'), ('Low', '488.6'), ('Close', '496.0001'), ('Volume', '816880')]),
OrderedDict([('Date', '7/12/2006'), ('Open', '495.2'), ('High', '497.3'), ('Low',
'487.1001'), ('Close', '488.3'), ('Volume', '1374150')]), OrderedDict([('Date',
'7/13/2006'), ('Open', '488'), ('High', '488'), ('Low', '478.3'), ('Close', '478.7'),
('Volume', '1633189')]), OrderedDict([('Date', '7/14/2006'), ('Open', '478.5001'),
('High', '480.0999'), ('Low', '474.1'), ('Close', '475.8'), ('Volume', '1539689')]),
OrderedDict([('Date', '7/17/2006'), ('Open', '469.1'), ('High', '469.5'), ('Low',
'463.3'), ('Close', '463.9999'), ('Volume', '3265409')]), OrderedDict([('Date',
'7/18/2006'), ('Open', '464.2'), ('High', '468.9999'), ('Low', '462.2'), ('Close',
'465.5'), ('Volume', '1655100')]), OrderedDict([('Date', '7/19/2006'), ('Open',
'468.5001'), ('High', '475.0999'), ('Low', '468.3'), ('Close', '472.5'), ('Volume',
'2621339')]), OrderedDict([('Date', '7/20/2006'), ('Open', '472.5'), ('High', '474.5'),
('Low', '470.5'), ('Close', '471.1'), ('Volume', '1597130')])])
```

In Listing 19.8, we go one step further with our code. In this listing, we add the logic to compute the total of the closing prices across the dataset.

LISTING 19.8

Using our list from reading a CSV file to calculate the closing price

```
def read_csv(filepath,delimiter=","):
    import csv
    dataset = list()
    with open(filepath) as f:
        csv_file = csv.DictReader(f, delimiter=delimiter)
        for row in csv_file:
            dataset.append(row)
    return dataset

dataset = read_csv("data/stocks.csv")
total = 0
for row in dataset:
  total += float(row["Close"])
  print("Close: " + str(row["Close"]))
  print("----")print(total)
```

You can see that most of this code is similar to the previous listings. After using our read_csv function to convert the CSV data to a list, we use a for loop to total and print each closing value in our dataset. We then print the total of all the values. Note that because we are using the stocks.csv file, the output is a long list:

```
Close: 18.5
Close: 18.65
Close: 19.24
Close: 19.24
Close: 19.13
Close: 19.25
Close: 19
Close: 19
Close: 18.1
Close: 19.43
Close: 19.4
Close: 19.08
Close: 19.03
Close: 19.32
...
...
Close: 7.55
Close: 10.02
Close: 10.08
Close: 11.14
Close: 11.07
Close: 11.11
Close: 10.88
Close: 11.28
----
15290.700000000004
```

In our ERP banking application, we often have large transaction lists that we need to review for accuracy as well as for fraud. In order to process datasets, we need to be able to view the file as a whole. Taking the entire CSV file as a data source via Python can enable us to better process our data.

USING WRITEROW()

We can use the `writerow()` method of the `writer` class to write data to a file row by row in write mode.

In our ERP application, we will often want to store our data locally. For instance, we may want to create a local copy of the customer transaction queries made in the day to discover any anomalies. In order to do this, we will want to save the data locally for further analysis. We can use the writer method `writerow()` in the `csv` module to write a row of data (usually iterable such as a list or list of lists) as a CSV file as shown in Listing 19.9.

LISTING 19.9

Using `writerow`

```python
import csv

row_1 = ["employee_id","first_name","last_name"] # header row
row_2 = ["EMP2345235636","robert","balti"] # first row
row_3 = ["EMP2498799899","mark","smith"] # second row
row_4 = ["EMP2498989890","mary","caldwell"] # third row


with open('data/employee.csv', 'w') as csv_file: # open file in write mode
    # use the writer class to create a writer object
    # that we will use to write data into the file
    writer = csv.writer(csv_file,delimiter=',')
    writer.writerow(row_1) # writing the header row
    writer.writerow(row_2) # writing the first row
    writer.writerow(row_3) # writing the second row
    writer.writerow(row_4) # writing the third row

f = open('data/employee.csv', 'r')
print(f.read())
f.close()
```

In Listing 19.9 we define a series of rows, starting with a header row. We then open a CSV file in write mode and iterate through the data one row at a time to add the data to the file. The data should be entered into the dataset as a list; otherwise, words will be separated into their individual characters.

We use the "w" parameter with open, which will either overwrite an existing file or create a new file in the given path. In this example, the file does not yet exist, so Python creates a new file and adds the data to that file.

In the last three lines of code in this listing, we open our new employee.csv file and print its content. We see that all four rows were created:

```
employee_id,first_name,last_name

EMP2345235636,robert,balti

EMP2498799899,mark,smith

EMP2498989890,mary,caldwell
```

In Listing 19.10 we provide a second example of using the `writerow()` method. This time, we prompt the user to enter the data that will be added to a CSV file. Values will be collected until the user enters **quit**.

LISTING 19.10

Prompting the user for data for a CSV file

```python
import csv
with open('user_input.csv', 'w', newline='') as csv_file:

    while True:
        user_input = input("Please enter text to add to file [enter quit to exit]: ")
        if user_input.lower() == 'quit':
            break
        else:
            writer = csv.writer(csv_file,delimiter=',')
            writer.writerow([user_input])

f = open('user_input.csv', 'r')
print(f.read())
f.close()
```

In this listing we are overwriting or creating a new file named user_input.csv. The user is asked for input text that will be added to our file. The user will continue to be prompted to input text until they enter **quit**, at which time, the existing contents of the file are displayed as such:

```
Please enter text to add to file [enter quit to exit]: Banana Cream Pie
Please enter text to add to file [enter quit to exit]: Cherry Pie
Please enter text to add to file [enter quit to exit]: Apple Pie
Please enter text to add to file [enter quit to exit]: Dutch Apple Pie
Please enter text to add to file [enter quit to exit]: Rhubarb Pie
Please enter text to add to file [enter quit to exit]: Sweet Potato Pie
Please enter text to add to file [enter quit to exit]: quit
Banana Cream Pie
Cherry Pie
Apple Pie
Dutch Apple Pie
Rhubarb Pie
Sweet Potato Pie
```

> **TIP** It is always useful to tell the user how to get out of a loop.

APPENDING DATA

If we open a file in append mode, we can use the writer.writerow() method to add data to a file row by row without affecting existing data. In Listing 19.11 we open the employee.csv file in append mode rather than write mode. The new data will be added to the end of the existing file without deleting any content that was already there.

LISTING 19.11

Appending data to a CSV file

```
import csv
row_1 = ["EMP4564576566","rodney","evans"] # first row
row_2 = ["EMP9807976875","lesa","clapper"] # second row
row_3 = ["EMP4564564566","mario","cruz"]   # third row

# open file in append mode, which will add the data at the end of the file
with open('data/employee.csv', 'a') as csv_file:

    # use the writer class to create a writer object
    # that we will use to write data into the file
    writer = csv.writer(csv_file,delimiter=',')
    writer.writerow(row_1) # writing the first row
    writer.writerow(row_2) # writing the second row
    writer.writerow(row_3) # writing the third row

f = open('data/employee.csv', 'r')
print(f.read())
f.close()
```

You can see that to open in append mode, we simply change the parameter we are passing when we open the file to 'a'. This tells the file to append instead of overwrite. When we run the listing, we can see that the data from running Listing 19.9 still exists, and our three new rows are added to the end:

```
employee_id,first_name,last_name

EMP2345235636,robert,balti

EMP2498799899,mark,smith

EMP2498989890,mary,caldwell

EMP4564576566,rodney,evans

EMP9807976875,lesa,clapper

EMP4564564566,mario,cruz
```

With the ability to both create new files and append to existing files, we are now able to give our programs flexibility to overwrite or add to a file. In Listing 19.12, we use the os module to determine if a file exists. If the file does not exist, then we create a new file that is opened in write mode. If the file does exist, then we open the existing file for appending data. The rest of the functionality is similar to Listing 19.10.

LISTING 19.12

Append or overwrite?

```
import os,csv

while True:
  if os.path.exists('data/user_input.csv'):
    user_prompt= input("The file exists, what data would you like to append? [type
quit to exit]: ")
    if user_prompt.lower() == 'quit':
      break
    else:
      with open('data/user_input.csv', 'a') as csv_file:
        writer = csv.writer(csv_file,delimiter=',')
        writer.writerow([user_prompt]) # writing the first row
  else:
    f = open('data/user_input.csv','w')
    print("The file data/user_input.csv does not exist. It has been created.")

f = open('data/user_input.csv','r')
print(f.read())
f.close()
```

The output from this listing depends on whether you select to append or overwrite. In the following execution, we chose to append to the file:

```
The file exists, what data would you like to append? [type quit to exit]: Peach Pie
The file exists, what data would you like to append? [type quit to exit]: Apple Pie
The file exists, what data would you like to append? [type quit to exit]: quit
Banana Cream Pie

Cherry Pie

Apple Pie

Dutch Apple Pie
```

```
Rhubarb Pie

Sweet Potato Pie

Peach Pie

Apple Pie
```

In our ERP banking application, it's important to keep logs and records of transactions so that data can be traced and tracked in the future. Appending data to the file allows us to add additional information to a file, such as the next row of data for the log.

WRITING ROWS AS LISTS

We can use the `writerows()` method within the `writer` class to write several rows to the file at once if the dataset includes identifiable objects that it can treat as rows. For example, a list could be used to write multiple rows at once.

In Listing 19.13, we create a list named `dataset` that itself includes multiple lists. Each of the embedded lists represents a row of data, so when we use `writer.writerows`, each nested list is added to the file as a new row of data. It is important to note that the values in each nested list must be in the same order as the columns in the CSV file; otherwise, the data will not be structured correctly in the updated file.

LISTING 19.13

Writing multiple rows to a file at once

```
import csv

dataset = [["EMP9807976877","vicki","gallegos"],["EMP9807976872","hector","bowen"],
           ["EMP4564564598","cassandra","wang"]]

# open file in append mode, which will add the data at the end of the file

with open('data/employee.csv', 'a') as csv_file:
    # use the writer class to create a writer object
    # that we will use to write data into the file
    writer = csv.writer(csv_file,delimiter=',')
    # write multiple rows at once using writerows
    writer.writerows(dataset)
```

```
f = open('data/employee.csv', 'r')
print(f.read())
f.close()
```

Again, `dataset` is a list of lists with each nested list being a separate row for our data file. Three lists are created within the `dataset` list, which will get added to the existing `employee.csv` file that was used in Listing 19.11. The file is opened for appending, a writer is created with a comma delimiter, and then `writerows()` is called to add the values in `dataset` to the file. When we print the contents of our file, we see that the three new rows have been appended all with just one call to `writerows()`:

```
employee_id,first_name,last_name

EMP2345235636,robert,balti

EMP2498799899,mark,smith

EMP2498989890,mary,caldwell

EMP4564576566,rodney,evans

EMP9807976875,lesa,clapper

EMP4564564566,mario,cruz

EMP9807976877,vicki,gallegos

EMP9807976872,hector,bowen

EMP4564564598,cassandra,wang
```

In our ERP application, the quantity of our daily customer transaction queries can be large, into the hundreds or thousands or more. We may want to save all the transactions in a CSV file for further analysis. We can do this easily using the `writerows()` method of the writer object in Python.

WRITING ROWS FROM DICTIONARIES

We can use the `DictWriter` class to write dictionary objects as rows to a CSV file. When defining the dictionary objects, we use the column header labels as keys and associate a value with each key. The `DictWriter` class interprets the keys and adds the data to the correct column. This means that as long as each key: value pair is identified correctly, the data will be structured correctly in the final version of the file.

We can see this in action in Listing 19.14, where we create three dictionary objects and add each object to a CSV file as a separate row.

LISTING 19.14

Adding dictionary objects to a CSV file

```
import csv

# create three rows of data; item order is not important because each dictionary
# uses keys to identify each value
row_1 = {"employee_id":"EMP4564576566","first_name":"rodney","last_name":"evans"}
row_2 = {"first_name":"lesa","last_name":"clapper","employee_id":"EMP9807976875"}
row_3 = {"employee_id":"EMP4564564566","last_name":"cruz","first_name":"mario"}

fieldnames = ["employee_id","first_name","last_name"]

with open('data/employee.csv', 'w') as csv_file:
    writer = csv.DictWriter(csv_file,delimiter=',',fieldnames=fieldnames)
    writer.writeheader()
    writer.writerow(row_1) # write the first row
    writer.writerow(row_2) # write the second row
    writer.writerow(row_3) # writethe third row

f = open('data/employee.csv', 'r')
print(f.read())
f.close()
```

We start by creating three dictionary objects (row_1, row_2, and row_3) that each contain a row of data for our CSV file. Note that when we create each row of data, item order is not important because in a dictionary we use the keys to identify each value.

When we open the writer object using DictWriter(), we add a parameter called fieldnames that we assign the list of fieldnames (in this case also called fieldnames). This is in addition to the file handle (csv_file) and delimiter (',') parameters we've used before.

With our new file opened, we first write the headers to the file with a call to the method writeheader(). We can then write each of our dictionaries as a row and the data will be assigned to the proper columns as can be seen from the output:

```
employee_id,first_name,last_name

EMP4564576566,rodney,evans

EMP9807976875,lesa,clapper

EMP4564564566,mario,cruz
```

As a second example of writing dictionaries to a CSV file, in Listing 19.15, we will write a script that creates a CSV file called `transactions.csv`, which will contain information about customer card transactions. It includes the following attributes for the transactions:

- Date
- Customer
- Merchant
- Total Amount

In this listing, we use a dictionary to define the data for each transaction and then add each dictionary as a separate row in the CSV file. This script also checks to see if the file exists, and if it does, it appends the data without the headers.

LISTING 19.15

Adding transactions via dictionaries

```
import csv,os

count = 0
filename='data/transactions.csv'
dataset = {}

trans_date = input("Please enter the transaction date: ")
customer = input("Enter the customer: ")
merchant = input("Enter the merchant name: ")
total = input("Enter the total of the transaction: ")

input_data = {"trans_date":trans_date,"customer":customer,
"merchant":merchant,"total":total}
print(input_data)

fieldnames = ["trans_date","customer","merchant","total"]

# Open file in append mode, which will add the data at the
# end of the  file
if os.path.exists(filename):
    with open(filename, 'a') as csv_file:
        writer = csv.DictWriter(csv_file,fieldnames=fieldnames)
        writer.writerow(input_data)
else:
```

```python
    with open(filename, 'w') as csv_file:
        writer = csv.DictWriter(csv_file,fieldnames=fieldnames)
        writer.writeheader()
        writer.writerow(input_data)

# Print out the data in the file:
f = open('data/transactions.csv', 'r')
print(f.read())
f.close()
```

When you run this listing the first time, you should see something similar to the following:

```
Please enter the transaction date: 12/12/2021
Enter the customer: John P. Smith
Enter the merchant name: The World Bank of Money
Enter the total of the transaction: 13.45
{'trans_date': '12/12/2021', 'customer': 'John P. Smith', 'merchant': 'The World Bank
of Money', 'total': '13.45'}
trans_date,customer,merchant,total

12/12/2021,John P. Smith,The World Bank of Money,13.45
```

If you run the listing a second time, you'll see that the new information entered by the user is appended to the file:

```
Please enter the transaction date: 12/13/2021
Enter the customer: Paul E. Pocket
Enter the merchant name: City Grocery Store
Enter the total of the transaction: 132.91
{'trans_date': '12/13/2021', 'customer': 'Paul E. Pocket', 'merchant': 'City Grocery
Store', 'total': '132.91'}
trans_date,customer,merchant,total

12/12/2021,John P. Smith,The World Bank of Money,13.45

12/13/2021,Paul E. Pocket,City Grocery Store,132.91
```

In our ERP banking application, our data may be in the form of dictionaries. For instance, we may have key: value pairs of information such as name, employee ID, address, or department. We can save the information stored in our Python dictionary object locally using the DictWriter class in the Python csv module.

SUMMARY

In this lesson we continued learning about working with files but transitioned to working with CSV files (.csv), which include records organized into columns like tables and are often generated by structured databases. Throughout this lesson, we discovered how to use Python scripts to read these files, add (or append) content to an existing CSV file, and create new CSV files.

Now that you have completed Lesson 19, you should be able to:

- Open, read, and display information from files in a .csv format.

- Append content to an existing .csv file.

- Replace data in an existing .csv file with new data.

EXERCISES

The following exercises will allow you to demonstrate your ability to achieve the objectives for this chapter. Unless otherwise specified, you may use any of the files provided in the book to complete these activities, create your own files, or find files that are available online. You should complete each exercise and make sure that the code runs without errors. The exercises include:

Exercise 1: Reading Lines

Exercise 2: Company Stocks

Exercise 3: Rearranging Files

Exercise 4: Pop Music Evolution

Exercise 5: All About Cars

Exercise 1: Reading Lines

Write a function that prompts the reader for an integer n and reads the first n lines of the stocks.csv file. Include a creative way to handle cases where n is greater than the number of lines available in the file.

Exercise 2: Company Stocks

In this exercise create a file called company-stocks.csv that includes three columns:

- **company_name:** The name of the company

- **purchase_date:** The purchase date of the stock

- **shares:** The number of shares purchased

Create a script that performs the following tasks:

- Prompt the user for a company name, purchase date, and number of shares for five different companies.
- Add each company's information to a list and add each list to a collection of lists.
- After all data has been collected from the user, append the new data to `company_stocks.csv` and display the file's contents to the user.

The data entries should be realistic, even if the data is not real.

Exercise 3: Rearranging Files

Write a function that completes the following steps:

- Open and read a CSV file.
- Count the number of rows in the file.
- Split the file into three separate CSV files so that each file includes approximately the same number of rows.
- Reassemble the three CSV files into a new file with the pieces in a different order from the original.
  - For example, if the original is split into Part 1, Part 2, and Part 3, the new file could contain the same content in the order Part 3, Part 1, Part 2.

The code should be as automated as possible, so that the user simply has to identify the original file and does not need to know how many lines of text the file includes.

> **NOTE** Exercise 3 is not overly practical; however, it is a great exercise to practice opening, manipulating, writing, and closing CSV files.

Exercise 4: Pop Music Evolution

For this exercise, use the `evolutionPopUSA_MainData.csv` file, which you can find on Figshare at `https://figshare.com/articles/dataset/Main_Dataset_for_Evolution_of_Popular_Music_USA_1960_2010_/1309953`. Take some time to review the information about the dataset on that page before completing this activity.

Write a program to read the collection and find the following information:

- Find out if there are any artists that had songs on the Pop USA playlist in two different decades.
- Identify the artist with the most songs on the Pop USA playlist.

- Identify the cluster with the most songs.
- Identify the genres within each cluster.
- Identify the era with the most songs.

Exercise 5: All About Cars

This exercise uses the car_data.csv file that is located in the data folder in the JobReadyPython.zip file that can be downloaded from www.wiley.com/go/JobReadyPython.

Save the linked file to your computer and extract the CSV file it contains before using it. Be sure to put the extracted file in an appropriate directory so that Python can access it. Complete the following steps using the data in the car_data.csv file:

1. Create a function that reads the car_data.csv file into a list. Each element in the list should be a dictionary where the keys are the column names, and the values are the corresponding elements in each column.

2. Create a function that uses the filter function to identify all records in the car_data.csv file with a specific make, based on user input. For instance, if the user inputs "Audi," the function should return all Audi cars in the car_data.csv file.

3. Create a function that uses the filter function to identify all fuel-efficient cars. A fuel-efficient car is a car with a city mileage greater than 35 MPG.

4. Create a function that uses the filter function to identify all the cars that have a horsepower greater than 100.

5. Using the map function, compute the cost of driving 100 miles in the city with each car. Prompt the user to input a current gasoline cost per gallon.

6. Using the reduce function, identify the average city MPG and highway MPG across all cars.

7. Using the reduce function, identify the average cost of all cars in the database.

> **NOTE** If you don't recall the details of using filter, map, and reduce functions, then revisit Lesson 13.

Lesson 20
Processing JSON Files

This is the third lesson on working with files using Python. In the previous two lessons, we learned about working with basic text files and with CSV files. In this lesson, the focus shifts to working with JSON files, which can represent unstructured datasets and with key:value pairs. Like with the other file formats, we can use Python scripts to read JSON files, add (or append) content to an existing file, and create new files.

LEARNING OBJECTIVES

By the end of this lesson, you will be able to:

- Open, read, and display JSON files.
- Append content to an existing JSON file.
- Replace data in an existing JSON file with new data.

PROCESSING JSON FILES

Python has a built-in package called JavaScript Object Notation (JSON), which can be used to work with JSON data. The abbreviation is pronounced like the name "Jason." We use JSON to store unstructured datasets in a format that allows us to transfer data from one system to another, in the same way we use CSV to transfer structured datasets.

We say that JSON is unstructured because we can create records that include different kinds of data in the same dataset, unlike a CSV file where each row includes a similar set of data based on the column headers. For example, if we build a dataset for social media posts, some posts will have text content, some will include images, some will tag other people, and any post can include any or all of these features.

JSON format is similar in structure to a Python dictionary. Each entry in the dataset includes key:value pairs, where each key is unique to that record.

CREATING A JSON FILE WITH DUMP()

As with other file types, we can open a JSON file in write mode using the option "w". If the named file exists, the existing file will be deleted and replaced with the new file. We can serialize Python objects into JSON-encoded data using the dump() function from the json module.

In Listing 20.1, we create a dictionary and add some data to it. We then use the json .dump() function to export the data to a new JSON file in the data subdirectory.

LISTING 20.1

Creating a JSON file from Python dictionaries

```python
import json

# Create a list of dictionaries
data = []
data.append({"name":"Andre Richards","DOB":"10/10/1979"})
data.append({"name":"Melinda Jefferson","DOB":"12/31/1979"})
```

```
with open('data/person.json', 'w') as outfile:
    json.dump(data, outfile)

# Print the file's contents
f = open('data/person.json', 'r')
print(f.read())
f.close()
```

This script creates a list of dictionaries called data, which represent a list of items that will be stored in the file. Two dictionary items are included. Next in the script, the JSON file is opened for writing. You can see that the file is opened in the same way previous lessons have opened files. In this case, the handle created to work with our file is outfile:

```
with open('data/person.json', 'w') as outfile:
```

With the file open, json.dump() is called with the dictionaries (data) passed as the first parameter and the file handle (outfile) as the second. This writes our dictionary items to the file as JSON data. The rest of the listing simply reopens the file and prints the contents, which should look like the following:

```
[{"name": "Andre Richards", "DOB": "10/10/1979"}, {"name": "Melinda Jefferson", "DOB": "12/31/1979"}]
```

CONVERTING TO JSON WITH DUMPS()

We can use json.dumps() to convert a Python dictionary into a JSON-encoded string object. We can do this by passing a dictionary object to json.dumps(), which then returns a string.

In Listing 20.2, we start with a dictionary that includes one entry for one person. Note that this data is unstructured because one of the values (roles) is a list of values. We use the json.dumps() function to convert the dictionary into a string object that we can display to the user.

LISTING 20.2

Creating a JSON file with unstructured data

```
import json

json_dict = {
```

```
    "first_name": "Robert",
    "last_name": "Balti",
    "role": ["Manager", "Lead Developer"],
    "age": 34
}

# convert a dictionary into a string object that we can display.
json_data = json.dumps(json_dict)

print(json_dict)        # dict
print(type(json_dict))

print(json_data)        # string
print(type(json_data))
```

Note that we are simply manipulating our data in this listing and are not writing to a file. We start by creating a dictionary called `json_dict`. We then use the `json.dumps()` function to convert the dictionary to a JSON-encoded string, which is assigned to the variable `json_data`. In the script, we print the values stored in each of these two variables along with their data types so you can see what they truly are:

```
{'first_name': 'Robert', 'last_name': 'Balti', 'role': ['Manager', 'Lead
Developer'], 'age': 34}
<class 'dict'>
{"first_name": "Robert", "last_name": "Balti", "role": ["Manager", "Lead
Developer"], "age": 34}
<class 'str'>
```

In our ERP application, we will often have data that is unstructured and of varying lengths. For instance, we may have transaction histories of our customers but not all customers would have performed the same number of transactions. In such a case, we can store our data as a dictionary where the keys are transaction number history for individual customers. We can then serialize the transaction history dictionary into JSON-encoded data using the `json` module in Python.

FORMATTING JSON DATA

We can use custom indenting to make the output of JSON data easier to read. Listing 20.3 is similar to Listing 20.2, except that we add an `indent` value in the `dumps()` function. This causes each data item in our encoded JSON string to appear on a separate line in the output, with each line indented four spaces. The result is easier to read than having all data on a single line.

LISTING 20.3

Formatting our output with indent

```
import json

json_dict = {
    "first_name": "Robert",
    "last_name": "Balti",
    "role": ["Manager", "Lead Developer"],
    "age": 34
}

json_data = json.dumps(json_dict,indent = 4)

print(json_data)
print(type(json_data))
```

You can see that we added `indent = 4` to the `json.dumps()` function call. When `json_data` is now printed, four spaces will be added for indents, plus each value is on its own line. You can see that this output is much easier to read than the output from the previous listing:

```
{
    "first_name": "Robert",
    "last_name": "Balti",
    "role": [
        "Manager",
        "Lead Developer"
    ],
    "age": 34
}
<class 'str'>
```

Note that you can change the value assigned to `indent` and the output will be formatted accordingly. For example, changing to `indent = 10` adds additional spaces, but otherwise the output is the same:

```
{
          "first_name": "Robert",
          "last_name": "Balti",
          "role": [
                    "Manager",
                    "Lead Developer"
          ],
```

```
        "age": 34
    }
    <class 'str'>
```

While it's no problem for a computer to read data in many formats, there are many times when we need humans to read data in a user-friendly format. Our ERP application will often have to export logs or provide a console to troubleshoot, so making this output more readable is important for efficiency. The indent ability with JSON data makes it more usable by humans, which leads to faster coding.

USING JSON.LOADS()

We can use the `json.loads()` function to convert a JSON-encoded object or file into a Python dictionary. In Listing 20.4, we create a dictionary, transform the dictionary into a JSON-encoded string, and convert the string back to a Python dictionary.

LISTING 20.4

Converting a JSON-encoded object to a Python dictionary

```python
import json

json_dict = {
    "first_name": "Robert",
    "last_name": "Balti",
    "role": ["Manager", "Lead Developer"],
    "age": 34
}

# Convert a dictionary into a JSON formatted string object.
json_data = json.dumps(json_dict)
print(json_data)
print(type(json_data)) # string

# Convert a JSON encoded object into a python dictionary.
python_dict = json.loads(json_data)
print(python_dict)
print(type(python_dict)) # dict
```

As we can see in the output, Python treats each object as a different data class, although the content looks identical for both objects:

```
{'first_name': 'Robert', 'last_name': 'Balti', 'role': ['Manager', 'Lead
Developer'], 'age': 34}
<class 'str'>
{'first_name': 'Robert', 'last_name': 'Balti', 'role': ['Manager', 'Lead
Developer'], 'age': 34}
<class 'dict'>
```

In Listing 20.5 we take JSON data and again convert it into a dictionary. We then print the user's email address from the Python dictionary data.

LISTING 20.5

Converting from JSON to a dictionary

```python
import json

x = """{
    "Name": "Cheyanne Kemp",
    "Contact Number": 7867567898,
    "Email": "ckemp@gmail.com",
    "Services":["Checking", "Savings", "Auto Loan"]
}"""

user_data = json.loads(x)
print(user_data['Email'])
```

Don't get confused by all of the double quotes. The three quotes before and after our data indicates to Python that this is a JSON-enabled string, which is being assigned to x. We then use `json.load()` to load this string into `user_data`. The `load()` function converts it to a dictionary. The values, such as the email address, can then be printed from the dictionary. In this case, the output is:

```
ckemp@gmail.com
```

As we pass around serialized JSON objects in our ERP application, we may also want to occasionally convert the JSON-encoded string objects back into Python dictionaries to further perform operations that we can only perform on a dictionary. In this scenario, we need to extract the email address for mailings. We can achieve this using the `loads()` function from the Python `json` module.

ITERATING THROUGH JSON DATA

We can use a `for` loop to iterate through the contents of a JSON file. In Listing 20.6 we display the contents of the JSON file by iterating through its contents to display each JSON object separately, without converting the data to a dictionary.

LISTING 20.6

Iterating through a JSON file

```
import json

with open('data/prize.json','r') as jsonfile:
    # use the json module with the load function
    # to read the entire content of the json file
    data = json.load(jsonfile)

# iterate through the file and display each json object separately.
for k in data['prizes']:
    print(k)
```

This script loads a JSON file and then simply iterates through the opened file printing each row of data within `'prizes'`. The results include:

```
{"year":"2018","category":"physics","overallMotivation":"\"for groundbreaking
inventions in the field of laser
physics\"","laureates":[{"id":"960","firstname":"Arthur","surname":"Ashkin","motivation":
"\"for the optical tweezers and their application to biological
systems\"","share":"2"},{"id":"961","firstname":"G\u00e9rard","surname":"Mourou","moti
vation":"\"for their method of generating high-intensity, ultra-short optical
pulses\"","share":"4"},{"id":"962","firstname":"Donna","surname":"Strickland","motivat
ion":"\"for their method of generating high-intensity, ultra-short optical
pulses\"","share":"4"}]},{"year":"2018","category":"chemistry","laureates":[{"id":"963
","firstname":"Frances H.","surname":"Arnold","motivation":"\"for the directed
evolution of enzymes\"","share":"2"},{"id":"964","firstname":"George
P.","surname":"Smith","motivation":"\"for the phage display of peptides and
antibodies\"","share":"4"},{"id":"965","firstname":"Sir Gregory
P.","surname":"Winter","motivation":"\"for the phage display of peptides and
antibodies\"","share":"4"}]},{"year":"2018","category":"medicine","laureates":[{"id"
:"958","firstname":"James P.","surname":"Allison","motivation":"\"for their discovery of
cancer therapy by inhibition of negative immune
regulation\"","share":"2"},{"id":"959","firstname":"Tasuku","surname":"Honjo","motivation":
"\"for their discovery of cancer therapy by inhibition of negative immune
regulation\"","share":"2"}]},

...
```

{"year":"1901","category":"physics","laureates":[{"id":"1","firstname":"Wilhelm Conrad","surname":"R\u00f6ntgen","motivation":"\"in recognition of the extraordinary services he has rendered by the discovery of the remarkable rays subsequently named after him\"","share":"1"}]},{"year":"1901","category":"chemistry","laureates":[{"id":"160", "firstname":"Jacobus Henricus","surname":"van 't Hoff","motivation":"\"in recognition of the extraordinary services he has rendered by the discovery of the laws of chemical dynamics and osmotic pressure in solutions\"","share":"1"}]},{"year":"1901","category":"medicine","laureates":[{"id":" 293","firstname":"Emil Adolf","surname":"von Behring","motivation":"\"for his work on serum therapy, especially its application against diphtheria, by which he has opened a new road in the domain of medical science and thereby placed in the hands of the physician a victorious weapon against illness and deaths\"","share":"1"}]},{"year":"1901","category":"literature","laureates":[{"id":"569" ,"firstname":"Sully","surname":"Prudhomme","motivation":"\"in special recognition of his poetic composition, which gives evidence of lofty idealism, artistic perfection and a rare combination of the qualities of both heart and intellect\"","share":"1"}]},{"year":"1901","category":"peace","laureates":[{"id":"462"," firstname":"Jean Henry","surname":"Dunant","share":"2"},{"id":"463","firstname":"Fr\u00e9d\u00e9ric", "surname":"Passy","share":"2"}]}]}

As an additional example of iterating through JSON data, Listing 20.7 iterates through a list of bank transactions found in the file `bank_transactions.json`. The script uses a `for` loop to iterate through the list of transactions and prints out the high-dollar-amount withdrawals over $650,000.

LISTING 20.7

Iterating through a JSON file of bank transactions

```
import json

filename = 'data/bank_transactions.json'

with open(filename,'r') as jsonfile:
  data = json.load(jsonfile)

for each in data:
  if each['WITHDRAWAL AMT'] != '':
    val = float(each['WITHDRAWAL AMT'])
    if val > 650000:
      print(each['Account No'], "===>", val)
```

In this script you can see that we open the file to read and load the contents into a variable called `data`. Using a `for` loop, we then iterate through each row of data. For each row, we check to see if the withdrawal amount is not blank. If it is not blank, then we set `val` to the withdrawal amount converted to a floating-point number. The script then checks to see if `val` is greater than 650000. If so, it is displayed; otherwise, the loop iterates to the next row of information.

The resulting output is:

```
409000611074' ===> 654498.0
409000611074' ===> 710800.0
409000611074' ===> 823240.0
409000611074' ===> 785049.0
409000611074' ===> 793251.0
409000611074' ===> 717850.0
409000611074' ===> 709200.0
409000611074' ===> 689650.0
```

Listing 20.8 is almost the same as Listing 20.7. This time, we create a script that uses the `bank_transactions.json` file to extract and add the withdrawal amounts as well as total the balances from all accounts.

LISTING 20.8

Iterating for totals

```
import json

filename = 'data/bank_transactions.json'

with open(filename,'r') as jsonfile:
  data = json.load(jsonfile)

total = 0
total_balance = 0

for each in data:
  if each['WITHDRAWAL AMT'] != '':
    total +=  float(each['WITHDRAWAL AMT'])
```

```
    if each['BALANCE AMT'] != '':
      total_balance +=  float(each['BALANCE AMT'])

print("Total Withdrawals: ", total)
print("Total of Balances: ", total_balance)
```

From this script, the total amount withdrawn and the total of all balances across all accounts is displayed:

```
Total Withdrawals:  70887681.0
Total of Balances:  861383887.0
```

Many applications that encounter disparate or separate architecture will pass information through common data methods such as JSON. In our ERP application, there are systems that require us to send and receive JSON data in certain functions. When receiving a large set of JSON data, we can use the looping methods in Python to make it easier to parse and access the data in the JSON file.

READING AND WRITING JSON DATA

In Python, we can use the `json` module to read and write data in JSON format. To display the data from the dictionary, we can use the `pprint()` function, which formats the data to make it easier to read.

To illustrate writing JSON data using this "pretty print" function, we'll use the example included in the dataset you downloaded at the start of the lesson. In Listing 20.9, we open a JSON file, use `json.load()` to convert the content into a dictionary, and then use `pprint` to display the data from the dictionary in a human-readable format.

> **NOTE** To better understand what `pprint()` does, you may want to open the raw JSON file on your computer to see how the data is stored in its original format.

LISTING 20.9

Using pprint

```
import json

from pprint import pprint

with open('data/prize.json','r') as jsonfile:
```

```
    data = json.load(jsonfile) # load the json content and serialize it.
print(type(data)) #dict
pprint(data)       # print the entire file content.
```

To use `pprint`, we need to import it from the `pprint` module. We do this with the command:

```
from pprint import pprint
```

After our imports, we open the `prize.json` file in the `data` folder. As a reminder, this file needs to be downloaded as mentioned earlier in the lesson. With the file opened, we use `json.load` to read the contents of the JSON file into a dictionary called `data`. With the data loaded, we can confirm the data type of data by printing it. We can then print all the data from the file using the `pprint` function. The resulting output is:

```
<class 'dict'>
{'prizes': [{'category': 'physics',
             'laureates': [{'firstname': 'Rainer',
                            'id': '941',
                            'motivation': '"for decisive contributions to the '
                                          'LIGO detector and the observation '
                                          'of gravitational waves"',
                            'share': '2',
                            'surname': 'Weiss'},
                           {'firstname': 'Barry C.',
                            'id': '942',
                            'motivation': '"for decisive contributions to the '
                                          'LIGO detector and the observation '
                                          'of gravitational waves"',
                            'share': '4',
                            'surname': 'Barish'},
                           {'firstname': 'Kip S.',
                            'id': '943',
                            'motivation': '"for decisive contributions to the '
                                          'LIGO detector and the observation '
                                          'of gravitational waves"',
                            'share': '4',
                            'surname': 'Thorne'}],
             'year': '2017'},
            {'category': 'chemistry',
             'laureates': [{'firstname': 'Jacques',
                            'id': '944',
                            'motivation': '"for developing cryo-electron '
```

```
                                        'microscopy for the high-resolution '
                                        'structure determination of '
                                        'biomolecules in solution"',
                        'share': '3',
                        'surname': 'Dubochet'},
                       {'firstname': 'Joachim',
                        'id': '945',
                        'motivation': '"for developing cryo-electron '
                                        'microscopy for the high-resolution '
                                        'structure determination of '
                                        'biomolecules in solution"',
                        'share': '3',
                        'surname': 'Frank'},
                       {'firstname': 'Richard',
                        'id': '946',
                        'motivation': '"for developing cryo-electron '
                                        'microscopy for the high-resolution '
                                        'structure determination of '
                                        'biomolecules in solution"',
                        'share': '3',
                        'surname': 'Henderson'}],
          'year': '2017'},

  [Results truncated for brevity]

          {'category': 'medicine',
           'laureates': [{'firstname': 'Emil Adolf',
                          'id': '293',
                          'motivation': '"for his work on serum therapy, '
                                          'especially its application against '
                                          'diphtheria, by which he has opened '
                                          'a new road in the domain of medical '
                                          'science and thereby placed in the '
                                          'hands of the physician a victorious '
                                          'weapon against illness and deaths"',
                          'share': '1',
                          'surname': 'von Behring'}],
            'year': '1901'},
          {'category': 'literature',
           'laureates': [{'firstname': 'Sully',
                          'id': '569',
                          'motivation': '"in special recognition of his '
                                          'poetic composition, which gives '
                                          'evidence of lofty idealism, '
```

```
                                   'artistic perfection and a rare '
                                   'combination of the qualities of '
                                   'both heart and intellect"',
                      'share': '1',
                      'surname': 'Prudhomme'}],
         'year': '1901'},
        {'category': 'peace',
         'laureates': [{'firstname': 'Jean Henry',
                       'id': '462',
                       'share': '2',
                       'surname': 'Dunant'},
                      {'firstname': 'Frédéric',
                       'id': '463',
                       'share': '2',
                       'surname': 'Passy'}],
         'year': '1901'}]}
```

The dataset in the `prize.json` file includes winners of Nobel Prizes from 1901 through 2017. Because of the output's layout, it is easy to see that different datasets are nested inside other datasets, including information about different prizes in each year and lists of who won the same prize in the same year. The key:value layout also makes it easy to understand what each piece of data represents.

SUMMARY

In this lesson, the focus shifted to working with JSON files, which can represent unstructured datasets and with key:value pairs. In this lesson, we saw how we can create JSON serialized string objects such as transaction history of all the customers by using the `dump()` function in the `json` module. We saw how we can also read in our saved JSON file as a dictionary for further analysis using the `load()` function in the `json` module. Finally, a new printing function was introduced that allows for "pretty" printing of many Python objects.

Now that you have completed Lesson 20, you should be able to:

- Open, read, and display JSON files.

- Append content to an existing JSON file.

- Replace data in an existing JSON file with new data.

EXERCISES

The following exercises are provided to allow you to demonstrate the objectives for this lesson. You should complete each exercise and make sure that the code runs without errors. The exercises include:

Exercise 1: Company Bank Account

Exercise 2: Formatted Account Information

Exercise 3: Nobel Prizes

Exercise 4: New York Restaurants

Exercise 5: Movies

Exercise 1: Company Bank Account

Create a dictionary that represents a company bank account with fields for customer_ID, name, and account number. Use the `json.dumps()` function to convert the dictionary into a JSON-encoded object.

Exercise 2: Formatted Account Information

Update the company account script from the last practice activity to include the `indent` option to make the output easier to read.

Exercise 3: Nobel Prizes

For this activity, download and use the file `prize.json` found in the download file for this book. You can also find a copy of the file at `https://the-software-guild.s3.amazonaws.com/techstart-1909/data-files/prize.json`. As mentioned in the lesson, this dataset includes information about Nobel Prizes, including the laureates who received each prize, when the prize was awarded, and the category of the prize.

Write a program to analyze the data in this file to find the following information:

- Identify the most recent year in the dataset when someone received a Nobel Prize.

- Identify the earliest year when someone received a Nobel Prize.

- Identify the category with the highest number of prizes.

- Identify the laureate with the highest number of prizes.

- Identify the laureate who won the most recent prize in peace.

- Identify the laureate who won the most recent prize in medicine.

- Identify the year when the most laureates jointly won the same prize in the same year.

- How many prizes have been given in the economics category?

- How many prizes have been given in the peace category?

- How many prizes have been given in the literature category?

TIP Open the JSON file and examine it before starting this activity. This will help you identify where to find the data you need to answer the questions.

Exercise 4: New York Restaurants

For this activity, use the file `restaurant.json` included in the download files for this book. Download it if you do not already have a copy.

This dataset includes records of restaurants in New York City, including where each restaurant is located, what kind of cuisine it serves, and its customer ratings. Here is a sample record:

```
{"address": {"building": "1007", "coord": [-73.856077, 40.848447], "street": "Morris
Park Ave", "zipcode": "10462"}, "borough": "Bronx", "cuisine": "Bakery", "grades":
[{"date": {"$date": 1393804800000}, "grade": "A", "score": 2}, {"date": {"$date":
1378857600000}, "grade": "A", "score": 6}, {"date": {"$date": 1358985600000}, "grade":
"A", "score": 10}, {"date": {"$date": 1322006400000}, "grade": "A", "score": 9},
{"date": {"$date": 1299715200000}, "grade": "B", "score": 14}], "name": "Morris Park
Bake Shop", "restaurant_id": "30075445"}
```

Use Python to analyze the data in this file and find the following information:

- Compute the average score for each restaurant.

- Compute the minimum score for each restaurant.

- Compute the maximum score for each restaurant.

- Compute the average score for each type of cuisine in each borough.

- Compute the minimum score for each type of cuisine in each borough.

- Compute the maximum score for each type of cuisine in each borough.

Exercise 5: Movies

In this exercise, start by downloading Rand.fun's Movie JSON dataset from `https://github.com/randfun/movies-dataset/blob/master/movies.json`. Use the dataset to answer the following questions:

- How many movies are included in the file?
- In what year was the movie *A Separation* made?
- How many movies has Martin Scorsese directed?

After answering the questions, look through the raw dataset and generate five more questions about the data. Then write code to answer those questions.

PART V

Data Analysis and Exception Handling

Lesson 21: Using Lambdas

Lesson 22: Handling Exceptions

Lesson 23: Pulling It All Together: Word Analysis in Python

Lesson 24: Extracting, Transforming, and Loading with ETL Scripting

Lesson 25: Improving ETL Scripting

Lesson 21
Using Lambdas

In this lesson, we will learn ways to analyze data to create meaningful business reports based on that data.

LEARNING OBJECTIVES

By the end of this lesson, you will be able to:

- Create lambda functions.
- Explain how a lambda function uses input values.
- Use a lambda function as part of a defined function.
- Use Python's `map()` function to apply a function to each element of an iterable object.
- Use Python's `filter()` function to identify specific elements in a collection that meet defined criteria and extract those elements to a new collection.
- Use Python's `reduce()` function to apply an operation sequentially to the elements in a collection.

Rather than creating a named function, it is sometimes useful to create a short function and embed it as part of a larger function. Lambda functions allow us to do this. A lambda function is a small anonymous function that allows us to create expressions within other functions.

Because iteration is a fundamental task in Python, there are several iteration functions that automatically move through a series of values in a collection, stopping only when the last value in the collection has been processed. There are a few key terms you should be aware of as you work through this lesson:

- **Anonymous function:** A function definition that is not bound to an identifier.
- **Lambda function:** An anonymous function that can take several arguments but can have only one expression.

- **map():** The map() function returns a map object after applying the given function to each item of a given iterable function.
- **reduce():** The reduce() function is a mathematical technique called to an iterable that reduces it to a single cumulative value.

> **NOTE** This lesson uses the file stocks.csv, which can be found in the data folder of the JobReadyPython.zip file found at www.wiley.com/go/jobreadypython. You can save this file to your computer and extract the files to an appropriate folder on your computer.

CREATING A LAMBDA FUNCTION

We create a lambda function using the keyword lambda. The function can include any number of arguments, but it can include only one expression. The format of creating a lambda is:

```
lambda arguments : expression
```

In Listing 21.1 we create a lambda function called x that takes one argument called a. Its expression is a + 10, which adds 10 to the value of the argument.

LISTING 21.1

Using a lambda function

```
x = lambda a : a + 10
print(x(5))
```

After creating the lambda, we assign it to x. This means that x is now a lambda function and can be used like a normal function. In the listing, we then call x with the value of 5 and get 15 as the result.

In Listing 21.2, we create another simple lambda function. In this one, we input x and return the square of x.

> **NOTE** In Python, use a ** b to express a^b.

LISTING 21.2

Creating a lambda for power

```
x = lambda a : a ** 2
print(x(10))
```

You can see that the lambda is set up the same way as the previous listing. The result of calling x(10) will be 100.

As we analyze our ERP application data, we may find ourselves often writing small functions to perform a certain task such as calculating the sum of the transaction history for a customer over the past week. Lambda functions in Python provide us with a short syntactic way to do this as an alternative to writing these small functions.

WORKING WITH MULTIPLE INPUTS

A lambda function can include multiple inputs. In this case, when we use the function, the argument values we provide at runtime are provided in the same order in which the inputs are defined in the lambda function, as shown in Listing 21.3.

LISTING 21.3

Using multiple inputs with a lambda function

```
x = lambda a, b : a * b
print(x(5, 6))
```

Here, we create a lambda function that takes two arguments (a and b) and outputs the product of the arguments. We provide the values 5 and 6 when we run the program, so the lambda output is 5 * 6, or 30.

Again, the order in which we present the values that the lambda function uses is important. This importance is not obvious when we add or multiply numbers because addition and multiplication are commutative operations (meaning that the result is the same regardless of the order in which the values are used in the operation). However, for operations that are not commutative, like subtraction or division, you get different results if the values are in a different order. In Listing 21.4 we have two identical lambda functions, but we present the values in a reversed order, so the outputs are different.

LISTING 21.4

Order of parameters matters

```
x = lambda a, b : a / b
print(x(6, 5))

y = lambda a, b : a / b
print(y(5, 6))
```

When we run this listing, we see that the order matters because switching the order of the parameters passed to the lambda changes the results:

```
1.2
0.8333333333333334
```

This is a little clearer if we apply the code in Listing 21.4 to a more specific example, as shown in Listing 21.5.

LISTING 21.5

Items per person

```
PerPerson = lambda items, people : items / people
print(PerPerson(20, 5))   # Correct
print(PerPerson(5, 20))   # Wrong
```

This time, we call the lambda PerPerson because it calculates how many items each person receives. If we have 20 items and 5 people, you can see that the order we pass the values must match the order that was created in the lambda or we get a wrong answer. The output from running Listing 21.5 is:

```
4.0
0.25
```

The correct answer is that each person would get 4 items, not a fourth of an item.

We can create a lambda with more than two arguments as well as with values other than numbers. Listing 21.6 presents another example, this time using multiple strings.

LISTING 21.6

Lambda to concatenate strings

```
x = lambda a, b, c: a + " " + b + " " + c
print(x("This", "String", "Is Concatenated."))
```

This lambda function isn't doing much, but it does illustrate that we can use more than two arguments, and that they don't have to be numbers. In this case, the lambda function concatenates three input strings and adds a space between them. It then is used to print the three strings to the screen, resulting in the following output:

```
This String Is Concatenated.
```

In our ERP banking application, the data analysis task might require us to provide more than one input. In Python, lambda functions allow us to provide more than one input parameter similar to a regular function in Python.

> **NOTE** Using the lambda function reduces the amount of code required in the end and provides a faster route for developers in certain instances.

PLACING LAMBDA FUNCTIONS INSIDE A FUNCTION

One reason to use a lambda function is to define a function that should be part of another function. In Listing 21.7, we create a function named myfunc that includes a lambda function.

LISTING 21.7

Using a lambda inside another function

```
def myfunc(n):
    return lambda a : a * n

doubler = myfunc(2) # we set the value of n

print(doubler(11)) # we set the value of a
```

The myfunc function accepts one argument, n, and the lambda function accepts another argument, a. When we call the function to create the doubler variable, we include a value for n. In this case we provide the value of 2.

When we print the value of doubler, we provide the value for a. When we then call doubler with the value of 11, the result is the output of 22.

As a second example, in Listing 21.8 we create a function called pow_n that computes the power of n of an input number a.

LISTING 21.8

Creating a lambda function within a function

```
def pow_n(n):
  return lambda a: a ** n

pow_2 = pow_n(2)
print(pow_2(6))
```

In this case, the pow_n function simply returns a lambda function that calculates the power of a number. We use this function to create the lambda function called pow_2 that sets the value of n to be equal to 2. We then pass the value of 6 to pow_2, getting the result of 6 to the power of 2, which is 36.

> **NOTE** Practice with the functions in Listings 21.7 and 21.8 with different values until you are sure you understand how the runtime values map to the function arguments.

In our ERP application, we may have certain tasks that we would write functions to perform. For instance, we may have to update our local database and remote database with new customer transactions. We could write two separate functions, local_update() and remote_update(), that are called by a higher-order function, update_all_database(), every time a customer makes a transaction. Instead, we can improve the readability of our code by using lambda functions that perform the local and remote update task within our higher-order function.

USING THE MAP() FUNCTION

Python's map() function allows us to apply a function to each element of an iterable object as part of the iteration process. The map() function takes two arguments: a defined function and an iterable object, such as a list, tuple, dictionary, or set. The output is a map object that contains the elements of the original object, after applying the specified function to those elements.

In Listing 21.9 we define a function to_upper_case that converts string characters to uppercase. We then use the map() function to apply the to_upper_case function to each item in a list. The final map object is converted back to a list.

LISTING 21.9

Converting a characters to uppercase

```
def to_upper_case(s):
    return str(s).upper()

names=['haythem','mike','james']
print(names)

names_upper = map(to_upper_case, names) # apply to_upper_case function to each
                                        # element in names
print(type(names_upper))

names_upper_list = list(names_upper) # convert the names_upper map object to a
                                     # python list.
print(names_upper_list)
print(type(names_upper_list))
```

This listing starts by defining a function called to_upper_case() that takes a single parameter, which is converted to uppercase and returned. We then define a simple list of names called names that are printed to the screen.

We then call map() and pass the to_upper_case() function and names list. The map() function applies the to_upper_case() function to each element in the names list and returns the result as a map as shown by printing the type of names_upper. Finally, the names_upper map object is converted to a Python list, which is then printed, along with its type. The final output is:

```
['haythem', 'mike', 'james']
<class 'map'>
['HAYTHEM', 'MIKE', 'JAMES']
<class 'list'>
```

In Listing 21.10, we have another example that applies map() to the data within a CSV file.

LISTING 21.10

Using map on a CSV file

```python
def fromCSV(path,delimiter,quotechar):
    import csv  # import the csv module
    data=list() # convert the CSV data into a list
    with open(path, newline='') as csvfile: # open the file
        filecontent = csv.DictReader(csvfile, delimiter=delimiter,
quotechar=quotechar)
        # access the content of the file
        for row in filecontent:  # iterate through the rows
            data.append(row)     # save each row as a dictionary
                                 # item in the data list
    return data


def extract_month(row):
    # input is the entire row of data
    # extract the month from the date field
    # add the month field to the row and return the row
    value = row['Date']
    MM=""
    # split function in python used to divide strings based on some delimiter
    a = value.split("/")
    MM = a[0]
    #implement logic here
    new_row = row.copy()
    new_row.update({'Month':MM})
    return new_row

data=fromCSV(path='data/stocks.csv',delimiter=',',quotechar='|')
print(data[0])

data_mapped = map(extract_month,data)
data_mapped_list = list(data_mapped)
print(data_mapped_list[0])
```

This program includes multiple steps:

- We define a `fromCSV` function that imports the contents of a CSV file as a list of dictionaries, wherein each row in the original file is a dictionary that uses the column names as keys associated with the data values.

- We also define an `extract_month` function, which looks at the date value in each dictionary item, splits the value using / as the delimiter, extracts the first value as the month, and appends that value as a new item in the original data.

- We use the `fromCSV` function to convert the data from the named CSV file to a list of dictionary values. We then apply `extract_month` as a mapped function on the new list.
- Finally, we display the first item for each list.

The output from running this listing is:

```
OrderedDict([('Date', '7/7/06'), ('Open', '492.7'), ('High', '495.9'), ('Low',
'490.0999'), ('Close', '490.8'), ('Volume', '807950')])
OrderedDict([('Date', '7/7/06'), ('Open', '492.7'), ('High', '495.9'), ('Low',
'490.0999'), ('Close', '490.8'), ('Volume', '807950'), ('Month', '7')])
```

It is not uncommon to have data analysis as a part of an application, including our ERP banking application. In data analysis, often we will have to perform some form of data cleaning. For instance, we may be interested in the full names of our customers, but those were provided to us only as separate first and last names. We can write a function to concatenate first and last names to give our customer's full name. We can then use the built-in `map()` function in Python to apply the transformation to our entire dataset.

COMBINING MAP AND LAMBDA FUNCTIONS

We can combine `map` and lambda functions to create powerful, customized operations. For example, we might have two separate lists that we want to combine, one containing employee names and another containing their IDs. We can use the `map()` function in combination with a custom lambda function to perform this task efficiently in Python.

In the example in Listing 21.11, we start with a list that includes four numbers and a tuple that also includes four numbers. We define a lambda function that takes as input a value from the list and a value from the tuple and returns the product of those values.

We then apply the `map()` function with the `lambda` function to iterate through the list and tuple, pairing the values respectively. The results are saved to a new list that includes the product of each pair of numbers.

LISTING 21.11

Using lambdas and map together

```
list_numbers = [1, 2, 3, 4]
tuple_numbers = (5, 6, 7, 8)
print(list_numbers)
print(tuple_numbers)
```

```
map_iterator = map(lambda x, y: x + y, list_numbers, tuple_numbers)

map_list= list(map_iterator) # convert map output to a list

print(map_list)
```

Again, note that the map( ) function includes a lambda function that calculates the sum of two values. The output from this listing is:

```
[1, 2, 3, 4]
(5, 6, 7, 8)
[6, 8, 10, 12]
```

As a second example, Listing 21.12 computes the result of the exchange rate multiplied against the transaction amount values from a list and tuple.

LISTING 21.12

Summing exchange rate and transaction amounts

```
exchange_rate = [1.25, 2, 1.3, 1.18]
transaction_amt = (5, 6, 7, 8)
print(exchange_rate)
print(transaction_amt)

map_iterator = map(lambda x, y: x * y, exchange_rate, transaction_amt)

map_list= list(map_iterator)
print(map_list)
```

This listing works in a similar way to Listing 21.11. The lambda is passed to the map( ) function along with the two sets of values that will be used: the exchange_rate list and the transaction_amt tuple. The output when this listing is executed is:

```
[1.25, 2, 1.3, 1.18]
(5, 6, 7, 8)
[6.25, 12, 9.1, 9.44]
```

USING THE FILTER() FUNCTION

The filter() function takes as input a condition that can be evaluated as True or False and an iterable object, such as a list or dictionary. It applies the condition to each element in the object and returns those elements that evaluate as True for the condition.

In the simple example in Listing 21.13, we want to find all names that start with "h" in the list.

LISTING 21.13

Using filter()

```
def initial_h(dataset):
    for x in dataset:
        if str.lower(x[0]) == "h": # normalize the case of the
                                   # first letter and look for 'h'
            return True
        else:
            return False

names=['Haythem','Mike','James','Helen','Mary']
print(names)

# extract the True results from the initial_h function to a new filter object
names_filtered = filter(initial_h,names)
print(type(names_filtered))

# convert the filter object to a list object
names_filtered_list = list(names_filtered)
print(type(names_filtered_list))

print(names_filtered_list)
```

We start by defining an initial_h function that looks at each item in a dataset and identifies the values that start with "h." We do this by checking the first position of each item after converting it to lowercase. For each item checked in the dataset either True or False is returned.

We use the initial_h function in a filter on a names dataset to extract the names that return True in the function to a new filter object, which we then convert to a list. The output from this listing shows the initial list data, the type that was returned from the filter, the type of our converted filter, and then the final output of running the filter:

```
['Haythem', 'Mike', 'James', 'Helen', 'Mary']
<class 'filter'>
<class 'list'>
['Haythem', 'Helen']
```

In Listing 21.14, we show a second function being used to filter the same list of data as the previous listing. This time, the script defines a function that takes as input a list of names and returns all names that include the letter "e" at any position in the name.

LISTING 21.14

Filtering for names containing an "e"

```
def contains_e(dataset):
     if 'e' in dataset:
       return True
     else:
       return False

names=['Haythem','Mike','James','Helen','Mary']
print(names)

names_filtered = filter(contains_e,names)
print(type(names_filtered))

names_filtered_list = list(names_filtered)
print(type(names_filtered_list))

print(names_filtered_list)
```

The output is similar to that of the previous listing, except names that contain the lowercase letter "e" are returned:

```
['Haythem', 'Mike', 'James', 'Helen', 'Mary']
<class 'filter'>
<class 'list'>
['Haythem', 'Mike', 'James', 'Helen']
```

In our ERP application, we will perform various kinds of filtering operations. For instance, we may be interested in knowing how many customers opened their account with us on a particular date. We may further want to know, of those customers, how many of them live in a particular state. We can perform such filtering tasks using the built-in filter() function in Python.

COMBINING A FILTER AND A LAMBDA

We can combine the filter() function with a lambda function to create more complicated filters. In the example in Listing 21.15, we import the data from the stocks.csv file we used earlier. This data is imported into a new list, where each row in the original file is a dictionary object in the list.

Using a lambda function with the filter() function, we then filter the data in the list to output only those records where the open price is lower than the close price. The lambda function uses the key values Open and Close to create the comparison used by the filter() function. The result is a filter object that includes only those items that meet the criteria in the lambda function.

As a last step, we convert the filter object to a list object and display the filtered results from the dataset.

LISTING 21.15

Using a filter and lambda on our stocks.csv data

```
def fromCSV(path,delimiter,quotechar):
    import csv # import the csv module
    data=list() # any data we will read will be returned in a list
    with open(path, newline='') as csvfile: #o pen the file
        filecontent = csv.DictReader(csvfile, delimiter=delimiter,
quotechar=quotechar)
        # access the content of the file
        for row in filecontent: # iterate through the rows
            data.append(row) # save the rows in the data list. Each row
                             # is a dictionary
    return data

data=fromCSV(path='data/stocks_short.csv',delimiter=',',quotechar='|')

# filter all elements in data where the open price is lower than the close price
data_filtered = filter(lambda x: x['Open'] < x['Close'], data)
print(type(data_filtered))

data_filtered_list = list(data_filtered) # convert the filter object into a list
for row in data_filtered_list: # display each element in the filtered list
    print(row)
```

The output from running this listing using the `stocks.csv` file is:

```
<class 'filter'>
OrderedDict([('Date', '7/10/2006'), ('Open', '493.3'), ('High', '496.4'), ('Low',
'491.0001'), ('Close', '493.4'), ('Volume', '838869')])
OrderedDict([('Date', '7/11/2006'), ('Open', '493.4'), ('High', '496.7999'),
('Low', '488.6'), ('Close', '496.0001'), ('Volume', '816880')])
OrderedDict([('Date', '7/18/2006'), ('Open', '464.2'), ('High', '468.9999'),
('Low', '462.2'), ('Close', '465.5'), ('Volume', '1655100')])
OrderedDict([('Date', '7/19/2006'), ('Open', '468.5001'), ('High', '475.0999'),
('Low', '468.3'), ('Close', '472.5'), ('Volume', '2621339')])
```

In our ERP banking application, we may be interested in notifying our customers if they spent more than they deposited in a particular month. To do this, we can compare their incoming transactions to the opening and closing balance for the month and notify our customers accordingly. We can achieve this in Python using the `filter()` function with custom lambda functions to perform the filtering.

USING THE REDUCE() FUNCTION

We use Python's `reduce()` function to calculate a sequential value on a set of individual values. For example, given a collection of numbers, we can use the `reduce()` function to calculate the sum of those numbers. The function will perform the calculation by iterating through the numbers in order, calculating the sum of the first two values, adding the third value to that sum, and so on, until it has included each number in the set in the calculation.

The `reduce()` function was built into Python 2. However, in Python 3, it was moved to the `functools` module. As a result, we must include an `import` statement before we can use it in a script.

The `reduce()` function takes two required arguments: a function and a series of values that the function will apply to. It returns a single value, regardless of the individual items in the original dataset.

In Listing 21.16, we use the `reduce()` function to multiply all the numbers within the `list_numbers` list together. We do this by using a lambda function that multiplies the numbers in pairs.

LISTING 21.16

Multiplying numbers together

```
from functools import reduce

list_numbers = [2, 4, 6, 8]
```

```
product = reduce(lambda x, y: x * y,list_numbers)

print(type(product))

print(product)
```

As mentioned, the lambda function works by multiplying two numbers together. It starts with the first two values and then works from there:

- **2 * 4 = 8:** The product of the first two values
- **8 * 6 = 48:** The product of the first product and the third value
- **48 * 8 = 384:** The product of the second product and the fourth value

The result is an integer that equals 2 * 4 * 6 * 8. The full output from the listing is:

```
<class 'int'>
384
```

TIP It is always helpful to let the user know how to exit a loop.

In Listing 21.17, we create another script that is very similar to the previous listing. This time, our script prompts the user for a series of numbers and determines the sum of all the values entered.

LISTING 21.17

Using reduce and a lambda to calculate a sum

```
from functools import reduce

value_list = []

while True:
  user_input = input("Enter the deposits to add to the series to sum [type quit
to exit]: ")
  if user_input.lower() == 'quit':
    break
  else:
    value_list.append(int(user_input))

product = reduce(lambda x, y: x + y,value_list)

print("The total is: " + str(product))
```

This listing starts by importing `reduce` from the `functools` module. It then sets up an empty list, `value_list`. The user is prompted to enter deposit numbers one-by-one. Once they are done, they can enter "**quit**." The `reduce()` function is then used with a lambda function to determine the sum of the values. The following is one example of running the script:

```
Enter the deposits to add to the series to sum [type quit to exit]: 300
Enter the deposits to add to the series to sum [type quit to exit]: 250
Enter the deposits to add to the series to sum [type quit to exit]: 199
Enter the deposits to add to the series to sum [type quit to exit]: 42
Enter the deposits to add to the series to sum [type quit to exit]: 100
Enter the deposits to add to the series to sum [type quit to exit]: quit
The total is: 891
```

In our banking ERP application, we will want to display the total account balance for our customers. This is the sum of all the transactions performed by the customer. We can achieve this using the `reduce()` function from the built-in `functools` module in Python.

Specify an Initial Value

While `reduce()` requires at least a function and a dataset on which to perform the function, we can optionally include an initial value as a third argument:

```
reduce(function, dataset[, initial value])
```

Listing 21.18 is the same as the example, except that we include an initial value of 5.

LISTING 21.18

Starting with an initial value

```
from functools import reduce

list_numbers = [2, 4, 6, 8]

product = reduce(lambda x, y: x * y,list_numbers,5) #initial value = 5

print(type(product))

print(product)
```

When we specify an initial value, the reduce() function starts with the initial value, pairs it with the first value in the collection, and applies the function to that pair. It then continues through the rest of the values normally. Specifically, in this case, the reduce() function applies the following steps:

- **5 * 2 = 10:** The initial value of 5 is multiplied by the first value in the set, 2, giving the initial product
- **10 * 4 = 40:** The initial product and the third item
- **40 * 6 = 240:** The product of the previous operation and the third value
- **240 * 8 = 1920:** The product of the previous operation and the fourth value

The result is an integer that equals 5 * 2 * 4 * 6 * 8 as shown in the output:

```
<class 'int'>
1920
```

In Listing 21.19, we modify the script in Listing 21.17. This time the script prompts the user to enter the previous balance for an account, and then to enter each of the deposits that has been made since that time. The reduce() function is then used to add all the entered deposits to provide a new total balance.

LISTING 21.19

Summing the total account balance

```
from functools import reduce

value_list = []
prev_bal = int(input("Enter your previous balance: "))

while True:
  user_input = input("Enter the deposits to add to the series to sum [type quit
to exit]: ")
  if user_input.lower() == 'quit':
    break
  else:
    value_list.append(int(user_input))

product = reduce(lambda x, y: x + y,value_list,prev_bal)
print("New balance is: " + str(product))
```

This following is an example of the output produced by running this script:

```
Enter your previous balance: 23100
Enter the deposits to add to the series to sum [type quit to exit]: 300
Enter the deposits to add to the series to sum [type quit to exit]: 250
Enter the deposits to add to the series to sum [type quit to exit]: 199
Enter the deposits to add to the series to sum [type quit to exit]: 42
Enter the deposits to add to the series to sum [type quit to exit]: 100
Enter the deposits to add to the series to sum [type quit to exit]: quit
New balance is: 23991
```

In our ERP application, we may want to inform our customers of their balance every month. To calculate the balance, we take the previous month's closing balance and add all the transactions for the new month. Then, we can use the reduce() function from the functools module with the previous month's closing balance as the initial value.

Using reduce() with Comparison Operations

The reduce() function always handles the values in the dataset sequentially and in pairs. This means that we can also use it to perform comparison operations like max and min, where the result is a single value derived from a collection of values.

In Listing 21.20 we want to find the highest value in a collection of values. The result will be one of the original values, rather than a collective value calculated from all values.

LISTING 21.20

Finding the highest value in a collection of values

```
from functools import reduce

list_numbers =  [1,20,300,560,4]

max_element =reduce(lambda a,b : a if a > b else b,list_numbers)

print(max_element)
```

Specifically, we use a comparison statement in a lambda function that compares each value in the original collection to the next value in the collection, and then keeps the higher of the two values for the next comparison. Given the numbers 1, 20, 300, 560, and 4, the reduce function will return the following:

- The larger of the first two numbers, 1 and 20: 20
- The larger of the previous result and the third number, 20 and 300: 300

- The larger of the previous result and the fourth number, 300 and 560: 560

- The larger of the previous result and the fifth number, 560 and 4: 560

The result is the integer value 560.

As a second example, we will again look at deposits to an account. In Listing 21.21, we create a script that outputs the lowest deposit in a series of deposit values input by the user.

LISTING 21.21

Finding the lowest value

```
from functools import reduce

value_list = []

while True:
  user_input = input("Enter the deposits to determine the lowest deposit [type
stop to exit]: ")
  if user_input.lower() == 'stop':
    break
  else:
    value_list.append(int(user_input))

if len(value_list) > 0:
  product = reduce(lambda x, y: x if y > x else y,value_list)
else:
  product = "Nothing."

print("The values you entered were: "+ str(value_list))
print("The lowest value is: " + str(product))
```

This script accepts values from the user until the user enters "**Stop**" (in any letter case). Once the user enters "**Stop**," the script checks to confirm that a value was entered (the length of our value_list is greater than 0). If values were entered, then reduce is called to determine the lowest value in the list. The following shows an example of running the script:

```
Enter the deposits to determine the lowest deposit [type stop to exit]: 100
Enter the deposits to determine the lowest deposit [type stop to exit]: 200
Enter the deposits to determine the lowest deposit [type stop to exit]: 500
Enter the deposits to determine the lowest deposit [type stop to exit]: 299
Enter the deposits to determine the lowest deposit [type stop to exit]: 42
Enter the deposits to determine the lowest deposit [type stop to exit]: 300
Enter the deposits to determine the lowest deposit [type stop to exit]: stop
The values you entered were: [100, 200, 500, 299, 42, 300]
The lowest value is: 42
```

SUMMARY

In this lesson, we explored ways to analyze data to create business reports that include meaningful information.

Now that you have completed Lesson 21, you should be able to:

- Create lambda functions.
- Explain how a lambda function uses input values.
- Use a lambda function as part of a defined function.
- Use Python's `map()` function to apply a function to each element of an iterable object.
- Use Python's `filter()` function to identify specific elements in a collection that meet defined criteria and extract those elements to a new collection.
- Use Python's `reduce()` function to apply an operation sequentially to the elements in a collection.

EXERCISES

The following exercises are provided to allow you to demonstrate the objectives for this lesson. You should complete each exercise and make sure that the code runs without errors. The exercises include:

Exercise 1: Computing the Square Root

Exercise 2: Converting a Text File to Uppercase

Exercise 3: Determining Prime

Exercise 4: Identifying Absolute Value

Exercise 5: Highest Number

Exercise 6: Lowest Number

Exercise 7: Last Key

Exercise 8: Highest Value

Exercise 9: Sum of Even

Exercise 10: Sum of Positive Numbers

Exercise 11: Highest Stock Market Volume

Exercise 12: Bad Stock Market Day

Exercise 13: Highest Opening Price

Exercise 14: Highest Price at Closing

Exercise 15: Self-Assessment

Exercise 1: Computing the Square Root

Create a script that uses the map() function to compute the square root of each value in an input set of integers.

Exercise 2: Converting a Text File to Uppercase

Create a script that uses the map() function to convert the contents of a text file into uppercase.

Exercise 3: Determining Prime

Create a script that uses the map() function to determine which integers are prime numbers in an input list of integers.

Exercise 4: Identifying Absolute Value

Create a script that uses the map() function to compute the absolute value of each integer in an input list.

Exercise 5: Highest Number

Create a script that uses the reduce() function to compute the highest number in a tuple.

Exercise 6: Lowest Number

Create a script that uses the reduce() function to compute the lowest number in a tuple.

Exercise 7: Last Key

Create a script that uses the reduce() function to identify the key in a dictionary that is last in alphabetical order. For example, if you had the input of:

```
dict_my = {"elephant":1, "zebra":4, "panther":5}
```

The output would be:

```
zebra
```

In this case, "zebra" is the key that appears last in alphabetical order.

Exercise 8: Highest Value

Create a script that uses the `reduce()` function to identify the highest value in a dictionary. For example, if the input was:

```
dict_my = {"elephant":1, "zebra":4, "panther":5}
```

Then the output would be:

```
panther
```

In this case, "panther" has the highest value, 5.

Exercise 9: Sum of Even

Create a script that uses the `reduce()` function to compute the sum of all even numbers in a list of numbers. For example, given the list [3, 4, 5, 9, 6], the output should be 10 (because 4 and 6 are the only even numbers in the list, and 4 + 6 = 10).

Exercise 10: Sum of Positive Numbers

Create a script that uses the `reduce()` function to compute the sum of all positive numbers within a list of numbers. For example, the input [1, 2, –1, –2, 1] should output 4 (1 + 2 + 1).

Exercise 11: Highest Stock Market Volume

Create a script that uses the `reduce()` function to compute the trading day where the highest volume was recorded in the `stocks.csv` file. You can use any functions that are appropriate for the task, but you must include the `reduce()` function at least once.

Display the results in a user-friendly format.

Exercise 12: Bad Stock Market Day

Create a script that uses the `filter()` function to identify all records in the `stocks.csv` file where the opening price is higher than the closing price.

Exercise 13: Highest Opening Price

Create a script that uses the `filter()` function to identify all records in the `stocks.csv` file where the highest price of the day is the open price.

Exercise 14: Highest Price at Closing

Create a script that uses the filter() function to identify all records in the stocks.csv file where the highest price of the day is the close price.

Exercise 15: Self-Assessment

This exercise is provided as a self-assessment, allowing you to check your knowledge and readiness for the next lesson. For this exercise, create a program that includes lambda functions as part of other functions. Create a program that includes the following:

- Write a function named dateReturn that accepts one datetime parameter value.
  - Include a lambda function that extracts and returns the date from the dateReturn function's parameter value.
- Write a function named timeReturn that accepts one datetime parameter value.
  - Include a lambda function that extracts and returns the time from the timeReturn function's datetime value.
- Write another function named oneWord that accepts a single string input value.
  - Include a lambda function that extracts and returns the first word in the input string.

The dateReturn and timeReturn functions can use the same datetime value. The string used for the oneWord function can be any string that includes multiple words, using spaces to delineate the words.

If you want to challenge yourself, you can do the following optional steps:

- Add user prompts for the datetime value(s) and string that are used in the functions.
- Modify the oneWord function so that it returns a random word from the string.

Lesson 22
Handling Exceptions

Errors detected during the program execution are called *exceptions*. Specifically, an exception is an event that occurs during the execution of a program, disrupting the normal flow of the program's instructions. Error detection is distinguished from detection of syntax errors (like incorrect indents or missing colons), which prevent the code from running at all.

LEARNING OBJECTIVES

By the end of this lesson, you will be able to:

- Define custom exception messages that will display when Python encounters an error in the code.
- Use try:except to display a message based on the type of error Python encounters.
- Use try:except:finally to continue running a script after Python has encountered an error.

Exception handling is one of the most important features of programming, allowing developers to handle runtime errors caused by exceptions. In this lesson, we will explore exception handling and use examples to demonstrate how to handle exceptions in Python. Exceptions can be handled by implementing proper exception-handling techniques within the code itself. Python allows programmers to implement their own exception-handling techniques as well as to take advantage of built-in exception handlers. Key terms related to this lesson that you should be aware of are the following:

- **Exception handling** is code designed to handle interruptions in the normal flow of the program execution.
- **Try block** is code that allows developers to test a code block for errors.
- **Except statements** handle the error encountered in the code.

BUILT-IN EXCEPTIONS

Some exceptions are common enough that they are built into Python by default. These include the following:

- Missing files
- Data mismatches for conversions or imports
- Divide by zero errors

It is mathematically impossible to divide any value by zero, so Python has a built-in exception named ZeroDivisionError when a program has this error. We can see this exception when we run the simple one-line program in Listing 22.1.

LISTING 22.1

Division by zero exception

```
a = 1/0   # This will throw a division by zero exception
```

When we run the program, the output includes the name of the error (in this case, ZeroDivisionError) and the default message associated with that error (division by zero):

```
--------------------------------------------------------------------

ZeroDivisionError                 Traceback (most recent call last)

<ipython-input-1-87bc6b39f555> in <module>()
----> 1 a = 1/0 #this will throw a division by zero exception
ZeroDivisionError: division by zero
```

In Listing 22.2, we create a Python script that can be used to produce other types of built-in exceptions. Examples include missing files, bad conversion, and import errors. Remove the # in front of the line to see the error code. The code will only generate one error at a time, so you will need to replace the # to see the other errors.

LISTING 22.2

Exceptions in Python

```
#file = open('nonexistant_file.txt') #FileNotFound error
#a = 1/0
#string = 'string'; string/1
```

> **NOTE** As you uncomment each line of code in Listing 22.2, you'll generate a different error.

It is possible to write programs that handle selected exceptions. For example, the accounting module of our ERP application may attempt to generate a 1095 tax form for an employee who does not have company-provided insurance. Because the total annual premiums are equal to zero, and it is mathematically impossible to divide any value by zero, Python will throw an error rather than stop processing.

WORKING WITH TRY AND EXCEPT

We can use `try` and `except` to help identify errors and add a more user-friendly way to handle those errors. For example, if the user inputs data that results in a `ZeroDivisionError`, we would prefer that the user be informed about the problem and how to get around it, rather than displaying the default error message.

In Listing 22.3, we create an operation that could result in a `ZeroDivisionError`. Instead of simply running the operation as we did in the previous example, we embed it in a `try:except` statement.

LISTING 22.3

Handling a ZeroDivisionError exception

```
a = 1
b = 0

try: # check that the operation is valid
  x = a/b
except ZeroDivisionError as e: # The type of exception is division by zero.
  # print a custom message when the execption occurs
  print("Oops! We cannot divide a number by zero. Try again...")
  print(format(e)) #print the exception error message
```

In this listing, we embed the operation in a `try` statement. This tells Python to attempt to run the operation, and the program will output the result if it does not encounter any errors. If the operation does report an exception, Python will implement the `except` part of the statement.

The `except` part of the statement executes only if the `try` statement throws a `ZeroDivisionError` exception. In this case, it displays a user-friendly message about what caused the error and how to avoid it, along with Python's built-in message for the same error:

```
Oops! We cannot divide a number by zero. Try again...
division by zero
```

Listing 22.4 is a second example of using the `try:except` statement. This time we create a script that opens the uploaded text file (`data/bank_transacts.txt`) and defines a user-friendly exception message that displays if the file does not exist. When you run this listing, you should test using both a valid path and an invalid path.

LISTING 22.4

Handling FileNotFoundError

```
try:
  file_object = open("data/bank_transacts.txt",'r')
except FileNotFoundError as e:
 print("The file was not found")
 print("The error was:\n" + str(e))
```

When this listing is run without the file existing, the following is displayed:

```
The file was not found
The error was:
[Errno 2] No such file or directory: 'data/bank_transacts.txt'
```

> **TIP** To identify Python's name for an error (as well as the built-in message), run the program in a way that it produces the error(s) you want to catch. Use Python's output on the error to build the except statement.

In our ERP application, consider this scenario. When there is an attempt to update a customer record for Gussie Jones, a customer who no longer does business with the company, an exception is generated. Specifically, the try block will generate an exception, because x (Ms. Jones' customer ID) is not defined or not valid.

WORKING WITH MULTIPLE EXCEPTS

We can define a cascade of except statements to cover all the different exceptions that might occur in the code, as well as a generic except statement that will appear if the try statement throws an exception and none of the other except statements apply. When there are multiple except statements, only one will execute if there is an exception in the try statement.

In the example in Listing 22.3, we only looked at the ZeroDivisionError exception, which is actually less common than trying to perform a mathematical operation using a string value. In Listing 22.5, we add a second except statement for the built-in TypeError exception, which Python throws if the program uses a value that is the wrong type for the operation.

As with the previous example, we embed the division operation in a try statement, and we define two different except statements: the original ZeroDivisionError statement and a new `TypeError` statement. The exception statements will execute only if the operation in the `try` statement throws an exception, and only the one that matches the original `except` will execute.

One of the values provided as a variable is a string rather than a number. Because we cannot use string characters in a mathematical operation, Python throws a `TypeError` exception. As a result, the second `except` statement executes when we run the script.

LISTING 22.5

Adding muiltiple exceptions

```
import sys
a = 1
b = 'c'

try:
  x = a/b

# if we have a division by zero, this block will execute
except ZeroDivisionError as e:
  print("Oops, ZeroDivisionError! We cannot divide a number by zero. Try again...")

# if we have an error type (a non-valid integer such as char or string), this block will
# execute
except TypeError as t:
  print("Oops, TypeError! That was not a valid number. Try again...")

# the following will execute if the try statement fails with a different exception from
# those above
except:
  print("Unexpected error. Try again.", sys.exc_info()[0])
  raise
```

Because the value stored in b is not a number, we get a `TypeError` when this listing is executed. The resulting output after catching this error is:

```
Oops, TypeError! That was not a valid number. Try again...
```

In Listing 22.5, we don't check for errors until Python runs the operation. From a user perspective, though, it is often better to check values as they are entered by the user, so that the user has the opportunity to correct the input values before the program runs. In Listing 22.6, we update the listing to prompt the user to enter the values and then use exception handling to check the values to see that they are numbers and not equal to zero.

LISTING 22.6

Validating user input

```
value_1 = input("Please enter a number: ")
value_2 = input("Please enter a second number [do not enter 0]: ")
try:
 x = int(value_1)/int(value_2)
 print(x)
except ValueError:
  try:
   x = float(value_1)/float(value_2)
   print(x)
  except ValueError:
   try:
    x = float(value_1)
   except:
    print("The first value entered is not an integer or a float.")
   try:
    x = float(value_2)
   except:
    print("The second value entered is not an integer or a float.")
except ZeroDivisionError:
  print("Oops, there's a zero in the second value. You can't divide by zero.")
```

In walking through this script, we can see that the user is first prompted for our two numbers, value_1 and value_2. The script then tries to divide value_1 by value_2. If the division works, then the result is displayed. If not, then we check to see if the exception was a ValueError. If so, we try to do the division again, but this time we convert both values that were entered to float numbers. Again, if the division works, we print the result and are done. If not, we again check to see if a ValueError was thrown again indicating that at least one of the numbers is not a float or integer.

If we again have a ValueError, then we check to see which of the values is causing the problem. We first try to convert value_1 to a float, then we try to convert value_2 to a float. A message is displayed if either action causes an exception.

Finally, we also do a check (except) tied to the original division that checks to see if a ZeroDivisionError caused a problem. If so, we print an appropriate message. The following is the output from running the script several times:

```
Please enter a number: 10
Please enter a second number [do not enter 0]: 20
0.5

Please enter a number: 10
Please enter a second number [do not enter 0]: 20.0
0.5
```

```
Please enter a number: 10.0
Please enter a second number [do not enter 0]: 20.0
0.5

Please enter a number: a
Please enter a second number [do not enter 0]: b
The first value entered is not an integer or a float.
The second value entered is not an integer or a float.

Please enter a number: 10
Please enter a second number [do not enter 0]: b
The first value entered is not an integer or a float.

Please enter a number: 10
Please enter a second number [do not enter 0]: 0
Oops, there's a zero in the second value. You can't divide by zero.
```

As we update records in our ERP application remote database, we may run into several problems—connectivity issues, nonexistent database, duplicate entry, and so on. We can plan for all the various exceptions and handle them properly using multiple exceptions in Python. In our ERP banking application, we program it so that missing files are handled in such a manner to avoid causing any production outages.

COMBINING EXCEPTION TYPES

We can combine multiple exception types in the same except statement. Sometimes the exceptions raised might have a common way to handle the error. For instance, we might try to open a file that does not exist or add a record to a file that does not exist.

In Listing 22.7, we collapse the ZeroDivisionError and TypeError statements into a single except statement that handles both types of exceptions.

LISTING 22.7

Combining exceptions

```
a = 1
b = 'c'
try:
  x = a/b
except (ZeroDivisionError,TypeError) as e:
  print("Input is not a valid number")
  print(format(e))
```

You can see that to combine the errors, we place them in parentheses after the except keyword. The "as e" code provides a variable to store the actual exception that is thrown. We can see in the output that in this case, the exception thrown (and stored in e) is an unsupported operand type, or TypeError:

```
Input is not a valid number
unsupported operand type(s) for /: 'int' and 'str'
```

If you change value of b in the listing to 0, you'll see that e will then indicate a division by zero (ZeroDivisionError) error:

```
Input is not a valid number
division by zero
```

In Listing 22.8 a second example is presented that iterates through a list of values and returns only the valid numbers. By using a try:except the listing avoids ending early due to bad values.

LISTING 22.8

Checking a list for valid values

```
def check_numbers(input_list):
  list = []
  for x in input_list:
    try:
      a = float(x)
      list.append(x)
    except ValueError:
      try:
        a = int(x)
        list.append(x)
      except (ValueError,ZeroDivisionError,TypeError):
        print(x + " is not a valid number.")
    except (ZeroDivisionError,TypeError) as e:
      print(x + " is not a valid number.")
  return list


input_list = [1,'c',"Haythem",23,6,6.7,-1,"String"]
print(input_list)

# check_numbers should return a list that contains the valid numbers.
numbers = check_numbers(input_list)
print(numbers)
```

Looking at this listing, we see that it starts by defining our function, check_numbers, which iterates through a list of values that are supplied (input_list). Within the loop an attempt is made to convert each value to a float. If converted, it is appended to a new list called list.

If an exception happens, the code has two except statements that it can check against it. The first is for ValueError. If a ValueError exception happens, the code will try to convert the current value to an integer. If successful, the value is added to the list. The second except checks to see if the problem was a ZeroDivisionError or TypeError. If so, then a message is printed that the value couldn't be converted.

After defining the function, the code creates a list called input_list with a set of values. This is displayed to the screen before being passed to the check_numbers function. The results of the check_numbers function are printed, which shows the new list that contains only the numbers. The output is:

```
[1, 'c', 'Haythem', 23, 6, 6.7, -1, 'String']
c is not a valid number.
Haythem is not a valid number.
String is not a valid number.
[1, 23, 6, 6.7, -1]
```

USING MULTIPLE OPERATIONS IN A TRY

We can include several operations within the try statement, but Python will only display the except statement for the first error it encounters. Python only runs the operations in the try statement until it finds an error, and then it executes the except statement for that error. It ignores any subsequent errors in the try statement. To illustrate this, in Listing 22.9 we include two operations in the try statement.

LISTING 22.9

Using multiple try statements

```
import sys

b = 0
a = 1
c = 'd'

try:
    # This will throw an exception, which will trigger an except statement
    y = a/c
```

```
# This would also throw an exception, but python ignores it because
# it is the second exception

x = a/b
print(x)
print(y)

except ZeroDivisionError as e:
  print("Oops, ZeroDivisionError! We cannot divide by zero. Try again...")

except TypeError as t:
  print("Oops, TypeError! That was not a valid number. Try again...")

except:
  print("Unexpected error. Try again.", sys.exc_info()[0])
  raise
```

In this listing, the first operation (a/c) will throw a TypeError exception because it attempts to divide using a string character. The second operation (a/b) should throw a ZeroDivisionError because the divisor is zero. In this case, when we run the program, the result is a TypeError exception because that is the first error Python discovered. The output is:

```
Oops, TypeError! That was not a valid number. Try again...
```

It is also worth noting that once an exception occurs, the rest of the code within the try statement is also skipped. Processing of the code will return to the first line after the try block of code, not to any code within the try statement.

In Listing 22.9 we included a call to sys.exec_info()[0] as part of the print statement for an unexpected error. This provides additional information to the user about the unexpected error that occurred. We also needed to import the sys module to be able to get this additional information.

> **NOTE** As a challenge, can you add an operation to the try statement in Listing 22.9 that would cause the default except statement to execute, without changing either of the existing except statements?

USING THE RAISE KEYWORD

We can use the raise keyword to raise an exception manually. The concept of raising an exception means that the program's execution stops at that point. We can optionally include an associated message.

In the following line of code, we use `raise` to create an exception named `NameError` and associate the exception with a specific message:

```
raise NameError('Oswaldo Dunlap caused an Exception')
```

When this line of code is executed, Python stops at that point in the program and displays the `NameError` exception and the associated message:

```
---------------------------------------------------------------------------

NameError                         Traceback (most recent call last)

<ipython-input-14-13413f6f2d8f> in <module>()
----> 1 raise NameError('Oswaldo Dunlap caused an Exception')
NameError: Oswaldo Dunlap caused an Exception
```

Listing 22.10 includes three lines of code that are each commented out. These lines each use `raise` to define a type of exception other than `NameError`. You can uncomment each line and run the script to see the various exceptions displayed.

LISTING 22.10

Creating (raising) exceptions

```
print("starting...")
#raise ValueError("This is a custom ValueError.")
#raise TypeError("This is a raised TypeError.")
#raise ZeroDivisionError("I raised this ZeroDivisionError.")
print("...ending")
```

Remember, Python will only show one error at a time so remove the # to see an individual raised error. Note that once you remove the # from a line to raise an error, the program will no longer reach the second `print` statement.

Our ERP application code may be used by other employees in our company. In such a situation, if a user provides invalid input, we may want to manually raise an exception to let our users know what the error is. For instance, we may require that the transaction time always is specified with the corresponding time zone, and if the time zone is not provided, we can manually raise an exception.

EXPLORING THE GENERAL EXCEPTION CLASSES

Python includes a variety of general exception classes that are themselves divided into exception subclasses. For example, the `FileNotFoundError` exception is a subclass of a larger `IOError` exception class, while the `ModuleNotFoundError` exception is a subclass of the `ImportError` class.

When we define `except` statements, we can reference the class that a subclass belongs to instead of a specific subclass and get the same result. This is sometimes more efficient because the same exception class can include multiple subclasses, which reduces the number of `except` statements we need.

In the example in Listing 22.11 we create a `try` statement that includes the steps required to open and view the contents of a text file. We include an `except` statement for `IOError` exceptions that will execute if the file in the `try` statement does not exist in the specified path. This includes not only `FileNotFoundError` exceptions, but also other exceptions related to I/O processes, such as disk space problems or permission violations.

LISTING 22.11

Using the general IOError exception

```
try:
    f = open("data/another_file_do_not_exist.txt", "r")
    print(f.read())
    f.close()
except IOError as e:
    print("Oops! File Not Found.")
    print(format(e))
```

When you run this listing, if the file doesn't exist, the following will be displayed:

```
Oops! File Not Found.
[Errno 2] No such file or directory: 'data/another_file_do_not_exist.txt'
```

Listing 22.12 presents a second example where we attempt to import a package named `wrong_package`. Python throws an `ImportError` exception because the package does not exist, and we use the `except` statement to provide a custom error message.

LISTING 22.12

Trying to import a nonexistent package

```
try:
    import wrong_package
except ImportError as e:
    print("Oops! Module Not Found.")
    print(format(e))
```

The output from running this listing is the message we put into our except code:

```
Oops! Module Not Found.
No module named 'wrong_package'
```

If Python cannot find the specified file, the script should simply return "Unable to access file." In Listing 22.13, we expanded a script to open a file to something even more useful. In this code, a try:except statement has been added to handle cases where a file is missing by including an IOError exception type in an except statement. In such cases, a user-friendly message is displayed instead of the program stopping.

LISTING 22.13

Adding exception handling to opening a file

```
def read_csv(filepath,delimiter=","):
  import csv
  dataset = list()
  try:
    with open(filepath) as f: # Use open function to read the C.csv file
                              # and create a file object f

      # Use the reader function under the csv module to read the
      # file using comma a delimiter
      csv_file = csv.DictReader(f, delimiter=delimiter)

      # csv_file is an iterable object that we can iterate on using a for loop
      for row in csv_file:
        dataset.append(row)
    return dataset
  except IOError as e:
    print("Unable to access file.")

a = read_csv("file.txt","r") #do not change this line
```

This code creates a function called read_csv that opens a file to read. When the file is read into the program, the contents are placed in a dataset that is returned. Most importantly, the logic of opening and reading the file is placed within a try statement. If there is an IOError, then it triggers the except statement and a message is displayed before returning to the calling code. If this listing is run and there is not a file.txt file in the current directory, a simple message is displayed:

```
Unable to access file.
```

While trying to update a file in our ERP application, we may run into multiple errors, such as a nonexistent file, a permission error due to restricted access, or other errors. Since exceptions in Python follow hierarchy, instead of planning for all the various exceptions that could arise, we can use the parent class of our exceptions to capture all the possible errors. In this case, we would capture the `IOError`, which is the parent class of the `FileNotFoundError`.

ADDING FINALLY

We can use a finally statement with a `try:except` statement to execute a block of code whether an exception occurred or not.

In Listing 22.14 we include a finally statement that displays a message regardless of whether the `try` statement works. Specifically, we ask Python to open a file that does not exist, which triggers the `except` statement. Normally, Python would stop the script at that point, but instead, it will complete the finally statement even though the `try` statement threw an error.

LISTING 22.14

finally

```
try:
  f = open("data/text.txt", "r")
    # file does not exist so this line throws a FileNotFound exception
  print(len(f.read()))

# This except statement runs only if Python does not find the file
except IOError as e:
  print("Oops! File Not Found.")

# This finally statement runs whether or not Python finds
# the file
finally:
  print("Thanks for trying!")
```

If text.txt does not exist in the data folder, then the following output is displayed:

```
Oops! File Not Found.
Thanks for trying!
```

If `text.txt` does exist, then an output similar to the following is displayed. The number shown is the length of the file that was found. As you can see, the `finally` block ran in both cases.

```
72
Thanks for trying!
```

In our ERP application, we may try to open a file to update an entry. However, let's say while updating the entry, an exception occurs that exits the `try:except` block without updating the record in our file and in the process leaves our file open. We can solve this easily using `try:except:finally`. This enables us to close our file always, regardless of any exception that may come up in the `try` block.

SUMMARY

An exception is an event or error that occurs during the execution of a program that disrupts the normal flow of the program's instructions. Error detection is different from detection of syntax errors, which prevent the code from running at all. Exceptions can be used to give a custom error message to the user in order to make troubleshooting more intuitive.

Now that you have completed this lesson, you should be able to:

- Define custom exception messages that will display when Python encounters an error in the code.
- Use `try:except` to display a message based on the type of error Python encounters.
- Use `try:except:finally` to continue running a script after Python has encountered an error.

EXERCISES

The following exercises are provided to allow you to demonstrate the objectives for this lesson. In these exercises, you are asked to implement exception handling using the tools presented in this lesson. For example, update the scripts to handle cases like the following:

- Missing files
- Division by zero
- Conversion error

You should complete each exercise and make sure that the code runs without errors. The exercises include:

Exercise 1: Typing Numbers

Exercise 2: Current Value

Exercise 3: Reading Lines

Exercise 4: Concatenating Files

Exercise 5: Creating a List from a File

Exercise 6: Self-Assessment

For the file I/O activities, you are welcome to use any appropriate file, including files provided for other activities, files you download from a website, or files that you create for this activity. Be sure to use `try:except` and `try:except:finally` where appropriate.

Exercise 1: Typing Numbers

Create a program that prompts the user to enter a number and then displays the type of the number entered (e.g., complex, integer, or float). For example, if the user enters 6, the output should be `int`.

Implement appropriate exception handling for situations where the user enters a string that cannot be converted to a number.

Exercise 2: Current Value

Write a program that calculates and displays the current value of a deposit for a given initial deposit, interest rate, number of times interest is calculated per year, and the number of years since the initial deposit.

The program should prompt the user for each of the values and use the following formula to calculate the current value of the deposit:

$$V = P(1 + r/n)^{\wedge}nt$$

Where:

- V: Value
- P: Initial deposit
- r : Interest rate as a fraction (e.g., 0.05)
- n : The number of times per year interest is calculated
- t : The number of years since the initial deposit

The program should display each of the values entered in a meaningful way so that the user can easily see what each value represents, along with the results of the calculation.

Implement appropriate exception handling for each input where the user might enter a string value that cannot be used as a number. In particular, consider the following:

- The user enters a percentage value like "5%" instead of "0.05" for the interest rate.
- The user enters "0" for *n*, resulting in a division by 0 error.

Exercise 3: Reading Lines

Write a function that prompts the reader for an integer *n* and reads the first *n* lines of a file. Include a creative way to handle cases where n is greater than the number of lines available in the file.

Add exception handling for these cases:

- The user enters something other than an integer for *n*.
- The file cannot be located.

Exercise 4: Concatenating Files

Write a function that takes as input the path to two text files and concatenates the files into a single new file. Include exception handling for problems with one or both input files.

Exercise 5: Creating a List from a File

Write a function that reads a text file line by line, stores each line in a list, and then returns the list. Add exception handling for problems with the file.

Exercise 6: Self-Assessment

This exercise is provided as a self-assessment, allowing you to check your knowledge of the material you've learned. This assessment combines concepts presented in the module in a single program without the guidance provided in the lesson activities.

Review the content and examples for this lesson as necessary to complete this exercise. In this assessment, you will update an existing script to include appropriate exception handling.

Consider the class in Listing 22.15, which includes two methods, `fromCSV` and `fromJSON`, that allow us to read data from CSV and JSON files, respectively. The current version of the code doesn't deal with missing file exceptions. Implement the necessary exceptions to display a custom error message when the file is missing.

- The program must display a meaningful message to the user and allow the user to enter another path without exiting the program.

- If the user enters a new path, the program must check the new path for errors and respond appropriately.

- The program must include an option for the user to quit the program if they cannot provide a correct path.

You can use any CSV and JSON file you wish for testing, including files used elsewhere in this book, files you find online, or files you create.

LISTING 22.15

Self-assessment code

```
# Update the following code according to the instructions above.

class extract:
  def fromCSV(self, file_path, delimiter = ",", quotechar = "|"):
    if not file_path:
      raise Exception("You must provide a valid file path.")
    import csv
    dataset = list()
    with open(file_path) as f:
      csv_file = csv.DictReader(f, delimiter = delimiter,quotechar = quotechar)
      for row in csv_file:
        dataset.append(row)
    return dataset

  def fromJSON(self, file_path):
    if not file_path:
      ·raise Exception("You must provide a valid file path.")
    import json
    dataset = list()
    with open(file_path) as json_file:
      dataset = json.load(json_file)
    return dataset

e = extract()
dataset1 = e.fromCSV(file_path="data/missing_file.csv")
dataset2 = e.fromJSON(file_path="data/missing_file.json")
```

Pulling It All Together: Word Analysis in Python

In this lesson, we will apply what we've learned up to this point to perform a common text analysis process using Python. Specifically, we will build a project that takes a dataset and analyzes it to calculate the number of times each word appears.

LEARNING OBJECTIVES

By the end of this lesson, you will have learned to build a project that can:

- Read a JSON file that contains a list of online ecommerce reviews.
- Tokenize each review in the dataset.
- Compute word count in each review in the dataset.

EXAMINE THE DATA

When we start any data analysis process, the first step is to ensure that the data is in a format that our system can use and that the data is available for use. For our project, we will need to download the data. We will use the Digital Music review set from Julian McCauley's Amazon product data website, which you can find at http://jmcauley .ucsd.edu/data/amazon/. This file, reviews.json, can also be found in the data folder of the downloadable zip file for this book (JobReadyPython.zip) available at www.wiley. com/go/jobreadypython.

The reviews.json file is in a modified JSON format. If you open the extracted file using any text editor, the first two records look like the following:

```
{"reviewerID": "A3EBHHCZ06V2A4", "asin": "5555991584", "reviewerName": "Amaranth
\"music fan\"", "helpful": [3, 3], "reviewText": "It's hard to believe \"Memory of
Trees\" came out 11 years ago;it has held up well over the passage of time.It's Enya's
last great album before the New Age/pop of \"Amarantine\" and \"Day without rain.\"
Back in 1995,Enya still had her creative spark,her own voice.I agree with the reviewer
who said that this is her saddest album;it is melancholy,bittersweet,from the opening
title song.\"Memory of Trees\" is elegaic&majestic.;\"Pax Deorum\" sounds like it is
from a Requiem Mass,it is a dark threnody.Unlike the reviewer who said that this has a
\"disconcerting\" blend of spirituality&sensuality;,I don't find it disconcerting at
all.\"Anywhere is\" is a hopeful song,looking to possibilities.\"Hope has a place\" is
about love,but it is up to the listener to decide if it is romantic,platonic,etc.I've
always had a soft spot for this song.\"On my way home\" is a triumphant ending about
return.This is truly a masterpiece of New Age music,a must for any Enya fan!",
"overall": 5.0, "summary": "Enya's last great album", "unixReviewTime": 1158019200,
"reviewTime": "09 12, 2006"}
{"reviewerID": "AZPWAXJG90JXV", "asin": "5555991584", "reviewerName": "bethtexas",
"helpful": [0, 0], "reviewText": "A clasically-styled and introverted album, Memory of
Trees is a masterpiece of subtlety.  Many of the songs have an endearing shyness to
them - soft piano and a lovely, quiet voice.  But within every introvert is an
inferno, and Enya lets that fire explode on a couple of songs that absolutely burst
with an expected raw power.If you've never heard Enya before, you might want to start
with one of her more popularized works, like Watermark, just to play it safe.  But if
you're already a fan, then your collection is not complete without this beautiful work
of musical art.", "overall": 5.0, "summary": "Enya at her most elegant",
"unixReviewTime": 991526400, "reviewTime": "06 3, 2001"}
```

Each record is enclosed in curly brackets ({ }), and the records are separated by new lines. In standard JSON, each record would be enclosed in square brackets ([ ]). Our code will need to take this into account when we import the data to be analyzed.

The fields in each record include a name and value using a colon (:) as the separator:

```
"reviewerID": "A3EBHHCZO6V2A4"
```

The fields are separated by commas:

```
"reviewerID": "A3EBHHCZO6V2A4", "asin": "5555991584"
```

For this analysis, we are most interested in the reviews themselves. The review of the first record looks like:

```
"reviewText": "It's hard to believe \"Memory of Trees\" came out 11 years ago;it has
held up well over the passage of time.It's Enya's last great album before the New
Age/pop of \"Amarantine\" and \"Day without rain.\" Back in 1995,Enya still had her
creative spark,her own voice.I agree with the reviewer who said that this is her
saddest album;it is melancholy,bittersweet,from the opening title song.\"Memory of
Trees\" is elegaic&majestic.;\"Pax Deorum\" sounds like it is from a Requiem Mass,it
is a dark threnody.Unlike the reviewer who said that this has a \"disconcerting\"
blend of spirituality&sensuality;,I don't find it disconcerting at all.\"Anywhere is\"
is a hopeful song,looking to possibilities.\"Hope has a place\" is about love,but it
is up to the listener to decide if it is romantic,platonic,etc.I've always had a soft
spot for this song.\"On my way home\" is a triumphant ending about return.This is
truly a masterpiece of New Age music,a must for any Enya fan!"
```

You can see that in addition to words, the text includes punctuation. While we can use spaces as one option for separating and identifying distinct words in the data, we can also use punctuation.

Because the focus of our project is to count the number of times a word appears, we have another problem with the raw data. Some words are capitalized while others are not. Keeping in mind that Python is case-sensitive, we also want to normalize the text so that it is all in lowercase, so that both "hope" and "Hope" are considered the same word.

READ THE DATA

Now that we have looked at the data and identified what we want our code to do, we're ready to start writing code. Create two new files in the same folder where the `.json` data file is stored:

- `main.py`
- `lib.py`

> **NOTE** If you are using Jupyter Notebook, create the `main` file as a Jupyter Notebook file (`.ipynb`) and create the `lib.py` file as a Python file in the same folder.

The `main` file will include the main commands of the program, while we will use the `lib` file to define the functions that we want the main program to execute. We could use a single file for all the code, but separating the main code from the functions keeps the code more organized.

We'll start with the `lib` file. We've identified that we want the program to import the data and save it to a new list that we can analyze in Python. We can add the code shown in Listing 23.1 to the `lib.py` file. This creates our new function.

LISTING 23.1

The start of our lib.py file

```
import json

def read_json_file(path):
    dataset = list()
    with open(path) as json_file:
        for line in json_file:
            dataset.append(json.loads(line))
    return dataset
```

In this code, we import Python's JSON package to manage the JSON input. We then create the `read_json_file` function that takes a file path as input. An empty list named `dataset` is then created before data is read into the list. As data is read, each line of text (each review) in the JSON file is converted to a dictionary (using `json.loads`) and then the dictionary (the review) is added to the dataset. The function returns a list in which each item in the list is a record from the original JSON file.

This function won't run on its own, though. We must add it to the main file for it to work. Listing 23.2 presents the code for our `main.py` file.

LISTING 23.2

The main function to run function to read a JSON file

```
from lib import *

dataset = read_json_file("reviews.json") #read file
print(dataset[0])
```

Here, we start by importing the `lib` file. Because that file is in the same folder as the code files, we only need the filename here. If the file were in a different location, we would need a more detailed path so that Python could find it.

We then call the `read_json_file` function from `lib` and provide the filename as the path. The results are stored in a new variable named `dataset`. Finally, we include a `print` statement to display the first item in the new list to verify that the output is as expected.

After adding the code, run `main.py`. The output should display the first record from the original JSON file as shown:

```
{u'reviewerID': u'A3EBHHCZO6V2A4', u'asin': u'5555991584', u'reviewerName': u'Amaranth
"music fan"', u'helpful': [3, 3], u'reviewText': u'It\'s hard to believe "Memory of
Trees" came out 11 years ago;it has held up well over the passage of time.It\'s
Enya\'s last great album before the New Age/pop of "Amarantine" and "Day without
rain." Back in 1995,Enya still had her creative spark,her own voice.I agree with the
reviewer who said that this is her saddest album;it is melancholy,bittersweet,from the
opening title song."Memory of Trees" is elegaic&majestic.;"Pax Deorum" sounds like it
is from a Requiem Mass,it is a dark threnody.Unlike the reviewer who said that this
has a "disconcerting" blend of spirituality&sensuality;,I don\'t find it disconcerting
at all."Anywhere is" is a hopeful song,looking to possibilities."Hope has a place" is
about love,but it is up to the listener to decide if it is romantic,platonic,etc.I\'ve
always had a soft spot for this song."On my way home" is a triumphant ending about
return.This is truly a masterpiece of New Age music,a must for any Enya fan!',
u'overall': 5.0, u'summary': u"Enya's last great album", u'unixReviewTime':
1158019200, u'reviewTime': u'09 12, 2006'}
```

We need to tweak the function a little to make it more user-friendly. When we ask the user to input a file, any of three things can happen:

1. They enter a complete and correct path, which works the way we expect it to.

2. They forget to enter a path.

3. They enter the wrong path.

Our current code can't handle user input errors well, so the program will simply crash if the input doesn't meet the expectations. In Listing 23.3, we'll address the missing path first.

LISTING 23.3

Dealing with a missing path

```
def read_json_file(path):
    if not path:
        raise Exception("You must provide a valid file path.")
    dataset = list()
    with open(path) as json_file:
        for line in json_file:
            dataset.append(json.loads(line))
    return dataset
```

In this update to the lib.py file, we've added a check to determine if the file (path) exists. If it does not, an exception is thrown.

Once you've updated your lib.py file to match the code from Listing 23.3, you can also then remove the filename from main.py as shown in Listing 23.4 and run the program again.

LISTING 23.4

Updating main to receive a blank (bad) file

```
dataset = read_json_file("") #read file
print(dataset[0])
```

Because there isn't a file being passed that can be found, the program should print out the exception message defined in the code as such:

```
Exception: You must provide a valid file path.
```

Next, let's address the problem if the input file is not a JSON file, using a try-except block. Listing 23.5 updates the read_json_file function to include exception handling for a couple of errors.

LISTING 23.5

Adding exception handling to our function

```
def read_json_file(path):
    if not path:
        raise Exception("You must provide a valid file path.")
    try:
        dataset = list()
        with open(path) as json_file:
            for line in json_file:
                dataset.append(json.loads(line))
    except (IOError, OSError):
        raise Exception("You must provide a valid JSON file.")
    return dataset
```

In our new read_json_file function, we embed the existing code in a try block. We then create a user-friendly message that will display to the user if the path value is not correct and does not point to a JSON file. We can update our main file to run the code with a slightly different filename such as the one shown in Listing 23.6.

LISTING 23.6

Using a slightly different filename

```
dataset = read_json_file("reviews.json") #read file
print(dataset[0])
```

When Listing 23.6 executes, Python will display the message we defined for an invalid file:

```
Exception: You must provide a valid JSON file.
```

Whether an invalid filename or an invalid JSON file, the program will end gracefully, allowing the user to restart the program to try again.

TOKENIZE THE DATASET

In order to tokenize the dataset (meaning tokenizing each review in the dataset), we will adopt the following layered logic:

- First, implement a function that *tokenizes an input string*.

- Input for this function is a simple string.
- This function will form the base of the next two functions.
- Second, implement a function that *tokenizes an input review* from our dataset.
  - Input for this function is a single review (dictionary) from our dataset.
  - This function will simply identify the review text in the review and call the first function to tokenize the text.
  - This function will also add the tokenized words to the review in a new key that we will provide.
- Finally, implement a function that *tokenizes the entire dataset* by iterating through each review in the dataset and tokenizing it.
  - Input for this function is the dataset we read from the JSON file.
  - This function will leverage the second function to tokenize each review in the dataset.

Tokenize an Input String

The function to tokenize an input string is the simplest function in terms of input. It accepts as input a string and returns a list that represents the words in the string with the order preserved. This function should split the string into words based on spaces or punctuation.

We can simplify the problem by first identifying punctuation marks and replacing each with a space. This allows us to be able to then split based solely on spaces. Let's consider the following example:

```
"Hello, Sean! -How are you?"
```

The first step would be to replace the punctuation with a space. This results in the following string:

```
Hello  Sean   How are you
```

Next, we can use the `split` function to split the string based on spaces and get the list of words in the string, which will be the following:

```
['Hello', 'Sean', 'How', 'are', 'you']
```

The logic of this function is as follows:

1. Convert the input text string to lowercase.

2. Identify/replace punctuation with a space in the string.

3. Split the string into words based on spaces.

We can add this functionality with a new `tokenize` function that is shown in Listing 23.7. This function should be added to the `lib.py` file.

LISTING 23.7

A new tokenize function

```
import re
import json

def tokenize(text):
    if type(text) != str:
        raise Exception("Text must be a string")
    text_lower = text.lower()
    text_clean = re.sub("[^\w\s]", " ",text_lower)
    words = text_clean.split()
    return words
```

In simple terms, the `tokenize` function accepts a string input and returns a list of words from the string. Looking closer, however, the `tokenize` function performs the following steps:

1. Check that the input is a string and stop the program if it is not.

2. Convert the text in the string to lowercase.

3. Replace each punctuation symbol with a space. One of the main issues with tokenization is that we must be able to split the string based on spaces or punctuation. In order to overcome this issue, we identify each punctuation mark and replace it with a space, so we only have to split based on spaces. We do not need to keep track of punctuation after the tokenization so it's appropriate to replace each punctuation mark in the text with a space.

4. Split the string into individual words based on spaces.

The `lower` and `split` methods are included in Python's string class; however, the process of removing the punctuation characters uses **regular expressions**, often also called **regex**.

Regex is a standard that developers use frequently for searching through strings. In fact, most modern search engines use regex as a standard part of their matching process. We won't go into details about regex but for the purpose of this lesson, we will leverage it to identify punctuation and replace it with a space. In this case, we are using Python's regex library (re) to search for punctuation marks and the sub method to substitute a space for those punctuation marks:

```
re.sub("[^\w\s]", " ",text_lower)
```

Because re is an external library, we must also include an import statement at the top of the lib.py file by the import that was added for JSON earlier:

```
import re
import json
```

In order to understand what is happening with regex, let's consider the snippet of code in Listing 23.8. This is not part of our main project, but rather a simple example using regular expressions.

LISTING 23.8

Using a regular expression

```
import re

text = "Hello, Sean! —How are you?"
print(text)
text_clean = re.sub("[^\w]", " ",text)
print(text_clean)
words = text_clean.split()
print(words)
```

In this code, we define a variable called text where we store a simple string. We then print the string.

We then apply a regular expression (regex) to replace each punctuation mark with a space using the sub method from the regex library. The sub function requires the that we pass a regex pattern, which identifies what we want to find. In this case we use [^\w]. Many standard patterns exist in regex. You can visit https://www.regexlib.com/?Aspx AutoDetectCookieSupport=1 to view many regex patterns that can be used to identify phone numbers, emails, or any other pattern in a string. In our case [^\w] identifies any non-word character (which includes punctuation) in the string.

The second parameter in the call to `re.sub` is the value to be used to replace each identified item in the string. In this case we are replacing each value with an empty space. Finally, the third parameter of the call to `re.sub` is the string that we want to search with the regex expression.

With the punctuation removed using the regular expression, we can simply split the string based on spaces to get the list of words from the string using the `split` method. The full output from the listing is:

```
Hello, Sean! -How are you?
Hello Sean   How are you
['Hello', 'Sean', 'How', 'are', 'you']
```

NOTE It is beyond the scope of this book to cover regular expressions in detail. You can find other books on regular expressions such as *Beginning Regular Expressions* by Andrew Watt or you can review online resources such as `www.regexlib.com`.

Tokenize an Input Review

We also need a function that tokenizes a review, which means that the function will take a review as input (in the form of a dictionary), and then it will execute the `tokenize` function we just wrote on the key where the text is stored. To do this, add the code in Listing 23.9 to the `lib.py` file.

LISTING 23.9

The function to tokenize a review

```
def tokenize_review(review):
    if type(review) != dict:
        raise Exception("Review must be a dictionary")
    new_review = review.copy()
    words= tokenize(new_review[TEXT_KEY])
    new_review[WORDS_KEY] = words
    return new_review
```

This code block takes in review data formatted as a dictionary. It then copies the original review data into a new dictionary called `new_review`:

```
new_review = review.copy()
```

In the next step, the words are determined by using the `tokenize` function we created previously (Listing 23.7). In this case, we provide the review text stored in the TEXT_KEY as input.

We need to define the values `TEXT_KEY` and `WORDS_KEY`. At the top of `lib.py`, add the definitions as shown in Listing 23.10.

LISTING 23.10

Adding constants to the `lib.py` file

```
import re
import json

TEXT_KEY='reviewText'
WORDS_KEY = 'words'
```

As you can see, the `TEXT_KEY` simply contains `reviewText`, which represents the key where the review text is stored. By defining the `TEXT_KEY`, if we end up with another dataset with different column names, we can simply change this value to point to the new key where the text is stored.

The `WORDS_KEY` constant simply refers to the new key where we want to store the list of words from each review. In our case, we will store the list of words in a key named `words`.

Tokenize the Entire Dataset

The last step is to implement the code that will iterate through the entire dataset, tokenize each review, and store the words in an attribute. In order to do that, we will implement the `tokenize_dataset` function shown in Listing 23.11.

LISTING 23.11

Tokenizing the dataset

```
def tokenize_dataset(dataset):
    if type(dataset) != list:
```

```
        raise Exception("Dataset must be a list")
    result = list(map(tokenize_review, dataset))
    return result
```

The `tokenize_dataset` function accepts the dataset as an input and will iterate through it to tokenize each review. To do that, we can leverage the `map` function. The `map` function allows us to execute a function on each item of a list (or any iterator). In other words, we can leverage the `map` function to execute the `tokenize_review` function so it is executed on each review in the dataset (without implementing an explicit `for` loop).

We can do this by simply calling `map`, as such:

```
map(tokenize_review, dataset)
```

This will cause the `tokenize_review` to execute on each review in the `dataset`. The result is an iterator, which we can convert into a list by doing the following:

```
result = list(map(tokenize_review, dataset))
```

Using the Tokenize Functions

With the three functions now created to tokenize an input string, a review, and the entire dataset, we are ready to see them in action using our reviews dataset. Start by updating the code in `main.py` as shown in Listing 23.12.

LISTING 23.12

Tokenizing our reviews dataset

```
from lib import *

dataset = read_json_file("/Users/haythembalti/Downloads/reviews.json")
print(dataset[0])

dataset_tokenized = tokenize_dataset(dataset)
print("Words of the first review:")
print(dataset_tokenized[0]['words'])
print("Words of the second review:")
print(dataset_tokenized[1]['words'])
print(type(dataset_tokenized))
```

You can run this listing to tokenize the dataset. The tokenized data will include letters and numbers, but no punctuation marks. The resulting list includes only the words from the reviewText field.

COUNT THE WORDS IN EACH REVIEW

Now that each review in the dataset is tokenized, we can proceed to compute the word count in each review. The word count is simply the frequency of occurrence of each unique word in the review. In order to achieve that, we will adopt the same logic as the tokenize step. That is, we will build three functions as follows:

- First, a function that computes the *word count of an input list of words*. This function takes as input a list of words, iterates through them, and computes the frequency of occurrence of each unique word in the input list.

- Second, a function that computes the *word count from an input review* from our dataset. This function takes as input a review from our dataset and computes the word count for that review (using the words we derived from the tokenization step).

- Finally, a function that computes the *word count of each review in the dataset*. This function takes as input the dataset of reviews and simply iterates through each review and computes the word count for that review.

Word Count for an Input List of Words

Again in lib.py, add the compute_word_count function shown in Listing 23.13. Place it under the existing code.

LISTING 23.13

The compute_word_count function

```
def compute_word_count(words):
    if type(words) != list:
        raise Exception("Words must be a list")
    word_count= dict()
    for word in words:
        if word in word_count:
            word_count[word] = word_count[word]+1
        else:
            word_count[word]=1
    return word_count
```

In this function, we create a dictionary named `word_count` and add the words from a list to the dictionary. The dictionary uses the word itself as the key, and the corresponding value will be the number of times that word appears in the dictionary.

As we loop through the list of words in each review, the function checks to see if each word is already in the dictionary. If it is, it finds that word in the dictionary and increases the corresponding count by 1. If not, it adds the word to the dictionary with a count value of 1.

Word Count an Input Review

We use a separate `compute_word_count_review` function as shown in Listing 23.14 to pull in the words from the review. Using the same logic as the `tokenize_review`, we are building a word count function that will compute the word count of an input review (as dictionary).

LISTING 23.14

compute_word_count_review

```
def compute_word_count_review(review):
    if type(review) != dict:
        raise Exception("Review must be a dictionary")
    new_review = review.copy()
    word_freq= compute_word_count(new_review[WORDS_KEY])
    new_review[WORD_COUNT_KEY] = word_freq
    return new_review
```

The function simply checks that the input is a dictionary review. Next, it copies the review into a new review and calls the `compute_word_count` function:

```
word_freq= compute_word_count(new_review[WORDS_KEY])
```

Notice that we are using the constant `WORDS_KEY`, which refers to the key name where the words of each review are stored. In our case, it is `words`.

Finally, we store the `word_count` into a new key in the `new_review`:

```
new_review[WORD_COUNT_KEY] = word_freq
```

In this case, we use the `WORD_COUNT_KEY` as the variable where we store the key name for the word count. `WORD_COUNT_KEY` needs to be added with the other constants at the top of `lib.py`, as indicated in Listing 23.15.

LISTING 23.15

Current list of constants in lib.py

```
TEXT_KEY='reviewText'
WORDS_KEY = 'words'
WORD_COUNT_KEY = 'word_count'
```

Finally in compute_word_count_review function we will return new_review, which contains the previous review data as well as the new field we just computed (word count). In other words, the word_count of each review will be stored now in a key called word_count.

Word Count for the Dataset

Similar to the tokenize functions, the last step is to implement the function that will compute the word count for the entire dataset. This function will take as input the dataset, iterate through it, and for each review, compute the word count. As with the tokenize function, we can do this by simply using the map function as shown in Listing 23.16.

LISTING 23.16

The compute_word_count_dataset function

```
def compute_word_count_dataset(dataset):
    if type(dataset) != list:
        raise Exception("Dataset must be a list")
    result = list(map(compute_word_count_review, dataset))
    return result
```

In the compute_word_count_dataset, we again use a map function and create a list. The map function takes as input the compute_word_count_review function, which will be executed on every element in the list dataset.

In order to see everything in action, go back to main.py and add the code in Listing 23.17 to the end of the file.

LISTING 23.17

Updating main to count the words

```
dataset_word_count = compute_word_count_dataset(dataset_tokenized)
print("Word count for first review:")
```

```
print(dataset_word_count[0]['word_count'])
print("Word count for second review:")
print(dataset_word_count[1]['word_count'])
```

As you can see, each review in the `dataset_word_count` includes the word count key, which stores the frequency of occurrence of words in each review.

When you run the final listings, the output should look similar to the following:

```
{'reviewerID': 'A2IBPI20UZIR0U', 'asin': '1384719342', 'reviewerName': 'cassandra tu
"Yeah, well, that\'s just like, u...', 'helpful': [0, 0], 'unixReviewTime':
1393545600, 'reviewText': "Not much to write about here, but it does exactly what it's
supposed to. filters out the pop sounds. now my recordings are much more crisp. it is
one of the lowest prices pop filters on amazon so might as well buy it, they honestly
work the same despite their pricing,", 'overall': 5.0, 'reviewTime': '02 28, 2014',
'summary': 'good'}
Words of the first review:
['not', 'much', 'to', 'write', 'about', 'here', 'but', 'it', 'does', 'exactly',
'what', 'it', 's', 'supposed', 'to', 'filters', 'out', 'the', 'pop', 'sounds', 'now',
'my', 'recordings', 'are', 'much', 'more', 'crisp', 'it', 'is', 'one', 'of', 'the',
'lowest', 'prices', 'pop', 'filters', 'on', 'amazon', 'so', 'might', 'as', 'well',
'buy', 'it', 'they', 'honestly', 'work', 'the', 'same', 'despite', 'their', 'pricing']
Words of the second review:
['the', 'product', 'does', 'exactly', 'as', 'it', 'should', 'and', 'is', 'quite',
'affordable', 'i', 'did', 'not', 'realized', 'it', 'was', 'double', 'screened',
'until', 'it', 'arrived', 'so', 'it', 'was', 'even', 'better', 'than', 'i', 'had',
'expected', 'as', 'an', 'added', 'bonus', 'one', 'of', 'the', 'screens', 'carries',
'a', 'small', 'hint', 'of', 'the', 'smell', 'of', 'an', 'old', 'grape', 'candy', 'i',
'used', 'to', 'buy', 'so', 'for', 'reminiscent', 's', 'sake', 'i', 'cannot', 'stop',
'putting', 'the', 'pop', 'filter', 'next', 'to', 'my', 'nose', 'and', 'smelling',
'it', 'after', 'recording', 'dif', 'you', 'needed', 'a', 'pop', 'filter', 'this',
'will', 'work', 'just', 'as', 'well', 'as', 'the', 'expensive', 'ones', 'and', 'it',
'may', 'even', 'come', 'with', 'a', 'pleasing', 'aroma', 'like', 'mine', 'did', 'buy',
'this', 'product']
<class 'list'>
Word count for first review:
{'not': 1, 'much': 2, 'to': 2, 'write': 1, 'about': 1, 'here': 1, 'but': 1, 'it': 4,
'does': 1, 'exactly': 1, 'what': 1, 's': 1, 'supposed': 1, 'filters': 2, 'out': 1,
'the': 3, 'pop': 2, 'sounds': 1, 'now': 1, 'my': 1, 'recordings': 1, 'are': 1, 'more':
1, 'crisp': 1, 'is': 1, 'one': 1, 'of': 1, 'lowest': 1, 'prices': 1, 'on': 1,
'amazon': 1, 'so': 1, 'might': 1, 'as': 1, 'well': 1, 'buy': 1, 'they': 1, 'honestly':
1, 'work': 1, 'same': 1, 'despite': 1, 'their': 1, 'pricing': 1}
Word count for second review:
{'the': 5, 'product': 2, 'does': 1, 'exactly': 1, 'as': 4, 'it': 6, 'should': 1, 'and':
3, 'is': 1, 'quite': 1, 'affordable': 1, 'i': 4, 'did': 2, 'not': 1,
'realized': 1, 'was': 2, 'double': 1, 'screened': 1, 'until': 1, 'arrived': 1, 'so':
```

```
2, 'even': 2, 'better': 1, 'than': 1, 'had': 1, 'expected': 1, 'an': 2, 'added': 1,
'bonus': 1, 'one': 1, 'of': 3, 'screens': 1, 'carries': 1, 'a': 3, 'small': 1, 'hint':
1, 'smell': 1, 'old': 1, 'grape': 1, 'candy': 1, 'used': 1, 'to': 2, 'buy': 2, 'for':
1, 'reminiscent': 1, 's': 1, 'sake': 1, 'cannot': 1, 'stop': 1, 'putting': 1, 'pop':
2, 'filter': 2, 'next': 1, 'my': 1, 'nose': 1, 'smelling': 1, 'after': 1, 'recording':
1, 'dif': 1, 'you': 1, 'needed': 1, 'this': 2, 'will': 1, 'work': 1, 'just': 1,
'well': 1, 'expensive': 1, 'ones': 1, 'may': 1, 'come': 1, 'with': 1, 'pleasing': 1,
'aroma': 1, 'like': 1, 'mine': 1}
```

SUMMARY

In this lesson, we were able to implement a tokenizer/word counter from scratch using built-in Python libraries. Tokenization and word count are both important concepts used in many data analysis tasks such as topic detection.

Now that you have completed Lesson 23, you should be able to:

- Read a JSON file that contains a list of online ecommerce reviews.

- Tokenize each review in the dataset.

- Compute word counts in each review in the dataset.

Listings 23.18 and 23.19 contain the complete code for the lib.py and main.py files.

As a challenge, you can build on the code to implement a function that will compute the word count across the entire dataset. You could use a function that takes the dataset as input. The function could return a dictionary where the key is a unique word in the dataset and the value is the frequency of occurrence of that word across all reviews.

LISTING 23.18

The completed lib.py file

```
import re
import json

TEXT_KEY='reviewText'
WORDS_KEY = 'words'
WORD_COUNT_KEY = 'word_count'

def read_json_file(path):
    if not path:
        raise Exception("You must provide a valid file path.")
    try:
        dataset = list()
```

```python
        with open(path) as json_file:
            for line in json_file:
                dataset.append(json.loads(line))
        return dataset
    except (IOError, OSError):
        raise Exception("You must provide a valid JSON file.")


def compute_word_count(words):
    if type(words) != list:
        raise Exception("Words must be a list")
    word_count= dict()
    for word in words:
        if word in word_count:
            word_count[word] = word_count[word]+1
        else:
            word_count[word]=1
    return word_count


def compute_word_count_review(review):
    if type(review) != dict:
        raise Exception("Review must be a dictionary")
    new_review = review.copy()
    word_freq= compute_word_count(new_review[WORDS_KEY])
    new_review[WORD_COUNT_KEY] = word_freq
    return new_review


def compute_word_count_dataset(dataset):
    if type(dataset) != list:
        raise Exception("Dataset must be a list")
    result = list(map(compute_word_count_review, dataset))
    return result


def tokenize(text):
    if type(text) != str:
        raise Exception("Text must be a string")
    text_lower = text.lower()
    text_clean = re.sub("[^\w]", " ",text_lower)
    words = text_clean.split()
    return words


def tokenize_review(review):
    if type(review) != dict:
        raise Exception("Review must be a dictionary")
    new_review = review.copy()
```

```
    words= tokenize(new_review[TEXT_KEY])
    new_review[WORDS_KEY] = words
    return new_review

def tokenize_dataset(dataset):
    if type(dataset) != list:
        raise Exception("Dataset must be a list")
    result = list(map(tokenize_review, dataset))
    return result
```

LISTING 23.19

The completed main.py file

```
from lib import *

#read dataset
dataset = read_json_file("reviews.json")
print(dataset[0])

#tokenize dataset
dataset_tokenized = tokenize_dataset(dataset)
print("Words of the first review:")
print(dataset_tokenized[0]['words'])
print("Words of the second review:")
print(dataset_tokenized[1]['words'])
print(type(dataset_tokenized))


#compute word count
dataset_word_count = compute_word_count_dataset(dataset_tokenized)
print("Word count for first review:")
print(dataset_word_count[0]['word_count'])
print("Word count for second review:")
print(dataset_word_count[1]['word_count'])
```

Lesson 24

Extracting, Transforming, and Loading with ETL Scripting

In this and the next lesson, we will build on everything we've learned throughout this book and create a Python script we can use to automate processes related to extracting data from one source, transforming that data to meet the needs of a data scientist, and load the data into a data source accessible to the data scientist.

LEARNING OBJECTIVES

By the end of this lesson, you will be able to:

- Describe a variety of activities related to ETL.
- Leverage Python to extract, transform, and load data from various sources.

- Use Python to create a script that extracts data from one location, transforms the data as necessary, and loads the transformed data into a separate database.
- Leverage Python and object-oriented programming concepts to create a reusable and compact ETL library.

> **NOTE** This lesson uses files located in the Lesson24 folder of the file that you can download from www.wiley.com/go/jobreadypython.

ETL SCRIPTING IN PYTHON

Data engineers use extract-transform-load (ETL) processes widely in data warehouses to move data between databases, servers, and machines. ETL processes are an intersection of process engineering and technology. It is important to think about ETL processes as actual processes and not as physical implementations of the data. An ETL process can be used in the following situations:

- Access data in a source database or other storage location and load it into a different database or storage location. This process is equivalent to a simple copy and paste of the data from source to target.

- Access data in the source database or storage, perform some transformation to meet the schema of the target table, and then store the data in the target table. An example of this situation is extracting data from an OLTP database, performing some transformation on the data to meet the schema of the target database, then loading the transformed data into the target database. More specifically, a database of prices stored as dollar values could be pulled, each price could be converted to a different monetary type, and then the updated prices could be loaded into a new database.

- Extract data that is not stored in a database and move that data to a database. Examples include information stored in text files, spreadsheets, and similar unorganized files. The data is transformed into a format that can be stored in a temporary database and loaded to the target database.

DESIGN AND IMPLEMENT CUSTOM ETL SCRIPTS

As mentioned, an ETL process has three steps: extract, transform, and load. One of the most common tasks for a data engineer is designing and implementing ETL processes. We will learn how to design and develop a simple ETL tool.

Before we can start to build an ETL script, we must establish the requirements for our ETL tool. Following is a list of requirements that we will start with.

1. **Extract** must be able to access data from a variety of data sources, including:

   - CSV files
   - SQL tables
   - MongoDB collections
   - JSON files

2. **Transform** must support several transformations on the data, including:

   - Basic data transformation, such as:
     - Data resizing and reshaping rows (e.g., selecting a limited number of columns from the original data)
     - Converting and parsing data (e.g., converting a string into an integer or parsing the number part of a string)
   - Column transformation
   - Header manipulation (e.g., changing the column headers)
   - Sorting data
   - Grouping data
   - Concatenating data
   - Detecting and removing duplicates
   - Filling in missing values and replacing erroneous values

3. **Load** must support saving data to a variety of data formats, including:

   - CSV files
   - SQL tables
   - NoSQL tables
   - JSON files

The script must support adding new extract, transform, and load functions. For instance, in the future, we might add an Oracle server to our data infrastructure, so we need to write specific extract and load functions that allow us to retrieve and store data on the SQL server. To this end, we must use object-oriented and functional programming to design a flexible ETL tool.

Throughout this lesson, we will implement our own ETL tool that satisfies these requirements. We will learn to design flexible modules that will allow us to extend and improve our ETL tools. In the rest of this lesson, we will lay down the design for our ETL tool as well as implement extract, transform, and load capabilities.

THE EXTRACT CLASS

Because an ETL process has three main components, it is logical to create a separate class for each activity. We will start with the `extract` class and define methods that will allow it to extract data from a variety of sources.

In Listing 24.1, we simply create placeholders for the `extract` class and some basic extraction methods for common file types we have already identified. This structure allows us to easily add additional methods if we later need to start with a different data source from those we already know about.

LISTING 24.1

`extract.py`: The extract class shell

```
class extract:
    def fromCSV(self):
        pass

    def fromJSON(self):
        pass

    def fromMYSQL(self):
        pass

    def fromMONGODB(self):
        pass
```

As we move forward, we will write code that references separate Python packages rather than including all required code in the current block here. These package files will be saved using the `.py` filename extension, independently of any code running in the current window, but in the same folder as the current code. Create a new file named `extract.py` in the same folder as your code files for this lesson and add the template code from Listing 24.1 to that file.

Adding the `extract.fromCSV` Method

We can use inheritance to create the `extract` class, which will contain all the methods needed to extract data from different sources. We will start with the `fromCSV` method, which we can use to extract data from any CSV file.

NOTE We will use the `extract.fromCSV` method as a model for extracting data from other types of sources.

In Listing 24.2 we create a new method inside the `extract` class that we saw in Listing 24.1. This method takes arguments for the file path, the way the data is delimited (using comma as the default delimiter), and the way quotations are defined. This function performs the following tasks:

- It displays a user-friendly message if the file path is not valid.

- It uses the built-in `csv.DictReader` method to read the contents of the CSV file.

- It stores the results in a list named `dataset`.

The script in Listing 24.2 also displays the contents of the extracted dataset to verify that it works as expected. We use a CSV file called `got_chars.csv` that you can download from `https://the-software-guild.s3.amazonaws.com/datascience/track1-1909/got_chars.csv`; however, you can use any available CSV file to test the script.

LISTING 24.2

Creating the fromCSV method

```
class extract:
    def fromCSV(self, file_path, delimiter = ",", quotechar = "|"):
        if not file_path:
            raise Exception("You must provide a valid file path.")
        import csv
        dataset = list()
        with open(file_path) as f:
            csv_file = csv.DictReader(f, delimiter = delimiter, quotechar = quotechar)
            for row in csv_file:
                dataset.append(row)
        return dataset

    def fromJSON(self):
        pass

    def fromMYSQL(self):
        pass

    def fromMONGODB(self):
        pass
```

```
e = extract()
dataset = e.fromCSV(file_path="data/got_chars.csv")
for row in dataset:
    print(row)
```

> **NOTE** You can also pull the got_chars.csv file from the data folder in the JobReadyPython.zip file available at www.wiley.com/go/JobReadyPython.

Using got_chars.csv, the output from running the script is:

```
OrderedDict([('actor', 'Sean Bean'), ('character', '"Eddard ""Ned"" Stark"'),
('first_appearance', '1')])
OrderedDict([('actor', 'Mark Addy'), ('character', 'Robert Baratheon'),
('first_appearance', '1')])
OrderedDict([('actor', 'Nikolaj Coster-Waldau'), ('character', 'Jaime Lannister'),
('first_appearance', '1')])
OrderedDict([('actor', 'Michelle Fairley'), ('character', 'Catelyn Stark'),
('first_appearance', '1')])
OrderedDict([('actor', 'Lena Headey'), ('character', 'Cersei Lannister'),
('first_appearance', '1')])
OrderedDict([('actor', 'Emilia Clarke'), ('character', 'Daenerys Targaryen'),
('first_appearance', '1')])
    [ ... ]
OrderedDict([('actor', 'Dean-Charles Chapman[d]'), ('character', 'Tommen Baratheon'),
('first_appearance', '1')])
OrderedDict([('actor', 'Tom Wlaschiha[e]'), ('character', "Jaqen H'ghar"),
('first_appearance', '1')])
OrderedDict([('actor', 'Michael McElhatton'), ('character', 'Roose Bolton'),
('first_appearance', '2')])
OrderedDict([('actor', 'Jonathan Pryce'), ('character', 'The High Sparrow'),
('first_appearance', '5')])
OrderedDict([('actor', 'Jacob Anderson'), ('character', 'Grey Worm'),
('first_appearance', '3')])
```

After verifying that the fromCSV method works as expected, add the updated code to your extract.py file created in Listing 24.1 at the beginning of this lesson.

Creating the extract.fromJSON Method

We can also implement a fromJSON method to extract data from JSON files. In Listing 24.3, we create a new script with the extract class that adds the new fromJSON method following the same pattern we used for fromCSV. We then test the method using a person.json file that you can find in the download file for this lesson.

LISTING 24.3

The `fromJSON` method

```
class extract:
    def fromCSV(self, file_path, delimiter = ",", quotechar = "|"):
        if not file_path:
            raise Exception("You must provide a valid file path.")
        import csv
        dataset = list()
        with open(file_path) as f:
            csv_file = csv.DictReader(f, delimiter = delimiter,quotechar = quotechar)
            for row in csv_file:
                dataset.append(row)
        return dataset

    def fromJSON(self, file_path):
        if not file_path:
            raise Exception("You must provide a valid file path.")
        import json
        dataset = list()
        with open(file_path) as json_file:
            dataset = json.load(json_file)
        return dataset

    def fromMYSQL(self):
        pass

    def fromMONGODB(self):
        pass


e = extract()
dataset = e.fromJSON(file_path = "data/person.json")
print(dataset)
print(len(dataset))
```

When this is executed with the `person.json` file, the output is:

```
[{'name': 'Hermione Granger', 'DOB': '09/19/1979'}, {'name': 'Ronald Weasley',
'DOB': '03/01/1980'}, {'name': 'Draco Malfoy', 'DOB': '06/05/1980'}]
3
```

You can test the `extract.fromJSON` method using a different JSON file of your choice. After verifying that the `fromJSON` method works as expected, add the updated code to your `extract.py` file created at the beginning of this lesson.

Creating the `extract.fromMySQL` Method

We can now create a new method to extract data from a MySQL database. The code examples in this lesson assume that MySQL is using the following settings:

- host: `localhost`
- username: `root`
- password: `admin`

You may need to adjust the code if your MySQL server uses different login settings.

We cannot follow the same pattern we used for CSV and JSON files because extracting data from a MySQL database is more complicated than simply reading a local file. In this case, we will add a new `fromMYSQL` method to the `extract` class to perform the following steps:

- Define the arguments for the method, including information about how to connect to the MySQL server, what database to use, and what query will pull the correct data from the database.
- Use PyMySQL to retrieve the data using the defined connection parameters.
- Save the retrieved data to a list.
- Commit the changes in the database.
- Close the connection to the database and the database itself.

To test this script, you must have the PyMySQL package installed as well as have a MySQL server running on `localhost`, with a database named `vinylrecordshop` and a table named `artist`.

Installing the PyMySQL Package

If you do not have PyMySQL installed, you will need to install it to run the `fromMySQL` method in the `extract` class. To install, run the following at the command line:

```
python3 -m pip install PyMySQL
```

Once installed, you should follow the prompt on upgrading as well.

Once you have the PyMySQL package installed and the MySQL database set up, then you are ready to create the `fromMYSQL` method in your `extract` class. Listing 24.4 contains the new `fromMYSQL` method along with a few lines of code to test it.

LISTING 24.4

The fromMySQL method in the extract class

```
class extract:
    def fromMYSQL(self, host, username, password, db, query):
        if not host or not username or not db or not query:
            raise Exception("Please make sure that you input a valid host, username, \
password, database, and query.")
        import pymysql
        db = pymysql.connect(host = host, user = username, password =
password, db = db,
                            cursorclass = pymysql.cursors.DictCursor)
        cur = db.cursor()
        cur.execute(query)
        dataset = list()
        for r in cur:
            dataset.append(r)
        db.commit()
        cur.close()
        db.close()
        return dataset
```

```
e = extract()
query = "select * from artist;"
dataset = e.fromMYSQL(host = "localhost", username = "root", password = "admin",
                      db = "vinylrecordshop",query = query)
print(dataset)
print(len(dataset))
```

Verify that the script works using other MySQL tables and/or queries. Note that the query is a variable on its own, so you could update the query to display all available tables in the database, retrieve only specific fields from a table, sort the retrieved data, or do any other valid MySQL statement. The output from running the listing as presented should be:

```
[{'artist_id': 1, 'fname': 'John', 'lname': 'Lennon', 'isHallOfFame': 0},
{'artist_id': 2, 'fname': 'Paul', 'lname': 'McCartney', 'isHallOfFame': 0},
{'artist_id': 3, 'fname': 'George', 'lname': 'Harrison', 'isHallOfFame': 0},
{'artist_id': 4, 'fname': 'Ringo', 'lname': 'Starr', 'isHallOfFame': 0}, {'artist_
id': 5, 'fname': 'Denny', 'lname': 'Zager', 'isHallOfFame': 0}, {'artist_id': 6,
'fname': 'Rick', 'lname': 'Evans', 'isHallOfFame': 0}, {'artist_id': 10, 'fname':
'Van', 'lname': 'Morrison', 'isHallOfFame': 0}, {'artist_id': 11, 'fname':
'Judy', 'lname': 'Collins', 'isHallOfFame': 0}, {'artist_id': 12, 'fname':
'Paul', 'lname': 'Simon', 'isHallOfFame': 0}, {'artist_id': 13, 'fname': 'Art',
'lname': 'Garfunkel', 'isHallOfFame': 0}, {'artist_id': 14, 'fname': 'Brian',
'lname': 'Wilson', 'isHallOfFame': 0}, {'artist_id': 15, 'fname': 'Dennis',
'lname': 'Wilson', 'isHallOfFame': 0}, {'artist_id': 16, 'fname': 'Carl',
'lname': 'Wilson', 'isHallOfFame': 0}, {'artist_id': 17, 'fname': 'Ricky',
'lname': 'Fataar', 'isHallOfFame': 0}, {'artist_id': 18, 'fname': 'Blondie',
'lname': 'Chaplin', 'isHallOfFame': 0}, {'artist_id': 19, 'fname': 'Jimmy',
'lname': 'Page', 'isHallOfFame': 0}, {'artist_id': 20, 'fname': 'Robert',
'lname': 'Plant', 'isHallOfFame': 0}, {'artist_id': 21, 'fname': 'John Paul',
'lname': 'Jones', 'isHallOfFame': 0}, {'artist_id': 22, 'fname': 'John', 'lname':
'Bonham', 'isHallOfFame': 0}, {'artist_id': 23, 'fname': 'Mike ', 'lname':
'Love', 'isHallOfFame': 0}, {'artist_id': 24, 'fname': 'Al ', 'lname': 'Jardine',
'isHallOfFame': 0}, {'artist_id': 25, 'fname': 'David', 'lname': 'Marks',
'isHallOfFame': 0}, {'artist_id': 26, 'fname': 'Bruce ', 'lname': 'Johnston',
'isHallOfFame': 0}]
23
```

After verifying that the fromMYSQL method works as expected in Listing 24.4, you should add the updated code to your extract.py file created earlier. Your extract.py file should now look similar to Listing 24.5.

LISTING 24.5

The current extract class

```python
class extract:
    def fromCSV(self, file_path, delimiter = ",", quotechar = "|"):
        if not file_path:
            raise Exception("You must provide a valid file path.")
        import csv
        dataset = list()
        with open(file_path) as f:
            csv_file = csv.DictReader(f, delimiter = delimiter,quotechar = quotechar)
            for row in csv_file:
                dataset.append(row)
        return dataset

    def fromJSON(self, file_path):
        if not file_path:
            raise Exception("You must provide a valid file path.")
        import json
        dataset = list()
        with open(file_path) as json_file:
            dataset = json.load(json_file)
        return dataset

    def fromMYSQL(self, host, username, password, db, query):
        if not host or not username or not db or not query:
            raise Exception("Please make sure that you input a valid host, \
            username, password, database, and query.")
        import pymysql
        db = pymysql.connect(host = host, user = username, password = password, db = db,
                             cursorclass = pymysql.cursors.DictCursor)
        cur = db.cursor()
        cur.execute(query)
        dataset = list()
        for r in cur:
            dataset.append(r)
        db.commit()
        cur.close()
        db.close()
        return dataset

    def fromMONGODB(self):
        pass
```

Creating the `extract.fromMongoDB` Method

Finally, we will add the `fromMongoDB` method to the `extract` class. To test this script, which is shown in Listing 24.6, you must have a MongoDB server running on localhost, with a database named `amazon_records` and a collection named `musical_instruments`. If you do not have this database and collection, follow the steps in the sidebar before completing this step.

Import Data to MongoDB

See Appendix E for instructions on installing MongoDB. Appendix F provides instructions on how to import data into a MongoDB database.

The `fromMONGODB` method's code presented in Listing 24.6 assumes that the MongoDB server uses the following connection settings:

- host: `localhost`
- port: `27017`
- username: `admin`
- password: `admin`

You will need to revise the code if your settings are different. Alternatively, you may use the following command in MongoDB to create an administrator account that you can use to connect to MongoDB so that you can use the credentials in the code provided in this lesson:

```
use admin;
db.createUser({user: "admin",pwd: "admin",roles: [ { role:
"userAdminAnyDatabase", db: "admin" } ]});
```

LISTING 24.6

Adding the `fromMONGODB` method

```
class extract:
    def fromMONGODB(self, host, port, username, password, db, collection, query = None):
        if not host or not port or not username or not db or not collection:
            raise Exception("Please make sure that you input a valid host, username, \
            password, database, and collection name")
```

```
        import pymongo
        client = pymongo.MongoClient(host = host, port = port,username  = username,
password = password)
        tmp_database = client[db]
        tmp_collection = tmp_database[collection]
        dataset = list()
        if query:
            for document in tmp_collection.find(query):
                dataset.append(document)
            return dataset
        for document in tmp_collection.find():
                dataset.append(document)
        return dataset

e = extract()

#update the values here based on your own mongodb options if necessary
dataset = e.fromMONGODB(host = "localhost", port = 27017, username = "admin",
                       password = "admin", db = "amazon_reviews",
                       collection = "musical_instruments")
print(len(dataset))
print(dataset[0])
```

The output from running the listing against the `musical_instruments` collection in the `amazon_reviews` database should be:

```
10261
{'_id': ObjectId('5d8d0bcedc1e820e19de743b'), 'reviewerID': 'AJNFQI3YR6XJ5',
'asin': 'B00004Y2UT', 'reviewerName': 'Fender Guy "Rick"', 'helpful': [0, 0],
'unixReviewTime': 1353024000, 'reviewText': "I now use this cable to run from the
output of my pedal chain to the input of my Fender Amp. After I bought Monster Cable
to hook up my pedal board I thought I would try another one and update my guitar. I
had been using a high end Planet Waves cable that I bought in the 1980's... Once I
found out the input jacks on the new Monster cable didn't fit into the Fender Strat
jack I was a little disappointed... I didn't return it and as stated I use it for the
output on the pedal board. Save your money... I went back to my Planet Waves Cable...I
payed $30.00 back in the eighties for the Planet Waves which now comes in at around
$50.00. What I'm getting at is you get what you pay for. I thought Waves was a lot of
money back in the day...but I haven't bought a guitar cable since this one...20 plus
years and still working...Planet Waves wins.", 'overall': 3.0, 'reviewTime': '11 16,
2012', 'summary': "Didn't fit my 1996 Fender Strat..."}
```

You can use the script to extract data from another MongoDB collection. For example, a default MongoDB setup will include a database named `local` with a collection named `startup_log` that stores data about user logins.

Verify the `extract.py` Module

To this point, we have run Python code exclusively as scripts within the IDE. However, we can also store reusable code as Python modules—files stored outside of the current code but that we can call as needed when we run the code.

At this point, your `extract.py` file should include code for all four methods, as shown in Listing 24.7. If any of the methods are missing at this point, update the contents of the file before going to the next step.

LISTING 24.7

The current status of the extract class

```
class extract:
    def fromCSV(self, file_path, delimiter = ",", quotechar = "|"):
        if not file_path:
            raise Exception("You must provide a valid file path.")
        import csv
        dataset = list()
        with open(file_path) as f:
            csv_file = csv.DictReader(f, delimiter = delimiter,quotechar = quotechar)
            for row in csv_file:
                dataset.append(row)
        return dataset

    def fromJSON(self, file_path):
        if not file_path:
            raise Exception("You must provide a valid file path.")
        import json
        dataset = list()
        with open(file_path) as json_file:
            dataset = json.load(json_file)
        return dataset

    def fromMYSQL(self, host, username, password, db, query):
        if not host or not username or not db or not query:
            raise Exception("Please make sure that you input a valid host, \
                username, password, database, and query.")
        import pymysql
        db = pymysql.connect(host = host, user = username, password = password,
                            db = db, cursorclass = pymysql.cursors.DictCursor)
```

```
        cur = db.cursor()
        cur.execute(query)
        dataset = list()
        for r in cur:
            dataset.append(r)
        db.commit()
        cur.close()
        db.close()
        return dataset

    def fromMONGODB(self, host, port, username, password, db,
                    collection, query = None):
        if not host or not port or not username or not db or not collection:
            raise Exception("Please make sure that you input a valid host,
                            username, password, database, and collection name")
        import pymongo
        client = pymongo.MongoClient(host = host, port = port,username  = username,
                                     password = password)
        tmp_database = client[db]
        tmp_collection = tmp_database[collection]
        dataset = list()
        if query:
            for document in tmp_collection.find(query):
                dataset.append(document)
            return dataset
        for document in tmp_collection.find():
                dataset.append(document)
        return dataset
```

Using Our Script as an External Module

When we save the script as a separate file with a .py extension, we can include the new class in other scripts by using the statement:

```
from extract import extract
```

The code in Listing 24.8 calls the external package and retrieves the data from a CSV file. Save this code in the same directory folder where you have extract.py, but use a different filename. Note how much more streamlined our working code is when we use external packages instead of inline scripts.

LISTING 24.8

Using our script as an external module

```
from extract import extract

e = extract()
dataset = e.fromCSV(file_path="data/got_chars.csv")
for row in dataset:
    print(row)
```

This code simply extracts data from the `got_chars.csv` file and prints its contents as was done earlier with Listing 24.2. This listing, however, is more streamlined.

THE TRANSFORM CLASS

Once the `extract` class works as expected and we have the `extract.py` module ready to use, we can start building the `transform` class.

Data engineering processes frequently involve moving data from one storage structure to another storage structure. For example, we may have existing data stored as a CSV or JSON file, but the data scientists we are working with want the data stored in a relational database like MySQL or SQL Server.

Because of this, the second step of the ETL process is transform, which means that after we extract data from the source files, we change the data to match the target specifications and store the transformed data in a temporary location until we can load the data into the target storage. Transformation includes steps such as renaming columns, removing columns we do not need, and changing the data itself.

As with the earlier extract steps, we want to automate this process as much as possible, so we will build a Python class that can perform these steps for us and save the class as an external Python module.

Defining the `transform` Class

We start by creating a `transform` class template that outlines the steps we plan to use when transforming the extracted data. We create a class template with the following steps:

- Retrieve some records from the top of the extracted dataset
- Retrieve some records from the end of the extracted dataset

- Rename one or more columns
- Remove one or more unnecessary columns
- Transform the data itself

Listing 24.9 contains the base shell for our `transform` class. This script should be created as a new file named `transform.py` and saved in the same folder you are using for these code files.

LISTING 24.9

`transform.py`—the shell for the transform class

```
class transform:
    def head(self, dataset, step): #return the top N records from the dataset
        pass

    def tail(self): #return the last N records from the dataset
        pass

    def rename_attribute(self): #rename a column in the dataset
        pass

    def remove_attribute(self): #remove a column from the dataset
        pass

    def rename_attributes(self): #rename a list of columns in the dataset
        pass

    def remove_attributes(self): #remove a list of columns in the dataset
        pass

    def transform(self):
        pass
```

This code doesn't do anything visible at this time; however, you should add the code to create the template and verify that it runs without errors. We will update this file as we build each of the methods in this class.

Creating the head and tail Methods

We start by retrieving only a few records from the top of the extracted dataset and from the end of the extracted dataset. Data engineers often work with extremely large datasets, and it could be time consuming to use the entire dataset if we just want to verify that the dataset exists or verify what is in it.

We can use steps like this for any of the following:

- To confirm that there is data in the dataset

- To see what columns or attributes exist in the dataset

- To determine what the columns or attributes are named

- To examine what kind of data is in each column or attribute

In the example in Listing 24.10, we start by importing the extract class in extract.py. We then create separate head and tail functions to retrieve a user-specified number of records from the dataset.

LISTING 24.10

Defining head and tail methods

```
from extract import extract #import our custom built extract module

class transform:
    #return the top N records from the dataset
    def head(self, dataset, step):
        if not dataset:
            raise Exception("Dataset cannot be empty.")
        if step < 1:
            raise Exception("The step value must be positive.")
        return dataset[0:step]

    #return the last N records from the dataset
    def tail(self, dataset, step):
        if not dataset:
            raise Exception("Dataset cannot be empty.")
        if step < 1:
            raise Exception("The step value must be positive.")
        return dataset[len(dataset) - step:len(dataset)]

    def rename_attribute(self): #rename a column in the dataset
        pass

    def remove_attribute(self): #remove a column from the dataset
        pass

    def rename_attributes(self): #rename a list of columns in the dataset
        pass
```

```
    def remove_attributes(self): #remove a list of columns in the dataset
        pass

    def transform(self):
        pass

e = extract()
# connect to mongodb; change values if necessary
dataset = e.fromMONGODB(host = "localhost", port = 27017, username = "admin",
                        password = "admin", db = "amazon_reviews",
                        collection = "musical_instruments")

t = transform()
dataset_1 = t.head(dataset = dataset, step = 5) # retrieve the top 5 records
                                                # in the dataset
print("Top 5 records in the dataset:")
for row in dataset_1:
    print(row['_id'])

dataset_2 = t.tail(dataset = dataset, step = 5) #retrieve the bottom 5 records
                                                #in the dataset
print("\nBottom 5 records in the dataset:")
for row in dataset_2:
    print(row['_id'])
```

We test this code by retrieving data from the MongoDB database, amazon_reviews. We then use the head method to get the top 5 records, which then have their IDs printed. This is followed by using the tail method to get the bottom 5 records, which then have their IDs printed. The output from running this code is:

```
Top 5 records in the dataset:
5d8d0bcedc1e820e19de743b
5d8d0bcedc1e820e19de743c
5d8d0bcedc1e820e19de743d
5d8d0bcedc1e820e19de743e
5d8d0bcedc1e820e19de743f

Bottom 5 records in the dataset:
5d8d0bcfdc1e820e19de9c4b
5d8d0bcfdc1e820e19de9c4c
5d8d0bcfdc1e820e19de9c4d
5d8d0bcfdc1e820e19de9c4e
5d8d0bcfdc1e820e19de9c4f
```

After testing the code in Listing 24.11, you should update your transform.py file to
include the head and tail methods. Your transform.py file should currently look like
Listing 24.11.

LISTING 24.11

The updated transform.py file

```python
class transform:
    def head(self, dataset, step): #return the top N records from the dataset
        if not dataset:
            raise Exception("Dataset cannot be empty.")
        if step < 1:
            raise Exception("The step value must be positive.")
        return dataset[0:step]

    def tail(self, dataset, step): #return the last N records from the dataset
        if not dataset:
            raise Exception("Dataset cannot be empty.")
        if step < 1:
            raise Exception("The step value must be positive.")
        return dataset[len(dataset) - step:len(dataset)]

    def rename_attribute(self): #rename a column in the dataset
        pass

    def remove_attribute(self): #remove a column from the dataset
        pass

    def rename_attributes(self): #rename a list of columns in the dataset
        pass

    def remove_attributes(self): #remove a list of columns in the dataset
        pass

    def transform(self):
        pass
```

Renaming a Column

One common transformation step is to rename columns or attributes for extracted data. For example, the original name may conflict with the name of an existing column in the target dataset, or we may simply want to use a more descriptive name. In the code in Listing 24.12, we rename a single column in the target dataset and assign it a different name in the temporary data store created during the transform process.

LISTING 24.12

Renaming a column

```
from extract import extract #import our custom built extract module

class transform:
    #return the top N records from the dataset
    def head(self, dataset, step):
        if not dataset:
            raise Exception("Dataset cannot be empty.")
        if step < 1:
            raise Exception("The step value must be positive.")
        return dataset[0:step]

    #return the last N records from the dataset
    def tail(self, dataset, step):
        if not dataset:
            raise Exception("Dataset cannot be empty.")
        if step < 1:
            raise Exception("The step value must be positive.")
        return dataset[len(dataset) - step:len(dataset)]

    #rename a column in the dataset
    def rename_attribute(self, dataset, attribute, new_attribute):
        if not dataset:
            raise Exception("Dataset cannot be empty.")
        if not attribute:
            raise Exception("The attribute key must be a valid key.")
        new_dataset = list()
        for row in dataset:
            if attribute in row.keys():
                val = row[attribute]
                new_row = row.copy()
                del new_row[attribute]
```

```
                    new_row[new_attribute] = val
                    new_dataset.append(new_row)
            else:
                    raise Exception("Operation is not possible because the \
column " + str(column_name) + " does not exist in one of the rows \
in the dataset")
        return new_dataset

e = extract()
dataset = e.fromCSV(file_path="data/got_chars.csv")
print("Dataset before renaming the column:")
print(dataset[0])

t = transform()
new_dataset = t.rename_attribute(dataset = dataset, attribute = "character",
new_attribute = "character_name")
print("\nDataset after renaming the column:")
print(new_dataset[0])
```

In this listing we use the `got_chars.csv` file that we've used before. Using the `rename_attribute` method, we change the name of the `character` column to `character_name`. We print out the first row of the dataset before and after the transform so that the change can be seen as shown in the following output:

```
Dataset before renaming the column:
{'first_appearance': '1', 'character': '"Eddard ""Ned"" Stark"', 'actor':
'Sean Bean'}

Dataset after renaming the column:
{'first_appearance': '1', 'actor': 'Sean Bean', 'character_name': '"Eddard
""Ned"" Stark"'}
```

Update your `transform.py` file to include the `rename_attribute` method.

Removing a Column from the Data Source

Another common transformation step is to remove one or more attributes from the original data source. Note that this process does not change the original dataset, which we typically want to preserve in case we need it for other uses in the future. Instead, it removes the attribute from the temporary dataset created in the transform process.

In the example in Listing 24.13, we create a `remove_attribute` method in the `transform` class and then use it to remove the `Open` column.

LISTING 24.13

Removing items in the transform class

```
from extract import extract #import our custom built extract module

class transform:

    #return the top N records from the dataset
    def head(self, dataset, step):
        if not dataset:
            raise Exception("Dataset cannot be empty.")
        if step < 1:
            raise Exception("The step value must be positive.")
        return dataset[0:step]

    #return the last N records from the dataset
    def tail(self, dataset, step):
        if not dataset:
            raise Exception("Dataset cannot be empty.")
        if step < 1:
            raise Exception("The step value must be positive.")
        return dataset[len(dataset) - step:len(dataset)]

    #rename a column in the dataset
    def rename_attribute(self, dataset, attribute, new_attribute):
        if not dataset:
            raise Exception("Dataset cannot be empty.")
        if not attribute:
            raise Exception("The attribute key must be a valid key.")
        new_dataset = list()
        for row in dataset:
            if attribute in row.keys():
                val = row[attribute]
                new_row = row.copy()
                del new_row[attribute]
                new_row[new_attribute] = val
                new_dataset.append(new_row)
            else:
                raise Exception("Operation is not possible because the column " + \
                            str(column_name) \
                            + " does not exist in one of the rows in
the dataset")
        return new_dataset
```

```
    #remove a column from the dataset
    def remove_attribute(self, dataset, attribute):
        new_dataset = list()
        for row in dataset:
            new_row = row
            if attribute in new_row.keys():
                del new_row[attribute]
                new_dataset.append(new_row)
        return new_dataset

e = extract()
dataset = e.fromCSV(file_path = "data/stocks.csv")
print("Original dataset:")
print(dataset[0])

t = transform()
new_dataset = t.remove_attribute(dataset = dataset, attribute = "Open")
print("\nTransformed dataset:")
print(new_dataset[0])
```

You can see that this listing calls the `remove_attribute` method and indicates the `Open` attribute should be removed from the dataset called `dataset`. When you run this listing against the `stocks.csv` file that you used in previous lessons, you should see output similar to the following:

```
{'Volume': '2799073', 'High': '20.1', 'OpenInt': '0', 'Low': '17.6', 'Date':
'2018-10-02', 'Close': '18.5', 'Open': '20'}

Transformed dataset:
{'Volume': '2799073', 'High': '20.1', 'OpenInt': '0', 'Low': '17.6', 'Date':
'2018-10-02', 'Close': '18.5'}
```

Update your `transform.py` file to include the `remove_attribute` method. Your `transform.py` file should now look like Listing 24.14.

LISTING 24.14

The current transform.py file

```
class transform:

    #return the top N records from the dataset
    def head(self, dataset, step):
```

```
            if not dataset:
                raise Exception("Dataset cannot be empty.")
            if step < 1:
                raise Exception("The step value must be positive.")
            return dataset[0:step]

    #return the last N records from the dataset
    def tail(self, dataset, step):
        if not dataset:
            raise Exception("Dataset cannot be empty.")
        if step < 1:
            raise Exception("The step value must be positive.")
        return dataset[len(dataset) - step:len(dataset)]

    #rename a column in the dataset
    def rename_attribute(self, dataset, attribute, new_attribute):
        if not dataset:
            raise Exception("Dataset cannot be empty.")
        if not attribute:
            raise Exception("The attribute key must be a valid key.")
        new_dataset = list()
        for row in dataset:
            if attribute in row.keys():
                val = row[attribute]
                new_row = row.copy()
                del new_row[attribute]
                new_row[new_attribute] = val
                new_dataset.append(new_row)
            else:
                raise Exception("Operation is not possible because the \
column " + str(column_name) + " does not exist in one of the rows \
in the dataset")
        return new_dataset

    #remove a column from the dataset
    def remove_attribute(self, dataset, attribute):
        new_dataset = list()
        for row in dataset:
            new_row = row
            if attribute in new_row.keys():
                del new_row[attribute]
                new_dataset.append(new_row)
        return new_dataset
```

```
    def rename_attributes(self): #rename a list of columns in the dataset
        pass

    def remove_attributes(self): #remove a list of columns in the dataset
        pass

    def transform(self):
        pass
```

Renaming Multiple Columns

While it is useful to rename a single column in the temporary dataset, it is even more useful to be able to rename multiple columns. We can modify the code from the previous example to allow an indefinite number of columns to be renamed. In the example in Listing 24.15, we create the `rename_attributes` method that will allow us to rename any number of columns during the transform process.

To get this effect, we create a list to hold the names of the existing columns and a second list to hold the new column names. We verify that the number of columns named is the same for both lists, and then we use a `for` loop to replace each attribute name in the same order in which they are provided when the method is implemented.

LISTING 24.15

Renaming multiple columns

```
from extract import extract #import our custom built extract module

class transform:
    #return the top N records from the dataset
    def head(self, dataset, step):
        if not dataset:
            raise Exception("Dataset cannot be empty.")
        if step < 1:
            raise Exception("The step value must be positive.")
        return dataset[0:step]

    #return the last N records from the dataset
    def tail(self, dataset, step):
        if not dataset:
            raise Exception("Dataset cannot be empty.")
        if step < 1:
```

```python
            raise Exception("The step value must be positive.")
        return dataset[len(dataset) - step:len(dataset)]

#rename a column in the dataset
def rename_attribute(self, dataset, attribute, new_attribute):
    if not dataset:
        raise Exception("Dataset cannot be empty.")
    if not attribute:
        raise Exception("The attribute key must be a valid key.")
    new_dataset = list()
    for row in dataset:
        if attribute in row.keys():
            val = row[attribute]
            new_row = row.copy()
            del new_row[attribute]
            new_row[new_attribute] = val
            new_dataset.append(new_row)
        else:
            raise Exception("Operation is not possible because the column " + \
                            str(column_name) \
                            + " does not exist in one of the rows in the dataset.")
    return new_dataset

#remove a column from the dataset
def remove_attribute(self, dataset, attribute):
    new_dataset = list()
    for row in dataset:
        new_row = row
        if attribute in new_row.keys():
            del new_row[attribute]
            new_dataset.append(new_row)
    return new_dataset

 #remove multiple columns from the dataset
def rename_attributes(self,dataset,attributes,new_attributes):
    if not attributes or not new_attributes:
        raise Exception("The attributes cannot be empty.")
    if len(attributes) != len(new_attributes):
        raise Exception("The number of new column names must match the number of \
        existing column names.")
    new_dataset = list()
    for row in dataset:
        new_row = row
        for i in range(0,len(attributes)):
```

```
            attribute = attributes[i]
            new_attribute = new_attributes[i]
            if attribute in new_row.keys():
                val = row[attribute]
                del new_row[attribute]
                new_row[new_attribute] = val
            else:
                raise Exception("Operation is not possible because the key " + \
                                str(key)+ \
                        " does not exist in one of the rows in the dataset.")
        new_dataset.append(new_row)
    return new_dataset

e = extract()
dataset = e.fromCSV(file_path="data/stocks.csv")
print("Original dataset:")
print(dataset[0])


t = transform()
new_dataset = t.rename_attributes(dataset = dataset, attributes = ["Open","Close"],
                                new_attributes = ["open_price", "close_price"])
print("\nUpdated dataset:")
print(new_dataset[0])
```

Our new `rename_attributes` method is tested by renaming two columns, `Open` and `Close`, in the `stocks.csv` file. The output is:

```
Original dataset:
{'Volume': '2799073', 'High': '20.1', 'OpenInt': '0', 'Low': '17.6', 'Date':
'2018-10-02', 'Close': '18.5', 'Open': '20'}

Updated dataset:
{'open_price': '20', 'Volume': '2799073', 'High': '20.1', 'OpenInt': '0',
'Low': '17.6', 'Date': '2018-10-02', 'close_price': '18.5'}
```

Update your `transform.py` file to include the new `rename_attributes` method.

Removing Multiple Columns

We often want to exclude multiple columns from the original dataset in the transformation process. The existing `remove_attribute` method works for a single column, but we can also create a method that can remove an indefinite number of columns.

In Listing 24.16, we add a `remove_attributes` method so that the user can name any number of columns to be removed from the extracted dataset. The new method uses a `for` loop to update the dataset.

LISTING 24.16

Removing multiple columns

```
from extract import extract #import our custom built extract module

class transform:
    #return the top N records from the dataset
    def head(self, dataset, step):
        if not dataset:
            raise Exception("Dataset cannot be empty.")
        if step < 1:
            raise Exception("The step value must be positive.")
        return dataset[0:step]

    #return the last N records from the dataset
    def tail(self, dataset, step):
        if not dataset:
            raise Exception("Dataset cannot be empty.")
        if step < 1:
            raise Exception("The step value must be positive.")
        return dataset[len(dataset) - step:len(dataset)]

    #rename a column in the dataset
    def rename_attribute(self, dataset, attribute, new_attribute):
        if not dataset:
            raise Exception("Dataset cannot be empty.")
        if not attribute:
            raise Exception("The attribute key must be a valid key.")
        new_dataset = list()
        for row in dataset:
            if attribute in row.keys():
                val = row[attribute]
                new_row = row.copy()
                del new_row[attribute]
                new_row[new_attribute] = val
                new_dataset.append(new_row)
```

```
                else:
                    raise Exception("Operation is not possible because the column " + \
                                    str(column_name) + \
                                    " does not exist in one of the rows in the dataset.")
        return new_dataset

    #remove a column from the dataset
    def remove_attribute(self, dataset, attribute):
        new_dataset = list()
        for row in dataset:
            new_row = row
            if attribute in new_row.keys():
                del new_row[attribute]
                new_dataset.append(new_row)
        return new_dataset

    def rename_attributes(self,dataset,attributes,new_attributes):
        if not attributes or not new_attributes:
            raise Exception("The attributes cannot be empty.")
        if len(attributes) != len(new_attributes):
            raise Exception("The number of new column names must match the number of \
            existing column names.")
        new_dataset = list()
        for row in dataset:
            new_row = row
            for i in range(0,len(attributes)):
                attribute = attributes[i]
                new_attribute = new_attributes[i]
                if attribute in new_row.keys():
                    val = row[attribute]
                    del new_row[attribute]
                    new_row[new_attribute] = val
                else:
                    raise Exception("Operation is not possible because the key " + \
                                    str(key)+ \
                                    " does not exist in one of the rows in the dataset.")
            new_dataset.append(new_row)
        return new_dataset

    #remove a column from the dataset
    def remove_attributes(self, dataset, attributes):
        if not dataset:
            raise Exception("Dataset cannot be empty")
        if not attributes:
            raise Exception("The list of attributes cannot be empty.")
        new_dataset= list()
```

```
        for row in dataset:
            new_row = row
            for attribute in attributes:
                if attribute in new_row.keys():
                    del new_row[attribute]
            new_dataset.append(new_row)
        return new_dataset


e = extract()
dataset = e.fromCSV(file_path = "data/stocks.csv")
print("Original dataset:")
print(dataset[0])

t = transform()
new_dataset = t.remove_attributes(dataset = dataset, attributes = ["Open","Close"])
print("\nTransformed dataset:")
print(new_dataset[0])
```

We again run this script against the `stocks.csv` file. This time instead of renaming the `Open` and `Close` attributes, we remove them as can be seen in the output:

```
Original dataset:
{'Volume': '2799073', 'High': '20.1', 'OpenInt': '0', 'Low': '17.6', 'Date': '2018-10-02',
'Close': '18.5', 'Open': '20'}

Transformed dataset:
{'Volume': '2799073', 'High': '20.1', 'OpenInt': '0', 'Low': '17.6', 'Date': '2018-10-02'}
```

Once again, update your `transform.py` file to include the new `remove_attributes` methods. At this time, your `transform.py` file should look similar to Listing 24.17.

LISTING 24.17

The current transform.py file

```
class transform:
    #return the top N records from the dataset
    def head(self, dataset, step):
        if not dataset:
            raise Exception("Dataset cannot be empty.")
        if step < 1:
            raise Exception("The step value must be positive.")
```

```python
        return dataset[0:step]

    #return the last N records from the dataset
    def tail(self, dataset, step):
        if not dataset:
            raise Exception("Dataset cannot be empty.")
        if step < 1:
            raise Exception("The step value must be positive.")
        return dataset[len(dataset) - step:len(dataset)]

    #rename a column in the dataset
    def rename_attribute(self, dataset, attribute, new_attribute):
        if not dataset:
            raise Exception("Dataset cannot be empty.")
        if not attribute:
            raise Exception("The attribute key must be a valid key.")
        new_dataset = list()
        for row in dataset:
            if attribute in row.keys():
                val = row[attribute]
                new_row = row.copy()
                del new_row[attribute]
                new_row[new_attribute] = val
                new_dataset.append(new_row)
            else:
                raise Exception("Operation is not possible because the column " + \
                            str(column_name) + \
                            " does not exist in one of the rows in the dataset.")
        return new_dataset

    #remove a column from the dataset
    def remove_attribute(self, dataset, attribute):
        new_dataset = list()
        for row in dataset:
            new_row = row
            if attribute in new_row.keys():
                del new_row[attribute]
            new_dataset.append(new_row)
        return new_dataset

    def rename_attributes(self,dataset,attributes,new_attributes):
        if not attributes or not new_attributes:
            raise Exception("The attributes cannot be empty.")
        if len(attributes) != len(new_attributes):
            raise Exception("The number of new column names must match the number of \
            existing column names.")
```

```python
        new_dataset = list()
        for row in dataset:
            new_row = row
            for i in range(0,len(attributes)):
                attribute = attributes[i]
                new_attribute = new_attributes[i]
                if attribute in new_row.keys():
                    val = row[attribute]
                    del new_row[attribute]
                    new_row[new_attribute] = val
                else:
                    raise Exception("Operation is not possible because the key " + \
                                    str(key)+ \
                                " does not exist in one of the rows in the dataset.")
            new_dataset.append(new_row)
        return new_dataset

    #remove a column from the dataset
    def remove_attributes(self, dataset, attributes):
        if not dataset:
            raise Exception("Dataset cannot be empty")
        if not attributes:
            raise Exception("The list of attributes cannot be empty.")
        new_dataset= list()
        for row in dataset:
            new_row = row
            for attribute in attributes:
                if attribute in new_row.keys():
                    del new_row[attribute]
            new_dataset.append(new_row)
        return new_dataset
```

Transforming the Data

The final step in the transform process is to make changes to the data so that the data meets the needs of the target database. This can include transformations like:

- Rounding numeric values
- Changing the case of string values
- Concatenating string values
- Deconstructing strings or datetime values
- Removing out-of-range values, such as nulls or values that are too high or too low for the target specifications
- Converting strings to numbers or vice versa

The exact transformations depend both on what the original data looks like and the needs of the data scientists who will use the extracted data. The transformation itself will include not only a new method in the transform class, but also one or more functions that the method can call to transform the data.

In Listing 24.18 we create a new transform method inside the transform class. This new method will import from the extracted dataset, store the transformed data in a new column in the temporary dataset, and apply a named function to the values in one column of the extracted dataset. Note the use of the *args argument here, which allows the script to handle any number of values in the named column.

We also create one function, round_price, that is set up to round the given value to the nearest integer. When we implement the method, we ask the program to round all values in the Open column and to store the updated values in a new open_price_rounded column. Note that the transformed dataset includes both the original Open column and the new open_price_rounded column.

LISTING 24.18

Transforming the data with round_price

```
from extract import extract #import our custom built extract module

class transform:
    #return the top N records from the dataset
    def head(self, dataset, step):
        if not dataset:
            raise Exception("Dataset cannot be empty.")
        if step < 1:
            raise Exception("The step value must be positive.")
        return dataset[0:step]

    #return the last N records from the dataset
    def tail(self, dataset, step):
        if not dataset:
            raise Exception("Dataset cannot be empty.")
        if step < 1:
            raise Exception("The step value must be positive.")
        return dataset[len(dataset) - step:len(dataset)]

    #rename a column in the dataset
    def rename_attribute(self, dataset, attribute, new_attribute):
        if not dataset:
            raise Exception("Dataset cannot be empty.")
        if not attribute:
```

```python
            raise Exception("The attribute key must be a valid key.")
        new_dataset = list()
        for row in dataset:
            if attribute in row.keys():
                val = row[attribute]
                new_row = row.copy()
                del new_row[attribute]
                new_row[new_attribute] = val
                new_dataset.append(new_row)
            else:
                raise Exception("Operation is not possible because the column " + \
                                str(column_name) + \
                                " does not exist in one of the rows in the dataset.")
        return new_dataset

    #remove a column from the dataset
    def remove_attribute(self, dataset, attribute):
        new_dataset = list()
        for row in dataset:
            new_row = row
            if attribute in new_row.keys():
                del new_row[attribute]
                new_dataset.append(new_row)
        return new_dataset

    def rename_attributes(self,dataset,attributes,new_attributes):
        if not attributes or not new_attributes:
            raise Exception("The attributes cannot be empty.")
        if len(attributes) != len(new_attributes):
            raise Exception("The number of new column names must match the number of \
            existing column names.")
        new_dataset = list()
        for row in dataset:
            new_row = row
            for i in range(0,len(attributes)):
                attribute = attributes[i]
                new_attribute = new_attributes[i]
                if attribute in new_row.keys():
                    val = row[attribute]
                    del new_row[attribute]
                    new_row[new_attribute] = val
                else:
                    raise Exception("Operation is not possible because the key " + \
                                    str(key)+ \
                                    " does not exist in one of the rows in the dataset.")
            new_dataset.append(new_row)
        return new_dataset
```

```python
        #remove a column from the dataset
        def remove_attributes(self, dataset, attributes):
            if not dataset:
                raise Exception("Dataset cannot be empty")
            if not attributes:
                raise Exception("The list of attributes cannot be empty.")
            new_dataset= list()
            for row in dataset:
                new_row = row
                for attribute in attributes:
                    if attribute in new_row.keys():
                        del new_row[attribute]
                new_dataset.append(new_row)
            return new_dataset

    def transform(self, dataset, attribute, new_attribute, transform_function, *args):
        if not dataset:
            raise Exception("Dataset cannot be empty.")
        if not attribute or not new_attribute:
            raise Exception("The input attribute cannot be empty.")
        if not transform_function:
            raise Exception("The transform_function cannot be None.")
        new_dataset = list() #output of this function
        for row in dataset:  #iterate through the input data
            t = transform_function(row[attribute], *args) #apply transformation function
                                                #on column
            z = row.copy()
            z.update({new_attribute:t}) #create new column in the data
            new_dataset.append(z)
        return new_dataset

def round_open_price(value, *args):
    return round(float(value))


e = extract()
dataset = e.fromCSV(file_path="data/stocks.csv")
print("Original dataset:")
print(dataset[0])
t = transform()
new_dataset = t.transform(dataset = dataset, attribute = "Open",
                          new_attribute = "open_price_rounded",
                          transform_function = round_open_price)
print("\nTransformed dataset:")
print(new_dataset[0])
```

When this listing is run, the transform and rounding methods will be applied to attributes in the stocks.csv file:

```
{'Volume': '2799073', 'High': '20.1', 'OpenInt': '0', 'Low': '17.6', 'Date':
'2018-10-02', 'Close': '18.5', 'Open': '20'}

Transformed dataset:
{'Volume': '2799073', 'High': '20.1', 'OpenInt': '0', 'Low': '17.6', 'Date':
'2018-10-02', 'Close': '18.5', 'Open': '20', 'open_price_rounded': 20.0}
```

At this point, you can update your transform.py file to include the new transform method as shown in Listing 24.19.

LISTING 24.19

The completed transform.py file

```
class transform:
    #return the top N records from the dataset
    def head(self, dataset, step):
        if not dataset:
            raise Exception("Dataset cannot be empty.")
        if step < 1:
            raise Exception("The step value must be positive.")
        return dataset[0:step]

    #return the last N records from the dataset
    def tail(self, dataset, step):
        if not dataset:
            raise Exception("Dataset cannot be empty.")
        if step < 1:
            raise Exception("The step value must be positive.")
        return dataset[len(dataset) - step:len(dataset)]

    #rename a column in the dataset
    def rename_attribute(self, dataset, attribute, new_attribute):
        if not dataset:
            raise Exception("Dataset cannot be empty.")
        if not attribute:
            raise Exception("The attribute key must be a valid key.")
        new_dataset = list()
        for row in dataset:
```

```python
            if attribute in row.keys():
                val = row[attribute]
                new_row = row.copy()
                del new_row[attribute]
                new_row[new_attribute] = val
                new_dataset.append(new_row)
            else:
                raise Exception("Operation is not possible because the column " + \
                                str(column_name) + \
                                " does not exist in one of the rows in the dataset.")
        return new_dataset

    #remove a column from the dataset
    def remove_attribute(self, dataset, attribute):
        new_dataset = list()
        for row in dataset:
            new_row = row
            if attribute in new_row.keys():
                del new_row[attribute]
            new_dataset.append(new_row)
        return new_dataset

    def rename_attributes(self,dataset,attributes,new_attributes):
        if not attributes or not new_attributes:
            raise Exception("The attributes cannot be empty.")
        if len(attributes) != len(new_attributes):
            raise Exception("The number of new column names must match the number of \
            existing column names.")
        new_dataset = list()
        for row in dataset:
            new_row = row
            for i in range(0,len(attributes)):
                attribute = attributes[i]
                new_attribute = new_attributes[i]
                if attribute in new_row.keys():
                    val = row[attribute]
                    del new_row[attribute]
                    new_row[new_attribute] = val
                else:
                    raise Exception("Operation is not possible because the key " + \
                                    str(key)+ \
                                    " does not exist in one of the rows in the dataset.")
            new_dataset.append(new_row)
        return new_dataset
```

```
#remove a column from the dataset
def remove_attributes(self, dataset, attributes):
    if not dataset:
        raise Exception("Dataset cannot be empty")
    if not attributes:
        raise Exception("The list of attributes cannot be empty.")
    new_dataset= list()
    for row in dataset:
        new_row = row
        for attribute in attributes:
            if attribute in new_row.keys():
                del new_row[attribute]
        new_dataset.append(new_row)
    return new_dataset

def transform(self, dataset, attribute, new_attribute, transform_function, *args):
    if not dataset:
        raise Exception("Dataset cannot be empty.")
    if not attribute or not new_attribute:
        raise Exception("The input attribute cannot be empty.")
    if not transform_function:
        raise Exception("The transform_function cannot be None.")
    new_dataset = list() #output of this function
    for row in dataset: #iterate through the input data
        t = transform_function(row[attribute], *args) #apply transformation
                                                       #function on column
        z = row.copy()
        z.update({new_attribute:t}) #create new column in the data
        new_dataset.append(z)
    return new_dataset
```

At this point, we have finished building the `transform` class and the `transform.py` file is ready to use in the load step of the ETL process. Verify that you have both the `extract.py` file and the `transform.py` file in the same folder before continuing to the next part of this lesson.

THE LOAD CLASS

The final step of an ETL process is to load the transformed data into a relatively permanent storage location so that data scientists and other users can access the data and use it as they need to. As with the `extract` class we've already defined, we want our ETL script to be able to put the transformed data into a variety of data formats, including CSV, JSON, MySQL, and MongoDB. In the process, we will save the transformed data to an external file.

Note that the data format we use to load the data does not have to be the same as the format we started with. In fact, it is common for an ETL process to change the data format to better meet the needs of the data scientists who will use the data. For example, we may have a pool of data in a MongoDB collection, but there is another process that uses data in CSV or JSON format. While the transform class manages most of the changes needed to move data from one format to another, the load class must be able to save the data to the target format.

Let's start with a template that outlines the steps we want to include in the load class. Create a new file named load.py in the same folder as the existing extract.py and transform.py files and add the code in Listing 24.20 to this new file.

LISTING 24.20

load.py—the template for the load class

```python
class load:
    def toCSV(self):
        pass

    def toJSON(self):
        pass

    def toMYSQL(self):
        pass

    def toMONGODB(self):
        pass
```

Going from top to bottom, we'll start with the toCSV method in the new load class.

Creating the `load.toCSV` Method

In Listing 24.21 we add the first method to the load class, toCSV, which will load our dataset to a CSV file. You can update your load.py file to include the toCSV method.

LISTING 24.21

The toCSV method

```
class load:
    def toCSV(self, file_path, dataset):
        if not dataset:
            raise Exception("Input dataset must have at least one item.")
        if not file_path:
            raise Exception("You must provide a valid CSV file path.")
        import csv
        with open(file_path, 'w') as csvfile:
            fieldnames = dataset[0].keys()
            writer = csv.DictWriter(csvfile, fieldnames = fieldnames)
            writer.writeheader()
            writer.writerows(dataset)

    def toJSON(self):
        pass

    def toMYSQL(self):
        pass

    def toMONGODB(self):
        pass
```

Listing 24.22 shows this method in action: we can use the extract class to import data from the existing stocks.csv file to a copy of that file, also in CSV format. Note that we do not actually transform the data in any way in this example, and the result should be an exact copy of the file we started with.

LISTING 24.22

Using the toCSV method

```
from extract import extract #import our custom built extract module

class load:
    def toCSV(self, file_path, dataset):
        if not dataset:
            raise Exception("Input dataset must have at least one item.")
```

```
        if not file_path:
            raise Exception("You must provide a valid CSV file path.")
        import csv
        with open(file_path, 'w') as csvfile:
            fieldnames = dataset[0].keys()
            writer = csv.DictWriter(csvfile, fieldnames = fieldnames)
            writer.writeheader()
            writer.writerows(dataset)

    def toJSON(self):
        pass

    def toMYSQL(self):
        pass

    def toMONGODB(self):
        pass

e = extract()
dataset = e.fromCSV(file_path = 'data/stocks.csv',delimiter = ',')

l = load()
l.toCSV(file_path = "data/stocks_copy.csv", dataset = dataset)
```

After running this script, verify that the new file exists in the appropriate location on your computer.

You can update this code to include a transform step in the process. For example, you could rename one or more of the existing columns, exclude one or more columns from the original dataset, or round the values in one of the columns.

Creating the load.toJSON Method

Next, let's add a method that will put the extracted data in a JSON file. The new toJSON method in the load class shown in Listing 24.23 outputs the extracted dataset to a new JSON file.

LISTING 24.23

The updated load class with the toJSON method

```
class load:
    def toCSV(self, file_path, dataset):
        if not dataset:
```

```
        raise Exception("Input dataset must have at least one item.")
    if not file_path:
        raise Exception("You must provide a valid CSV file path.")
    import csv
    with open(file_path, 'w') as csvfile:
        fieldnames = dataset[0].keys()
        writer = csv.DictWriter(csvfile, fieldnames = fieldnames)
        writer.writeheader()
        writer.writerows(dataset)

def toJSON(self, file_path, dataset):
    if not dataset:
        raise Exception("Input dataset must have at least one item.")
    if not file_path:
        raise Exception("You must provide a valid JSON file path.")
    import json
    with open(file_path, 'w') as jsonfile:
        json.dump(dataset, jsonfile)

def toMYSQL(self):
    pass

def toMONGODB(self):
    pass
```

You should update your load.py file to include the new toJSON method.

In Listing 24.24 we use the toJSON method. Again, no transformation steps are included here. We simply extract the data from a CSV file and add the same data to a JSON file.

LISTING 24.24

Using the toJSON method

```
from extract import extract #import our custom built extract module

class load:
    def toCSV(self, file_path, dataset):
        if not dataset:
            raise Exception("Input dataset must have at least one item.")
        if not file_path:
            raise Exception("You must provide a valid CSV file path.")
        import csv
        with open(file_path, 'w') as csvfile:
            fieldnames = dataset[0].keys()
```

```
            writer = csv.DictWriter(csvfile, fieldnames = fieldnames)
            writer.writeheader()
            writer.writerows(dataset)

    def toJSON(self, file_path, dataset):
        if not dataset:
            raise Exception("Input dataset must have at least one item.")
        if not file_path:
            raise Exception("You must provide a valid JSON file path.")
        import json
        with open(file_path, 'w') as jsonfile:
            json.dump(dataset, jsonfile)

    def toMYSQL(self):
        pass

    def toMONGODB(self):
        pass

e = extract()
dataset = e.fromCSV(file_path = 'data/stocks.csv', delimiter = ',')

l = load()
l.toJSON(file_path = "data/stocks_copy.json", dataset = dataset)
```

After running the script, verify that the new stocks_copy.json file exists in the target location on your computer. As stated, when presenting the toCSV method, you can update this code to include a transform step between the extract and the load processes.

Creating the load.toMYSQL Method

Update your load.py file to include the toMYSQL method. Your load.py file should now look like Listing 24.25.

LISTING 24.25

Updating the load class to include the toMYSQL method

```
class load:
    def toCSV(self, file_path, dataset):
        if not dataset:
```

```python
            raise Exception("Input dataset must have at least one item.")
        if not file_path:
            raise Exception("You must provide a valid CSV file path.")
        import csv
        with open(file_path, 'w') as csvfile:
            fieldnames = dataset[0].keys()
            writer = csv.DictWriter(csvfile, fieldnames = fieldnames)
            writer.writeheader()
            writer.writerows(dataset)

    def toJSON(self, file_path, dataset):
        if not dataset:
            raise Exception("Input dataset must have at least one item.")
        if not file_path:
            raise Exception("You must provide a valid JSON file path.")
        import json
        with open(file_path, 'w') as jsonfile:
            json.dump(dataset, jsonfile)

    def toMYSQL(self, host, username, password, db, table, dataset):
        if not dataset:
            raise Exception("Input dataset must have at least one item.")
        if not db:
            raise Exception("You must input a valid database name.")
        if not table:
            raise Exception("You must input a valid table name")
        import pymysql
        db = pymysql.connect(host = host, user=username, password = password, db = db,
                             cursorclass = pymysql.cursors.DictCursor)
        cur = db.cursor()
        for row in dataset:
            placeholder = ", ".join(["%s"] * len(row))
            stmt = "insert into {table} ({columns}) values ({values});".
format(table=table, columns=",".join(row.keys()), values = placeholder)

            cur.execute(stmt, list(row.values()))
        db.commit()
        cur.close()
        db.close()

    def toMONGODB(self):
        pass
```

Because the load process will add data to an existing table, open a MySQL instance and run the code in Listing 24.26 to set up a target database and table. Our next example in Listing 24.27 will load data into this new table.

LISTING 24.26

Creating a target database and table to load

```
DROP DATABASE IF EXISTS test;
CREATE DATABASE test;

USE test;

CREATE TABLE cstocks(
    date VARCHAR(10) NOT NULL,
    open FLOAT(10) NOT NULL,
    high FLOAT(10) NOT NULL,
    low FLOAT(10) NOT NULL,
    close FLOAT(10) NOT NULL,
    volume INT(10) NOT NULL
);

SHOW TABLES;
```

This is straightforward SQL code for creating a database called test and adding a table called cstocks to it. If you already have a database called test, it will be overwritten.

The new toMYSQL method accepts the values needed to connect to the database, as well as the name of the target database and table. It then reads the data from the existing CSV file and inserts the rows into the target table, without changing any of the original data.

Note that because this script simply inserts data into the target table, it will add the data from the source dataset each time it runs. You may want to delete the existing data in the table if you run the script more than a couple of times.

LISTING 24.27

Using the toMYSQL method

```
from extract import extract #import our custom built extract module

class load:
    def toCSV(self, file_path, dataset):
```

```python
        if not dataset:
            raise Exception("Input dataset must have at least one item.")
        if not file_path:
            raise Exception("You must provide a valid CSV file path.")
        import csv
        with open(file_path, 'w') as csvfile:
            fieldnames = dataset[0].keys()
            writer = csv.DictWriter(csvfile, fieldnames = fieldnames)
            writer.writeheader()
            writer.writerows(dataset)

    def toJSON(self, file_path, dataset):
        if not dataset:
            raise Exception("Input dataset must have at least one item.")
        if not file_path:
            raise Exception("You must provide a valid JSON file path.")
        import json
        with open(file_path, 'w') as jsonfile:
            json.dump(dataset, jsonfile)

    def toMYSQL(self, host, username, password, db, table, dataset):
        if not dataset:
            raise Exception("Input dataset must have at least one item.")
        if not db:
            raise Exception("You must input a valid database name.")
        if not table:
            raise Exception("You must input a valid table name")
        import pymysql
        db = pymysql.connect(host = host, user=username, password = password, db = db,
                             cursorclass = pymysql.cursors.DictCursor)
        cur = db.cursor()
        for row in dataset:
            placeholder = ", ".join(["%s"] * len(row))
            stmt = "insert into {table} ({columns}) values ({values});".
format(table=table, columns=",".join(row.keys()), values = placeholder)

            cur.execute(stmt, list(row.values()))
        db.commit()
        cur.close()
        db.close()

e = extract()
dataset = e.fromCSV(file_path = 'data/stocks.csv', delimiter = ',')

l=load()
```

```
#change these values if necessary to connect to your MySQL instance
l.toMYSQL(host = "localhost", username = "root", password = "admin",
db = "test", table = "cstocks", dataset = dataset)
```

After running the script, use the following command in MySQL to verify that the data was added correctly to the table:

```
SELECT * FROM cstocks LIMIT 10;
```

Creating the Load.toMONGODB Method

Finally, let's look at loading data into a MongoDB database. Update your load.py file to include the toMONGODB class as shown in Listing 24.28. This listing now contains the code to do all the loads that were originally presented in Listing 24.1.

LISTING 24.28

The updated load class with all methods completed

```
class load:
    def toCSV(self, file_path, dataset):
        if not dataset:
            raise Exception("Input dataset must have at least one item.")
        if not file_path:
            raise Exception("You must provide a valid CSV file path.")
        import csv
        with open(file_path, 'w') as csvfile:
            fieldnames = dataset[0].keys()
            writer = csv.DictWriter(csvfile, fieldnames = fieldnames)
            writer.writeheader()
            writer.writerows(dataset)

    def toJSON(self, file_path, dataset):
        if not dataset:
            raise Exception("Input dataset must have at least one item.")
        if not file_path:
            raise Exception("You must provide a valid JSON file path.")
        import json
```

```
        with open(file_path, 'w') as jsonfile:
            json.dump(dataset, jsonfile)

    def toMYSQL(self, host, username, password, db, table, dataset):
        if not dataset:
            raise Exception("Input dataset must have at least one item.")
        if not db:
            raise Exception("You must input a valid database name.")
        if not table:
            raise Exception("You must input a valid table name")
        import pymysql
        db = pymysql.connect(host = host, user=username, password = password, db = db,
                             cursorclass = pymysql.cursors.DictCursor)
        cur = db.cursor()
        for row in dataset:
            placeholder = ", ".join(["%s"] * len(row))
            stmt = "insert into {table} ({columns}) values ({values});".format(table=table,
                    columns=",".join(row.keys()), values = placeholder)

            cur.execute(stmt, list(row.values()))
        db.commit()
        cur.close()
        db.close()

    def toMONGODB(self, host, port, username, password, db, collection, dataset):
        if not dataset:
            raise Exception("Input dataset must have at least one item.")
        if not db:
            raise Exception("You must input a valid database name.")
        if not collection:
            raise Exception("You must input a valid collection name.")
        import pymongo
        client = pymongo.MongoClient(host = host, port = port, username = username,
                                     password = password)
        tmp_database = client[db]
        tmp_collection = tmp_database[collection]
        tmp_collection.insert_many(dataset)
```

In Listing 24.29, we extract the same stocks.csv file we have used in earlier steps, and we load the data into a new MongoDB collection. Because MongoDB allows us to create a database or a collection by simply naming them, we do not have to set up the database ahead of time.

LISTING 24.29

Using the `toMONGODB` method

```
use test
db.dropDatabase()
from extract import extract #import our custom built extract module

class load:
    def toCSV(self, file_path, dataset):
        if not dataset:
            raise Exception("Input dataset must have at least one item.")
        if not file_path:
            raise Exception("You must provide a valid CSV file path.")
        import csv
        with open(file_path, 'w') as csvfile:
            fieldnames = dataset[0].keys()
            writer = csv.DictWriter(csvfile, fieldnames = fieldnames)
            writer.writeheader()
            writer.writerows(dataset)

    def toJSON(self, file_path, dataset):
        if not dataset:
            raise Exception("Input dataset must have at least one item.")
        if not file_path:
            raise Exception("You must provide a valid JSON file path.")
        import json
        with open(file_path, 'w') as jsonfile:
            json.dump(dataset, jsonfile)

    def toMYSQL(self, host, username, password, db, table, dataset):
        if not dataset:
            raise Exception("Input dataset must have at least one item.")
        if not db:
            raise Execption("You must input a valid database name.")
        if not table:
            raise Exception("You must input a valid table name")
        import pymysql
        db = pymysql.connect(host = host, user=username, password = password, db = db,
                        cursorclass = pymysql.cursors.DictCursor)
        cur = db.cursor()
        for row in dataset:
            placeholder = ", ".join(["%s"] * len(row))
            stmt = "insert into {table} ({columns}) values ({values});".format(table=table,
                    columns=",".join(row.keys()), values = placeholder)
```

```
            cur.execute(stmt, list(row.values())))
        db.commit()
        cur.close()
        db.close()

    def toMONGODB(self, host, port, username, password, db, collection, dataset):
        if not dataset:
            raise Exception("Input dataset must have at least one item.")
        if not db:
            raise Exception("You must input a valid database name.")
        if not collection:
            raise Exception("You must input a valid collection name.")
        import pymongo
        client = pymongo.MongoClient(host = host, port = port, username = username,
                                password = password)
        tmp_database = client[db]
        tmp_collection = tmp_database[collection]
        tmp_collection.insert_many(dataset)

e = extract()
dataset = e.fromCSV(file_path = 'data/stocks.csv', delimiter = ',')

l=load()
#change values here as necessary for your MongoDB instance
l.toMONGODB(host = "localhost", port = 27017, username = "admin", password = "admin",
        db = "test", collection = "cstocks", dataset = dataset)
```

After running the script, you can verify that the data was added to the collection using a MongoDB client command:

```
use test
db.cstocks.find()
```

However, each time we run this script, the entire set of data will be loaded into the cstocks collection, meaning that there will be duplicate data if you run this script more than once. As you test things with MongoDB, you may want to use a MongoDB client to drop the test database periodically.

As mentioned with the other examples, you can add a transform step to change the data between the extract and the load.

We should now have basic scripts for all three ETL steps. Verify that you have all three files at this point, all in the same folder on your computer:

- extract.py
- transform.py
- load.py

SUMMARY

At this point you have the core classes needed to automate processes related to extracting data from one source, transforming that data to meet the needs of a data scientist, and loading the data into a data source accessible to the data scientist. In the next lesson, we'll add additional functionality to improve these classes.

Now that you have completed Lesson 24, you should be able to:

- Describe a variety of activities related to ETL.

- Leverage Python to extract, transform, and load data from various sources.

- Use Python to create a script that extracts data from one location, transforms the data as necessary, and loads the transformed data into a separate database.

- Leverage Python and object-oriented programming concepts to create a reusable and compact ETL library.

EXERCISES

The following exercises are provided to allow you to demonstrate the objectives for this lesson. Write code for each of the following scenarios, using the existing ETL script to extract, transform, and load the data as requested for each activity. Unless otherwise specified, you may use any file of the appropriate type to test the code. After the next lesson, additional exercises will be presented that review this lesson as well. The exercises here are:

Exercise 1: Transforming CSV to CSV

Exercise 2: Transforming CSV to JSON

Exercise 3: Transforming JSON to CSV

Exercise 4: Transforming JSON to JSON

Exercise 5: Removing an Attribute

Exercise 6: Renaming an Attribute

Exercise 7: Confirming an Attribute

Exercise 1: Transforming CSV to CSV

Write a Python program that prompts the user for the path of an existing CSV file and copies the data from that file into a new CSV file.

Exercise 2: Transforming CSV to JSON

Write a Python program that prompts the user for the path of an existing CSV file and copies the data from that file into a new JSON file.

Exercise 3: Transforming JSON to CSV

Write a Python program that prompts the user for the path of an existing JSON file and copies the data from that file into a new CSV file.

Exercise 4: Transforming JSON to JSON

Write a Python program that prompts the user for the path of an existing JSON file and copies the data from that file into a new JSON file.

Exercise 5: Removing an Attribute

Write a Python program that performs the following tasks:

- Prompts the user for the path of an existing CSV file and an attribute in that file
- Reads the data from the file
- Removes the specified attribute
- Saves the transformed data to a new CSV file

Exercise 6: Renaming an Attribute

Write a Python program that performs the following tasks:

- Prompts the user for the path of an existing CSV file, an attribute in that file, and a new name for the same attribute
- Reads the data from the file
- Renames the specified attribute
- Saves the transformed data to a new CSV file

Exercise 7: Confirming an Attribute

Write a Python program that performs the following tasks:

- Prompts the user for the path of an existing file of any data type
- Prompts the user for the name of an attribute
- Checks whether or not the named attribute exists in the data source
- Prints a user-friendly response to inform the user whether the attribute exists in the data source

Lesson 25
Improving ETL Scripting

From Lesson 24, we have a basic ETL script that can be used to extract data from a variety of sources, perform basic transformations on the extracted data, and load the transformed data into a variety of target datasets. In this lesson, we will tweak the existing script to make it more efficient and easier to use.

LEARNING OBJECTIVES

By the end of this lesson, you will be able to:

- Set up Python classes to use static methods.
- Add exception handling to the existing `extract` class.
- Update the `extract` class to allow a developer to add custom extract methods.

CONVERTING TO STATIC METHODS FOR THE EXTRACT CLASS

Static methods, much like class methods, are methods that are bound to a class rather than its object. They do not require a class instance creation, so they are not dependent on the state of the object. To make the methods in our classes more flexible, we will add @staticmethod to each method in our classes.

Update the extract class to include @staticmethod with each method in the class, as shown in Listing 25.1. You should also remove the self argument from each method because it is not needed when we use static methods.

LISTING 25.1

Converting classes to static in the extract class

```python
class extract:
    @staticmethod
    def fromCSV(file_path, delimiter = ",", quotechar = "|"):
        if not file_path:
            raise Exception("You must provide a valid file path.")
        import csv
        dataset = list()
        with open(file_path) as f:
            csv_file = csv.DictReader(f, delimiter = delimiter,quotechar = quotechar)
            for row in csv_file:
                dataset.append(row)
        return dataset

    @staticmethod
    def fromJSON(file_path):
        if not file_path:
            raise Exception("You must provide a valid file path.")
        import json
        dataset = list()
        with open(file_path) as json_file:
            dataset = json.load(json_file)
        return dataset
```

```python
    @staticmethod
    def fromMYSQL(host, username, password, db, query):
        if not host or not username or not db or not query:
            raise Exception("Please make sure that you input a valid host, username, \
                             password, database, and query.")
        import pymysql
        db = pymysql.connect(host = host, user = username, password = password,
                             db = db, cursorclass = pymysql.cursors.DictCursor)
        cur = db.cursor()
        cur.execute(query)
        dataset = list()
        for r in cur:
            dataset.append(r)
        db.commit()
        cur.close()
        db.close()
        return dataset

    @staticmethod
    def fromMONGODB(host, port, username, password, db, collection, query = None):
        if not host or not port or not username or not db or not collection:
            raise Exception("Please make sure that you input a valid host, \
            username, password, database, and collection name")
        import pymongo
        client = pymongo.MongoClient(host = host, port = port,username  = username,
                                     password = password)
        tmp_database = client[db]
        tmp_collection = tmp_database[collection]
        dataset = list()
        if query:
            for document in tmp_collection.find(query):
                dataset.append(document)
            return dataset
        for document in tmp_collection.find():
                dataset.append(document)
        return dataset

dataset = extract.fromCSV(file_path = "data/stocks.csv")
print(dataset[0])
```

This script includes the updated script class along with two additional lines of code to extract the data from the `stocks.csv` file we've used in previous lessons and to print the first row of the dataset:

```
{'Volume': '2799073', 'High': '20.1', 'OpenInt': '0', 'Low': '17.6', 'Date':
'2018-10-02', 'Close': '18.5', 'Open': '20'}
```

Once you confirm that this listing runs as expected, you should update your `extract.py` file to use `@staticmethod` with each method in the `extract` class. Remember to remove the `self` argument from each method in the process.

Verify that the updated code works to extract data from a variety of file types. You can do this using by running the script in Listing 25.2 in the same folder as your `extract.py` file. The code again extracts from the `stocks.csv` file; however, you should also practice extracting JSON, MySQL, and MongoDB data.

LISTING 25.2

Using the updated `extract.py` file

```
from extract import extract

dataset = extract.fromCSV(file_path = "data/stocks.csv")
print(dataset[0])
```

CONVERTING TO STATIC METHODS FOR THE TRANSFORM CLASS

The next step is to create static methods in the `transform` class, too. Add `@staticmethod` to each method in the `transform` class and remove the `self` argument for each method as shown in Listing 25.3.

LISTING 25.3

Converting classes to static in the transform class

```
from extract import extract

class transform:
    #return the top N records from the dataset
```

```python
    @staticmethod
    def head(dataset, step):
        if not dataset:
            raise Exception("Dataset cannot be empty.")
        if step < 1:
            raise Exception("The step value must be positive.")
        return dataset[0:step]

    #return the last N records from the dataset
    @staticmethod
    def tail(dataset, step):
        if not dataset:
            raise Exception("Dataset cannot be empty.")
        if step < 1:
            raise Exception("The step value must be positive.")
        return dataset[len(dataset) - step:len(dataset)]

    #rename a column in the dataset
    @staticmethod
    def rename_attribute(dataset, attribute, new_attribute):
        if not dataset:
            raise Exception("Dataset cannot be empty.")
        if not attribute:
            raise Exception("The attribute key must be a valid key.")
        new_dataset = list()
        for row in dataset:
            if attribute in row.keys():
                val = row[attribute]
                new_row = row.copy()
                del new_row[attribute]
                new_row[new_attribute] = val
                new_dataset.append(new_row)
            else:
                raise Exception("Operation is not possible because the column "
                        + str(column_name)
                        + " does not exist in one of the rows in the dataset.")
        return new_dataset

    #remove a column from the dataset
    @staticmethod
    def remove_attribute(dataset, attribute):
        new_dataset = list()
        for row in dataset:
            new_row = row
            if attribute in new_row.keys():
                del new_row[attribute]
```

```python
                new_dataset.append(new_row)
        return new_dataset

    @staticmethod
    def rename_attributes(dataset, attributes, new_attributes):
        if not attributes or not new_attributes:
            raise Exception("The attributes cannot be empty.")
        if len(attributes) != len(new_attributes):
            raise Exception("The number of new column names must match the number of \
            existing column names.")
        new_dataset = list()
        for row in dataset:
            new_row = row
            for i in range(0,len(attributes)):
                attribute = attributes[i]
                new_attribute = new_attributes[i]
                if attribute in new_row.keys():
                    val = row[attribute]
                    del new_row[attribute]
                    new_row[new_attribute] = val
                else:
                    raise Exception("Operation is not possible because the key "
                                    + str(key)+
                                    " does not exist in one of the rows in the dataset.")
            new_dataset.append(new_row)
        return new_dataset

    #remove a column from the dataset
    @staticmethod
    def remove_attributes(dataset, attributes):
        if not dataset:
            raise Exception("Dataset cannot be empty.")
        if not attributes:
            raise Exception("The list of attributes cannot be empty.")
        new_dataset= list()
        for row in dataset:
            new_row = row
            for attribute in attributes:
                if attribute in new_row.keys():
                    del new_row[attribute]
            new_dataset.append(new_row)
        return new_dataset
```

```
    @staticmethod
    def transform(dataset, attribute, new_attribute, transform_function, *args):
        if not dataset:
            raise Exception("Dataset cannot be empty.")
        if not attribute or not new_attribute:
            raise Exception("The input attribute cannot be empty.")
        if not transform_function:
            raise Exception("The transform_function cannot be None.")
        new_dataset = list() #output of this function
        for row in dataset: #iterate through the input data
            t = transform_function(row[attribute], *args) #apply transformation
                                                    #function on column

            z = row.copy()
            z.update({new_attribute:t}) #create new column in the data
            new_dataset.append(z)
        return new_dataset


def round_open_price(value,*args):
    return round(float(value))



dataset = extract.fromCSV(file_path = "data/stocks.csv")
print(dataset[0])
new_dataset = transform.transform(dataset = dataset, attribute = "Open",
                                  new_attribute = "open_price_rounded",
                                  transform_function = round_open_price)
print(new_dataset[0])
```

This script again provides the static update in the transform class and includes a bit of additional code to open the stocks.csv file to test a transform method. When you run this script, you should see the first line from the dataset with the Open attribute renamed to open_price_rounded:

```
{'Volume': '2799073', 'High': '20.1', 'OpenInt': '0', 'Low': '17.6', 'Date': '2018–10–
02', 'Close': '18.5', 'Open': '20'}
{'Volume': '2799073', 'High': '20.1', 'OpenInt': '0', 'Low': '17.6', 'Date': '2018–10–
02', 'Close': '18.5', 'Open': '20', 'open_price_rounded': 20.0}
```

Update your transform.py file so that each method is static and remove the self argument from each method. Save the changes to the file and verify that you can use it instead of the complete script in the code shown in Listing 25.4. This change does the same thing as Listing 25.3 but uses the import of the transform class.

LISTING 25.4

Testing the new transform.py file

```
from extract import extract
from transform import transform

def round_open_price(value,*args):
    return round(float(value))


dataset = extract.fromCSV(file_path = "data/stocks.csv")
print(dataset[0])

new_dataset = transform.transform(dataset = dataset, attribute = "Open",
                                  new_attribute = "open_price_rounded",
                                  transform_function = round_open_price)
print(new_dataset[0])
```

After verifying that the script works, change the script to extract data from other sources and perform other transformations on the extracted data. For example:

- Extract data from `vinyldatabase.artists` in MySQL, renaming one or more columns.
- Extract data from `data.json`, removing one or more columns.
- Extract only the first ten records from `amazon_reviews.musical_instruments` in MongoDB.

Converting to Static Methods for the load Class

Finally, we also want to make each of the methods in the `load` class static. Add `@staticmethod` to each method in the `load` class and remove all `self` arguments as shown in Listing 25.5. Verify that the updated code works to extract a CSV file and create a duplicate of that file with a new filename.

LISTING 25.5

Converting classes to static in the load class

```
from extract import extract

class load:
```

```python
    @staticmethod
    def toCSV(file_path, dataset):
        if not dataset:
            raise Exception("Input dataset must have at least one item.")
        if not file_path:
            raise Exception("You must provide a valid CSV file path.")
        import csv
        with open(file_path, 'w') as csvfile:
            fieldnames = dataset[0].keys()
            writer = csv.DictWriter(csvfile, fieldnames = fieldnames)
            writer.writeheader()
            writer.writerows(dataset)

    @staticmethod
    def toJSON(file_path, dataset):
        if not dataset:
            raise Exception("Input dataset must have at least one item.")
        if not file_path:
            raise Exception("You must provide a valid JSON file path.")
        import json
        with open(file_path, 'w') as jsonfile:
            json.dump(dataset, jsonfile)

    @staticmethod
    def toMYSQL(host, username, password, db, table, dataset):
        if not dataset:
            raise Exception("Input dataset must have at least one item.")
        if not db:
            raise Exception("You must input a valid database name.")
        if not table:
            raise Exception("You must input a valid table name")
        import pymysql
        db = pymysql.connect(host = host, user=username, password = password,
                             db = db, cursorclass = pymysql.cursors.DictCursor)
        cur = db.cursor()
        for row in dataset:
            placeholder = ", ".join(["%s"] * len(row))
            stmt = "insert into {table} ({columns}) values
({values});".format(table=table,
                    columns=",".join(row.keys()), values = placeholder)

            cur.execute(stmt, list(row.values()))
        db.commit()
        cur.close()
        db.close()
```

```
@staticmethod
def toMONGODB(host, port, username, password, db, collection, dataset):
    if not dataset:
        raise Exception("Input dataset must have at least one item.")
    if not db:
        raise Exception("You must input a valid database name.")
    if not collection:
        raise Exception("You must input a valid collection name.")
    import pymongo
    client = pymongo.MongoClient(host = host, port = port, username = username,
                                 password = password)
    tmp_database = client[db]
    tmp_collection = tmp_database[collection]
    tmp_collection.insert_many(dataset)


dataset = extract.fromCSV(file_path="data/ stocks.csv")
load.toCSV(file_path="data/stocks_copy.csv",dataset=dataset)
```

When you execute this listing, you should find that the stocks.csv file is copied. A new file called stocks_copy.csv should now be included in your folder.

Update your load.py file so that each method is static and remove the self argument from each method. Save the changes to the file and verify that it works correctly using the code in Listing 25.6, which does the same as the previous listing, but using an import.

LISTING 25.6

Testing the new load.py file

```
from extract import extract
from load import load

dataset = extract.fromCSV(file_path="data/stocks.csv")
load.toCSV(file_path="data/stocks_copy.csv",dataset=dataset)
```

Adding Exception Handling in the extract Class

Next, we will look at how we can improve exception handling in the extract class. We added some basic exception statements in our original script, primarily to ensure that the script includes the name of a file. We can add additional, more detailed error messages to help users understand problems that might happen during the extract process.

Let's look first at the `fromCSV` method. We already have one exception message that Python will display if the user fails to provide a value for a file path:

```
def fromCSV(file_path, delimiter = ",", quotechar = "|"):
    if not file_path:
        # message to display if the user fails to provide a file path at all
        raise Exception("You must provide a valid file path.")
```

However, that exception only checks that a value was provided and does not apply if the user provides an invalid file path. It's possible that the user might ask for a file that does not exist, and we want to provide a user-friendly message when that happens. We will add a try–except statement that references Python IO and OS modules and that returns an error if the file path is not valid:

```
try:
    import csv
    dataset = list()
    with open(file_path) as f:
        csv_file = csv.DictReader(f, delimiter = delimiter, quotechar = quotechar)
        for row in csv_file:
            dataset.append(row)
    return dataset
except (IOError, OSError):
    raise Exception("You must provide a valid CSV file.")
```

In the try step, the code attempts to export the named file to a new dataset. If the try step fails, Python will display the message in the except step. In the code in Listing 25.7, we provide an incorrect filename to generate the expected error message.

LISTING 25.7

Testing our new exception for incorrect filenames

```
class extract:
    @staticmethod
    def fromCSV(file_path, delimiter = ",", quotechar = "|"):
        if not file_path:
            # message to display if the user fails to provide a file path at all
            raise Exception("You must provide a valid file path.")
        try:
            import csv
            dataset = list()
```

```python
        with open(file_path) as f:
            csv_file = csv.DictReader(f, delimiter = delimiter,
                                      quotechar = quotechar)
            for row in csv_file:
                dataset.append(row)
        return dataset
    except (IOError, OSError):
        raise Exception("You must provide a valid CSV file.")


@staticmethod
def fromJSON(file_path):
    if not file_path:
        raise Exception("You must provide a valid file path.")
    import json
    dataset = list()
    with open(file_path) as json_file:
        dataset = json.load(json_file)
    return dataset


@staticmethod
def fromMYSQL(host, username, password, db, query):
    if not host or not username or not db or not query:
        raise Exception("Please make sure that you input a valid host, username, \
                        password, database, and query.")
    import pymysql
    db = pymysql.connect(host = host, user = username, password = password,
                         db = db, cursorclass = pymysql.cursors.DictCursor)
    cur = db.cursor()
    cur.execute(query)
    dataset = list()
    for r in cur:
        dataset.append(r)
    db.commit()
    cur.close()
    db.close()
    return dataset


@staticmethod
def fromMONGODB(host, port, username, password, db, collection, query = None):
    if not host or not port or not username or not db or not collection:
        raise Exception("Please make sure that you input a valid host, username, \
        password, database, and collection name")
    import pymongo
    client = pymongo.MongoClient(host = host, port = port,username  = username,
                                 password = password)
```

```
        tmp_database = client[db]
        tmp_collection = tmp_database[collection]
        dataset = list()
        if query:
            for document in tmp_collection.find(query):
                dataset.append(document)
            return dataset
        for document in tmp_collection.find():
                dataset.append(document)
        return dataset

dataset = extract.fromCSV(file_path="data/wrong_name.csv")
print(dataset[0])
```

When you run this script using the bad file (data/wrong_name.csv), the exception is tripped, but this time, you get a clearer message saying you must provide a valid CSV file. Your output should look similar to the following:

```
Traceback (most recent call last):
  File "test.py", line 65, in <module>
    dataset = extract.fromCSV(file_path="data/wrong_name.csv")
  File "test.py", line 16, in fromCSV
    raise Exception("You must provide a valid CSV file.")
Exception: You must provide a valid CSV file.
```

You should apply the same exception handling and user-friendly messaging to each of the methods in the extract class's code. Within each method, add the current code inside a try statement, following the model given in the example for CSV files. With each method, you will want to add an appropriate except message such as the ones suggested here:

For the fromJSON method you can use:

```
except (IOError, OSError):
    raise Exception("You must provide a valid JSON file.")
```

For the fromMYSQL method you can use:

```
except pymysql.InternalError as error:
    print(error)
    raise Exception("Error while reading data from MySQL.")
```

For the fromMONGODB method you can use:

```
except pymongo.errors.PyMongoError as e:
    print(e)
    raise Exception("Error while reading data from MongoDB.")
```

You should update each method independently of the others. After each update, check to make sure that the code works as expected, using both valid and invalid values for the data source, before updating the next method. Listing 25.8 shows the updated class code that should now be in the extract.py file.

LISTING 25.8

The updated extract.py code with additional exception handling

```
class extract:
    @staticmethod
    def fromCSV(file_path, delimiter = ",", quotechar = "|"):
        if not file_path:
            # message to display if the user fails to provide a file path at all
            raise Exception("You must provide a valid file path.")
        try:
            import csv
            dataset = list()
            with open(file_path) as f:
                csv_file = csv.DictReader(f, delimiter = delimiter,
                                            quotechar = quotechar)
                for row in csv_file:
                    dataset.append(row)
            return dataset
        except (IOError, OSError):
            raise Exception("You must provide a valid CSV file.")


    @staticmethod
    def fromJSON(file_path):
        if not file_path:
            raise Exception("You must provide a valid file path.")
        try:
            import json
            dataset = list()
            with open(file_path) as json_file:
                dataset = json.load(json_file)
            return dataset
        except (IOError, OSError):
            raise Exception("You must provide a valid JSON file.")
```

```python
    @staticmethod
    def fromMYSQL(host, username, password, db, query):
        if not host or not username or not db or not query:
            raise Exception("Please make sure that you input a valid host, username, \
                            password, database, and query.")
        try:
            import pymysql
            db = pymysql.connect(host = host, user = username, password = password,
                                 db = db, cursorclass = pymysql.cursors.DictCursor)
            cur = db.cursor()
            cur.execute(query)
            dataset = list()
            for r in cur:
                dataset.append(r)
            db.commit()
            cur.close()
            db.close()
            return dataset
        except pymysql.InternalError as error:
            print(error)
            raise Exception("Error while reading data from MySQL.")


    @staticmethod
    def fromMONGODB(host, port, username, password, db, collection, query = None):
        if not host or not port or not username or not db or not collection:
            raise Exception("Please make sure that you input a valid host, username, \
            password, database, and collection name")
        try:
            import pymongo
            client = pymongo.MongoClient(host = host, port = port,username  = username,
                                         password = password)
            tmp_database = client[db]
            tmp_collection = tmp_database[collection]
            dataset = list()
            if query:
                for document in tmp_collection.find(query):
                    dataset.append(document)
                return dataset
            for document in tmp_collection.find():
                    dataset.append(document)
            return dataset
        except pymongo.errors.PyMongoError as e:
             print(e)
             raise Exception("Error while reading data from MongoDB.")
```

With the extract class updated, we can now do something similar with the load class. You can find the code for the updated load class that includes the appropriate try-except statements for generating appropriate, user-friendly error messages for common error types in Listing 25.9. You should test the updated code with a variety of load options to confirm that the exception handling is in place correctly.

LISTING 25.9

Additional exception handling in the load class

```
from extract import extract

class load:
    @staticmethod
    def toCSV(file_path, dataset):
        if not dataset:
            raise Exception("Input dataset must have at least one item.")
        if not file_path:
            raise Exception("You must provide a valid CSV file path.")
        import csv
        with open(file_path, 'w') as csvfile:
            fieldnames = dataset[0].keys()
            writer = csv.DictWriter(csvfile, fieldnames = fieldnames)
            writer.writeheader()
            writer.writerows(dataset)

    @staticmethod
    def toJSON(file_path, dataset):
        if not dataset:
            raise Exception("Input dataset must have at least one item.")
        if not file_path:
            raise Exception("You must provide a valid JSON file path.")
        import json
        with open(file_path, 'w') as jsonfile:
            json.dump(dataset, jsonfile)

    @staticmethod
    def toMYSQL(host, username, password, db, table, dataset):
        if not host or not username or not db or not query:
            raise Exception("Please make sure that you input a valid host, username, \
                            password, database, and query.")
        try:
            import pymysql
```

```
            db = pymysql.connect(host = host, user = username, password = password,
                                  db = db, cursorclass = pymysql.cursors.DictCursor)
            cur = db.cursor()
            cur.execute(query)
            dataset = list()
            for r in cur:
                dataset.append(r)
            db.commit()
            cur.close()
            db.close()
            return dataset
        except pymysql.InternalError as error:
            print(error)
            raise Exception("Error while reading data from MySQL.")

    @staticmethod
    def toMONGODB(host, port, username, password, db, collection, dataset):
        if not host or not port or not username or not db or not collection:
            raise Exception("Please make sure that you input a valid host, username, \
            password, database, and collection name")
        try:
            import pymongo
            client = pymongo.MongoClient(host = host, port = port,username  = username,
                                         password = password)
            tmp_database = client[db]
            tmp_collection = tmp_database[collection]
            dataset = list()
            if query:
                for document in tmp_collection.find(query):
                    dataset.append(document)
                return dataset
            for document in tmp_collection.find():
                    dataset.append(document)
            return dataset
        except pymongo.errors.PyMongoError as e:
            print(e)
            raise Exception("Error while reading data from MongoDB.")
```

Creating a Custom Extractor for the extract Class

Developers often want to implement their own custom Python function that can read data from a specific data source. For example, we might want to use our ETL script to read data from XML files. While we could add a new `fromXML` method to the current script, it would be much more flexible to have a custom extractor that will allow us to extract from any data source in the future, without having to update the script for every possible data source type. Adding a custom extractor will allow us to define the data source type when we execute the program.

Python allows us to create standalone functions and then use other functions to call and execute those standalone functions. We will take advantage of this feature to create a custom extractor method.

In Listing 25.10 we define a function to extract a dataset from an XML file. This is a standalone function that receives an XML file that contains news and media items and returns a dataset.

LISTING 25.10

Custom class to extract from an XML file

```
def xml_extractor(xmlfile):
    import xml.etree.ElementTree as ET
    # create element tree object
    tree = ET.parse(xmlfile)
    # get root element
    root = tree.getroot()
    # create empty list for news items
    newsitems = []
    # iterate news items
    for item in root.findall('./channel/item'):
        # empty news dictionary
        news = {}
        # iterate child elements of item
        for child in item:
            # special checking for namespace object content:media
            if child.tag == '{http://search.yahoo.com/mrss/}content':
                news['media'] = child.attrib['url']
            else:
                news[child.tag] = child.text.encode('utf8')
        # append news dictionary to news items list
        newsitems.append(news)
    # return news items list
    return newsitems
```

The xml_extractor function takes a file path as input and returns a list of items similar to the other extract methods we have already used. In the process, it takes advantage of Python's built-in ElementTree XML API, which is designed to parse data in XML format.

After parsing the data, it stores and returns the data in a new list named newsitems. You could rewrite this method to extract data from an XML file in any manner that fits your need.

> **NOTE** You can learn more about the ElementTree XML API at https://docs.python.org/3/library/xml.etree.elementtree.html.

We will use the xml_extractor function with a new custom function in our extract class.

In the script provided in Listing 25.11, we update the current extract class with a new method, fromCustom, which is shown in Listing 25.11. The fromCustom extractor method takes as input a custom extractor standalone function (xml_extractor) whose goal is to read XML data.

Note the following differences between the fromCustom method and the other methods we have already used:

- The new method does not include a path argument. Instead, we expect the standalone function to identify the source file.

- The new method does not check for exceptions except to be certain that the dataset is a list. We can incorporate data-specific exception handling in the standalone function.

- The fromCustom method uses **kwds to allow for an indefinite number of arguments, depending on the values provided by the standalone function.

The code for our fromCustom method is in Listing 25.11.

LISTING 25.11

The fromCustom method

```
# new custom extract method
@staticmethod
def fromCustom(custom_extractor,**kwds):

    #this will execute the custom_extractor and store the data in dataset.
    dataset = custom_extractor(**kwds)

    #if the type of dataset is not a list then we need to throw an error
    if type(dataset)!= list:
        raise ValueError("Output data from extract step should be a list of items.")
    return dataset
```

To execute the `xml_extractor` function defined in Listing 25.10, we pass it to the `fromCustom` method in the `extract` class along with the path of the XML file we want to use:

```
dataset = extract.fromCustom(xml_extractor,xmlfile="data/newsfeed.xml")
```

The result is that the `dataset` variable will contain the data from the XML file. We can use other standalone functions to read data from other sources, such as HDFS/Hadoop, and use that data in our ETL script. This approach allows us to easily extend the ETL library without having to modify the existing code.

In Listing 25.12 we create a script that contains the extract code with the new `fromCustom` method and the `xml_extractor` function. The listing uses a file named `newsfeed.xml`, which you can find in the download file for this book.

LISTING 25.12

Using the fromCustom method

```
class extract:
    @staticmethod
    def fromCSV(file_path, delimiter = ",", quotechar = "|"):
        if not file_path:
            raise Exception("You must provide a valid file path.")
        import csv
        dataset = list()
        with open(file_path) as f:
            csv_file = csv.DictReader(f, delimiter = delimiter,quotechar = quotechar)
            for row in csv_file:
                dataset.append(row)
        return dataset

    @staticmethod
    def fromJSON(file_path):
        if not file_path:
            raise Exception("You must provide a valid file path.")
        import json
        dataset = list()
        with open(file_path) as json_file:
            dataset = json.load(json_file)
        return dataset

    @staticmethod
    def fromMYSQL(host, username, password, db, query):
        if not host or not username or not db or not query:
```

```python
            raise Exception("Please make sure that you input a valid host, username, \
                            password, database, and query.")
        import pymysql
        db = pymysql.connect(host = host, user = username, password = password,
                            db = db, cursorclass = pymysql.cursors.DictCursor)
        cur = db.cursor()
        cur.execute(query)
        dataset = list()
        for r in cur:
            dataset.append(r)
        db.commit()
        cur.close()
        db.close()
        return dataset


    @staticmethod
    def fromMONGODB(host, port, username, password, db, collection, query = None):
        if not host or not port or not username or not db or not collection:
            raise Exception("Please make sure that you input a valid host, username, \
            password, database, and collection name")
        import pymongo
        client = pymongo.MongoClient(host = host, port = port,username  = username,
                                    password = password)
        tmp_database = client[db]
        tmp_collection = tmp_database[collection]
        dataset = list()
        if query:
            for document in tmp_collection.find(query):
                dataset.append(document)
            return dataset
        for document in tmp_collection.find():
                dataset.append(document)
        return dataset


    # new custom extract method
    @staticmethod
    def fromCustom(custom_extractor,**kwds):
        #we do not check for path. Path must be defined in the standalone function.

        #this will execute the custom_extractor and store the data in dataset.
        dataset = custom_extractor(**kwds)
        #if the type of dataset is not a list then we need to throw an error
        if type(dataset)!= list:
            raise ValueError("Output data from extract step should be a list
of items.")
        return dataset
```

```
#standalone function to extract data from XML
def xml_extractor(xmlfile):
    import xml.etree.ElementTree as ET
    # create element tree object
    tree = ET.parse(xmlfile)
    # get root element
    root = tree.getroot()
    # create empty list for news items
    newsitems = []
    # iterate news items
    for item in root.findall('./channel/item'):
        # empty news dictionary
        news = {}
        # iterate child elements of item
        for child in item:
            # special checking for namespace object content:media
            if child.tag == '{http://search.yahoo.com/mrss/}content':
                news['media'] = child.attrib['url']
            else:
                news[child.tag] = child.text.encode('utf8')
        # append news dictionary to news items list
        newsitems.append(news)
    # return news items list
    return newsitems

dataset = extract.fromCustom(xml_extractor,xmlfile="data/newsfeed.xml")
print(dataset[0])
```

When this script is run with the `newsfeed.xml` file, the following output should be displayed:

```
{'description': 'India vs West Indies: Catch all the action of the second ODI between
the two teams in Trinidad through our live blog', 'pubDate': 'Sun, 11 Aug 2019
06:14:53 GMT ', 'title': "India vs West Indies Live Score: Gayle, Lewis begin Windies'
280-run chase", 'media':
'https://www.hindustantimes.com/rf/image_size_630x354/HT/p2/2019/08/11/Pictures/cricket-
windies-ind-t20i_709f7352-bc5f-11e9-b550-1b3b7c3fb345.jpg', 'link':
'https://www.hindustantimes.com/cricket/india-vs-west-indies-live-score-2nd-odi-at-
port-of-spain-ind-wi-cricket-scorecard-updates-virat-kohli-and-co-look-to-draw-first-
blood/story-DVNTZ4yPVpuicNdrJnrwHP.html', 'guid':
'https://www.hindustantimes.com/cricket/india-vs-west-indies-live-score-2nd-odi-at-
port-of-spain-ind-wi-cricket-scorecard-updates-virat-kohli-and-co-look-to-draw-first-
blood/story-DVNTZ4yPVpuicNdrJnrwHP.html'}
```

Once you confirm that the fromCustom method works you should update your copy of extract.py to include the method. You can then modify Listing 25.12 to import the extract class as shown in Listing 25.13.

LISTING 25.13

Using fromCustom via an imported extract class

```
from extract import extract

def xml_extractor(xmlfile):
    import xml.etree.ElementTree as ET
    # create element tree object
    tree = ET.parse(xmlfile)
    # get root element
    root = tree.getroot()
    # create empty list for news items
    newsitems = []
    # iterate news items
    for item in root.findall('./channel/item'):
        # empty news dictionary
        news = {}
        # iterate child elements of item
        for child in item:
            # special checking for namespace object content:media
            if child.tag == '{http://search.yahoo.com/mrss/}content':
                news['media'] = child.attrib['url']
            else:
                news[child.tag] = child.text.encode('utf8')
        # append news dictionary to news items list
        newsitems.append(news)
    # return news items list
    return newsitems

dataset = extract.fromCustom(xml_extractor,xmlfile="data/newsfeed.xml")
print(dataset[0])
```

SUMMARY

With this lesson now complete, your basic ETL script has become a lot more robust. It can now be used to extract data from a variety of sources, perform basic transformations on the extracted data, and load transformed data into a variety of target datasets. With the tweaks you made in this lesson, the program is less prone to an error if a database doesn't exist, plus you added functionality that will allow for new extractions to be created without having to change your extract script.

Now that you have completed Lesson 25, you should be able to:

- Set up Python classes to use static methods.

- Add exception handling to the existing `extract` class.

- Update the `extract` class to allow a developer to add custom extract methods.

These last two lessons have used what you learned throughout this book to walk you through building a simple reusable library that performs common extract, transform, and load operations. You have now learned the foundational elements of Python and how to leverage them to create complex scripts and applications.

EXERCISES

The following exercises are provided to allow you to use the improved ETL tool shown in this lesson. Write code for each of the following scenarios, using the existing ETL script to extract, transform, and load the data as requested for each activity. Unless otherwise specified, you may use any file of the appropriate type to test the code.

Exercise 1: Revisiting Lessons Learned

Exercise 2: Day of Week

Exercise 3: Date Validity

Exercise 4: Listing Duplicates

Exercise 5: Removing Duplicates

Exercise 6: Transforming Names

Exercise 1: Revisiting Lessons Learned

Update the exercises from Lesson 24 to use the updated ETL classes you created in this lesson. Make sure that all lessons work as expected.

Exercise 2: Day of Week

Write a Python program that extracts data from a data file containing a date (such as `stocks.csv`), transforms the data to include a new attribute with the corresponding day of the week for each date (e.g., Monday, Tuesday, etc.), and adds the transformed data to a new file of the same data type. You may need to search the internet to find out how to extract a weekday from a date.

Exercise 3: Date Validity

Write a Python program that extracts data from a data file containing a date (such as `stocks.csv`) and checks that all rows include valid dates. The program should display a validation warning message if there are any rows that contain invalid dates or an appropriate user-friendly message if all dates are valid.

Exercise 4: Listing Duplicates

Write a Python program that reads a data file, identifies duplicate records in the data file, and prints a list of the duplicate records.

Exercise 5: Removing Duplicates

Write a Python program that reads a data file, identifies duplicate records in the data file, removes duplicates, and saves the new dataset in a new file.

> **TIP** Make sure that you leave one copy of each duplicate record.

Exercise 6: Transforming Names

Write a Python program that reads any type of data file that contains two string/text fields, such as first name and last name. The program should concatenate the two string attributes into a single field (such as full name), remove the original string fields, and save the transformed data in a new file whose data type is different from that of the original data file. The new concatenated field should include any appropriate spaces or punctuation.

PART VI

Appendices

Appendix A: Flowcharts

Appendix B: Creating Pseudocode

Appendix C: Installing MySQL

Appendix D: Installing Vinyl DB

Appendix E: Installing MongoDB

Appendix F: Importing to MongoDB

Appendix A: Flowcharts

:Flowcharts allow us to visualize how the application will flow from one instruction to the next, from start to finish. Building a flowchart before we start to code a program helps ensure that we don't skip any steps in the program and gives us a tool to easily communicate those steps to others.

FLOWCHART BASICS

One of the interesting things about programming is how surprisingly simplistic computers and programs really are. Even though we can create massive-scale programs that perform complex tasks, there are really only three things a program can do:

Sequence: Execute a series of statements in order

Branch: Follow a specific path based on a defined condition

Loop: Repeat a series of instructions until a condition is met

We use the term **flow of control** to define the path that a program takes from one instruction to the next, and we use a flowchart to visualize the flow of control. Another important term is **algorithm**. While TV shows and movies make algorithms sound like very technical things that only a software developer could understand, an algorithm is really just a well-defined set of instructions that a computer or similar machine can follow to reach a desired output. In other words, we use flowcharts to diagram algorithms.

Sequences

By default, the simplest path in an algorithm is to move sequentially from one statement to the next. For example, in the following pseudocode, we have two statements:

```
greeting = "Hello, world!"
print(greeting)
```

The program would process the first statement (which defines greeting) and then print the value of greeting. This control structure is called a **sequence**.

As shown in Figure A.1, sequences are the easiest control structure to understand because they simply execute statements in the order they are given. The computer reads the code left-to-right, top-to-bottom, just like reading a book. Ultimately, the program's instructions that do the actual work required will be organized into sequences. A sequence can become quite large as methods can call other methods and objects may need to sub some of their work out to other objects.

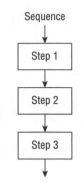

Figure A.1: A sequence

As an example, consider the workflow of completing a purchase on an ecommerce website. When you hit the checkout button, the program will complete a series of steps that need to be done across multiple objects. The top object generally controls the workflow of the checkout process, but sub-sequences could include:

1. Logging in

2. Entering payment information

3. Sending payment information to the payment processor/bank

4. Notifying the warehouse of the order

5. Notifying the shipping company to pick up the order

6. Emailing the customer a confirmation

And so on.

A skilled developer will lay out each of these processes in detail before they begin to write code. They will separate the code into methods and objects that group related things together while keeping in mind ease of maintenance and testability. Each step in a sequence may end up calling other sequences.

Branches

In a **branch** situation, the program reaches a point where there are two or more possible next steps, and it must evaluate a condition to determine which path to take. Branches are always based on a question that can be answered as either True or False. In most instances, the True case determines the default sequence that the program will follow.

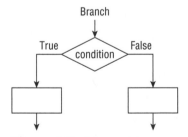

Figure A.2: A branching program flow

There can also be a False case where a different sequence can be followed. Figure A.2 shows a branching program flow.

A branch case can be as simple as logging in to a website. In a branching flowchart, a diamond represents the condition that will determine which branch the flow of control will follow. For example, "Are the username and password correct?" If True, take the user to their home page. If False, display an error and prompt the user to try again.

Loops

In a **looping** situation, we continue to run a sequence of instructions until some condition is met. We do this frequently in our daily lives. When washing our hands, our condition is, "Are my hands clean yet?" If not, then we will keep scrubbing until they are clean.

There are several different varieties of loops in software development. Some loops will run a specific number of times, like looping through the number of characters in a string of text. If we know how many characters are in the string, we know how many times we want to loop.

In other cases, we don't know in advance how many times we will need to loop. In the previous website example, the user may enter their username and password correctly the first time, but because humans are imperfect creatures, they may not enter the information correctly until the second time or the tenth time. In these cases, we would want to structure the loop to continue until they get it right.

A loop includes a branch, but the sequence following the branch returns to the branch. Figure A.3 presents a looping program flow.

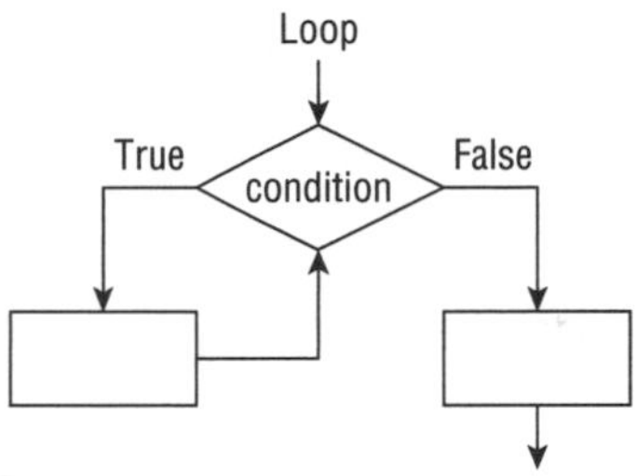

A loop will continue until a specified condition is met. Once the condition is met, the loop ends, and the flow of control moves to the next block of instructions in the program.

Figure A.3: A looping program flow

One thing to watch out for is endless (or infinite) loops. It is quite possible to define a loop's condition such that the condition can never be met (like defining a log-in loop to require both a username and password but failing to ask the user to enter the password). In that case, the loop will run indefinitely until something else stops it.

COMMON FLOWCHARTING SHAPES

Using our flow of control structures and branch statements, we can come up with some very interesting algorithms. In fact, as we pointed out earlier, even the most complex scenarios must ultimately break down into these three structures.

While there are many symbols available to use in flowcharts, the most common include:

Oval: Indicates the start and end points of an algorithm

Rectangle: Indicates an instruction that the computer must complete

Parallelogram (a tilted rectangle): Input and output

Diamond: A condition

We also use one-sided arrows to indicate the order in which the steps will be completed. Technically, a flowchart can be oriented in any way because the arrows define the order in which the steps will be completed, but they are most commonly oriented from top to bottom (so the program starts at the top and ends at the bottom) or left to right. Larger flowcharts can include a combination of top-to-bottom and left-to-right orientation, as well as right-to-left if it makes the flowchart easier to read.

Flowcharts can certainly be written out by hand, although it's often best to use pencil, a whiteboard, or another erasable medium to make corrections easily. There are also several software options, including Draw.io, recently renamed to Diagrams (`https://app.diagrams.net`), which is a free online diagramming tool, and LucidChart (`www.lucidchart.com`), which is a paid program that includes a free option. Microsoft Office products (including Visio, Word, and PowerPoint) also include flowchart tools, as does Drawings in Google Drive (`https://drive.google.com`).

> **NOTE** The focus of a flowchart is to give you a visual aid for your logic.

Flowcharting Example

Now let's look at how we might use a flowchart to diagram a simple algorithm. Consider a method that requires the user to enter an odd number. The steps for this might include:

1. Declare variables to store keyboard input and parsed number
2. Start loop
   1. Prompt user to enter an odd number
   2. Read input from keyboard
   3. If the input is a number
      - If the number is odd
        - Exit loop
      - If the number is not odd
        - Inform user the number is not odd
        - Restart the loop
   4. If the input is not a number
      - Inform user that input is not a number
      - Restart loop
3. Return the number

So, we have a loop that should run until an odd number is entered. Checking for an odd number requires two checks: first, that it is a numeric entry and second, that the parsed number is odd.

The preceding text is a form of **pseudocode**, which can be used to supplement (or even replace) flowcharts in early development processes. Pseudocode sounds technical (like *algorithm*), but it really refers to the process of writing out a program's steps using a more natural human language that anyone can understand. We can then translate the pseudocode into the programming language of choice (such as C#, Java, or Python) once we are sure we have identified all the required steps.

In the pseudocode, each indentation in the text represents a code block, and each of those blocks will be a shape in the flowchart. A flowchart representing the steps in this algorithm might look like Figure A.4.

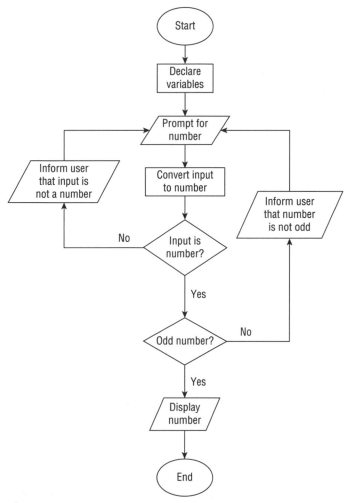

Figure A.4: A flowchart of our pseudocode

> **TIP** We recommend using the minimum number of symbols possible and focusing instead on the logical flow.

Additional Flowchart Elements

Flowcharting isn't an exact science. There aren't really any standards for every possible situation, so be guided by your team and your personal preferences. Earlier four shapes were mentioned for flowcharting. Here is a little more detail on a few of the common symbols.

First, we have the flow line as shown in Figure A.5. This is used to indicate the flow of logic. Your code should always travel from one symbol to another following the arrow.

Indicates the flow of logic

Figure A.5: Flow line

When two lines meet, they'll either join or cross. If the two flow lines join together to then form a single line, it means that the two things have the same result. In the case where a line crosses another line, a bridge will be added so the two lines can continue on their different paths to different results. These flow line situations are illustrated in Figure A.6.

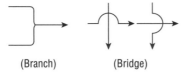

(Branch)   (Bridge)

Figure A.6: Branching (merging of two lines) and bridging flow lines

If multiple lines go to the same result, the lines will merge into one. Figure A.7 illustrates an example of merging flow lines.

(Multiple lines)

Figure A.7: Merging flow lines

A terminator is used to indicate the starting or stopping point in a flowchart. Figure A.8 illustrates terminators.

Indicates the starting or stopping
point of a flowchart

Figure A.8: Terminator

Next is the parallelogram, as shown in Figure A.9. It was mentioned earlier that the parallelogram is used for input and output. In the programs presented in this book, the parallelogram would be used to indicate interaction with the console. This would include input and printing actions.

Indicates user input and output

Figure A.9: Input/output parallelogram

The processing symbol as shown in Figure A.10 is used for math, logical operators, and method calls. These are typically code statements like `send email` or `check address` or `debit account`.

Math, logical operations,
and method calls

Figure A.10: Processing symbol

Lastly, we have the decision, which is a diamond, as shown in Figure A.11. Decisions can have two branches for true or false, yes or no, and so on. You can also use them to express more complex decisions like you would in a `switch` statement as shown in Figure A.12.

Branches to true/false, yes/no, etc.

Figure A.11: Decision symbol

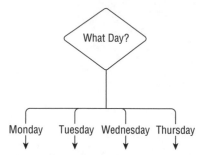

Figure A.12: Decisions

> **NOTE** The bottom line is that if you can't solve the problem on paper or on the whiteboard, then you can't solve it in code. Making sure that you can explain in plain English what your program is trying to do, at the very least to yourself, is an essential first step in thinking through the coding logic.

> **TIP** It's worth spending the time up front to plan things out. It will save lots of pain and frustration later.

Appendix B: Creating Pseudocode

Along with flowcharts, which we covered in Appendix A, developers frequently use pseudocode as a way to plan out and describe the instructions for a computer program before starting to write code for that program.

WHAT IS PSEUDOCODE?

Pseudocode is a representation of an algorithm using statements written within a natural language, but without the constraints of terminology and structure that are part of real programming languages. The prefix *pseudo-* comes from a Greek word that means "false," so pseudocode really means "false code."

You can think of pseudocode as a blend of normal human words and generic computer code. You can use `if` statements for conditionals, `while` and `for` statements for loops, and generic statements for declaring variables. The process is like creating a guide for your program. It will be a step-by-step process for your program when you start coding.

Although there are general recommendations for writing algorithms using pseudocode, the end result should be a sequence of steps that have the appearance and structure of programming code but are written so that humans can understand them. Teams of people often work on the same project, so it is a good idea to use simple and clear language in pseudocode without relying too much on abbreviations or terms that others may not easily understand. The individual statements can be complete sentences or simple phrases as long as they provide enough information to be clear.

For example, say you want to create a program that allows the user to select a shape, input some measurements, and get back the area of that shape. Here is one possible pseudocode solution:

```
Welcome user to your program
Display a list of shapes for the user (int or string input?)
    Square, rectangle, triangle, circle
Ask user to pick a shape
```

```
If shape is square, ask user for height
    Calculate and return area (height * height)
If shape is rectangle, ask user for height and width
    Calculate and return area (height * width)
If shape is triangle, ask user for base and height
    Calculate and return area (.5 * base * height)
If shape is circle, ask user for radius
    Calculate and return area (PI * radius * radius)
Show end of program message
```

Advantages of writing out pseudocode (and/or a flowchart) include all the following:

- You identify all instructions that the program will need to solve the problem, including input from the user and what the user will see when the program has finished running.

- You identify the variables, constants, and operations that the program will need.

- You create a structure that will work regardless of what the final program will look like or what language you will use to write it.

- Everyone on the development team can understand what the program will do, including designers who may not understand the programming language.

Pseudocode can also be in any human language. While you should use a common language like English for pseudocode that you will share with others, if you prefer to use a different language, you can write pseudocode in your own language for your own projects.

NOTE Meri Engle has a useful video that compares flowcharts and pseudocode that you can find at https://youtu.be/Qb2QrkrAfH8. This video contains suggestions for when to choose flowcharting versus pseudocode.

TIP Practice writing some pseudocode on your own. For example, you could write out instructions that a computer could use to make your favorite sandwich, wash dishes, or feed your pets. After writing out the instructions, ask someone else to read and follow them carefully. Did you miss any required steps?

Appendix C: Installing MySQL

MySQL is a **relational database management system (RDBMS)** that runs as a server providing multiuser access to multiple databases. Many Python programmers use MySQL with their Python applications. This appendix provides instructions for installing MySQL. By the end of this appendix, you should be able to have a MySQL database server and client working on your local system.

MySQL INSTALLATION

You can download and install MySQL using an installer. We're going to use MySQL's MSI installer to install MySQL to Windows. It installs everything we need for MySQL development and makes the 32-/64-bit decision for us.

> **NOTE** During installation, you will be asked to set the MySQL root user password. It is critical that you do *not* forget your root password. If you forget it, you won't be able to use your tools.

Download and Install MySQL

Browse to MySQL's download page at `https://dev.mysql.com/downloads/windows/installer/`. This should present you with options to select an MSI Installer. By default, Microsoft Windows should be selected for the Operating System. If you are using a different operating system, you can select it from the drop-down list. Note that this appendix will focus on Microsoft Windows; however, installing on other operating systems should be similar.

Two options are likely to be presented. Either download will work. The first is smaller because it fetches the necessary resources from the web. This means that the initial download is fast, but the installation process will take longer and require an internet connection throughout the process. The second includes all necessary resources. It will take longer to download, but once it is saved to your computer, you can install MySQL without being connected to the internet.

Choose the option that works best for you and click the appropriate *Download* button.

The MySQL site wants you to believe that an account is needed to download the software. While you can create an account if you think it will be useful, you can also simply click "*No thanks, just start my download*" under the login to save the file to a known location on your computer without creating an account.

When the download is complete, open the downloaded `mysql-installer-community-[version].msi` file to start the installer. This will start a wizard that you can step through. The installer will automatically check for problems, such as missing utilities or path conflicts. If you see an error, you will need to resolve the error before continuing the installation.

The following will help with selections you need to make during the installation:

- When prompted for a Setup Type, select *Developer Default* in the left column. This will install everything you need for development purposes.

- In the second dialog, review the products (tools) to be installed. You should see MySQL Server and MySQL Workbench included in the list, but it also includes connectors for a variety of languages, documentation for the current version of MySQL, and sample files that you can use to experiment with MySQL.

- Click *Execute* and relax. Installation takes a while. As the installation proceeds, you will see components being checked off the list as shown in Figure C.1.

> **NOTE** You can click the *Show Details* button to see the details of what is being installed.

If you see errors associated with any of the components, wait until everything else is installed and click the *Try Again* link for that component. If you still receive an error after the second try, click the *Show Details* button and scroll down (if necessary) to see the details of the error.

Configure MySQL

After the products are installed, you can click the *Next* button to continue to the *Product Configuration* options. For the most part, default options are sufficient. Click *Next* to start the product configuration options. The following will help in selecting options:

- If there is a *High Availability* option, use the default option Standalone MySQL Server / Classic MySQL Replication.

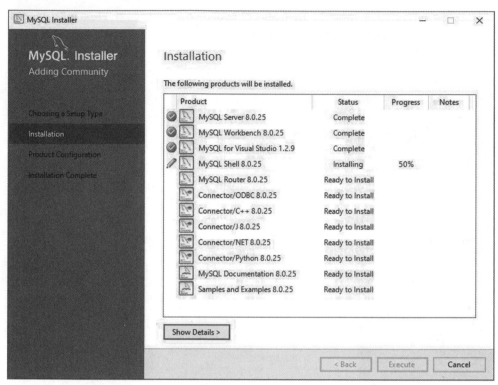

Figure C.1: MySQL Product installation

- Under *Type and Networking*, use the default options for Development Computer with TCP/IP, using the port number 3306, and open the Windows firewall port.

- For *Authentication Method*, we'll use the Legacy Authentication method. The stronger password encryption is a better option if you are running the MySQL server on a remote machine or if you are using sensitive data, but for the purposes of this book's lessons, we don't need that level of encryption.

- For *Accounts and Roles*, you will need to define a password for the root account. The root account is a "god" account that allows the user to do anything in the database, so in a typical installation that would include many users, this password should be extremely secure. In this case, you are doing a local install that only you can access, so a simple password is fine.

> **NOTE** Take note of the root password! You will need it later when you open MySQL.

- MySQL will run as a Windows Service and the default option to use the Windows Service named *MySQL80* and the standard system account is fine.

After all configuration options have been defined, click *Execute* on the Apply Configuration window. This will run through the steps as shown in Figure C.2 to configure the settings you selected.

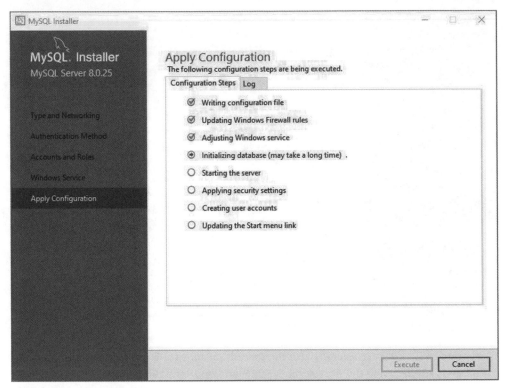

Figure C.2: Applying configuration settings

You should receive a message that the configuration was successful, and the *Finish* button should become available. If not, review the feedback, look over the configuration options again, and research ways to solve the problems.

Configure MySQL Router Options

When you click *Finish*, the installation wizard will return to the Product Configuration window and show that the configuration for MySQL Server is complete. Clicking the *Next* button will continue to the next item, which is the MySQL Router Configuration. The Router is only used for managing a database cluster, so we won't change anything here. You can click the *Finish* button on the MySQL Router Configuration page without making any changes.

Configure Samples and Examples

The installation wizard will again return to the Project Configuration window. Click *Next* to continue. You will be prompted to connect to the server.

At this point, a local MySQL Server should already be running. Enter the password you created for the **root** account and click *Check* to verify that you can connect to the server.

If everything is set up correctly and you entered the correct password, you will see a Connection succeeded message as shown in Figure C.3.

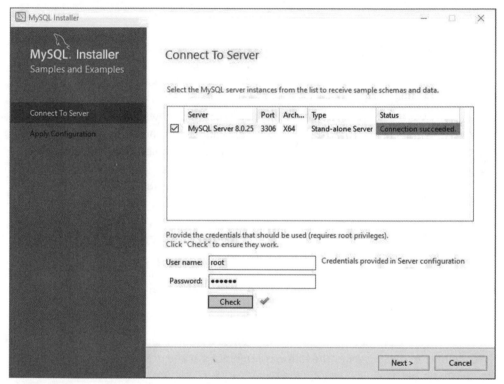

Figure C.3: Connecting successfully to the server

Click *Next* and then click *Execute* to apply the configurations you just defined. The installation wizard will install the Samples and Examples files and confirm that the configuration is complete. Click *Finish* to return to the Product Configuration window and then click *Next* to complete the installation.

The final step confirms that the installation is complete. Uncheck the boxes if you do not want to open MySQL Workbench or MySQL Shell immediately. You can then click *Finish* to close the wizard.

Installation and configuration are complete. You now have:

- The MySQL database server
- The MySQL shell: command-line query interface
- MySQL Workbench: GUI query interface and schema browser
- Documentation
- Samples
- MySQL connectors for various programming languages

VERIFY THE INSTALLATION

Let's use a command-line interface to verify that MySQL is installed and that you can connect to it. While MySQL Shell does provide a command-line interface for MySQL, it is not as straightforward as other options, including either the Windows Command Prompt or Windows PowerShell. We'll use the Command Line window for this step.

Start by determining where the `mysql.exe` file is on your computer. By default, it should be in `C:\Program Files\MySQL\MySQL Server 8.0\bin`, but if you installed the 32-bit version, it may be in `C:\Program Files (x86)\MySQL\MySQL Server 8.0\bin` instead. Once you have found the correct path, write it down or copy it to the Windows clipboard.

Open the Command Prompt by clicking the Start menu and keying **cmd** until you see *Command Prompt*. Click that option to open it.

In the Command Prompt, you need to navigate to the folder you just identified. Enter the following command, using the appropriate path for your computer:

```
cd C:\Program Files\MySQL\MySQL Server 8.0\bin
```

You should see the prompt in the Command Prompt window change to that directory.

To connect to MySQL, enter the following command at the prompt:

```
mysql -u root -p
```

This statement performs three tasks:

- It connects to MySQL.
- It identifies the user as root.
- It tells MySQL to prompt for the user password.

When you enter this command, you will see a password prompt as shown in Figure C.4.

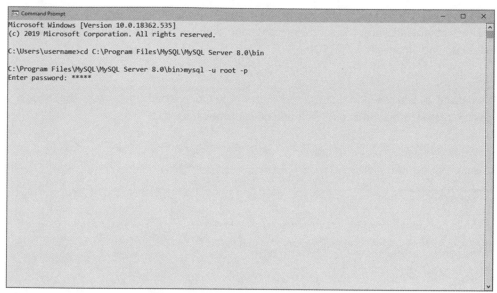

Figure C.4: Connecting to MySQL password prompt

Enter the password you set up during the installation process. In some versions, MySQL hides the password completely, so you may not see any sign that you have entered the password. If you enter the password correctly, you will see a MySQL prompt as shown in Figure C.5.

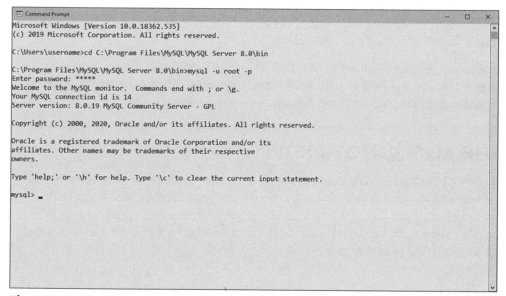

Figure C.5: The MySQL prompt

As noted by the MySQL welcome statement, commands end in ; or \g. We will use ; to end each command. Enter the following command, which will list all of the existing databases currently managed by MySQL:

```
show databases;
```

The databases you see (and that are shown in Figure C.6) are meta-databases that MySQL uses to track information about itself and how it is being used.

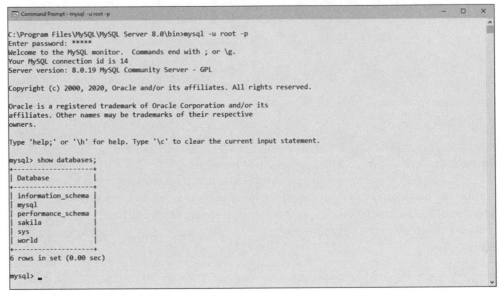

Figure C.6: The default meta-databases

If you were able to connect to MySQL and view the existing databases, you have installed MySQL and are set up for the lessons in this book. You can exit MySQL by entering quit; or by simply closing the Command Prompt window.

THE MySQL NOTIFIER

The MySQL data server is configured to start when your computer boots up and to always run in the background. If you want more control, consider installing the MySQL Notifier found at https://dev.mysql.com/downloads/windows/notifier/. The Notifier installs a system tray icon that shows the status of existing MySQL database servers and allows you to start and stop them.

Appendix D: Installing Vinyl DB

The Vinyl DB is a database that is used in the ETL program presented in Lessons 24 and 25 of this book. This appendix provides you with structure for the database and the code for a script you can use to create the SQL database.

DATABASE STRUCTURE

The database itself references the inventory for a vinyl record store that employees can use to look up songs, albums, and artists. The structure of the database is presented in Figure D.1.

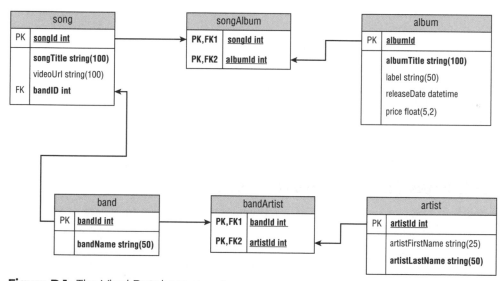

Figure D.1: The Vinyl Database structure

In list format, the database structure looks like the following:

```
song
      songId (PK) int
      songTitle string(100)
      videoUrl string(100)
      bandId (FK) int
songAlbum
      songId (PK, FK) int
      albumId (PK, FK) int
album
      albumId (PK) int
      albumTitle string(100)
      label string(50)
      releaseDate date
      price float(5,2)
band
      bandId (PK) int
      bandName string(50)
bandArtist
      bandId (PK, FK) int
      artistId (PK, FK) int
artist
      artistId (PK)
      artistFirstName string(25)
      artistLastName string(50)
```

CREATE THE DATABASE

The script in Listing D.1 creates the database. You can run this script in any MySQL interface, including MySQL Server with MySQL Workbench.

LISTING D.1

Script to create Vinyl Database

```
-- Running this script will DELETE the existing database and all data it contains.
-- Use with caution.

DROP DATABASE IF EXISTS vinylrecordshop;

CREATE DATABASE vinylrecordshop;

USE vinylrecordshop;
```

```
CREATE TABLE album (
    albumId INT AUTO_INCREMENT,
    albumTitle VARCHAR(100) NOT NULL,
    label VARCHAR(50),
    releaseDate DATE,
    price DECIMAL(5,2),
    CONSTRAINT pk_album
        PRIMARY KEY (albumId)
);

CREATE TABLE artist (
    artistId INT NOT NULL AUTO_INCREMENT,
    fname VARCHAR(25) NOT NULL,
    lname VARCHAR(50) NOT NULL,
    isHallOfFame TINYINT NOT NULL,
    CONSTRAINT pk_artist
        PRIMARY KEY (artistId)
);

CREATE TABLE band (
    bandId INT AUTO_INCREMENT,
    bandName VARCHAR(50) NOT NULL,
    CONSTRAINT pk_band
        PRIMARY KEY (bandId)
);

CREATE TABLE song (
    songId INT NOT NULL AUTO_INCREMENT,
    songTitle VARCHAR(100) NOT NULL,
    videoUrl VARCHAR(100),
    bandId INT NOT NULL,
    CONSTRAINT pk_song
        PRIMARY KEY (songId),
    CONSTRAINT fk_song_band
        FOREIGN KEY (bandID)
        REFERENCES band(bandId)
);

CREATE TABLE songAlbum (
    songId INT,
    albumId INT,
    CONSTRAINT pk_songAlbum
        PRIMARY KEY (songId, albumId),
    CONSTRAINT fk_songAlbum_song
        FOREIGN KEY (songId)
        REFERENCES song(songId),
```

```
            CONSTRAINT fk_songAlbum_album
                FOREIGN KEY (albumId)
                REFERENCES album(albumId)
);

CREATE TABLE bandArtist (
    bandId INT,
    artistId INT,
    CONSTRAINT pk_bandArtist
        PRIMARY KEY (bandId, artistId),
    CONSTRAINT fk_bandArtist_band
        FOREIGN KEY (bandId)
        REFERENCES band(bandId),
    CONSTRAINT fk_bandArtist_artist
        FOREIGN KEY (artistId)
        REFERENCES artist (artistId)
);

-- This script will add data to the tables created in the vinylrecordshop-schema script.
-- Add data to the primary tables first.

USE vinylrecordshop;

INSERT INTO album (albumId,albumTitle, releaseDate, price, label)
VALUES
    ROW (1,'Imagine','1971-9-9',9.99,'Apple'),
    ROW (2,'22525 (Exordium & Terminus)','1969-7-1',25.99,'RCA'),
    ROW (3,"No One's Gonna Change Our World",'1969-12-12',39.35,'Regal Starline'),
    ROW (4,'Moondance Studio Album', '1969-8-1',14.99,'Warner Bros'),
    ROW (5,'Clouds', '1969-5-1', 9.99,'Reprise'),
    ROW (6,'Sounds of Silence Studio Album', '1966-1-17',9.99,'Columbia'),
    ROW (7,'Abbey Road', '1969-1-10',12.99,'Apple'),
    ROW (9,'Smiley Smile', '1967-9-18',5.99,'Capitol');

INSERT INTO 'artist' VALUES
(1,'John','Lennon',1),(2,'Paul','McCartney',1),(3,'George','Harrison',1),(4,'Ringo','Sta
rr',1),(5,'Denny','Zager',0),(6,'Rick','Evans',0),(10,'Van','Morrison',1),(11,'Judy',
'Collins',0),(12,'Paul','Simon',1),(13,'Art','Garfunkel',0),(14,'Brian','Wilson',0),(
15,'Dennis','Wilson',0),(16,'Carl','Wilson',0),(17,'Ricky','Fataar',0),(18,'Blondie','
Chaplin',0),(19,'Jimmy','Page',0),(20,'Robert','Plant',0),(21,'John
Paul','Jones',0),(22,'John','Bonham',0),(23,'Mike ','Love',0),(24,'Al ',
'Jardine',0),(25,'David','Marks',0),(26,'Bruce ','Johnston',0);

INSERT INTO 'band' VALUES (1,'The Beatles'),(2,'Zager and Evans'),(3,'Van
Morrison'),(4,'Judy Collins'),(5,'Simon and Garfunkel'),(7,'Beach Boys'),(8,'Led
Zeppelin');
```

```
INSERT INTO 'song' VALUES (1,'Imagine','https://youtu.be/DVg2EJvvlF8',1),(2,'In the
Year 2525','https://youtu.be/izQB2-Kmiic',2),(3,'Across the
Universe','https://youtu.be/Tjq9LmSO1eI',1),(4,'Moondance','https://youtu.be/6lFxGBB4UG',
3),(5,'Both Sides Now','https://youtu.be/rQOuxByR5VI',4),(6,'Sounds of
Silence','https://youtu.be/qn0QBXMYXsM',5),(7,'Something','https://youtu.be/xLGe-
QzCK4Q',1),(9,'Good Vibrations','https://youtu.be/d8rd53WuojE',7),(10,'Come
Together','https://youtu.be/_HONxwhwmgU',1),(11,'Something','https://youtu.be/UKAp-
jRUp2o',1),(12,'Maxwell\'s Silver Hammer','https://youtu.be/YQgsob_o1io',1);

INSERT INTO 'bandartist' VALUES
(1,1),(1,2),(1,3),(1,4),(2,5),(2,6),(3,10),(4,11),(5,12),(5,13),(7,14),(7,15),(7,16
),(7,17),(7,18),(8,19),(8,20),(8,21),(8,22),(7,23),(7,24),(7,25),(7,26);

INSERT INTO 'songalbum' VALUES
(1,1),(2,2),(3,3),(4,4),(5,5),(6,6),(7,7),(9,9),(10,7),(11,7),(12,7);
```

> **NOTE** The script in Listing D.1 is available within the Appendix D folder
> found in the Lesson Listings folder of the JobReadyPython.zip file that can
> be downloaded from www.wiley.com/go/jobreadypython.

Appendix E: Installing MongoDB

This appendix provides instructions for downloading, installing, and running MongoDB using MongoDB Community Server. The instructions that follow assume that you are using Windows. If you are using Mac OS or Linux, please select the appropriate options for that OS.

INSTALLING MongoDB COMMUNITY SERVER

Because MongoDB is a server-based software package, you will need to install both a server that will run on your local computer and the client software that will access the local host. Let's start by installing the server.

Navigate to the MongoDB download page (`https://www.mongodb.com/try/download`) and click the option for MongoDB Community Server as shown in Figure E.1.

This will expand the MongoDB Community Server tab and present a form that can be used for selecting and downloading as shown in Figure E.2.

In the form on the right side, you will see drop-down options for selecting the version, platform, and package you want to download. Select the current version. You can then click the *Download* button to start the process of downloading the msi installation file for Windows.

> **NOTE** On the menu at the top of the page shown in Figure E.2 is an option for *Docs*. You can click *Docs* to see links to a variety of documents and support options that could be useful to you as a new user. You will find a number of how-to guides as well.

After the download is complete, open the saved file to start the installation. This will start the setup wizard as shown in Figure E.3.

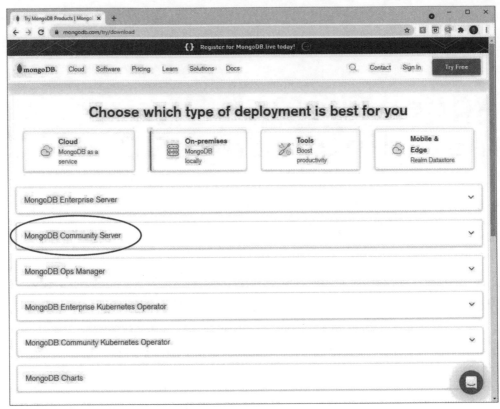

Figure E.1: Download page for MongoDB

Follow the prompts to perform a complete installation. When you are asked to set up a Service Configuration similar to what is shown in Figure E.4, select *Run service as a local or domain user*, using the following options:

- **Account Domain:** . (a period with no text)
- **Account Name:** The user account name that you use to log in to the computer you are using
- **Account Password:** The password that you use to log in to the computer you are using

All other options should use the default settings. Take note of the path to the Data Directory—you will need it to run MongoDB later. By default, it should be `C:\Program Files\MongoDB\Server\4.4\data`, although this may be slightly different on some machines and based on the current version at the time you download the file.

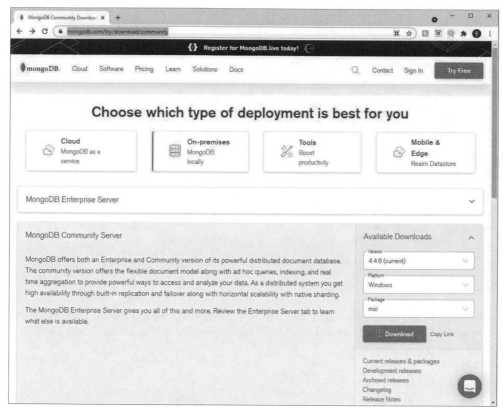

Figure E.2: MongoDB download form

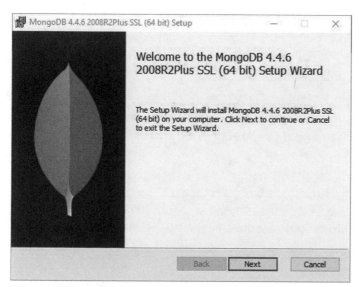

Figure E.3: MongoDB Setup Wizard

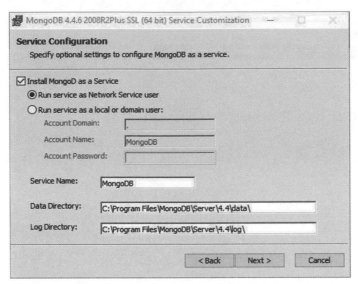

Figure E.4: Service Configuration dialog box

In the next step, you have the option to install MongoDB Compass, a GUI interface provided with MongoDB as shown in Figure E.5. This book will use only a text-based interface, so Compass is optional.

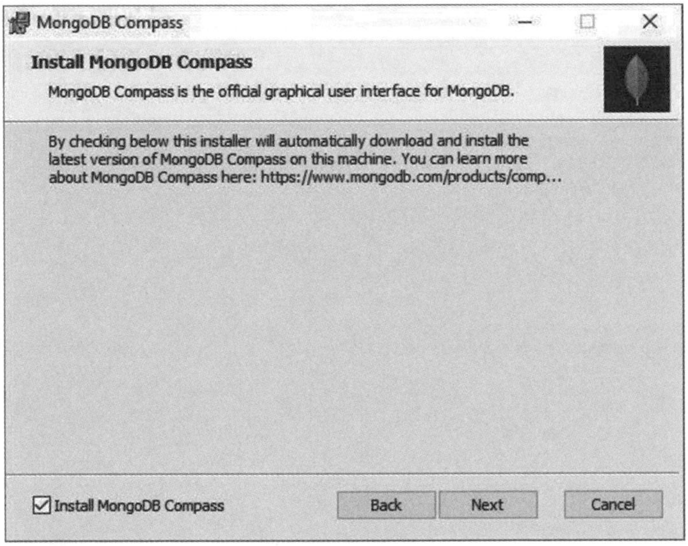

Figure E.5: Install MongoDB Compass window

For the remaining steps, use the default options and allow the installation process to run. As shown in Figure E.6, the installation wizard will show the status of the installation as it progresses.

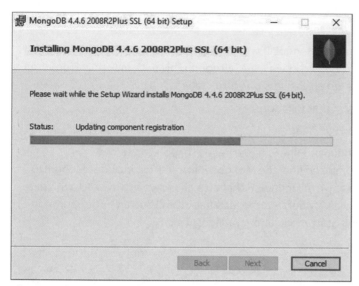

Figure E.6: Installation in progress

You will receive a confirmation once the installation process is complete as shown in Figure E.7.

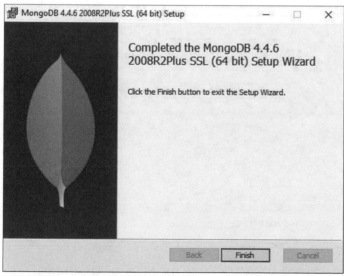

Figure E.7: Confirmation window

RUNNING MongoDB

Once you have MongoDB installed on the local computer, you can run the software using the following steps:

1. Open Windows File Explorer.

2. Navigate to the path where MongoDB was installed. By default, the path will be `C:\Program Files\MongoDB\Server\4.4`, although this path may be different on some machines and based on the version you installed.

3. Open the bin directory in that location.

4. Open the file named `mongo.exe`.

MongoDB will open in a command-line window, ready for you to use.

As an alternative to the command line, the MongoDB installation includes MongoDB Compass, a GUI interface as shown in Figure E.8 that also allows you to interact with databases stored on the local service. By default, the installation will add an option for *MongoDBCompass* to the Windows Start menu under *MongoDB Inc*.

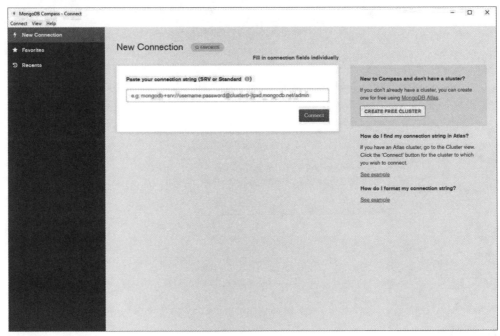

Figure E.8: The MongoDB Compass interface

NOTE For more information about Compass see the MongoDB Compass Documentation at `https://docs.mongodb.com/compass/master`.

Appendix F: Importing to MongoDB

In this appendix, we will learn how to use the mongoimport utility to move the contents of a JSON file into a collection in MongoDB. Specifically, we will import a dataset that contains user reviews for an ecommerce store to a MongoDB collection.

You will need to download a copy of this JSON file. You can find this file in the data directory of the JobReadyPython.zip file located at www.wiley.com/go/jobreadypython. You'll want to download the zip file and a save a copy of the data.json file to a known location on your computer.

To import a file into a MongoDB collection, we need to use the mongoimport utility in the Windows command line. This utility allows us to import data from popular file formats such as JSON, CSV, or TSV. Similarly, there is also a mongoexport utility that allows us to export the content of a collection into standard file formats such as JSON, CSV, or TSV.

Open the Windows command-line window:

1. Click the *Start* button or the Windows 10 search box.

2. Key the command **cmd** in the search box and select *Command Prompt* in the results.

NOTE It is assumed you have MongoDB installed. If not, see Appendix E for information on installing MongoDB.

On the command line, use the following command to navigate to the MongoDB bin directory. If necessary, adjust the path to reflect the correct path on your computer:

```
cd C:\Program Files\MongoDB\Server\4.0\bin
```

Enter the following command, using the appropriate path to the saved data.json file:

```
mongoimport --db amazon_reviews --collection musical_instruments --type json --file /PATH/TO/JSON/FILE/data.json
```

- We use `mongoimport` to copy the JSON file to a collection on MongoDB.

- `--db` refers to the database where the collection will be created. In this example, we are creating a new database called `amazon_reviews`.

- `--collection` refers to the collection name where the data will be stored. In this example, the table is called `musical_instruments`.

- `--type` refers to the file format. Here, we are using a JSON file, but we can also use other formats such as CSV and TSV.

- `--file` refers to the path where the JSON file is stored.

Figure F.1 shows how to import the JSON file using mongoimport. You can see that we successfully imported 10,261 reviews to the `musical_instruments` collection.

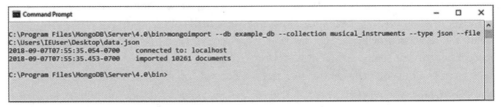

Figure F.1: Import confirmation

Switch back to the Mongo shell and confirm that the collection imported correctly:

```
> use amazon_reviews;
switched to db amazon_reviews
> db.musical_instruments.find();
```

If the collection imported correctly, you will see a partial set of the same data that appears in the original `data.json` file. Once you have confirmed that the data imported correctly, you can close the Windows command-line interface.

Index

A

a argument, 404
abbreviation: name pairs, 229
absolute path, 401
abstraction
    defined, 314
    as a principle of OOP, 314
account balance, summing, 483–484
Add file icon (Replit), 12
add( ) method
    example of, 297–298
    within a set, 262, 263
add_condiment method, 353
adding
    constants to lib.py file, 522
    content to text files, 412–415
    dictionary objects to CSV files,
        441–442
    drinks to order, 360–362
    exception handler to functions, 517
    exception handling to extract
        class, 594–601
    extract.fromCSV method, 534–535
    fromMONGODB method, 542–543
    methods to Person class, 320–321
    multiple exceptions, 496
    sides to order, 362–363
    transactions via dictionaries, 442–443
Adding Attributes exercise, 344–345
Adding New Names exercise, 280
algorithms
    defined, 613

purpose of, 102
    use of, 31–32
Alice's Adventures in Wonderland files, 400
All About Cars exercise, 446
All About You exercise, 203
Anaconda Distribution
    about, 14–15
    Jupyter Notebook installation, 15–16
and logic operation, 92
And the Total Is... exercise, 169
anonymous functions, 467
append( ) method
    within lists, 189
    tuples and, 214
appending data, 436–439
applying timestamps, 384–387
Are You Rich? exercise, 115
area of a circle, hard-coded constants
    within, 44
arguments
    arbitrary, 304–306
    defined, 296
    keyword, 306–308
arithmetic, dates and, 387–388
* (asterisk), within functions, 304
attributes
    adding, 344–345
    as a component of classes, 315
    datetime, 379–380
    defined, 314
    Person class with multiple, 318–319
average opening price, calculating, 429–430

B

\ (backslash), 54–55, 402
Bad Stock Market Day exercise, 488
banking application
    character storing and, 154–155
    classes representing employees
        in, 322–324
    classes with overriding in, 341–343
    clear() method within, 255
    comments within, 57
    comparative operators within, 96
    concatenating lists within, 197
    concatenating tuples within, 217
    debt ratio calculation example, 87–88
    default values within, 302–303
    defining function within, 300
    dictionary copying within, 251–252
    dictionary creation within, 226
    dictionary updating within, 247–249
    dictionary use within, 230, 235–236
    example of, 53–55
    functions within, 85
    get() method within, 240–241
    high wealth accounts within, 252–254
    identifying data types within, 72–74
    if statement use within, 105–107
    if-else statements within, 111–112
    input() function within, 58–59
    iterating through employees
        within, 165–167
    list accessing within, 183–184
    list creating within, 177–178
    list insertions within, 191–192
    list use within, 181–182, 190
    logic operations within, 94–95
    for loop within, 150–151
    menu selection capturing within, 60
    negative indexing with tuples within, 211
    in operator use within, 246
    PEMDAS within, 78–80
    pop() method within, 242–244
    regular tasks within, 300–301
    rounding within, 82–83
    sequence statements within, 103
    sets within, 261, 265, 266–267, 267–268,
        270, 271–272, 273–274, 277–278, 279
    simple interest calculation
        example, 88–89
    slice() function within, 188–189
    string splitting within, 154, 162–163
    strings within, 153
    tuple within, 207
    updating with numeric variables, 76–77
    username checking within, 108–109
    using class attribute in account class, 326
    using inheritance with tellers who are
        employees, 337–338
    using methods in, 321–322
    with variables and formatting, 63
    variables for, 71–72, 73–74
    while loop within, 148, 150–151
base class
    creating, 335
    defined, 334
Basic Inheritance exercise, 344
Beginning Regular Expressions (Watt), 521
bin function, 82
binary arithmetic operations, 70, 74–77
binary values, 39
body, loop, 145
bool() function, 90–92
Boolean data types, 89–92
Boolean values, 39
branches, in flowcharts, 613, 614–615
Broken Names exercise, 67
Broken Variables exercise, 67
Building a Burger Shop application
    creating classes, 351–352
    creating food_item class, 352–357
    creating main file, 357–364
    displaying output, 364
    planning code for, 350–351
    requirements for, 350
    tying code files together, 364–367
built-in exceptions, 492–493
built-in functions, 296
burger class, creating, 353–354

C

calculating
average opening price, 429–430
closing price, 433–434
difference in days, 388–390
sums, 481–482
camelCase, 34
`capitalize()` method, within sets, 274
case sensitivity
about, 34
of data entry, 156–157
example of, 55–56
of programming languages, 34
string searching and, 163
case structure, working with, 55–56
Cats or Dogs exercise, 115
`ceil(x)` function
defined, 83
use of, 85
characters
case ignoring of, 157
converting to uppercase, 473
slicing list of, 185
storing, 154–155
`check_numbers` function, 500
child class, creating, 335–336
class attributes
about, 324–325
`manager` class with, 325–326
static methods, 326–328
using in account class, 326
class methods, 316, 328–330
classes
base, 334, 335
`burger`, 353–354
child, 335–336
`combo`, 355
components of, 315–316
creating for Building a Burger Shop
application, 351–352
`datetime`, 372–376, 379–383
defined, 314
defining, 314–316
derived, 334
`DictReader`, 430–431
`DictWriter`, 440–443
`Director`, 338–340
`drink`, 354
`Employee`, 335, 336–337, 337–338,
338–340
`extract` (See `extract` class)
`food_item`, creating, 352–357
general exception, 502–505
`IOError` exception, 502–505
`load` (See `load` class)
`manager`, with class attribute, 325–326
`MathFormula`, 326–327, 328
`order`, 356–357
`parent`, 334, 335
`Person`, 317–321, 336–340
representing employees in banking
application, 322–324
`Sales`, 329
`side`, creating, 354–355
`Teller`, 337–338
`timedelta`, 387–388
`timestamp`, 384–387
`transform` (See `transform` class)
Classy Vehicles exercise, 331
`clear()` method
about, 254–255
defined, 225
within sets, 270–272
`close()` method, 403, 405
closing price, calculating, 433–434
code file
renaming (Replit), 11–12
saving locally (Replit), 12
code planning, for Building a Burger Shop
application, 350–351
`--collection`, 644
: (colon), within function code block, 297
columns
removing from data sources, 552–556
removing multiple, 558–561
renaming, 551–552
renaming multiple, 556–558

Combination of the Two exercise, 422
Combination of Them All exercise, 422
combo class, creating, 355
commands
    defined, 51
    print( ), 51–52, 62–63
    single-line, 51–52
comma-separated value (CSV) files
    appending data, 436–439
    creating dataset lists, 432–434
    iterating through, 427–429
    processing, 425–446
    reading, 426–430
    using DictReader class, 430–431
    using map( ) function on, 474–475
    using writerow( ) method, 434–436
    writing rows as lists, 439–440
    writing rows from dictionaries, 440–443
comments
    adding, 56–57
    defined, 50
Company Bank Account exercise, 461
Company Picnic exercise, 116
Company Stocks exercise, 444–445
comparative operators, 95–96
comparing
    dates, 382
    datetime values, 381–383
comparison operators
    about, 35–36
    using reduce( ) with, 484
Compass, 642
A Complete List Program exercise, 203–204
A Complete Tuple Program exercise, 220–221
computational thinking, 31–32
computer programming, future of, 30
computers
    binary language of, 33, 101
    functions of, 31
compute_sum( ) function, 305–306
compute_word_count function, 524–525
compute_word_count_dataset function, 526
compute_word_count_review
    function, 525–526

Computing the Square Root exercise,
    487
Concatenating Files exercise, 508
concatenating strings, 471
condition statement, 104
conditional operators
    defined, 102
    examples of, 106
conditional statements
    about, 106–107
    embedded, 112–114
    within income tax calculator
        exercise, 125–127
    list comprehension within, 199
configuring
    MySQL, 624–628
    MySQL router options, 626
    samples and examples, 627–628
Confirming an Attribute exercise, 584
Console window (Replit), 8
constants
    about, 44–46
    adding to lib.py file, 522
    in lib.py file, 526
constructors, 314
content
    adding to text files, 412–415
    limiting, 406–407
    overwriting of text files,
        415–417
control structures
    overview of, 101–102
    purpose of, 144
    selection, 102
    sequence, 102
converting
    characters to uppercase, 473
    to JSON files with dumps( )
        function, 449–450
    from JSON to dictionaries, 453
    JSON-encoded objects to dictionaries,
        452–453
    to static methods for extract class,
        586–588, 594–601

to static methods for `load` class, 592–594

to static methods for `transform` class, 588–592

Converting a Text File to Uppercase exercise, 487

`copy()` method, 225, 251–252

`cos(x)` function, 83

Count the Numbers exercise, 170

Counting exercise, 27–28

counting words in reviews, 524–528

Create Your Own Class exercise, 331

creating

    base class, 335

    `burger` class, 353–354

    child class, 335–336

    classes for Building a Burger Shop application, 351–352

    `combo` class, 355

    custom dates with named parameters, 381

    custom `datetime` objects, 380–381

    custom extractor for `extract` class, 601–607

    databases, 632–635

    dataset lists, 432–434

    `datetime`, 376

    dictionaries for rows in CSV files, 430–431

    `drink` class, 354

    `Employee` class, 336–337

    exceptions, 502

    `extract.fromJSON` method, 536–537

    `extract.fromMongoDB` method, 542–543

    `extract.fromMySQL` method, 538–539

    `food_item` class, 352–357

    `fromCSV` method, 535–536

    `head` method, 547–550

    JSON files with `dump()` function, 448–449

    lambda functions, 468–469

    lists from datasets, 432–433

    `load.toCSV` method, 570–572

    `load.toJSON` method, 572–574

    `load.toMONGODB` method, 578–581

    `load.toMySQL` method, 574–578

    main file, 357–364

    objects, 316–317

    `order` class, 356–357

    `order_once`, 358–359

    orders, 357–358

    parent class, 335

    `Person` object, 317–318

    `side` class, 354–355

    `tail` method, 547–550

    target database, 576

    text files, 417–418

    variables for dates, 372–376

    variables for time, 375–376

Creating a List from a File exercise, 508

Creating Tuples exercise, 219

CSV files. *See* comma-separated value (CSV) files

{} (curly brackets), 513

Current Value exercise, 98, 507–508

custom extractor, creating for `extract` class, 601–607

Customize installation link (Python), 25

D

Daily Tasks exercise, 47

data

    appending, 436–439

    examining, 512–513

    importing to MongoDB, 542

    reading, 514–517

    sequential flow of, 103

    structure of, 174–175, 224

    transforming, 563–567

data analysis and exception handling

    combining exception types, 498–500

    counting words in reviews, 524–528

    examining data, 512–513

    `except` statement, 493–495

    extracting, transforming, and loading (ETL) scripting, 531–584

    `FileNotFoundError`, 495

    `finally` statement, 505–506

general exception classes, 502–505

improving ETL scripting, 585–609

lambdas, 467–489

reading data, 514–517

tokenizing datasets, 517–524

`try` statement, 493–495

using multiple operations in a `try` statement, 500–501

using `raise` keyword, 501–502

Word Analysis in Python, 511–530

working with multiple excepts, 495–498

`ZeroDivisionError`, 492–500

data collections, as data type, 39–40

data types

    data collections as, 39–40

    date/time as, 39

    defined, 50, 70

    identifying, 72–74

    number, 70–72

    numbers within, 38–39

    overview of, 37–42

    review of, 70

    text within, 38

    true/false within, 39

    variables and, 43–44

databases, creating, 632–635

dataset lists, creating, 432–434

datasets

    creating lists from, 432–433

    tokenizing, 517–524, 522–523

    word count for, 526–528

Date Calculators exercise, 396–397

`date()` method, 375–376

date string, splitting, 377–379

Date Validity exercise, 609

dates and times

    about, 372

    applying timestamps, 384–387

    arithmetic and dates, 387–388

    calculating difference in days, 388–390

    comparing `datetime` values, 381–383

    creating custom `datetime` objects, 380–381

    as data type, 39

    getting current, 376–377

    getting started, 372–376

    splitting date strings, 377–379

    Universal Time Coordinated (UTC) format, 383–384

    using date without time, 390–391

    using `datetime` attributes, 379–380

    using time without date, 392–393

`datetime` class

    about, 372–375

    comparing values, 381–383

    creating, 376

    creating custom objects, 380–381

    extracting with attributes, 379–380

    using attributes, 379–380

`datetime` module, 372

`datetime.utcnow()` method, 383–384

Day of Week exercise, 608

`--db`, 644

debt ratio, calculating, 87–88

decimal values, 39

`def` keyword, within user-defined function, 297, 300–301

defining

    classes, 314–316

    `transform` class, 546–547

definite iteration

    defined, 145

    `for` loop and, 145–146

`del` keyword

    defined, 196

    tuples and, 215–216

    use of, 194

deleting

    removing *versus,* 194

    text files, 419–421

derived class, 334

designing custom ETL scripts, 532–534

desktop, of Replit, 8

Determining Prime exercise, 487

Diagrams, 616

dialog boxes

    Extension (Visual Studio Code), 22

    Files (Replit), 12

Sign-up (Replit), 6
Welcome (Replit), 7
diamonds, in flowcharts, 615–616, 619
dictionaries
    about, 224–226
    adding transactions via, 442–443
    clear() method within, 225
    clearing, 254–255
    converting from JSON to, 453
    converting JSON-encoded objects
        to, 452–453
    copy() method within, 225, 251–252
    creating, 226
    creating for rows in CSV files, 430–431
    creating JSON files from, 448–449
    defined, 174, 175, 224
    duplicating, 249–254
    generating, 227–230
    get() method within, 225, 239–241
    items() method within, 225, 234–239
    keys() method within, 225, 233–234, 245
    pop() method within, 225, 241–244, 254
    retrieving items from, 230–232
    separating, 237–239
    sets versus, 260
    update() method within, 225, 246–249
    updating referenced, 250–251
    values() method within, 225, 234–236
    working with items within, 232
    working with operators within, 245–246
    writing rows from, 440–443
DictReader class, 430–431
DictWriter class
    adding dictionary objects to CSV
        files, 441–442
    writing rows from dictionaries, 440–443
difference() method, within sets, 274–276
Digital Music review set, 512
Director class, 338–340
discard() method, within sets, 268–270
display() function
    default parameters and, 303
    overriding, 340–341
    overview of, 301–303, 307–308

display_customer_input()
    function, 304–305
display_info() method, 322
displaying
    date without time, 390–391
    output, 364
    time without date, 392–393
Displaying Dates exercise, 394–395
Displaying Text exercise, 66
Do the Math exercise, 99–100
docstrings, 296
documentation, importance of, 285
Dogs and Cats exercise, 345
"" (double quotes), 176
doubles, 39
downloading MySQL, 623–624
Drawings, 616
Draw.io, 616
drink class, creating, 354
drinks, adding to order, 360–362
dump() function, creating JSON files
    with, 448–449
dumps() function
    converting to JSON files with, 449–450
    formatting JSON data, 450–452
dynamic typing
    about, 43
    within Python, 61

E

e function, 83
elements, 175
ElementTreeXML API, 603
elif statement
    about, 109–110
    example of, 127
embedded conditions, 112–114
Employee class, 335, 336–337, 337–338,
    338–340
encapsulation
    defined, 314
    as a principle of OOP,
        314

end parameter, 185
Engle, Meri, 622
errors
    within IDEs, 10
    within numbers, 86
ETL scripting. *See* extracting, transforming,
    and loading (ETL) scripting
Everywhere That Mary Went... exercise,
    280–281
examining data, 512–513
except statement, 493–495, 503
exception handling. *See* data analysis and
    exception handling
exchange rates, summing, 476
exercises
    Adding Attributes, 344–345
    Adding New Names, 280
    All About Cars, 446
    All About You, 203
    Are You Rich?, 115
    Bad Stock Market Day, 488
    Basic Inheritance, 344
    Broken Variables, 67
    Cats or Dogs, 115
    Classy Vehicles, 331
    Combination of the Two, 422
    Combination of Them All, 422
    Company Bank Account, 461
    Company Picnic, 116
    Company Stocks, 444–445
    A Complete List Program, 203–204
    A Complete Tuple Program, 220–221
    Computing the Square Root, 487
    Concatenating Files, 508
    Confirming an Attribute, 584
    Converting a Text File to Uppercase, 487
    Count the Numbers, 170
    Counting, 27–28
    Create Your Own Class, 331
    Creating a List from a File, 508
    Creating Tuples, 219
    Current Value, 98, 507–508
    Daily Tasks, 47
    Date Calculators, 396–397

Date Validity, 609
Day of Week, 608
Determining Prime, 487
Displaying Dates, 394–395
Displaying Text, 66
Do the Math, 99–100
Dogs and Cats, 345
For Every Season..., 115–116
Everywhere That Mary Went..., 280–281
File System, 347
Finding the Largest, 310
Five Seconds in the Future, 395
Fixing the Code, 66–67
Fizz Buzz, 170–171
Follow the Comments, 66
Formatted Account Information, 461
Fruit Finder, 168
Fruity Code, 28
High and Low All in One, 257
Highest Number, 487
Highest Opening Price, 488
Highest Price at Closing, 489
Highest Stock Market Volume, 488
Highest Value, 488
Hourly Employees, 345–347
Identify the Numbers, 169
Identifying Absolute Value, 487
Integers Only, 98
It's Divisible, 169
Keeping It Short, 168
Last Key, 487
Leap Years, 395
Length without len( ), 170
Line by Line, 280
List Deletion, 203
List Modification, 203
Listing Duplicates, 609
Listing Lines, 422
Listing Text, 423
Longest Word, 422
Lower Numbers, 309
Lowest Number, 487
Manipulated Math, 97–98
Modifying Tuples, 219–220

Movies, 463
Multiplication Tables, 169
New York Restaurants, 462
Nobel Prizes, 461–462
One Letter at a Time, 170
The Past, 395
Playing with Numbers, 99
Pop Music Evolution, 445–446
Popping Accounts, 280
Prompting the User, 97
Python Programming, 47
Reading Lines, 422, 444, 508
Rearranging Files, 445
Removing an Attribute, 583
Removing Duplicates, 609
Renaming an Attribute, 583
Revisiting Lessons Learned, 608
Say Hello, 27
Self-Assessment, 257–258, 281,
    489, 508–509
Separating the High from the
    Low, 256–257
Separating Your Fruits, 168
Setting Future Days, 395
Shopping List, 203
Simple Calculator, 310
Simple Interest, 98
Streamlined Banking, 331
Street Addresses, 100
Sum of Even, 488
Sum of Positive Numbers, 488
Sum of Prime Numbers, 169–170
Text in Reverse, 423
This Will Be, 309–310
And the Total Is…, 169
Transforming CSV to CSV, 583
Transforming CSV to JSON, 583
Transforming JSON to CSV, 583
Transforming JSON to JSON, 583
Transforming Names, 609
True or False, 99
True or False Quiz, 115
Typing Numbers, 507
Unix Dates, 395

Using a Calculator in Class, 331–332
What's It Do?, 27
Where Are You?, 67
Where's Waldo, 220
Which Is Greater?, 310
Working with Text, 256
Yesterday, Today, and Tomorrow, 395
exists() method, 419
exit function, 296–297
Extension dialog box (Visual Studio Code), 22
Extension icon (Visual Studio Code), 22
extract class
    about, 534
    adding exception handling to, 594–601
    adding extract.fromCSV
        method, 534–536
    converting to static methods for,
        586–588, 594–601
    creating custom extractor for, 601–607
    creating extract.fromJSON
        method, 536–537
    creating extract.fromMongoDB
        method, 542–543
    creating extract.fromMySQL
        method, 538–540
    current, 541
    extract.py file, 534
    importing data to MongoDB, 542
    installing PyMySQL package, 538
    setting up VinylRecordShop
        database, 539
    using ETL script as external
        module, 545–546
    using fromCustom via imported, 607
    verifying extract.py module, 544–545
extract.fromCSV method, adding, 534–535
extract.fromJSON method, creating,
    536–537
extract.fromMongoDB method, creating,
    542–543
extract.fromMySQL method, creating,
    538–539
extracting, transforming, and loading
    (ETL) scripting

about, 532
adding exception handling in extract class, 594–601
converting to static methods for extract class, 586–588
converting to static methods for load class, 592–594
converting to static methods for transform class, 588–592
creating custom extractor for extract class, 601–607
designing and implementing custom scripts, 532–534
extract class, 534–546
improving, 585–609
load class, 569–581
transform class, 546–569
extracting, with datetime attributes, 379–380
extract_month function, 474
extract.py file
about, 534
with additional exception handling, 598–600
testing, 588
verifying module, 544–545

F

fabs(x) function, 83
False evaluation
from condition statements, 104, 105, 106–107
within sets, 265
within strings, 156
--file, 644
File System exercise, 347
FileNotFoundError exception, 495, 502–505
files
adding (Replit), 13
creating (Jupyter Notebook), 16–18
creating new (Replit), 12–13
opening, 504–505

opening existing (Jupyter Notebook), 20–21
Python, saving locally, 19–20
renaming (Jupyter Notebook), 18–19
renaming code (Replit), 11–12
saving code (Replit), 12
Files dialog box (Replit), 12
filter() function
combining with lambda() function, 479–480
using, 477–478
finally statement, 505–506
find_greater() function, 298–299
Finding the Largest exercise, 310
Five Seconds in the Future exercise, 395
Fixing the Code exercise, 66–67
Fizz Buzz exercise, 170–171
Flatland files, 400
float() function, 88–89
floats, 39, 70
floor(x) function
defined, 83
use of, 84
flow line, in flowcharts, 618
flow of control, 613
flowcharts
about, 613
additional elements, 618–620
benefits of, 104
branches, 613, 614–615
common shapes in, 615–620
example of, 104, 105, 616–618
for income tax calculator exercise, 120
loops, 613, 615
sequences, 613–614
folders, adding (Jupyter Notebook), 16–17
Follow the Comments exercise, 66
food_item class, creating, 352–357
For Every Season... exercise, 115–116
for loop
about, 145–146, 411, 433–434
example of, 254
keys() method and, 233–234
within list creation, 177

within a set, 261–262

while loop *versus,* 149–151

for operator, tuples and, 217–218

Formatted Account Information exercise, 461

formatting JSON data, 450–452

/ (forward slash), 402

fromCSV function, 474, 475

fromCSV method, creating, 535–536

fromCustom method, 603–607

fromMONGODB method, adding, 542–543

fromMySQL method, in extract class, 539–540

Fruit Finder exercise, 168

Fruity Code exercise, 28

function code blocks

    colon (:) within, 297

    defined, 296

functions

    about, 295–296, 308

    add(), 297–298

    adding exception handler to, 517

    anonymous, 467

    arbitrary arguments within, 304–306

    bin, 82

    bool(), 90–92

    built-in, 296

    ceil(x), 83, 85

    check_numbers, 500

    compute_sum(), 305–306

    compute_word_count, 524–525

    compute_word_count_dataset, 526

    compute_word_count_review, 525–526

    cos(x), 83

    creating to read characters from files, 407–408

    creating to read lines of text files, 409–410

    default input values within, 301–303

    defined, 81, 296

    defining in Python, 296–300

    display(), 301–303, 307–308, 340–341

    display_customer_input(), 304–305

    dump(), 448–449

    dumps(), 449–452

    e, 83

    exit, 296–297

extract_month, 474

fabs(x), 83

filter(), 477–480

find_greater(), 298–299

float(), 88–89

floor(x), 83, 84

fromCSV, 474, 475

gcd(x,y), 83

get_burger_order, 359–360

get_drink_order(), 360–362

get_side_order(), 362–363

head(), 407–408, 547–550

index(), 187

input(), 50, 57–60, 112, 402

int(), 88, 374

isqrt(x), 83

json.loads(), 452–453

lambda(), 475–476, 479–480

line_starts_with(), 411–412

list(), 244

load(), 453

map(), 468, 472–476

math, 81–83

math library, 83–85

myfunc, 471–472

my_function(), 306, 307

now(), 372, 376–377

open(), 402, 412

order_many, 360, 364

order_once, 358–359, 359–360

parameter syntax within, 303

pi, 84

placing lambda functions inside, 471–472

pow_n, 472

pow(x,y), 84

pprint(), 457–460

print(), 51–52, 62–63, 145, 403

read_csv, 432–434

read_json_file, 515–517

read_osv, 504–505

reduce(), 468, 480–485

round, 82

sin(x), 84

slice(), 187–189

sqrt(x), 84

syntax of, 300–301
tan(x), 84
today( ), 372, 376–377, 383
tokenize, 519–520, 521–522
tokenize_dataset, 522–523
tokenize_review, 523
for tokenizing reviews, 521–522
to_upper_case( ), 473
trunc(x), 84
user-defined, 296, 297
xml:extractor, 602–603

G

gcd(x,y) function, 83
get( ) method, 225, 239–241
get_burger_order function, 359–360
get_drink_order( ) function, 360–362
get_side_order( ) function, 362–363
got_chars.csv file, 535–536, 552

H

hard coding, with constants, 44
hash value, 105
head( ) function, 407–408, 547–550
header, loop, 145
Hello, World! phrase, 36–37
High and Low All in One exercise, 257
High Availability option, for MySQL, 624
Highest Number exercise, 487
Highest Opening Price exercise, 488
Highest Price at Closing exercise, 489
Highest Stock Market Volume exercise, 488
Highest Value exercise, 488
Hourly Employees exercise, 345–347

I

icons
    Add file (Replit), 12
    Extension (Visual Studio Code), 22
IDE. See integrated development
    environment (IDE)
Identify the Numbers exercise, 169

Identifying Absolute Value exercise, 487
IF, as reserved word, 35
if statement
    about, 374
    complexities of, 109
    for dictionary, 241
    example of, 105–106
    use of, 104
if-elif-else structure, within sets, 272, 274
if-else statements
    about, 108–109, 361
    example of, 111–112
    list comprehension within, 199
immutability, of tuples, 206, 213–216, 221
implementing custom ETL scripts, 532–534
import statement, 372, 520
importing
    data to MongoDB, 542
    to MongoDB, 643–644
improving extracting, transforming, and
    loading (ETL) scripting, 585–609
in operator
    within a set, 265
    tuples and, 217–218
    use of, 246
income tax calculator exercise
    application update within, 133–136
    calculating tax rate within, 124–132
    calculating taxable income
        within, 122–124
    conditional statement within, 125–127
    conversion additions within, 123–124
    elif statement within, 127
    gathering requirements for, 118–120
    input creation for, 120–122
    negative taxable income adjustments
        within, 134–136
    nested conditions within, 127–132
    program design within, 120
    standards for, 120
    user interface for, 119, 136–139
    values in use for, 119
indent, 451–452
index
    defined, 174
    for tuples, 209–210

index() function, 187
indexing
   of a list, 179–184
   negative, 210–211
inheritance
   about, 334–335
   at multiple levels, 338–340
   overriding methods, 340–343
   as a principle of OOP, 314
   using with tellers who are
      employees, 337–338
__init__ method, 317, 322, 324–325,
   337, 339, 340, 353–354, 380–381
input() function
   about, 402
   defined, 50
   example of, 112
   storing, 59–60
   use of, 57–59
input reviews
   tokenizing, 521–522
   word count for, 525–526
input strings, tokenizing, 518–521
inputs, working with multiple, 469–471
insert() method
   within lists, 190–192
   tuples and, 214
installing
   MongoDB Community Server, 637–642
   MySQL, 623–630
   PyMySQL package, 538
   Vinyl DB, 631–635
instance methods, 316
instantiation, 314
int() function, 88, 374
integers, 38, 70
Integers Only exercise, 98
integrated development environment (IDE).
   See also specific programs
   about, 284
   error indications within, 10
   indentation within, 145
   installing, 4
   syntax error within, 65

intersection() method, within
   sets, 277–278
IOError exception class, 502–505
isqrt(x) function, 83
items() method
   defined, 225
   example of, 244
   overview of, 234–236
iterating
   through CSV files, 427–429
   through JSON data, 454–457
   through text files, 410–412
   for totals, 456–457
iteration control structures
   about, 144
   through strings, 164–167
It's Divisible exercise, 169

J

Java, syntax variation of, 34
JavaScript Object Notation (JSON) files
   converting to, with dumps()
      function, 449–450
   creating with dump() function, 448–449
   formatting data, 450–452
   iterating through data, 454–457
   processing, 447–463
   reading, 515–516
   reading data, 457–460
   using json.loads() function, 452–453
   writing data, 457–460
JSON files. *See* JavaScript Object Notation
   (JSON) files
json.loads() function, 452–453
Jupyter Notebook
   about, 14–15
   file creation within, 16–18
   files, opening existing, 20–21
   folder adding within, 16–17
   installing, 15–16
   interface of, 16
   main file in, 357
   project file renaming within, 18–19

K

Keeping It Short exercise, 168
key: value method, keyword arguments and, 306
key: value pairs
    adding, 226
    within the dictionary, 225
keys, within dictionary, 225
keys() method
    defined, 225
    example of, 245
    review of, 236–239
    using, 233–234
keyword arguments
    about, 306
    arbitrary, 306–308
keywords
    in, 265
    about, 34–35
    def, 297, 300–301
    del, 194, 196, 215–216
    elif, 109–110
    self, 317

L

lambda() function
    combining with filter()
        function, 479–480
    combining with map() function,
        475–476
lambdas
    about, 467–468
    combining filter() and lambda()
        function, 479–480
    combining map() and lambda()
        function, 475–476
    creating lambda functions, 468–469
    placing lambda functions inside
        functions, 471–472
    using filter() function, 477–478
    using map() function, 472–475
    using reduce() function, 480–485
    working with multiple inputs, 469–471

Last Key exercise, 487
Leap Years exercise, 395
Legacy Authentication method, for
    MySQL, 625
len() method
    calculating length of sets with, 267
    within dictionary, 232
    exercise for, 170
    within lists, 179
    within tuples, 208
    use of, 152
Length without len() exercise, 170
lib.py file
    about, 514–517
    adding constants to, 522
    completed, 528–530
    current list of constants in, 526
limiting content, 406–407
Line by Line exercise, 280
lines, reading, 408–410
line_starts_with() function, 411–412
List Deletion exercise, 203
list() function, 244
List Modification exercise, 203
Listing Duplicates exercise, 609
Listing Lines exercise, 422
Listing Text exercise, 423
lists
    accessing end of, 183
    adding items to, 189–190
    checking for valid values, 499–500
    comprehension of, 197–199
    concatenating, 196–197
    conditional statements and, 199
    copying, 200–202
    creating, 175–178
    creating from datasets, 432–433
    defined, 174, 175, 224
    identification of, 264
    indexes, 179–182
    inserting items within, 190–192
    length determination for, 179
    negative indexing within, 182–184
    removing items from, 192–196
    slicing, 184–189

sorting, 199–200
structure of, 180
syntax of, 206
updating, 220
writing rows as, 439–440
writing to text files, 414–415
load class
about, 569–570
additional exception handling in, 600–601
converting to static methods for, 592–594
creating load.toCSV method, 570–572
creating load.toJSON method, 572–574
creating load.toMONGODB
method, 578–581
creating load.toMySQL method, 574–578
load.py file, 570
load() function, converting from JSON to
dictionaries, 453
load.py file
about, 570
testing, 594
load.toCSV method, creating, 570–572
load.toJSON method, creating, 572–574
load.toMONGODB method, creating, 578–581
load.toMySQL method, creating, 574–578
logic operations, 92–95
Longest Word exercise, 422
loop body, 145
loop header, 145
loops
for, 145–146, 149–151, 177, 233–234,
254, 261–262, 411, 433–434
about, 144
anatomy of, 144–145
defined, 146
ending, 168
in flowcharts, 613, 615
otr, 236
through strings, 164–167
while, 146–151, 236, 359, 374
lower() method
within sets, 266, 274
use of, 157
Lower Numbers exercise, 309
Lowest Number exercise, 487
LucidChart, 616

M

main file, creating, 357–364
main.py file
about, 514–517
completed, 530
updating to count words, 526–528
manager class, with class attribute, 325–326
Manipulated Math exercise, 97–98
map() function
combining with lambda()
function, 475–476
defined, 468
using, 472–475
math functions, 81–83
math library functions, 83–85
mathematical operations, 74–77
MathFormula class, 326–327, 328
McCauley, Julian, 512
memory, reserving, 42
menus, file (Replit), 11
methods
add(), 262, 263, 297–298
add_condiment, 353
adding to Person class, 320–321
append(), 189, 214
capitalize(), 274
class, 316, 328–330
clear(), 225, 254–255, 270–272
close(), 403, 405
as a component of classes, 316
copy(), 225, 251–252
date(), 375–376
datetime.utcnow(), 383–384
defined, 191, 319
difference(), 274–276
discard(), 268–270
display_info(), 322
exists(), 419
extract.fromCSV, 534–535
extract.fromJSON, 536–537
extract.fromMongoDB, 542–543
extract.fromMySQL, 538–539
fromCSV, 535–536
fromCustom, 603–607
fromMONGODB, 542–543

fromMySQL, in extract class, 539–540
get(), 225, 239–241
__init__, 317, 322, 324–325, 337, 339, 340, 353–354, 380–381
insert(), 190–192, 214
intersection(), 277–278
items(), 225, 234–236, 244
key: value, 306
keys(), 225, 233–234, 236–239, 245
Legacy Authentication, for MySQL, 625
len(), 152, 170, 179, 208, 232, 267
load.toCSV, 570–572
load.toJSON, 572–574
load.toMONGODB, 578–581
load.toMySQL, 574–578
lower(), 157, 266, 274
overriding, 340–343
pop(), 195, 196, 215, 225, 241–244, 254, 272, 280
pow, 326–327
range(), 186, 197–198
read(), 403, 405, 406–408
readline(), 408–410, 427, 428–429
remove(), 192–196, 215, 268–270, 419–421
remove_attribute, 552–556, 558–561
round_price, 563–567
set(), 262–263, 264
sort(), 200
split(), 153–154, 377–379, 518–519, 521
static, 326–328
staticmethod, 327–328
sub, 520–521
super(), 353
tail, 547–550
time(), 375–376, 392–393
toCSV, 571–572
toJSON, 572–574
toMONGODB, 580–581
toMySQL, 574–576, 576–578
type(), 176
union(), 278–279
update(), 225, 246–249
upper(), 158, 159

using in banking application, 321–322
values(), 225, 234–236
working with, 319–324
write(), 403, 413, 415–417
writeheader(), 441–442
writerow(), 434–436
writerows(), 439–440
writer.writerow(), 436–439
missing paths, 516
Modifying Tuples exercise, 219–220
ModuleNotFoundError exception, 502–503
MongoDB, importing to, 542, 643–644
MongoDB Community Server
    installing, 637–642
    running, 642
mongoimport, 644
Movies exercise, 463
multiline instruction, 54–55
Multiplication Tables exercise, 169
multiplying numbers, 480–481
myfunc function, 471–472
my_function() function, 306, 307
MySQL
    configuring, 624–628
    downloading, 623–624
    installing, 623–630
    MySQL Notifier, 630
    verifying installation, 628–630
MySQL Notifier, 630

N

\n (newline character), 413
naming conventions, 315
negative indexing
    of a list, 182–184
    in tuples, 210–211
nested conditions
    within income tax calculator exercise, 127–132
    working with, 109–112
New York Restaurants exercise, 462
\n (newline character), 413
Nobel Prizes exercise, 461–462
not logic operation, 92

now( ) function, 372, 376–377
number data types, 70–72
numbers
    as data type, 38–39
    multiplying, 480–481
    slicing list of, 186
numbers parameter, 298

O

object-oriented programming (OOP)
    about, 314
    class attributes, 324–330
    creating objects, 316–317
    incorporating, 313–332
    inheritance, 333–347
    principles of, 314
    working with methods, 319–324
objects
    creating, 316–317
    defined, 314
One Letter at a Time exercise, 170
one-sided arrows, in flowcharts, 616
OOP. See object-oriented programming
    (OOP)
open( ) function
    about, 402
    adding content to text files, 412
opening
    files, 504–505
    flatland01.txt file, 405–406
    text files, 404–406
operation
    defined, 35
    logic, 92–95
operators
    about, 35–36
    backslash, 54–55
    comparative, 95–96
    defined, 51
    for, 217–218
    in, 217–218, 246, 265
    +, 216
    working with, 245–246
or logic operation, 92

order class, creating, 356–357
order of operations, PEMDAS, 77–80
ordering combos, 363–364
order_many function, 360, 364
order_once function, 358–359, 359–360
orders, creating, 357–358
os module, 418–419
otr loop, 236
output, displaying, 364
output messages
    hard-coded constants within, 45–46
    improving, 291
    modifying, 287–288
ovals, in flowcharts, 615–616
overriding
    display method, 340–341
    methods, 340–343
overwriting contents of text files, 415–417

P

parallelograms, in flowcharts, 615–616, 619
parameters
    creating custom dates with named,
        381
    defined, 296
    end, 185
    numbers, 298
    order of, 470
    sep, 178
    start, 185
    step, 185
    syntax of, 303
    threshold, 298
parent class
    creating, 335
    defined, 334
PascalCasing, 34, 315
passwords
    case sensitivity of, 156–157
    tuple use for, 208–209
The Past exercise, 395
paths
    absolute, 401
    defined, 401

missing, 516
relative, 401
PEMDAS, 77–80
Person class
about, 336–337, 338–340
adding methods to, 320–321
creating, 317–318
with multiple attributes, 318–319
pi function, 84
Playing with Numbers exercise, 99
+ operator, tuples and, 216
polymorphism
defined, 314
as a principle of OOP, 314
pop( ) method
about, 241–244
defined, 196, 225
example of, 254
exercise for, 280
within lists, 195
within sets, 272
tuples and, 215
Pop Music Evolution exercise, 445–446
popping, removing *versus,* 195
Popping Accounts exercise, 280
symbol
within comments, 56
use of, 61
pow method, 326–327
pow_n function, 472
pow(x, y) function, 84
pprint( ) function, 457–460
PRINT
as reserved word, 35
single-line commands, 51–52
print( ) function
about, 403
displaying variables through, 62–63
loops and, 145
use of, 51–52
print statement
displaying split information within, 289
example of, 137
sep parameter within, 178
processing

CSV files, 425–446
JavaScript Object Notation (JSON)
files, 447–463
text files, 399–421
processing symbol, in flowcharts, 619
program, 30–31
programming, 30
programming languages
about, 32–37
case-sensitivity of, 34, 55–56
comparison operators of, 35–36
data types within, 37–42
operators within, 35–36
reserved words of, 34–35
space use within, 34
statements within, 33
syntax of, 33–34, 50
variables within, 37–42
Project Gutenberg, 400
Prompting for an Address lesson
accepting user input within, 285–286
adding period within, 292–293
displaying input value within, 286–287
displaying only house number, 290–291
displaying street name within, 291–292
getting started, 284–285
improving output within, 291
modifying the output within,
287–288
overview of, 283–284
splitting a text value within, 288–290
verification within, 287
Prompting the User exercise, 97
pseudocode
about, 617, 621–622
for income tax calculator exercise, 120
PyMySQL package, installing, 538
Python. *See also specific topics*
about, 4
Customize installation link of, 25
files, saving locally, 19–20
installing, 24–25
programming needs within, 4
syntax variation of, 34
Python Programming exercise, 47

Q

" (quotation marks)
  double, 176
  single, 176

R

r argument, 404
raise keyword, 501–502
range() method
  example of, 186
  within lists, 197–198
read() method
  about, 403, 405
  reading text files, 406–408
read_csv function, 432–434
reading
  comma-separated value (CSV)
    files, 426–430
  data, 514–517
  JavaScript Object Notation (JSON)
    files, 515–516
  JSON data, 457–460
  lines, 408–410
  text files, 406–408
Reading Lines exercise, 422, 444, 508
read_json_file function, 515–517
readline() method
  about, 408–410, 427
  iterating through CSV files, 428–429
read_osv function, 504–505
Rearranging Files exercise, 445
rectangles, in flowcharts, 615–616
reduce() function
  defined, 468
  summing account balance, 483–484
  using, 480–485
  using with comparison operations,
    484
redundancy checking, 296
regular expressions, 520–521
relative path, 401
remove() method
  defined, 196

deleting text files, 419–421
  within lists, 192–196
  within sets, 268–270
  tuples and, 215
remove_attribute method, 552–556,
  558–561
removing
  columns from data sources,
    552–556
  deleting versus, 194
  multiple columns, 558–561
  popping versus, 195
Removing an Attribute exercise, 583
Removing Duplicates exercise, 609
renaming
  columns, 551–552
  multiple columns, 556–558
Renaming an Attribute exercise, 583
Replit
  code file renaming within, 11–12
  code file saving within, 12
  creating account for, 5–7
  creating Python program within, 7–9
  desktop of, 8
  downloading project from, 13
  editor, 9
  error indicator within, 10
  files, creating, 12–13
  files menu within, 11
  help for, 14
  online use of, 4–6
  returning to, 13–14
  running Python program within, 9–10
  Shell tab within, 11–12
  Sign-up dialog box for, 6
  Welcome dialog box for, 7
reserved words, 34–35
return statement, exiting function
  through, 296–297
reviews, counting words in, 524–528
reviews dataset, tokenizing, 523–524
Revisiting Lessons Learned exercise, 608
root account, defining passwords for, 625
round function, 82
round_price method, 563–567

rows
    creating dictionaries for, in CSV
        files, 430–431
    writing as lists, 439–440
    writing from dictionaries, 440–443
running MongoDB Community Server, 642

S

`Sales` class, 329
Say Hello exercise, 27
selection control structure, 102, 144
selection statements, 103–106
`self` keyword, 317
Self-Assessment exercise, 257–258, 281,
    489, 508–509
; (semicolon), 52–54
`sep` parameter, 178
Separating the High from the Low exercise,
    256–257
Separating Your Fruits exercise, 168
sequence control structure, 102–103,
    144
sequence statements, 103
sequences, in flowcharts, 613–614
`set()` method, 262–263, 264
sets
    about, 260
    adding duplicates to, 264
    adding items to, 262
    calculating length of, 267–268
    clearing, 270–272
    combining, 278–279
    creating, 260–261
    creating an empty, 262–263
    defined, 174, 175, 224, 260
    deleting, 273–274
    deleting items from, 268–270
    determining difference
        between, 274–276
    dictionary *versus,* 260
    intersecting, 277–278
    looping through, 261–262
    popping items in, 272

retrieving items from, 261–262
searching items in, 265–267
understanding uniqueness
    within, 263–265
Setting Future Days exercise, 395
Setup wizard (Python), 25
Shell tab (Replit), 11–12
Shopping List exercise, 203
`side` class, creating, 354–355
sides, adding to order, 362–363
Simple Calculator exercise, 310
simple interest, calculating, 88–89
Simple Interest exercise, 98
' (single quotes), 176
single-line commands, 51–52
`sin(x)` function, 84
`slice()` function, 187–189
slice object, 187–189
snippet, 51
solution, 31
`sort()` method, within lists, 200
spaces, within syntax, 34
specifying initial values, 482–483
`split()` method, 153–154, 377–379,
    518–519, 521
splitting date string, 377–379
`sqrt(x)` function, 84
[] (square brackets), 513
`start` parameter, 185
statements
    about, 33
    `condition`, 104
    `elif`, 109–110, 127
    `except`, 493–495, 503
    finally, 505–506
    `if`, 104, 105–106, 109, 241, 374
    `if-else`, 108–109, 111–112, 199, 361
    `import`, 372, 520
    `print`, 137, 178, 289
    `return`, exiting function
        through, 296–297
    selection, 103–106
    `switch`, 619
    `try`, 493–495, 500–501, 503

TypeError, 495–496, 498–500, 501
  with, 427
static methods
  about, 316, 326–328
  converting to for extract class,
    586–588, 594–601
  converting to for load class, 592–594
  converting to for transform
    class, 588–592
static typing, 43–44
staticmethod method, 327–328
step parameter, 185
storing input
  overview of, 59–60
__str__ method, 353, 354
Streamlined Banking exercise, 331
Street Addresses exercise, 100
string data types
  defined, 70
  to user input, 86
strings
  comparison operators in, 155–157
  concatenating, 158–159, 471
  creating, 151–152
  inclusions within, 38
  iterating through, 164–167
  length determination of, 152–153
  limitations of, 174
  quotation mark use within, 176
  searching, 163–164
  slicing, 159–163
  splitting, 153–154
  storing characters within, 154–155
  within text, 38
style guides. See naming conventions
sub method, 520–521
Sum of Even exercise, 488
Sum of Positive Numbers exercise, 488
Sum of Prime Numbers exercise, 169–170
super() method, 353
switch statement, 619
syntax
  about, 33–34
  defined, 50
  error of, 65

of functions, 300–301
lists versus tuple, 206
of parameters, 303

T

tabs, Shell (Replit), 11–12
tail method, creating, 547–550
tan(x) function, 84
target database, creating, 576
tax rate, hard-coded constants within, 45
taxable income. See also income tax
  calculator exercise
    formula for, 122–123
    negative, 134
Teller class, 337–338
temporary code, testing with, 290
terminator, in flowcharts, 618–619
testing
  exceptions for incorrect filenames,
    595–598
  extract.py file, 588
  load.py file, 594
  transform.py file, 592
text, as data type, 38
text files
  about, 401–402
  adding content to, 412–415
  close() method, 403
  creating, 417–418
  deleting, 419–421
  input() function, 402
  iterating through, 410–412
  open() function, 402
  opening, 404–406
  overwriting content of, 415–417
  print() function, 403
  processing, 399–421
  read() method, 403
  reading, 406–408
  reading lines, 408–410
  using os module, 418–419
  write() method, 403
  writing to, 412–413

Text in Reverse exercise, 423
This Will Be exercise, 309–310
threshold parameter, 298
tilted rectangles, in flowcharts, 615–616
time() method, 375–376, 392–393
timedelta class, 387–388
times. *See* dates and times
timestamp class, 384–387
timestamps, applying, 384–387
toCSV method, 571–572
today() function
    about, 376–377
    date comparisons with, 383
    defined, 372
toJSON method, 572–574
tokenize function, 519–520, 521–522
tokenize_dataset function, 522–523
tokenize_review function, 523
tokenizing
    datasets, 517–524, 522–523
    input reviews, 521–522
    input strings, 518–521
    reviews dataset, 523–524
toMONGODB method, 580–581
toMySQL method, 574–576, 576–578
to_upper_case() function, 473
transactions
    adding via dictionaries, 442–443
    iterating through JSO files of, 455–456
    summing amounts, 476
    writing data to files, 413–414
transform class
    about, 546
    converting to static methods for, 588–592
    creating head method, 547–550
    creating tail method, 547–550
    defining, 546–547
    removing columns from data sources, 552–556
    removing multiple columns, 558–561
    renaming columns, 551–552
    renaming multiple columns, 556–558

transforming data, 563–567
transform.py file, 547, 550, 554–556, 561–563, 567–569
Transforming CSV to CSV exercise, 583
Transforming CSV to JSON exercise, 583
transforming data, 563–567
Transforming JSON to CSV exercise, 583
Transforming JSON to JSON exercise, 583
Transforming Names exercise, 609
transform.py file, 547, 550, 554–556, 561–563, 567–569, 592
True evaluation
    from condition statements, 104, 105, 106–107
    within sets, 265
    within strings, 156
True or False exercise, 99
True or False Quiz exercise, 115
true/false values
    as data type, 39
    logic operations, 92–94
trunc(x) function, 84
try statement
    about, 493–495
    IOError exception and, 503
    using multiple operations in a, 500–501
tuples
    about, 206
    concatenating of, 216–217
    creating, 206–207
    defined, 174, 175, 224
    immutability of, 206, 213–216, 221
    as immutable, 206
    index values of, 209–210
    length of, 208
    negative indexing in, 210–211
    passwords and, 208–209
    searching, 217–218
    slicing, 212–213
    syntax of, 206
    updating, 220
--type, 644
type() method, 176

TypeError statement, 495–496,
    498–500, 501
Typing Numbers exercise, 507

U

UI (user interface), for income tax calculator
    exercise, 119, 136–139
union() method, within sets, 278–279
Universal Time Coordinated (UTC) format,
    working with, 383–384
Unix Dates exercise, 395
update() method, 225, 246–249
updating main.py file to count
    words, 526–528
upper() method, 158, 159
user experience (UX), 286
user input
    about, 396
    accepting, 285–286
    defined, 50
    number use within, 86–89
    testing for, 258
    validating, 497–498
user interface (UI), for income tax calculator
    exercise, 119, 136–139
user-defined function
    declaring of, 297
    defined, 296
Using a Calculator in Class exercise, 331–332
UTC (Universal Time Coordinated) format,
    working with, 383–384
UX (user experience), 286

V

validating user input, 497–498
ValueError, 497–498
values
    binary, 39
    Boolean, 39
    checking lists for valid, 499–500
    within data types, 37
    finding highest in collections, 484–485

finding lowest, 485
    hash, 105
    specifying initial, 482–483
values() method
    defined, 225
    use of, 236–239
variables
    about, 40–42
    Boolean, 89–90
    creating for dates, 372–376
    creating for time, 375–376
    data types and, 43–44
    declaring, 42, 61, 64–65, 71
    defined, 50, 70, 174
    identifying type of, 72–73
    naming, 64–65, 166
    reserving memory within, 42
    string, 151–152
    tax calculations with, 130–131
    understanding types of, 61
    value display of, 62
verifying
    extract.py module, 544–545
    lists for valid values, 499–500
    MySQL installation, 628–630
Vinyl DB, installing, 631–635
VinylRecordShop database, setting up, 539
virtual reality, features of, 30
Visual Studio Code
    adding Python extension to, 22–24
    Extension icon within, 22
    obtaining, 21–22
    overview of, 21

W

w argument, 404
Watt, Andrew (author)
    Beginning Regular Expressions, 521
websites
    Alice's Adventures in Wonderland files, 400
    Anaconda, 15
    Compass, 642
    Diagrams, 616

Digital Music review set, 512
Drawings, 616
ElementTreeXML API, 603
Flatland files, 400
Jupyter Notebook Documentation, 20
LucidChart, 616
MongoDb Community Server, 637
MySQL, 623
MySQL Notifier, 630
Project Gutenberg, 400
Python, 24
Python documentation, 84
Replit, 5, 284
Visual Studio Code, 21
What's It Do exercise, 27
Where Are You? exercise, 67
Where's Waldo exercise, 220
Which Is Greater? exercise, 310
WHILE, as reserved word, 35
while loop
about, 146–149, 359, 374
example of, 236
iterating backward within, 148
for loop *versus*, 149–151
unexecutable, 148–149
whitespace, 153
windows, Console (Replit), 8
with statement, 427
Working with Text exercise, 256
write() method

about, 403, 413
overwriting content of text files, 415–417
writeheader() method, 441–442
writerow() method, 434–436
writerows() method, 439–440
writer.writerow() method, 436–439
writing
JSON data, 457–460
lists to text files, 414–415
rows as lists, 439–440
rows from dictionaries, 440–443
to text files, 412–413
transaction data to files, 413–414

X

x argument, 404
XML files, custom class to extract from, 602–603
xml:extractor function, 602–603

Y

Yesterday, Today, and Tomorrow exercise, 395

Z

zero-based indexing, 179
ZeroDivisionError, 492–500